PENNY WONG

ALSO BY MARGARET SIMONS

Six Square Metres: Reflections from a Small Garden (2015)

Kerry Stokes: Self-Made Man (2013)

Journalism at the Crossroads: Crisis and Opportunity for the Press (2012)

Malcolm Fraser: The Political Memoirs (2010)

The Content Makers: Understanding the Media in Australia (2007)

*Faith, Money and Power: What the Religious Revival Means
for Politics* (2007)

Latham's World: The New Politics of the Outsiders (2004)

Resurrection in a Bucket: The Rich and Fertile Story of Compost (2004)

The Meeting of the Waters: The Hindmarsh Island Affair (2003)

Fit to Print: Inside the Canberra Press Gallery (1999)

Wheelbarrows, Chooks and Children (1999)

The Truth Teller (1996)

The Ruthless Garden (1993)

PENNY WONG

PASSION AND PRINCIPLE

THE BIOGRAPHY BY

MARGARET SIMONS

Published by Black Inc.,
an imprint of Schwartz Books Pty Ltd
Level 1, 221 Drummond Street
Carlton VIC 3053, Australia
enquiries@blackincbooks.com
www.blackincbooks.com

9781760640859 (paperback)
9781743821145 (ebook)

 A catalogue record for this
book is available from the
National Library of Australia

Cover design by Akiko Chan
Cover photograph by Kristoffer Paulsen
Author photograph by Dave Tacon
Text design and typesetting by Tristan Main
Index by Kerry Anderson

Internal images reproduced courtesy of: Penny as a child; Francis, Jane, Penny and Toby;
Penny Wong class photo, all Penny Wong; Penny Wong and Peter Ker, Scotch College;
Penny Wong and family, Sabah Archives; maiden speech, Mark Graham / AAP; Penny
Wong and Quentin Bryce; Penny Wong and Kevin Rudd, both Alan Porritt / AAP;
Wong in Bali, Glen McCurtayne / Fairfax; Penny, Sophie and Alexandra, Penny Wong /
AAP; Julia Gillard and Alexandra, David Mariuz / AAP; Wong in Senate Estimates,
Lukas Coch / AAP; Penny Wong and Mathias Cormann, Mick Tsikas / AAP; Wong at
Parliament House, South Australia, Morgan Sette / AAP; Wong after postal survey results,
Andrew Meares / Fairfax; Penny and Hannah, Russell Millard / AAP; Penny Wong,
Anthony Albanese and Bill Shorten, Lukas Coch / AAP; Wong portrait, Tim Bauer.

Printed in Australia by McPherson's Printing Group.

CONTENTS

To Aidan and Willow,
and their generation

Preface

Penny Wong did not want this book to be written.

I first asked her office if she would cooperate with a biography in 2016. The reply came back firmly in the negative, and the idea was dropped.

I tried again, at the urging of Aviva Tuffield of Black Inc., in late 2017, after the positive result of the same-sex marriage national survey. Again, Penny Wong's office said that she would not cooperate.

This time, the publisher requested that I go ahead in any case. Partly this was because of the enormous interest in Penny Wong, one of our most fascinating but also most guarded politicians. As well, there was her activism on same-sex marriage – a fundamental social reform. She was increasingly important within Labor – the intellectual leader of the Left faction, and arguably the intellectual leader of the parliamentary party. She was shadow minister for foreign affairs and seemed likely to become minister, at a time of unprecedented difficulty and danger for Australia. There were good reasons to attempt a biography, whether or not she would cooperate.

For almost a year I researched the book without Penny Wong's cooperation, although many people I approached for interview asked her permission to speak to me, and she did not stand in their way. Penny Wong is private, they told me. She is shy.

There were some exchanges with her staff in which I gave assurances that I would not pursue anyone in her private life who indicated that they did not wish to speak with me. I also made it clear that while there would be some information on her private life in this book, that was not its focus. These discussions continued intermittently through-out the year.

In September 2018, with a large part of the book already drafted, I was invited to her Adelaide office for a meeting to discuss further coop-eration. She began by telling me that her hostility to this project might make our dealings difficult. She said she had felt me as 'a shadow in the corner of my life' through the previous year. She made it clear that in her view I had done something reprehensible in signing a contract to write this book when I knew she did not want it written. I told her the book was the publisher's idea, but that I was a willing recruit. I was doing it because I thought she was an important and interesting figure. In response I got the trademark Wong raised eyebrow, and a sceptical half-smile.

She gave me a hard time, while never raising her voice. Nevertheless, that first meeting did turn into a rushed kind of interview, in which I attempted – unsure if we would ever meet again – to pick the eyes out of the many things I wanted to ask her. At the end, she agreed to see me again.

In all, we had six interviews, each of about an hour and a half, between November 2018 and July 2019. Each but the last was in the sterile meeting room of her Adelaide office. The final interview was in an even more sterile meeting room in the Commonwealth Parliamentary Offices in Sydney. Penny Wong is far too smart to allow an unwelcome biographer the gift of an insight into her personal space – what she keeps on her office desk or in her home.

When each interview concluded, it was uncertain whether there would be another. It kept me on my toes. Once we were underway, though, things were easier. For the most part, we got on well. She spoke freely on most matters, and reluctantly and sparingly on her personal life. She declined to answer some questions – for example, on cabinet and shadow cabinet dealings, and actions by her fellow ministers in the Rudd–Gillard–Rudd governments. Any suggestion that I was straying too far into the personal was greeted with the Wong stare and what felt like a drop in the temperature of the room. She was usually in com-plete control, but at times became tearful or angry. At points, things felt like they were getting bogged down. She would give monosyllabic answers and start asking me questions – trademark characteristics of the media-trained politician. Then, suddenly, there would be a mini-speech: layered, complex and convincing, with not a word misplaced. It was clear she had used the previous moments to compose her thoughts. At those times, it was easy to see why she is renowned for her intellect. Her policy thinking was, at these moments, awesome in the true sense of the word, and of a calibre rarely encountered in political journalism.

The interviews were on the understanding that anything to be attributed to her would be cleared with her office before publication. This did not go entirely smoothly, largely because of delays in the post-election period. However, in the end the changes she requested were few and minor.

Requests to interview her parents and partner, Sophie Allouache, were firmly declined.

There are probably no advantages politically for Penny Wong in having a biography written now – and potentially some disadvantages. If she is to be foreign minister in a future Labor government, she will be under scrutiny both in Australia and overseas. As Leader of the Opposition in the Senate, she manages relationships between Labor and the minor parties and crossbenchers. Arming others with a detailed biography must be an alarming prospect.

Her reluctance to cooperate, she said to me at that first meeting in 2018, was mainly due to an inherent dislike of the spotlight. She told me she was an introvert. She spoke about how people such as her, who have suffered from prejudice, develop a closely guarded internal life.

In February 2019, there was a partial shift in attitude. She said that shortly before, she had been in a North Adelaide café with one of her daughters, six-year-old Alexandra. They had been on a shoe-buying expedition. Several people had approached her to wish her well, wanting to chat. 'I guess it's the demographic that likes me,' she remarked. After she had talked to her constituents, she apologised to her daughter for the intrusion on their private time. Alexandra responded that Penny should be glad and proud that people wanted to know her.

After that, just a few months before the publisher's already renegoti-
ated deadline, Penny Wong began to suggest people I should interview.
For the first time, her reluctant cooperation became something less
grudging.

Earlier, she had given some insight into her deep-seated objections
to this project. When the book came out, she said, it would give a version of her that she would have to deal with and live with and which
would be accepted as true – and it would not be how she saw herself.

I replied that there was always a gap between public image – how
journalists saw people – and self-image. She replied that it would not
be only a public image but 'your version of me'.

That, of course, is entirely correct. I don't apologise to Penny Wong
for this book, but I acknowledge the weight of her objections.

Historian and biographer Blanche Wiesen Cook has remarked that
for biographers all choices made in writing are autobiographical. So it
might be relevant that I, too, arrived in Adelaide at the age of eight and
was bullied at school – though in my case for an English accent rather
than because of racism. I went to the University of Adelaide, as a contemporary of Julia Gillard, ten years before Penny Wong. I have Jewish
ancestry. While I am not in any real sense Jewish, I was raised with a
strong awareness of the great evil of racism.

Wiesen Cook also says that biographers must necessarily believe that
it is possible for individuals to influence the political and social forces
in society. Otherwise, why devote time and effort to writing a life story?

That belief is another thing shared between this biographer and her
subject.

KINDRED OFFSPRING

When Penny Wong was twelve, she wrote a poem about a shark. She was a good poet for her age: that year she had two verses in the magazine of Adelaide's Scotch College – the wealthy private school that she attended on a scholarship.

Wong had arrived in Adelaide from Sabah, Malaysia, in spring 1976, when she was eight. The reason for the move – the break-up of the marriage between her Adelaide-born mother and Chinese-Malaysian father – was traumatic enough. But coming to Australia, it was as though she had moved to another planet – from the embracing, humid warmth of the city of Kota Kinabala, the capital of the state of Sabah, to an ordinary suburban house in Coromandel Valley, in the Adelaide Hills. Even though it was coming on summer, in the driest city in the driest state on the driest continent in the world, Wong often felt cold. 'Australia smelled dusty. It just looked different and smelled different, and the light was different,' she has recalled. 'I remember the first time I jumped into the sea here, and how cold it was … and me thinking, *what's wrong with the sea?*'[1]

In the new year, Penny and her younger brother, Toby, were enrolled at Coromandel Valley Primary School. As they followed their mother across the asphalt to the office to fill out the paperwork, students formed a crowd around them. 'They were saying "What is she?" and someone said, "She's Hong Kong-ese" … I realised for the first time that my race was something that other people would notice. That it was an issue.'

Today she is spare of speech when talking about the bullying she experienced at primary school. Partly it is because she doesn't like to remember how it felt. Partly it's because 'I don't like to repeat words of hate'.

By the time she moved to Scotch College, she had adopted a mantle of toughness. She had navigated the difference between Adelaide and Kota Kinabala, between who she was – a clever, quiet girl with a fiercely guarded internal life – and who she had to be. 'I did it by trying to be better than the people who were teasing me, so I have no doubt I became much more focused on studying, getting good marks, doing well on the sporting field, those sorts of things. I decided I was going to be better than them, and achieve in this field, and this field, and this field. I was trying to prove that I could succeed no matter what they said to me, and no matter what they thought of me. That I could do well no matter what they threw at me. It wasn't so much to get people to like me, to become my friend; it was that I wasn't going to allow them to keep me down.

'I didn't become insular. I've seen that happen with kids, but that wasn't my response. I just pretended to be confident, even when I wasn't. I learned to be steady and still, even when it felt very messy and difficult. You know, to hold yourself steady, even if your reactions are really strong and your emotions confused.'[2]

And so she wrote about the shark.

Beginning a biography of a politician with an evocation of a shark may seem provocative. The cliché demands we think of predators. That is not the intended implication here. What makes Penny Wong's childhood poem significant in retrospect is not that her subject is at the top of the food chain, but her admiration for the creature's strength, its sleekness, the way it is adapted to and moves cleanly through its environment – the way it inspires both fear and respect.

These are the words applied again and again to Wong, both by friends and enemies. She is clever. She can be politically aggressive, and ruthless, though it is rarely, if ever, personal. She is forensic, but also emotional – relatively easily moved to tears and to anger. She is hypervigilant for prejudice, for attempts to demean her, and more generally for persecution of the powerless. She is 'different'.

The nature of that difference – the nature of the woman behind the carefully curated public image – is one of the questions motivating this biography. Indeed, it is the justification for pursuing the book despite her objections. Penny Wong is now the undisputed intellectual leader of the Left faction of Australia's alternative government. She is an important friend and ally of the leader, Anthony Albanese. Other contenders for that title are seen as less politically adroit.

She may yet become our foreign minister at the most challenging time in recent decades – arguably in Australia's history. Until then, she will be shadow foreign minister and leader of Labor in the Senate – the latter role chiefly responsible for managing Labor's relationships with the Greens and the crossbench when the government doesn't have the numbers to pass legislation in its own right. Navigating all this is more than a management job. It demands both policy detail and a 'big picture', to adapt Paul Keating's phrase. It requires political aggression, yet also restraint when the national interest demands it. It requires leadership and people skills.

One of Penny Wong's strongest supporters, Labor factional chief and shadow minister for energy and climate change Mark Butler, says there is 'nothing Penny cannot do' – from deep, detailed policy work to the 'unappealing' business of machine politics. Hardly anyone doubts her competence.

Some accuse Wong of being overly politically cautious. Her former principal adviser John Olenich counters that given the composition of parliament in 2002, and even now, her very presence is radical. When she was elected a South Australian senator in 2001, she was the only person of Asian ancestry in parliament other than Senator Tsebin Tchen from Victoria, who was born in China, and Queensland MP Michael Johnson, whose mother was from Hong Kong. There was also a woman who worked in the library, and there were the cleaners. That was it for Asian faces. The newcomer was able to cope, she says, because of her school experiences: 'The hardest part of it is how you think about it internally, how you manage it inside you. I know I started to learn how to do that at school. In the end, politics isn't that different from the schoolyard.'[3] Olenich, when deciding whether he wanted to devote years of his life to being on her staff, considered that she was one of the first Asians and the first openly gay woman in a representative body, the Parliament of Australia, that in terms of gender and ethnicity was not representative at all. To him and to a generation of other young Labor members, it seemed that she represented a way forward – a reflection of a more modern, inclusive party and nation.

During the research for this biography, it was notable that Wong's political opponents – members of the Liberal Party interviewed on background – had only positive comments. 'The smartest person in the parliament,' said one. 'Someone you can deal with. She has integrity,' said another. There was also rueful respect for her savaging of government ministers appearing before Senate committees. Political journalists, too, spoke of her with respect. They saw her as principled, in politics for the 'right reasons', and as having exercised good judgement at key moments – for example, in advocating for Kevin Rudd to take Labor to a double-dissolution election over climate-change policy in 2009, advice he did not heed. As one put it, with conscious irony, she satisfies Kipling's description of 'a man': she has the ability to keep her head when all around are losing theirs. Notably, she emerges well from the memoirs of both Julia Gillard and Kevin Rudd, despite the poison between the two. Perhaps equally telling, the cleaner in charge of ministerial offices at Parliament House remembers Minister Wong always taking the time to talk and ask after her welfare.[4]

On the other hand, dig deeper and you hear about an unappealing aspect of Penny Wong. She can be worse than sharp to her staff and her colleagues. She does this in front of others, and she does not always apologise. Rather, she tends to rationalise her own behaviour. It is the same combativeness and temper that make her effective in opposition, but when turned on her own, it can be ugly. Those who have observed this remark that these episodes are usually related to her levels of fatigue. In their view, she doesn't manage fatigue well.

She works very hard indeed, starting in the early hours and finishing late. She over-prepares for media conferences, for Senate Estimates, for everything she does. She likes to feel more than across the material. She can be a control freak. A few times a year, when tired and stressed, she gets migraines severe enough to confine her to home. It is usually when approaching this kind of exhaustion that she shows her impatience and her acid tongue to those who work with her.

In many contexts Wong's aggression is a political strength. When ill-judged, it is also her main weakness. The aggression can undermine her reputation as a good negotiator. Only rarely do these ill-judged displays of temper become public. If they were on display more often, it is easy to imagine the fast erosion of her public popularity.

On the other hand, good staff stick with her, and are loyal. It is not her staff who complain about her temper. Rather, it is the people who have observed how, on occasions, she speaks to her team. She can be generous to her staff as well. She is known for taking them all out to lunch and picking up the considerable bill. Talented people want to work for her.

While she is personally and politically ambitious, she is not a psychopath or a narcissist. (These things need saying, in the era of Trump.) The strength and longevity of almost all her personal relationships attest to that. With her inner circle of friends and her family she is warm, devoted and fiercely protective. In these troubled times of populist politics, Penny Wong's is a different model of leadership. She is principled, intellectual, private, restrained and sane. Having eschewed populism, she is now popular – which is perhaps a cause for hope about our political processes.

The negative comments about Wong came almost exclusively from the losers and combatants in the internecine factional disputes within the Labor Party. 'I'd like to meet someone as smart as Penny Wong thinks she is,' said one. Woven through these comments – all from men – there was a strand of misogyny, though not obvious racism or prejudice based on sexual preference. There was resentment that Wong has a public profile as a darling of the left – an irony, given that if she has a political weakness it is her dislike of personal scrutiny. She is a private person.

There was resentment at the way she involves herself across the board, in areas beyond her shadow portfolio, and as Senate leader. She was key in knocking out the opposition to Anthony Albanese's becoming leader after the 2019 election defeat, for example. Her early declaration of support for Albanese made it much harder for others to contest. As well, she has earned enemies through her aggression in shadow cabinet and caucus. Her critics say there is a gap between her supporters' perceptions of her and who she actually is. They say she is not as left-wing as her fan club likes to think, and much more of a machine politician than the soft left fancies. A hip Melbourne café in the Green-leaning suburb of Brunswick serves an open sandwich called the Penny Wong, in tribute. It is vegan, with lentils, hummus, pumpkin, 'almond feta' and 'coconut bacon' on 'activated charcoal toast'. Food is important to Wong – tangled with love and memory. But it is difficult to imagine her ordering the sandwich that bears her name. When I told her about it, she asked how one activated charcoal (answer: you soak it).

There was talk, from Wong's Labor antagonists, of provoking her, in party-room and shadow cabinet meetings. She can be fierce in response. She does a good line in articulate rage.

In summary, Penny Wong is easy to like and demands admiration, but is also easy to fear.

Here is her shark poem, written as she was gaining a foothold in her new country, and delivering on her resolve to beat the bullies in every field of endeavour.

Menace of the deep
Man fears and hates you,
Yet admires you.
You slink through the water
Like a snake.
Cutting cleanly through the dark ocean.
Your skin like well-stretched leather,
Eyes that gleam like embers

In the murky water,
Razor-sharp teeth ready to rip and tear.
Little fish scuttle behind rocks,
Eels slither away in fear
As you glide above them.
Even the mighty whale
Will not tangle with you.
And Man, conqueror of all,
Dares not trespass
In your domain.

It is not unusual for children on the edge of adolescence, developing their sense of self and finding their voice, to focus on darkness and suffering. Wong had more reason to do so than most of her privileged classmates. Apart from her own pain, she had been raised with an awareness of the history and legacy of British colonialism, as well as war, invasion and death – and the luck and determination that lay behind her own family's survival.

Penny Wong was born in 1968 in North Borneo, which had recently become part of the new nation of Malaysia. Borneo and Australia seemed very different places to her, yet they were also, as an account of her father's professional life put it, 'kindred offspring' of the same colonial empire.[5] To Borneans of the post-war generation, engagement with Australia was both an expression of growing independence from colonial masters and an embrace of a more fortunate sibling. The strands of history are interwoven, and they meet in Penny Wong.

Wong, like most of us, tells well-honed stories about herself. In these, her main motivation for entering politics was to combat racism. Of course, it's more complicated than that, but the experience of racism formed her, and in more ways than she is aware. It is part of her family history. It is part of what made her, long before she walked through the schoolyard at Coromandel Valley Primary.

*

The sailors carried the settlers pickaback through the shallows to the beach. Before them stretched the Adelaide plains, punctuated with kangaroo grass and freshwater lagoons. There was a constant music of mosquitoes. The hills loomed blue in the distance. It was November 1836, on the cusp of a hot summer. The settlers travelled inland and pitched their tents in the shade of gum trees, including one that had been bowed into an arch by the south-westerly winds. The sandy soil was full of flies and fleas. Rats stole their supplies. Bullants and frogs came inside their tents, and one day the new colonial secretary, Robert Gouger, put his hand to the ground and almost touched a scorpion.[6] This site, though, had been chosen by Colonel William Light for a new settlement, the beginning of the colony of South Australia, founded upon idealism and a belief in the goodness of man. Christmas Day was intensely hot – more than 100 degrees Fahrenheit in the shade. A few days later, on 28 December, the new colony was proclaimed in the shade of the arched gum tree.

Watching the ceremony were Penny Wong's great-great-great-grandparents: 22-year-old Samuel Chapman and his wife, Charlotte,[7] and their infant daughter, also Charlotte. 'I always think it's amusing when people have a go at me, you know, all the racists? And I think, *on this side of my family, I go back further than you,*' says Wong. On her mother's side, she is as deeply rooted in Australia as is possible for someone not of Aboriginal ancestry. Her personal history and present geography are studded with the names resonant of that connection. Her electorate office is on Gouger Street – titled for the colonial secretary almost bitten by a scorpion in those first days on Holdfast Bay. When she studied at the University of Adelaide, she would have spent time in Elder Hall, which was named after the man, Thomas Elder, who employed her great-great-grandfather and opened up the state to agriculture. Her high school, Scotch College, was once home to the family of Scottish pioneer Robert Barr Smith, Elder's business partner, who was friend to her great-great-grandfather, and his son, her great-uncle. Most of this history does not weigh upon her. She learned some of the details of her mother's family during the interviews for this book.

The Chapmans had arrived with more than eighty other settlers aboard the *Cygnet*, which sailed from London in March 1836, travelling via Rio de Janeiro. Of the eighty-four passengers, fifty-two were 'adults conveyed by the emigration fund' and fifteen 'persons of a superior class'.[8] Included were surveyors contracted to assist Colonel Light in choosing and designing the new settlement.

The Chapmans were not of the 'superior class'. Samuel was a cabinetmaker. He and his wife were descended from farmers and artisans in Cambridgeshire and Surrey, the first generation to grow up amid the transformation of the Industrial Revolution, when the benefits of industrialisation were not yet felt by the poor. They suffered from low wages, poor diet and insecure employment – constantly at risk of sinking into the kind of poverty that Charles Dickens wrote about. The Chapmans crossed the world in search of new opportunity in a settlement that, it was promised, would be different to the eastern colonies of New South Wales or Port Phillip – South Australia would be idealistic, civilised, untouched by the convict taint.

There are glimpses of the Chapmans' voyage in the journal of Boyle Travers Finniss, who, two decades after serving as an assistant surveyor to Light, would become South Australia's first premier. On 7 April, after nearly three weeks at sea, he records that there are complaints about 'the dirt' below decks. The married passengers are referred to, Samuel Chapman among them. Later, there is a reference to the number of people who have fallen sick due to the foul air beneath the decks. Bilge water and vegetable matter had accumulated. Finniss laments that all married passengers are separated from the rest only by canvas, and that there are no tables at which to eat, 'making [t]heir berths a perpetual cook's shop. Meals going on at all hours must be productive of dirt and disorder'.[9]

The voyage was troubled. The crew staged a walk-off in Rio, and there was conflict between George Kingston, the deputy surveyor and head of Light's staff, and the captain, John Rolls. This delayed passage, and although the *Cygnet* had sailed a month before Light's ship, it arrived a month later – on 11 September 1836, arriving at Kangaroo Island. Light had already left to scout the coast and, having found the Torrens River, chosen his preferred site for the new settlement. The settlers were ordered to abandon their freshly established reed huts on the island and sail to Holdfast Bay in Gulf St Vincent – the site of the present-day suburb of Glenelg.

South Australia had been founded on a principle of being charitable to the 'native peoples', but it was already too late for any uncomplicated pursuit of that ideal. Sealers and whalers had been operating off the coast since the 1820s and had made occasional raids on Aboriginal camps, kidnapping women and taking them back to the islands. About six years before the *Cygnet*'s arrival, smallpox had spread along the Murray River from the colonies in eastern Australia. Many Aboriginal people had died, and the survivors bore the disease's telltale pockmarks. Indigenous society in the region was already stressed and traumatised. The first settlers at Holdfast Bay lived in fear of attack from the 'natives'. Yet relations were friendly enough between the two groups in late 1836. Aboriginal people arrived, were shown around the tents and huts, and shook hands with everyone. They were taken to the commissioner's stores and fitted out with trousers, flannel shirts and woollen caps.[10]

The idea for the new colony belonged to settler Edward Gibbon Wakefield. The existing Australian colonies had been used as a dumping ground for the criminal class. Wakefield wanted the colonisation of South Australia to be an antidote to pauperism: a settlement guided by a landed gentry. The problem, as for all colonialists, was how to work the land. Where was the labour to come from, if not from convicts? The answer was the sale of 'waste land' to migrants, whose work would allow the gentry to forge 'civilised life' with 'liberal feeling and polished manners'.[11]

The Chapmans likely responded to advertisements that began to appear in London in 1835 seeking free migrants from the ranks of 'small farmers and others ... persons of skill and industry and possessed by some capital but unable by the use of it to procure a comfortable livelihood'.

You naturally inquire, where is South Australia? What sort of place is the new colony? And what shall we do when we get there? I will tell you. Australia is a great big island, situated in the south sea or Indian Ocean. They used to call it New Holland.[12]

For the Chapmans, the South Australian dream worked out. In just one generation they were transformed from poverty to wealth. Today the Chapmans are one of the 'old Adelaide families' associated with privilege and establishment – although the monetary wealth had dissipated by the time Penny Wong's mother was born. By 1839, Samuel Chapman was a shopkeeper and licensed victualler, operating his business from public land.[13] By 1849, just thirteen years after arrival, he had a cabinetmaker's shop in Carrington Street. Chapman apparently had a talent for self-promotion. *The South Australian Register* recorded that he had submitted to the newspaper for appraisal a 'superb library chair, made to order' and later a library table with lion's paw feet.[14] The *Register* praised the 'beautiful execution' – the 'chaste beauty and masterly execution of the carvings' as well as the 'most effective' French polishing. 'We can only add that the colony may well be proud of those who, like Mr Chapman, can accomplish so much at so early a period of our history.'[15] Advertisements in the *Register* began to list the fact that furniture had been made by Chapman as a selling point at auctions.[16]

Charlotte Chapman died in 1876, and Samuel six years later. His obituary described him as 'a colonist of unblemished reputation' who was 'widely known and respected'.[17] He had had ten children – one of whom, a son, had died when only a year old. Eight were daughters, and they had married the children of other settlers, taken on new names and moved throughout the Adelaide plains and hills. It was his only surviving son, Alfred Stephen Chapman, who made the leap into wealth. As a teenager he had begun work for Elder & Co. – an agricultural company founded by Thomas Elder and his brother-in-law, Robert Barr Smith, which was settling the state's dry northern saltbush regions. In 1874 Elder made two large donations that helped the newly established University of Adelaide to gain quick renown. Barr Smith, too, was a philanthropist, and present-day Adelaide is dotted with his name. At Scotch College a young Penny performed in the Barr Smith

Theatre. At the University of Adelaide, she sat on the Barr Smith lawns and studied in the Barr Smith Library.

Alfred Chapman married Annie Horsley, an emigrant from London. By the time of his death in 1912, from typhoid, Chapman had served more than fifty-five years with the company and risen from office boy to manager. He was one of the best-known and most respected business-men in Adelaide. Barr Smith wrote a letter of eulogy:

> Looking back 50 years, when as a lad Mr. Chapman first came to the office of Elder and Co., my first impression of him then was his capacity and willingness for hard work. If any department was behind, and an assistant was required for night work, Mr. Chap-man presented himself, with the result that, going through all the departments in this way, he soon knew as much about them as the man in charge, and so when any one dropped out of his place in the office there never was any difficulty about replacing ... I fancy Mr. Chapman must have filled almost every post we had to give. Let me add that he has always had the strictest sense of honour and the most fair and reasonable consideration for everybody with whom he came in business contact.[18]

Alfred Chapman and Annie had eleven children. One, Alfred Horsley Chapman, followed his father into business at Elder, and became a member of the National Council of Wool Selling Brokers. Another son, Penny Wong's great-grandfather, Samuel William Chapman, farmed the property Edialta, in what is now the suburb of Cherry Gardens in Adelaide, a few minutes' drive from the primary school at which she was bullied.[19] Today Blackwood Golf Club covers part of the old property, and there is an Edialta Road. The rest has been subdivided for housing. This Samuel Chapman was the family's first politician – a councillor in what was then the Clarendon District.[20] His son, William, was Wong's grandfather, also a farmer. He married Esther Hannaford, from one of the wealthiest Adelaide land-owning families. In the family mythol-ogy, William was a simple farmer, but Wong's mother remembers him quoting poetry – Homer and Shakespeare – as he brought in the sheep and cattle. 'He was obviously extremely well read and extremely literate,' Wong remarks.

Her mother, Barbara Jane Chapman but always called Jane, was born in 1944, the middle daughter in a family of five girls. Their mother died in 1961, when Jane was a teenager, and their father a few years later, just before she turned twenty. The five sisters relied on one another for comfort and support. The family structure was set – a tight-knit, fiercely loyal group of women who looked out for their own. It was these women who embraced Jane, Penny and Toby when they landed back in Adelaide in 1976, and the Australian part of the Penny Wong story began. The family dynamic, Penny Wong says today, is matriarchal.

*

In 1838, two years after Samuel and Charlotte Chapman arrived in South Australia on the *Cygnet*, a British adventurer named James Brooke moored his boat in Kuching, Borneo – the third-largest island in the world and then part of an empire ruled over by the sultans of Brunei. The origins of the Sultanate are lost in history, but for as long as history records Borneo had faced outwards to the world – a trading nation set in the heart of the archipelagos of South-East Asia, between China and what today have become the Philippines and Indonesia. The sultans held sway over seaways and coastal merchant towns, leaving the jungled interior to the indigenous Dayak people. When Brooke arrived, they were in revolt against the sultan. Piracy and European trade were disrupting the maritime empire. Brooke helped the sultan defeat the rebellion and was rewarded with a parcel of land in the north-west, on which he established the Kingdom of Sarawak and founded a dynastic monarchy of so-called White Rajahs. This began the break-up of the island and its domination by outsiders. Today Borneo is split between Malaysia, Indonesia and the minuscule remnant of the Brunei empire, all but surrounded by Sarawak, the first White Rajah's creation.

By 1888, when Penny Wong's European ancestors were pushing into the Adelaide Hills, establishing farms and orchards, the British

North Borneo Company (BNBC) had been established under a royal charter to exploit the region's resources, with a concession granted by the Sultanate. Ceding land to the Europeans had become part of the accepted way of doing business in Borneo.

Wakefield and the founding fathers of South Australia had struggled with the problem of how to work the land without resorting to convict labour. The BNBC had the same problem – but it was in business, rather than governed by colonial idealism. The indigenous Dayak population was deemed unsuitable, and in any case there were not enough of them to build the railways and labour on the vast tobacco and timber plantations and in the tin mines. The company directors arrived at a different solution – the import of what were called Chinese 'coolies'.

Between 1881 and 1941, there were three different schemes to bring in Chinese labourers. In the first, between 1882 and 1886, five boatloads of mainly Cantonese migrants were shipped south. The composition of the cohort was all wrong. The company had recruited shopkeepers and artisans, who proved unable to make their way in an undeveloped country. By the beginning of the twentieth century, the emphasis had shifted decisively to the Hakka.[21]

The word 'hakka' means 'guest people'. It is a signal of their perpetual outsider status, both in China and in the many other regions of the world where, pushed out due to persecution and lured by opportunity, they have made their home. Less generous translations – 'outsiders', or words with a nuance of being unwelcome guests – are possible. Scholars suggest that the Hakka, despite their outsider identity, are not a separate ethnic group but Han Chinese who migrated from central to southern China, to the Cantonese areas of Guangdong, around the fourth century. As latecomers, they had to establish their communities on rugged, less fertile land. They were fringe dwellers and tenant farmers who over time established a distinct identity. They were proud, and could be prickly. It is said that although poor they were generally well educated, and often excelled in the imperial exams that were an essential requirement for advancement in China for many centuries. Hakka women were renowned for their stamina, and for doing strenuous farming work that in other communities was left to men. Hakka women did not bind their feet.

The Hakka are also notoriously political. For many centuries, they have been rebels.[22]

Confirming their outsider status, the Hakka of Guangdong in the late 1800s were largely Christian, and comparatively pro-European. Many had been converted by the Basel Mission, an evangelical missionary society that trained Dutch and British missionaries operating in India and China. In 1850, the Taiping Heavenly Kingdom – a Christian oppositional state led by Hakka revolutionary Hong Xiuquan – sought to overthrow the Qing Dynasty in an event that became known as the Taiping Rebellion. The rebels wanted land socialisation, the abolition of foot bindings, and the replacement of Buddhism and Confucianism with a version of Christianity. Once the insurgency was quashed, the Hakka were brutally persecuted. A generation later, in the Boxer Rebellion of 1900, an uprising against Christianity and European colonisation, most Hakka sided with the British. The patriotic Cantonese had even more reason to marginalise them. By the time the BNBC began offering free land to Chinese labourers, many Hakka had become religious and political refugees.

The Basel Mission ran a scheme for the BNBC in which the Hakka received passage and were leased land. Half of the land was devoted to cash crops: tobacco and rubber. The rest was available for the families to farm on a subsistence basis. Other workers, indentured to the British plantations, were treated like slaves. In 1891 most estates registered a death rate among workers of more than 20 per cent, with some as high as 40 per cent. Men and women were fodder for the economic machine of the empire. But the Hakka maintained connections with their families in China, and word spread fast. An old Chinese saying in Sabah is 'the tai-pan [foreign business owners] treat us like dogs'.[23] But the Hakka never accepted their subservience. Nor did they see themselves as inferior. That was not the Hakka way. British North Borneo soon found it harder to attract new migrants, which spurred an improvement in conditions. From 1921 Chinese settlers were encouraged to send for their relatives and friends back home, with the passage paid for by the company.

By the beginning of the 1930s, after half a century of continuous assisted immigration, there were 27,424 Hakka and 12,831 Cantonese in Borneo.[24] Together, Chinese migrants and their children may have accounted for nearly a quarter of the population. The Cantonese settled in the towns as merchants and artisans; the Hakka worked on the land and the estates. By now the Hakka were influential.[25] Their dialect had become the common language for the Chinese in Borneo. Their concerns were at the centre of political life. Their people sought opportunities for education and began to take up posts in the colonial administration. Today, Chinese make up almost one-sixth of Malaysian Borneo's population, but have much larger social and economic influence than those numbers indicate.

Exactly how Penny Wong's ancestors fit into this history is not known. Her grandmother was illiterate, and her father does not write Chinese script. Few written records were kept by those that preceded them. Almost an entire generation was wiped out in World War II, robbing their descendants of oral history.

A family tree of her father's patrilineal lineage shows the first known male ancestor as Wong Ling Kay, Penny Wong's great-grandfather.[26] Her father, Francis Yit Shing Wong, believes this man was a fisher who for many years travelled between southern mainland China and North Borneo before settling on the island. If this is accurate, on this side of the family Penny Wong is of Cantonese descent. But her most powerful understandings of her Chinese ancestry concern her Hakka grandmother, Lai Fung Shim, the second wife of her grandfather, Wong Yew Chung. Lai married at a time when it was normal for men to have at least two wives. Some might call her a concubine but, says Penny Wong, 'that is a very Western concept. In the Chinese tradition, the first marriage is the arranged marriage. The second match is for love.' The family lore is that Lai was the love of her husband's life. Of Lai's ancestry, little is known. She identified as Hakka, and it is almost certain she was descended from those brought out as part of the colonial project.

World War II saw an end to mass Chinese migration to Borneo. In late 1941 the Japanese invaded. Borneo was only a small part of what amounted to a Japanese empire, but it is known as its most terrible. The experience of Australian prisoners of war in Borneo – sent there by the Japanese to build an airstrip – is part of Australian mythology. The Sandakan death march, in which 2000 weak prisoners were forced to trudge along 260 kilometres of jungle tracks, is 'the greatest single atrocity committed against Australians in war', according to the Australian War Memorial. Of about a thousand Australians forced to make the trek, only six survived.[27]

The sufferings of the local Borneans have not made it into the Australian history books. About 16 per cent of the population were killed during the occupation.[28] The Hakkas bore the brunt. Before the war, true to their pro-British history, they had raised funds for the war effort, donating to the Spitfire Fund. Now, colonised by these new masters, they began to organise. Within six months of the occupation, they had formed a society: the Salvation of Overseas Chinese. Its inaugural meeting was held in the house of Wong Yun Tshin, then working for the Jesselton Ice and Power Co., a de facto electricity board.[29] (It is unlikely that this Wong is a relative of Penny. Wong is a common name.) Wong became the treasurer of the association. When the Japanese announced a plan to conscript Chinese men for military service and force Chinese women into sexual slavery, the society began to plan a rebellion. It was an extraordinary effort. Against the odds, the uprising succeeded in taking back Jesselton (Kota Kinabalu) from the Japanese, holding it for days. The recapture was brutal, the consequences awful. Entire village populations were killed. Many were tortured, which resulted in the uncovering of incipient plans for another rebellion. This, too, was ruthlessly put down through summary execution.[30]

Francis Yit Shing Wong, Penny Wong's father, was Lai Fung Shim's second-eldest child. According to his birth certificate he was born just before the Japanese occupation, on 25 July 1941. In fact, he believes he is at least a year or two older, and the certificate a later fabrication. He has dim memories of the war, more than would be expected if he was an infant. His main memory is hunger. Another is the strength of his mother.

They were living in Sandakan. Francis's father and most of the family had died, probably of beriberi and malnutrition, leaving Lai Fung Shim responsible for raising five children: Francis, his infant sister Sau Ying and brother Yit Hing, and his siblings by his father's first wife, half-brother Yet Leun and half-sister Sau Yu. He remembers his mother having a cut on her leg that wouldn't heal due to malnutrition. She would drag herself across the ground in search of food. Francis recalls being bitten in the face by a starving dog after he was told to guard some coconuts. With no medicines to treat the wound, it became dangerously infected. One day he was sitting by the road when a Japanese soldier noticed his swollen face. The soldier picked him up, put him on his bicycle and took him to a clinic, where the wound was treated. The soldier gave him a meal, returned him home and visited over the days ahead to dress the wound. Francis thinks this soldier probably saved his life. The lesson he drew, and passed on to Penny, was 'God may send an enemy to save you'.[31]

Only the male children survived the war. In these desperate circumstances the two sisters, mere infants, were abandoned by the side of a road. The hope was they would be taken in by another family that could feed them. Penny Wong is reluctant to have this fact printed. 'People will judge. And you can't judge what happens in that kind of deprivation.' At different times, the family has searched for them, without success.

Lai rarely spoke at length about what she had been through, but her characteristic response when anyone complained was, 'It can't be as bad as the war.' Wong feels the impact of this family memory. She refers to an ability to put aside her emotions, acquired partly at her grandmother's knee and partly through her experiences following the breakdown of her parents' marriage and the bullying at school. It is, she says, 'a habit or capacity which is not necessarily emotionally helpful but is quite useful'. When things are challenging, 'I just focus on doing for a bit. Doing what needs to be done. I feel later.'

It is normal in Chinese culture to show respect for elders, but in the Wong family it went further. Lai was not only the head of the family in which Penny grew up, but its saviour. She was venerated not only by her own descendants but also by her stepson and their families. She particularly loved Penny, the first female grandchild. Toby and Penny grew up calling her 'Poh Poh', their beloved grandmother. Only in adulthood did Wong realise that her full name – Penelope Ying-Yen Wong – had been chosen at her grandmother's request. She is named after Lai's first daughter, Sau Ying: the girl abandoned by the roadside and never heard from again.

Asked whether she identifies, on her father's side, as Malaysian, Chinese or Hakka, Wong is momentarily stumped. She dismisses the Malaysian identity. The culture in which she was raised was far removed from that of mainland Malaysia. The nation was barely a decade old when she was born. 'I grew up thinking of myself as half-Chinese and half-Australian,' she says. The Chinese identity does not imply any yearning for or loyalty to the present-day nation of China. Rather, it is an ethnic and cultural identification.

Her life story, and the way she talks about herself, makes another conclusion tempting. It is to her Hakka heritage that she frequently refers. This is both implicit and explicit. Within the family, it is said that Penny has inherited her grandmother's determination. It was her grandmother whom she referred to in her maiden speech, describing 'Madam Lai Fung Shim' as 'humble and compassionate but the strongest person I have ever known'.[32] The words 'guest people', with all their nuance, resonate with Penny Wong's childhood feelings of alienation. The Hakka are the strong, hardworking outsiders, the perpetual 'guests' who, with generations of discrimination and persecution behind them, have learned to show a tough face to the world. Through talent and determination, they end up at the centre of history. They initiate change, and they refuse to be only victims.

In these characteristics, along with the known facts of her ancestry, Penny Wong is surely Hakka.

*

In 1945 Sabah was liberated by the Australian 9th Division – the Rats of Tobruk – through three seaborne invasions involving more than 80,000 soldiers. To the Borneans the British were their former colonial masters, but the Australians were their liberators.

Borneans were left with a ravaged country. Roads, buildings and communication links had been destroyed. The BNBC lacked the resources to rebuild and handed North Borneo to the British Crown, which was preoccupied by its own post-war reconstruction. The young Francis Yit Shing Wong relied on a war victim fund for his early education. His mother worked as a domestic servant for a British family to support him and his brothers. It was always clear to him that the only path to improve his life was education: 'I had to do well to get out of the level of poverty … Circumstances make you the man you are. You have to give your best.'[33]

A photo shows Francis Wong, aged about fifteen, beside his mother. She is diminutive – a tiny woman in a patterned dress, the wartime trauma only a few years in her past. She is unsmiling, but he perches on the arm of her chair, bounding with optimism and energy.[34] Another shows him grinning broadly. The resemblance to Penny is striking.[35]

He was a scholarship boy, a border at the Sabah College Hostel, and by 1961, at the nominal age of twenty, a prefect. The hostel warden's written reference described him as having 'character and bearing', making him a 'leader among his fellow students … He is a young man who has a high sense of duty, which, I am sure, will bear him in good stead in the walk of life he may choose'.[36] Another reference, written by the headmaster of his high school, records him as having impressed with a 'discerning mind and a sensible approach to study'.[37] These references were written with a purpose. Francis Wong had applied to come to Australia to study under the Colombo Plan. It was to be the transformative opportunity of his life.

The first Colombo Plan ran for thirty years from its inception in 1951. At its core was a scheme in which the most academically able from emerging Asian and Pacific nations were sponsored to study in Commonwealth countries. It was not only philanthropic. Part of the motivation was an attempt to win the hearts and minds of young professionals as a safeguard against communism. In 1961 Francis arrived in Australia and enrolled in the recently established Bachelor of Architecture at the University of Adelaide. His student records show he was admitted on the strength of his school marks and a post-school certificate course.[38] He passed most of his subjects with credits or distinctions, and in 1965 was approved to do honours. He was by now something of a star, promoted as an exemplar of the Colombo Plan. *The Advertiser* carried an item headed 'University award to Asian', reporting that he had 'distinguished himself' by being recommended for the James Hardie Prize in architecture.[39] He was written up in the Sabah press as 'a future Sabah architect' who had done 'very well in his recent third-year examination'.[40] His honours thesis was a proposal for a technical college in Sabah. He explained in his thesis report that there were no facilities for higher education in Sabah.[41] Francis Wong was an optimist. His experiences in Australia had convinced him of the benefits of education, and of globalisation. Now, he was determined to make a contribution to the future of his country.

Jane Chapman must still have been grieving the death of her parents when, sometime in the early 1960s, a friend who was studying architecture at the University of Adelaide introduced her to Francis Yit Shing Wong. It apparently never occurred to Jane to allow race to be a barrier to love. Jane, according to Penny Wong, has never been racist. 'You know, some people have it, and some people don't have it, that sense of difference. She just doesn't have it.' As for her sisters, 'They loved Dad.'

Jane and Francis married before he had finished his degree. Jane changed her name to Wong and travelled with him back to his home. Staying in Australia was never an option for the new couple. The White Australia policy was still in force. Even if Francis had been able to find a way to settle in Australia, he was the hope of his mother, the consolation for all she had suffered, the realisation of a better future.

Francis Wong's degree was conferred on 10 May 1967, by which time the student who had entered university as a British subject in the protectorate of North Borneo was a citizen of the newly formed country of Malaysia. He was part of a generation of returning Colombo scholars, many of them with European wives, who saw it as their mission to rebuild Sabah and help to form the new nation.

In this new Malaysia the Chinese professionals of Borneo were at a triple disadvantage. First, they were remote from peninsular Malaysia. Second, they were mainly Christians in a Muslim-dominated nation. Third, the constitution gave ethnic Malays preference in education and employment. Chinese-Malaysians were second-class citizens. In this context, according to a history of architecture in Sabah, Francis Wong was 'the epitome of the manner of cosmopolitan, professional free-thinker, and agent of modernisation that the Australian training program had sought to produce'.[42] An Australian education, together with the fact that Colombo Plan students were selected purely on academic merit, was credited for infusing Sabah architecture with an egalitarian spirit and 'a peculiarly Australian preoccupation with fair play and the levelling of the field through rules of order and due process'. This was 'a hedge against possible political pressures and restrictions in a context of growing nationalist and racial chauvinism'.[43]

Francis Wong became one of Sabah's leading architects and a minor public figure. He played a role in the establishment of the Sabah chapter of the Malaysian Institute of Architects (Pertubuhan Akitek Malaysia, PAM) and served as its founding chairman. After practising as an architect, he became a property developer, a local government councillor and a lecturer at the Sabah Institute of Art. Reflecting later in life, he said, 'The influence of my university professors towards the value of education has come one full circle. It is now my turn to prepare the younger generation for globalisation. Without my professional training in Australia, I would not have achieved as much as a citizen of my country.'[44]

The lessons he drew from his Colombo Plan scholarship included the transformative effect of education, harnessed to a strong sense of obligation to hand on its benefits – to make a contribution. The beaming boy in the photo had grown into a man who believed in the generosity and essential goodness of Australia. Of the discrimination he suffered under the Malaysian constitution, he felt it was a matter of 'whatever it takes to keep the peace'. Wong remembers her father remarking that soon there would be no racism, because 'everyone will marry each other'. He was convinced of the benefits of globalisation and encouraged his children to think of themselves as citizens of the world.

Penny Wong's ability to take on her father's sunny optimism was challenged by the racism she suffered when she arrived in Australia. For much of her childhood, she was embattled and hypervigilant.

But on Anzac Day 1992, when Wong was twenty-three, prime minister Paul Keating gave a high-profile speech in Port Moresby about Australian identity and our place in Asia. He declared that the fall of Singapore was as important to the national story as Gallipoli. He spoke of the soldiers whose bodies lay in France and Belgium and the countries of the Middle East, but noted that Australia's war casualties 'also lie in Singapore and Malaysia, Burma, Borneo and the other countries of this region'. Those who fought in Korea, Malaya and Vietnam did so to secure a place in the Asia-Pacific for their country and its ideals.

Keating ended his speech with an appeal to a vision of modern Australia:

> Ladies and gentlemen, these days there is a relatively new memorial to the Anzac legend in Australia. Sitting on the hill near the new Parliament House, it is a modest monument inscribed with these words: 'Look around you – these are the things they believed in. In the end they believed in Australia – in the democracy they had built, in the life they had made there, and the future they believed their country held.'[45]

That same year, Wong took one of her regular trips to Kota Kinabalu, the capital of Sabah, to visit her father. She returned to Sydney's Kingsford Smith Airport on a hot summer day. When the wheels hit the tarmac, she thought, *This is my country now. This is my place.* 'It was the sense of a national identity that contemplated me that made the difference,' she recalled.[46] Penny Wong was now an Australian, both in ancestry and in the way she saw herself. Whether she realised it or not, she was the embodiment of and an agent for the broadening of Australian identity.

2

BUTTERFLIES AND BULLIES

There is a story Penny Wong tells – or not so much a story as a memory from her childhood – that evokes what it was like to be brought up in the tropics in a rapidly developing nation.

She was about six years old, playing in the double garage of her home in the new suburb of Friendly Garden, in Kota Kinabalu. Her younger brother, Toby, was with her. The house, newly built as a result of her father's improving fortunes, was on the edge of the city. Behind it was what Penny thought of as 'the jungle', although her father said it was merely the remains of an abandoned rubber plantation, rapidly being cleared to make way for new housing.

As the children played, rain began to fall. Tropical rain is a deluge. It slammed down. Amid the noise, something made the children look up at the ceiling to find it transformed into a jewel box of wall-to-wall butterflies – all sizes and colours. They had come in from the jungle for shelter. The image has never left Penny Wong. Today, she tells this story to her daughters.

Penelope Ying-Yen Wong was born in Kota Kinabalu on 5 November 1968, the year after her father's degree was awarded. Tobias To Pen Wong, always called Toby or Tobe, was born three years later. Her earliest memories are of Toby crawling across the wooden floors of their living room in an airy house on stilts – what Australians would call a Queenslander. This was where they lived until the move to Friendly Garden. She remembers Toby leaving a trail of dribble on the floor. Lai lived with them. Penny's father was working for a modest public service salary. It was her grandmother who looked after the children, together with a series of *amahs*, or nannies.

There is a photo of a young Penny Wong – perhaps three or four years old – with Lai. She is serving her grandmother tea. Penny wears a pink ruffled dress. She is kneeling on a cushion in front of the old woman, a tray solemnly extended. Lai is sitting ramrod straight, with a stern expression, her head inclined to the little girl. As Wong remarks, it is a moving picture because of the combination of Lai's pose and her obvious focus on the child: 'You can see she loves me, even though she is being strict.' Today, Wong keeps this image on her phone.

Penny Wong first visited Australia with her mother, Jane, on a three-month holiday in November 1970, arriving on her second birthday. They stayed with her Aunt Alison – Ally – in North Adelaide.[1] Penny was just beginning to speak, using a mixture of Chinese – probably Hakka dialect – and Malaysian Bahasa. Jane had to educate Ally on the words that meant a need to go to the toilet. But by the time Penny reached school age she had switched, apparently without difficulty, to speaking English. Her father was keen for her to do so. He wanted her to speak without an accent, which for him meant 'not like a Malaysian Chinese'. For Francis, English was the language of education and opportunity. Today, Penny Wong speaks very little Chinese. She says, 'I can't get the tones right.' She can understand parts of Bahasa – a unifying language of the region – but is not fluent.

Penny and Toby were brought up in a cultural, religious and ethnic melange. Her grandmother, unlike many Hakka, was Buddhist. She maintained a small altar and said a prayer before meals. 'It was nice, it grounded her,' says Wong. Her father identified with Catholicism, largely because he had attended Catholic schools and associated the religion with the opportunity for education. Her mother was not a believer but had been brought up Methodist. In their wider circle there was every kind of religion. They had friends who were Muslim (the family kept a separate wok to prepare halal food on social occasions). They also had friends who were Dayak, the indigenous inhabitants of Borneo, some of whom were Christian or Muslim, while others practised ancient animistic traditions. In this mix, Penny grew up with a strong sense of God – she says she has never doubted the existence of a divine force – but without any conviction that there was a single path to his favour. 'I always felt there were many paths to God ... I didn't have the sense that other faiths were inferior.'[2] The family celebrated Christmas, Chinese New Year and some Muslim religious festivals. The diversity did not seem unusual. She was used to hearing her parents rib each other about the cultural differences between them, but this was in good humour. Differences of race and culture carried no negative connotation in diverse Borneo, despite the discrimination written into the constitution of the new nation. Difference was simply part of the texture of everyday life.

Jane Wong, as she was now known, embarked upon her new life in Sabah with a fascination for Chinese culture and an openness to new experiences. She and Francis forged close links in particular with the Chinese and indigenous Kadazan communities, and Jane learned basic Cantonese. She embraced the close family dynamic. She and Francis mixed with members of the expatriate community, which included the foreign wives of other returned Colombo scholars. Nevertheless, it must have been challenging to establish a life in a new country.

Jane considered herself a feminist. On one of her journeys from Australia to Malaysia, she carried a copy of Germaine Greer's *The Female Eunuch* through customs from Australia to Malaysia. The cover featured a naked female torso hanging from a clothes rail, with handles on the hips – as though it were an item for male use and handling. The customs officer scratched out the image on the cover.[3]

Today, Wong says of her mother that she has an instinctive habit of taking the perspective of the person with less power. When her professional life developed after her return to Australia, she became known among campaigners for social justice in Adelaide – but she did not want her daughter to enter politics. Why? Because she feared the invasion of privacy that would result, says Wong. Jane did not want to be interviewed for this book.

Jane was in the public gallery when Wong gave her maiden speech in federal parliament in 2002. Wong looked up at her as she gave her tribute. 'Your intellect, mischievousness, sense of humour and unfailing love sustain me,' she said.[4] Others who know Jane emphasise her sense of humour, her quirkiness and her commitment to social justice. Later, Wong's stepchildren were to refer to Jane by the nickname 'the Goddess'.

It was Francis who pushed his children and had high ambitions for them. Coming from poverty, he was driven. He urged his kids to study and encouraged them to pursue excellence in all they did. He was later to recount that he told them success meant 'doing positive things to the limit of one's potential'. He would not give them money, but would give them all that he could in the way of education.[5] Jane was more relaxed. Penny Wong thinks today that her mother recognised her daughter's natural determination and adjusted her parenting as a result. 'She would talk to me about other measures of worth, rather than success. She would talk about my heart, or my spirit ... she wasn't didactic, and she wasn't pushy at all.'

Cooking was important in the Wong family home. Chinese families often weren't physically demonstrative, so food had a special place. Preparing food, her father used to say, was one of the ways in which you could show others your love. Almost all of Penny Wong's significant relationships seem linked to stories about cooking.

Little Penny liked superheroes. She had a Superman suit she wore frequently. She learned to read early – long before she started school – and had children's versions of Greek and Roman legends. When she wasn't Superman she was Perseus, slayer of monsters, or Theseus, founder of Athens and the great reformer. Penny was less interested in Hercules. She found him boring. One day Jane came home from work to find her young daughter perched on a windowsill of the stilted house, dressed as Superman. 'What are you doing there?' her mother asked. 'I'm going to fly down,' said Penny. Looking back, Penny regards her mother's response as restrained and wise. 'She knew me. She knew that if she told me I couldn't do it, that would only encourage me.' Instead, Jane suggested the flight should be delayed until after dinner. Food won out.

From the age of five Penny attended Kinabalu International School, established only three years before her enrolment to provide a

British-style education for expatriates and the emerging middle class. The ethnic melange continued there. The schoolyard had faces of every colour. Penny's best friend was white. The school motto was 'nurturing global citizens'.[6] The children were aware of the ethnic and cultural differences among their friends and family but it was, Penny remembers, 'difference without connotation. Nobody ever suggested it meant that people were lesser. It simply never occurred to me that race was an issue in that way until I came to Australia.'

*

In 1976, Penny's parents told her and Toby that they were separating and that the siblings would be moving to Australia with Jane. She can't remember now how she felt about the move beforehand, or how long it was between the announcement and their arrival in Adelaide. It seemed fast, as though within just a few days they left normal life and crashed into this new, colder and unfriendly place.

They stayed with their aunt Ally, until Penny's mother bought a cream-brick triple-fronted house in Coro Crescent, Coromandel Valley, in the Adelaide Hills – just a few kilometres from the farm that her grandfather and great-grandfather had once owned. Coromandel Valley was largely orchards and market gardens, but suburban Adelaide was rising up the hills to meet it. New housing subdivisions were being created, though it still felt like a country town.

Jane had limited cooking skills. Instead of the aromas and sounds of carefully prepared meals, it was sandwiches for lunch, meat and three veg in the evenings. The children didn't like it. Penny and Toby taught themselves to cook at an early age.[7]

The children weren't to know it, but the year after their arrival – 1977 – was a turning point in Australian migration. The year before, the first boatload of refugees from Vietnam had arrived. The last vestiges of the White Australia policy had been swept away by the Whitlam government, but Whitlam also cut immigration. It was therefore the Fraser government that gave multiculturalism form and definition. The government announced its decision to welcome many more refugees, and allow family reunions. By 1979 Asia had become the largest regional source of migrants, at 29 per cent, forever changing the nation. People of Asian descent now make up about 16 per cent of the population.[8] But when Penny and Toby were getting to know Coromandel Valley, theirs were the only Asian faces in the suburb.

When Penny went into their backyard one evening to call Toby in for dinner, the neighbour leaned over the back fence and shouted, 'Go back to where you came from, you slant-eyed little slut!' Wong still remembers her face, distorted in anger. Sometime after that Penny came home from a visit to Malaysia to find her mother and aunts scrubbing at the driveway. Anti-Asian slogans were painted on the footpath outside their home. The police were told, but if any action was taken the family never heard about it. She has since been told that the police suggested that the best solution was for them to move house.

Today, Coromandel Valley Primary School is part of an ordinary outer suburb. The orchards and farms have long since been built over. It is not a school with a deep sense of its own history. There are no old photos, or school annuals, or teachers still in touch who remember Penny and Toby Wong as children. The current teaching staff are aware, from comments she has made in interviews, that she wasn't happy there – but the school has changed dramatically since, they say. Some years ago European languages were dropped from the curriculum in favour of Japanese. In the library and in every classroom there are signs about how to demonstrate the school values – which include resilience, kindness, tolerance and embrace of difference. Penny Wong has been back in recent years to give a speech. She was moved to see, looking out at the school assembly, that the faces reflected multicultural Australia. 'It was a nice thing,' she says, 'hearing about the values they teach. And I thought, *things have changed.* It was quite healing.'

But as a child, school was a nightmare. The verbal bullying was constant, and sometimes turned physical. She approached each day as though going into battle, bracing herself mentally and physically. She learned to fight: 'I gave as good as I got.' If the teachers took any action to protect her and Toby from bullying, she doesn't remember it.

They felt entirely alone. She coped by trying not to respond or show her hurt. 'It was, "I'm never going to let you see, in any way, that this gets to me. I'm never going to let you see that I feel upset, or lonely, or shy."' She began to suffer from vicious migraines – so debilitating that she could barely stand and often had temporary losses of vision. Her mother took her for every kind of test, with no explanation to be found.

Jane tried to help with the bullying, offering one-line rejoinders. The aunts, particularly Ally, were a constant loving presence. Perhaps it is thanks to this support that Penny did not internalise the abuse, that her response was to deny her persecutors power over her. She learned to control her emotions and fiercely protect her thoughts, not to let those outside her family see what was going on inside. She found a steely resolve.

Jane began a bachelor's degree, followed by postgraduate qualifications, in social work. Meanwhile, by 1978 Francis Wong was at a turning point in his career – expanding from architectural practice into property development.[9] Their divorce was civilised; both parents worked hard at remaining on good terms. Whatever anger or hurt had caused their break-up, they did not allow it to affect their relationships with the children. Penny Wong says today that both her parents are remarkable. Not only did they marry at a time when much was against them doing so, but when they split they never argued – or at least not in a way the children were aware of. Neither ever criticised the other in front of the children. Penny and Toby flew back to Kota Kinabalu regularly to spend school holidays with their father. Penny remembers that her grandmother, Lai, used to kill and cook a chicken to celebrate their arrival. Francis took the children hiking up Mount Kinabalu, and on travels throughout South-East Asia.

A photo from 1983 shows Penny and Toby serving tea to their grandmother on the day of her seventieth birthday. Again, there is the tray of tea, and the diminutive grandmother. This time, though, something has shifted. Penny, now fifteen, meets her grandmother's eyes. She is clearly on the edge of adulthood. Toby stands slightly behind her, hands clasped behind his back. The old woman remains as she has ever been – strong, stern and loving, her back straight, her head inclined slightly towards her grandchildren.[10]

Francis Wong remarried to a Malaysian woman, Loris Lee, who had three children by a previous relationship with a New Zealander. In effect, Francis adopted them, then went on to father another two with Lee – a son, Wong Kein Peng, also called James, and a daughter, Wong Ying Soon, also called Jessica.[11] Today, Penny Wong considers herself one of seven. In the family, they don't parse between the steps and the halves – they are all brothers and sisters. There is an online family chat-room where they interact and share their news. She also remains in touch with her uncles – the two surviving children of her grandfather's first wife – and their children and grandchildren. A few years ago Francis moved to Australia, and Jessica is here as well. James runs an architec-tural practice in Kota Kinabalu.

Toby, though, was always the one closest to Penny – the sharer of early memories, the companion with whom she saw those butterflies, her ally in suffering during the early days in Australia. Toby and Penny were thrown together by their social isolation and by what became a vital mission to learn how to cook, to re-create the smells, flavours and good feelings that came with food. Toby used to say that, with food, you could make yourself feel good three times a day.[12]

Toby became a chef. Penny, too, is an accomplished cook. A few years ago she was asked, along with other parliamentarians, to provide a favourite recipe for a Labor Party fundraising book. She contributed 'Toby's Fish'.[13] It can be made with either fillets or whole fish, coated in rice flour, then fried until crisp. 'Lots' of ginger, chilli, the Malay-sian shrimp-paste condiment balachan, onion and tomatoes are fried, dressed with rice vinegar and soy sauce, and garnished with handfuls of coriander. The fish is placed on top. 'Toby's Fish' was also the rec-ipe Penny Wong cooked for the journalist Annabel Crabb when she took part in the ABC television series *Kitchen Cabinet*. Crabb described Wong as one of 'Australia's most guarded politicians' – without revealing to the audience that they had known each other since university days.[14] Penny Wong let her guard down while cooking for Crabb. She moved through the kitchen like a professional, tea towel slung over a shoulder, and talked about Toby, although she hadn't meant to. Toby's Fish was, she told Crabb, typical of the kind of simple, tasty food on which she had been raised in Malaysia. It was also a tribute to Toby – a sign of love. Perhaps it is also a tiny consolation for grief.

*

Adelaide is a small city – just big enough not to be a country town but not so large that the people who lead it, or who excel in it, can avoid knowing each other. The common pattern for its university graduates has been to move east for jobs. The city is ageing, and for nearly all of Penny Wong's life it has been the slowest-growing capital city on the Australian continent. When she was a teenager, the population had just topped a million. Today, when she represents her state in the Senate, it is just under 1.4 million.

Adelaide can feel like a city-state. More than three-quarters of the population of South Australia live in the capital. Beyond the Adelaide Hills there is marginal farming country, then desert.

But the city likes itself. Ever since its founding it has defined itself as different. It fancies itself less party-political and more cultured than its convict-founded sibling states. It is a state of social reform – the first to give women the vote, and the home of the progressive Dunstan government, in power when the Wong family arrived from Malaysia. Before Dunstan, the women of Adelaide used to wear white gloves when going to town; after Dunstan, they wore miniskirts and pantsuits. He decriminalised homosexuality, recognised Aboriginal land rights and enacted anti-discrimination laws. Penny Wong can be understood as one of the latest examples of the tradition of South Australian socially progressive reformers.

Yet, beneath this history, the politics can have a particular, internecine quality.

It is not hard for talented people to become big fish in this small pond. Rivals can't get away from one another. Certain restaurants and bars have a commonly recognised social significance. The journalists in

Adelaide have a saying. In any other part of Australia, if two people tell you something separately you are inclined to think it must be true. In Adelaide, it just means that sometime in the past week both have been drinking at the Exeter Hotel.

One of the first things that Adelaideans ask one another upon meeting is 'Where did you go to school?' It is the city's quintessential question: a way of placing people, a substitute for class. These days, the question is pitched ironically – but it still gets asked. If the answer is the name of a public school, the conversation quickly turns to a sympathetic discussion about social disadvantage. Sometimes the point will be made that former prime minister Julia Gillard went to Unley High School and despite this rose to the highest office in the land.

Penny Wong, though, has the ultimate 'correct' answer to the question. Her time at Coromandel Valley Primary School was limited. After a few years, she entered Scotch College – the most prestigious school in the city, and one of the wealthiest in the country.

The Chapmans of Jane's generation were not rich, but they were rooted in Adelaide society. They had resources, connections and a deep knowledge of how the city worked. Jane had had the resources to buy the house they were living in outright. Francis supplied the capital, through a family trust structure, to provide continued support for his children as his fortunes in Malaysia improved. Nevertheless, it is doubtful if Penny Wong could have attended Scotch if Jane had not organised for her to sit a scholarship test.

Wong does not remember the extent of the scholarship. If there were residual fees to be paid she never heard about it. She began in the middle school and, three years later, Toby started there as well.

Scotch College was founded as a school for Presbyterian boys in 1919. By the time Penny began there in 1980 it had become part of the Uniting Church of Australia, and had been taking girls for eight years. The campus was only a twenty-minute drive from home, but it could have been in a different country from the edge-of-suburban narrowness of Coromandel Valley. The campus hasn't fundamentally changed since she attended. It is a place of beauty, history and privilege, covering twenty hectares in Torrens Park, at the foot of the Adelaide Hills. At its heart lies a nineteenth-century mansion with a turreted tower, formerly the home of Robert Barr Smith, friend and employer of Penny Wong's maternal great-great-grandfather (not that she knew of the connection at the time of her attendance). Attached to the old building is a theatre, built by the Barr Smiths as an indulgence to their daughters, who liked to put on shows for their friends and family. It was a school tradition to climb to the rafters and carve your name. The words *Penny Wong* are said to be found somewhere near the roof.

The front verandah of the main building has views over a school chapel larger than most suburban churches, and beyond over playing fields and the northern suburbs of the city. Behind the main building are tennis courts, a swimming pool, a fully operational farm with a vineyard, more grand buildings and classrooms, and finally the Adelaide Hills. Further afield, there is an entire small island in Spencer Gulf, leased by the school for camps and excursions.

From the time she started at Scotch, Penny's life began to get better – much better. She entered as a bright kid fighting prejudice and determined to beat the bullies. She ended as a polished performer among the elite. For a Labor politician, having gone to Scotch College is a mixed blessing. Wong's critics in the Labor Party use it against her, at least behind her back. 'She speaks like a Scotch College prefect and she has the same attitudes,' said one. 'It's all rounded vowels and ruling-class arrogance.' Another described the Scotch College background as a political disadvantage – but for the saving grace that she was a scholarship girl.

According to Wong, when she was there the school reflected a particularly Adelaidean form of liberalism. The deputy principal at that time was Diana Hill, later president of UNICEF Australia and the wife of Robert Hill, who rose to be the minister for the environment and the minister for defence in the Howard government before being pushed out – reportedly because he was too far to the left. Diana Hill had been at the school since 1977, when girls were still a minority. She pushed Scotch to change the uniforms, language and facilities to make the environment more welcoming for girls and female staff, as well as advocating for a shift from a 'blokey' sports-oriented culture to one that valued academic excellence as well.[15] Diana Hill remains a friend of Wong's.

Scotch College, in Wong's experience, was less concerned with privilege and more with 'classic liberalism' or 'Steele Hall liberalism' – the latter a reference to the premier of South Australia and later senator who came from a humble farming background and modernised the state Liberal Party. Hall was one of those who crossed the floor in 1988 to oppose Liberal leader John Howard's move to make race a criterion for selecting migrants.

Penny thrived at Scotch. The bullying ceased. Partly, it was because the students were worldlier. As well, among the boarders were the children of wealthy Asians paying top dollar for the benefits of an elite Australian education. For a child who had already resolved to succeed, Scotch offered every opportunity.

The first substantial mention of Penny in the school magazine is in 1981, when she was twelve and in her second year at the school. She set a record in under-thirteen girls' javelin. She was also captain of her house, and wrote a report on the year's activities that recorded 'many enjoyable outings', including a cut lunch at the Scotch rowing shed on the River Torrens, and a roller-skating excursion followed by 'dinner at McDonald's, where most of us felt ill after eating too much'. Everyone had, she said, 'enjoyed the year immensely'. Her report is terribly jolly – exactly as one would expect from an average product of a privileged private school. Among her family and friends, Penny is described as a navigator of difference, a negotiator between positions. This glimpse suggests she had navigated the cultural distance and adopted the tone.

But there was a darker and more complex part of Penny Wong's twelve-year-old voice. This was also the year in which her poem about the shark was published in the school magazine. Along with it was another poem, titled 'Early Australia'. It was a distinctly anti-heroic take.

There is a stillness
As if the bush holds its breath.
The convicts, arriving,
Stagger off the ship
Dizzy, as if intoxicated still
by the foul smells of their vessel

And later, there is a whipping.

They receive their weekly rations
A meagre handful of flour
A few vegetables, a bit of salt pork.
Some try to steal more
And are caught.
They bare their backs,
to receive the brutal blows
And cry out in pain.
The overseer's voice chanting out the number of strokes.
33, 34, 35,
The numbers are spat out
like the crack of the whip.
49, 50.
The men do not move,
As if they do not know their ordeal is over.
Their backs are cut to shreds,
red, raw and bleeding.
It is over.
The convicts go back to work.
The guards hustle them along,
The Governor returns to his papers.
And the victims of the whipping
are dragged to a dark hut.
To lie in pain and agony
till the others are dismissed.[16]

It is an impressive poem for a twelve-year-old. It shows imagination, obviously, but also, one fancies, an early tendency to empathise with the downtrodden.

By the early years of secondary school, Penny had decided she wanted to be a doctor. Her father liked the idea.[17] She fancied she would work with Médecins Sans Frontières (Doctors Without Borders). Medicine seemed a natural ambition – partly because it was what bright Chinese children were supposed to do. But there was another motivation: she wanted her life to matter.

There is a term that Penny Wong uses a lot, in talking about herself and others. It is 'praxis'. During the interviews for this book, she spoke of a well-known public intellectual in the field of foreign policy. She described him as 'a clear and logical thinker, but he has no praxis'. It was a striking word to use – even a little pompous. Speaking of her high-school medical ambitions, she used it again: 'It was the idea of praxis.' What does she mean by the term? She refers to Marx, for whom praxis meant action oriented towards changing society. 'I'm not a Marxist in terms of outcome,' she says, 'but I think some of the analytical framework he used is valuable. I wanted to look in the mirror and feel like I was doing something that had meaning. And it didn't have meaning for me to make money or to get status or to do anything like that. I had no interest in that. I was not particularly entrepreneurial, and I had no interest in building a business or anything commercial ... I just wanted to do something that made me feel like my life had a kind of philosophical worth.' Becoming a doctor, working for Médecins Sans Frontières, spoke to her father's hopes, and to her own ambition.

Naturally, she studied physics, chemistry, biology and maths at school, as well as languages – but despite her medical ambitions, she is best remembered for her creative work. One of her former classmates, Shane Grant, remembers Penny as being, like him, in the school's 'nerdy intellectual clique'. They were both in the debating team and, in a self-conscious dig at the jocks, argued for warm-up tracksuits for debaters as well as footballers. 'I remember she supported our position, and we won.' But Penny was not only a nerd. True to her resolve to do everything well, she also excelled on the rowing team, and in netball.

In 1983 she won the school's creative writing prize as well as the academic prize for her year. She finished among the top five in cross-country, was on the athletics team and performed well in swimming. The poem that won her the creative writing prize was titled 'Age', and it displayed a characteristic combination of cool, cutting observation and empathy.

I sit with my friends,
At the back of the bus,
We chuckle at the old ones
Shuffling to and fro.
They are grey and withered,
We are young and healthy.
To us they look pathetic,
Objects of ridicule.
Then Melanie says
'We'll be like that some day,'
We look at her in horror,
'I'd rather die,' we say.
But we no longer laugh,
For now we realize,
Inevitably, we will become
Like the objects of our mirth,
We are laughing at ourselves.
We all grow old,
But those in youth
Disregard that fact,
View it with utter distaste.
Will we be like those,
Who dye their hair,
Who use Orlane's de-wrinkling cream,
Who paint their faces,
And wear young clothes,
Or will we just grow old? [18]

The next year, 1984, she won the Year 11 academic prize, and the Stroke of the Girls rowing trophy, represented the school in netball, toured New Caledonia as part of her French studies and wrote a skit based on her experiences. She played classical guitar and had begun to get involved in the school drama program.[19]

The Barr Smith Theatre had been renovated during her first two years at the school and now a dynamic drama teacher, Andrew Jefferis, took charge of the program. In Year 10, Penny had played the role of The Walrus in a version of *Alice in Wonderland* that had been rewritten by the students. She remembers little about it other than the hot, itchy suit. But the next year's program was more intellectually challenging. She was part of the production crew for a performance of George Orwell's *Nineteen Eighty-Four* – an appropriate piece given the year, and one that must have provoked reflections on the nature of totalitarian states.

After that, she began to both study and act in ambitious, complex plays. She took a leading role in one of the most conceptually and intellectually dense stage works of the twentieth century, Luigi Pirandello's *Six Characters in Search of an Author*. The play is a metadrama in which the characters wander around a set within a set, looking for an author to tell them what to do. According to the review published in the school magazine, the result 'assaulted the senses ... and the mind as well'. Penny gave a 'superb performance as the egotistical but interested producer and author for the Six Characters'.[20]

This was 1985, her last year at the school. She was one of two school captains, and co-captain of the rowing team. That year she also toured Ballarat with the hockey team, sang in the school choir and performed in as well as compered an orchestral concert.

Wong and her co-captain, Peter Ker, wrote an anodyne report about their year of, as they put it, 'trying to be responsible school leaders'. They had convened regular meetings with the school leadership team and attended an afternoon tea with the state governor, Sir Donald Dunstan (no relation to the former premier), and his wife, Lady Dunstan. 'Treading the hallowed halls of Government House was a memorable experience,' they wrote.[21]

Penny finished her Year 12 with a score that allowed her to enrol in any course of her choice. She applied for, and was easily accepted into, the University of Adelaide medical school.

Penny had already decided that she wanted to have a gap year. Helped by the school, she had applied for a scholarship to a volunteer exchange program run by the organisation AFS Australia. Eight Scotch College graduates, including Shane Grant, won places. The 1985 issue of the school magazine notes, 'Penny Wong and Shane Grant, who were both outstanding Drama students, will be spending a year in a destination as yet unknown. We would like to wish them all the best for their time overseas.'[22]

The reason her destination was not known was that she had decided to take a whole year off for travel. The University of Adelaide's medical school would not allow her to defer for more than one year. That ruled out the Northern Hemisphere – the most popular destination for Australian exchange students – because the academic years would not line up. There was little point, she thought, in going to South-East Asia, because she had already travelled there extensively. She asked for South America, and at the year's turn found out she would be going to Brazil.

*

By the time Penny Wong finished school, Jane Chapman had completed her bachelor's degree, followed by postgraduate qualifications in social work, and was employed at the Adelaide Central Mission. From the mid-1980s she also began to publish on the impact of sex-role stereotyping on couples therapy. She was part of a team that developed a non-sexist language policy for the leading *Australian Journal of Family Therapy*.[23] Over the next decade she was to become increasingly known and respected in her field, as well as a dedicated campaigner on feminist and social equality issues. She went on to complete two other bachelor's degrees and additional postgraduate qualifications.

Meanwhile, Toby Wong found his feet at Scotch College. He's there in some of the class photos, a round-faced child shorter than his peers and with a strong resemblance to his sister. He is remembered by his schoolfriends as charismatic, ready with jokes, anecdotes and ideas for adventure, frequently leading to trouble. If Penny was a nerd, Toby was cool. While Penny excelled at school, Toby did not. In the later years, he was increasingly absent. His drug problem was common knowledge among his classmates and, in the final years, he simply fell from view.

Around 1985, when Toby would have been about fifteen, the Adelaide journalist Stilgherrian was drinking in a Rundle Street hotel and discussing music with his friends. He remembers, 'Suddenly this lad turned to me and said, "Mate, your taste in music is fucked."'[24] Thus began a conversation that turned into a close friendship. Toby was a blues fan, and deeply knowledgeable about music. He was 'a bit of a ratbag. He was going to pubs when he was too young to be doing that', recalls Stilgherrian. Toby must still have been formally enrolled in school at this stage, because Stilgherrian remembers him being one of the presenters of *Rock'n'Roll High School* on the community radio station. As the name implies, the program was presented by secondary students. Stilgherrian and Toby talked about one day doing a show together that would shift between recipes and Southern blues.

By the time he was eighteen or nineteen, Toby was the front man of a blues band called Mr Wong and the Travelling Czechs. He was also a well-regarded chef – ahead of his time, according to Stilgherrian, in providing what would later be described as fusion food: East meets West. 'He was heaps of fun. He had one dish he put on at an Asian restaurant called Mr Wong's Authentic Malaysian Duck Pizza, and if anyone asked about the authenticity he'd come to the table and spin this great line of bullshit about Malaysia's hidden pizza tradition. He was really charismatic. I joked at the time that he had all the charisma that Penny didn't. She's charismatic now, but it took her a while to find that. Toby always had charisma.'

By the early 1990s, Toby was head chef at a restaurant on Hutt Street, and Stilgherrian had a flat nearby. He gave Toby his keys so he could use the place for a nap between the lunch and evening trades. 'So I arrived home early one day from work to find him going through my fridge and throwing things out. He'd grab things and say, "Mate, these are bullshit tomatoes. Don't buy shit like this." And he'd just throw them in the bin. I do miss him.'

Toby was ardent about food. Poor quality offended him; it could not be tolerated. Today, Stilgherrian credits Toby with teaching him how to cook well. 'It was all about using high-quality ingredients with respect, keep it simple, taste as you go, and understand your ingredients so you know what each thing does.' Toby was able to 'throw things together and make a wonderful meal in minutes'. On one occasion – backyard cricket with the boys – Stilgherrian arrived late and hungry. Toby went to fetch him a sandwich. 'He disappears inside, and five minutes later he gives me this beautiful sourdough with freshly grilled garfish.'

Toby later worked as a consultant, designing menus and helping pubs and restaurants to source quality ingredients at good prices. Stilgherrian remembers, 'It would go from ordinary greengrocer produce bought at full prices to an Italian market gardener calling at the back door with boxes of great tomatoes, or the Vietnamese market gardener with the box of greens.' South Australia legalised the sale of kangaroo meat for human consumption well ahead of other states. Toby was among the first to put it on restaurant menus. Once, Stilgherrian, Toby and Toby's girlfriend went to an Asian restaurant, and Toby noticed there were different prices on the menu for Western and Chinese customers. After giving the management a lecture, he then insisted on going into the kitchen to 'meet the fish' they were about to be served.

As the friendship developed, Toby told Stilgherrian that he had 'mood problems' and 'anger issues ... but he never let me see them'. The drug use, and all that went with it in the way of connections to the criminal world, became increasingly evident. But this was not unusual for chefs, who often used drugs to deal with the laborious physical work and the fatigue.

From the earliest days, says Stilgherrian, Toby would talk about Penny with love and pride. It was well recognised in the family, Toby said, that his sister was 'super smart' and going places. It was she who would please their father, Toby said. He characterised himself as a 'ratbag' and 'black sheep'.

In the mid-1990s Stilgherrian's journalistic career took him to Sydney and, about the same time, Toby Wong moved to Melbourne. The two of them lost touch.

*

Penny Wong's decision to go to Brazil in 1986 changed the direction of her life. The country was at a crucial point in its history. The year before, civilian government had been restored, ending a 21-year era of military rule. The new republic's constitution was being drafted. Under the military regime, the Catholic Church had assumed responsibility for providing services, often under threat of persecution, to the poor. Liberation theology – the synthesis of Christian belief and Marxist praxis – had its firmest grip in Latin America, and the Brazilian priest and theologian Leonardo Boff was among its best-known supporters, arguing for a grass-roots reinvention of the Church's hierarchy. He maintained that there was only one answer to the question of how to be a Christian in a world of destitution and injustice – by making common cause with the poor.

Wong learned the language, Portuguese, relatively easily, drawing on the French she had studied at school but also, she suspects, owing to a mental plasticity around language that came from her early bilingual years. Being relatively fluent meant she was able to form deeper connections with her host families and with other Brazilians than was often the case for foreign-language exchange students. Despite this, she did not engage at a formal level with national politics or theology. Rather, her experience of the country was direct, visceral and transformative.

For the first half of her stay, she was hosted by a committed Catholic family in the interior of Brazil. Her host volunteered at the local hospital and aged-care centre, and Penny went along with her. Given her medical ambitions, her experiences at the hospital proved unsettling. In later life, Penny Wong laughed this off as 'a bit of a problem with blood'.[25] That was true, but not the whole truth. She was forced to deal with the realities of medicine in a developing country. She discovered that she was not good at coping with them. She doubted her ability to deal with disease and death as the stuff of a career.

Penny had seen poverty before – both in Borneo and on her travels in South-East Asia – but here she was confronted for the first time by starvation. There was the sense that life was expendable, that the disenfranchised didn't matter to those with the power to save them. Yet even the poorest placed worship and the sacred at the centre of their lives. She sat in Catholic church services with her host family and saw, as she puts it now, what faith meant, and found herself 'tremendously moved'.[26] It caused her to reflect on her own faith – nominally Christian, refined by her education at a Uniting Church school, but still rooted in the melange of religions within her family. She had never doubted the existence of God or felt that she could live without the idea of a divine presence. In Brazil she was impressed by the power of faith and practice – praxis – in the grit of life.

For the last part of her time in Brazil she was based in Rio de Janeiro. There, she never ate in public without children approaching and begging to be allowed to finish her meal. She carried from Brazil to Adelaide two convictions. The first was that she was psychologically unsuited to medicine and would have to find another career. The second was a powerful reinforcement of what, when speaking intellectually, she calls praxis. In Brazil, she discovered there were only two options for the privileged: either you decide that the world is simply unfair and nothing can be done about it, or you decide that, because it is unfair, something must be done, and that this places a responsibility on you to act as best you can to achieve real change, rather than standing on the sidelines bemoaning the world.

*

David Penberthy, today a senior News Corp journalist and Adelaide radio presenter, remembers meeting Penny Wong in January 1987, at a weekend event held for about sixty returning exchange students in the southern Adelaide suburb of O'Halloran Hill. He had just landed from Mexico. The aim of the weekend was to help the students with re-entry to ordinary life – a bigger challenge for him and Penny, perhaps, than for most of the cohort, who had been to less confronting places such as Europe and the United States.

He and Penny both spoke to the group about their experiences, and afterwards got to chatting. Penberthy, the product of a state school in the working-class suburb of Mitchell Park, had enrolled in Arts at the University of Adelaide, hoping to do well enough to transition into an Arts/Law degree. Penny Wong was the dux of the elite Scotch College. Yet they found they had plenty in common. Like Wong, Penberthy had been radicalised by his experience overseas. She told him that she had decided she didn't want to pursue a career in medicine, but wanted to do something about social justice. She had changed her university enrolment to Arts/Law and had put herself down for a heavy dose of politics subjects in her first year, together with drama and Spanish – the first because she had loved it at school, the second an attempt to keep up with the closest thing she could find to Portuguese. At the end of the weekend, the two new friends agreed to catch up when university began.

3

BECOMING LABOR

Towards the end of 1988, Andrew Hamilton – a University of Adelaide medical student with a sardonic turn of phrase, a moneyed background and a lively social life – was in trouble. He had, like so many undergraduates, taken full advantage of the social opportunities at the university in the first three years of his degree. Now, about to enter the critical final years, including clinical practice, he had a string of narrow pass marks behind him. The dean took him aside and told him that he had to pull himself together. While technically he had passed, he would be given an examiner's fail and made to repeat the year. It was a blow – but also, he began to think, perhaps an opportunity.

Hamilton was toying with the idea of getting involved in politics. He was not a member of the Liberal Party, but was friends with another medical student, Andrew Southcott, who was enmeshed in party politics and would go on to be the federal Liberal member for the seat of Boothby. He also knew Christopher Pyne, who had just graduated from the university and joined the staff of Liberal senator Amanda Vanstone. With time on his hands, given that he would only be repeating subjects he had already passed, and with the encouragement of Southcott, Hamilton decided to run for the board of the Adelaide University Union. He was elected. Hamilton's decision brought him up against Penny Wong at the very beginning of her political career. She, too, had run for the board and been elected, representing Labor but also a broad coalition of progressive students.

Hamilton and Wong had known each other since childhood. Wong's

Aunt Kate, one of Jane's sisters, was the best friend of Hamilton's mother. He remembers Penny as always articulate, and always with a strong point of view. He quite liked her. But when they met again at university, they became political enemies.

At this time, student unionism was compulsory. Tertiary students were levied an annual fee that was used to help run campus services – cafeterias, sporting clubs and associations – as well as the student newspaper, *On Dit*. As well, the union financed the Students' Association, which was its political arm, advocating for the interests of students within the university and beyond.

The push to make student unionism voluntary was one of the defining causes of the times, and the foundation for many nascent political careers. The generation before Wong and Hamilton had cut their teeth on the issue. Voluntary student unionism had been part of Christopher Pyne's agenda when he had been at the university. At the University of Sydney, Tony Abbott had used his position as president of the Students' Representative Council to try to destroy compulsory campus unions. Peter Costello at Monash University had also opposed compulsory unionism. Julia Gillard had advocated for it at the University of Adelaide before moving to Melbourne to become the penultimate president of the Australian Union of Students.

The AUS – a national body made up of affiliated institution-based student unions – had collapsed under the weight of left-wing activism over the Middle East in 1984, when Penny Wong was in Year 11. Most students saw no reason why their fees should be spent on causes so remote, and a raft of campuses had disaffiliated. Gillard was later to recall that as a Labor student politician she had 'fought the wild Leftist tendencies' in student politics, making common cause with those who thought the AUS should be devoted to things students cared about – education and student services – rather than international issues.[1]

But Gillard and others had helped lay the groundwork for a replacement body: the National Union of Students. The NUS had been established the year before Penny Wong and Andrew Hamilton were elected to the board of the Adelaide University Union, which had

affiliated with the new body. The battle over compulsory student unionism was far from over.

In 1987 Christopher Pyne had fronted the Adelaide University Union
finance committee, where he had opposed the payment of honoraria to
elected student officials.[2] It was a strike against the professionalisation of
student politics. One of Pyne's antagonists was Andrew Lamb, a Centre
Left Labor member, who was on the board of the Adelaide University
Union and vice-president of the Students' Association. Lamb was in a
relationship with a young, non-party-aligned feminist called Natasha
Stott Despoja, who was also on the union board.

The issue that spurred Hamilton to step up into student politics, and
made his election possible, was a dispute over whether senior medical
students should be given discounted union fees on the ground that they
spent most of their time in hospitals and so couldn't use the campus facilities. There had been a referendum and a general student meeting on the
matter. In the elections, held in late 1988, the medical students got organised and won five positions on the twelve-member board, making them
the dominant faction. In alliance with the Liberals, led by Southcott, they
had the numbers. Apart from the Liberals, Labor and the medical students, there was a group of non-aligned students, Stott Despoja among
them. At the first meeting of the newly elected board in 1989, Penny
Wong proposed that Andrew Lamb be elected president. Andrew Hamilton stood against him and won. Labor and the left had lost the numbers.

It was the beginning of a months-long, bitterly fought war of attri-
tion, in which Penny and the other Labor members of the board were
determined to tear down Hamilton's presidency. They were relentless.
There were real issues at stake, including amalgamation of campuses,
award arrangements for union staff, and student fees, but Hamilton also
remembers long discussions about trivialities such as the colour of servi-
ettes at union events, and much carping. He felt that Penny leapt upon
any off-the-cuff remark he made. He was accused of sexism, constantly
chivvied and attacked. 'She used to use the word "outrageous" a lot,' he
recalls. 'As in, "That's outrageous, Andrew." She used the word "outrageous" in an outrageous fashion.'

The battle waged against Hamilton is recorded in excruciating detail in the minutes of the Adelaide University Union. Those opposed to his presidency, including Wong, argued that it was important every motion of no-confidence in the chair, every point of order, every motion that the motion be put, be recorded in detail. On several occasions, meeting time was taken up in discussing whether the minutes of the previous meeting were accurate. Hamilton was instructed to get quotes on better recording equipment so the minutes could be better kept. Sometimes one can sense, behind the deadpan recounting of these awful debates, the presence of the minute-taker. Once, she gets to speak – and remarks (minuting her own contribution) that she wouldn't need better recording equipment if only there were fewer interjections and less shouting.

Hamilton tried to convince the board that 'summary minutes', such as those done for the university's chief governing body, the University Council, would suffice. But he was opposed. Foreshadowed motions, points of order, withdrawn foreshadowed motions and debates about whether foreshadowed motions could be withdrawn were all to be minuted, and the resulting records now occupy boxes and boxes of space in the University of Adelaide archives – a depressing record of student politics at its worst, and unappealing political skills learned.

Penny, Lamb and their allies built and consolidated alliances with the independents and non-aligned student board members. By the middle of 1990, when they had amassed enough support to push through a motion of no-confidence in Hamilton's leadership, he found it almost a relief. He had dropped all thoughts of a political career. They killed that ambition in him.

Andrew Hamilton is now a leading Adelaide cardiologist and a specialist in the early detection of heart disease. He has a PhD and a long list of proud achievements, and is in the midstream of a glowing career. Asked to recall his battles with Penny Wong, he responds with something approaching post-traumatic stress. When he sees her on the television grilling some bureaucrat at Senate Estimates, or giving stick to the Liberals in the Senate, he feels a chill of recognition. It takes him back.

Does he still like her? He pauses and searches for tactful words. He respects her, but he remains attached to the opposite side of politics. 'Do I like what she stands for? No. Do I think she represents the people who vote for her well? Yes, she is an extraordinary politician. She was extraordinary back then, and today she outperforms most of the people in federal parliament.' He pauses again. 'But, you know, she actually is scary. You need to be careful when you talk to Penny. You can't be flippant on any topic because she'll pull you up immediately. She can be ferocious. Yes, there's something very scary about her.'

Today Wong remembers the battle in simple and unapologetic terms. Hamilton represented the Liberal agenda and was out to damage student unionism. He was also against fair treatment of union staff, in her view.

*

Penny Wong's university career did not start this way. In her first year on campus – 1987 – her politics were so far to the left of the Hawke government, which was re-elected to its third term that July, that she told her fellow students she could not possibly join the Labor Party.

David Penberthy was one of her early friends on campus, thanks to their encounter at O'Halloran Hill. Penberthy had been radicalised by Latin American politics. In his first year of university he joined, and ended up running, the local branch of the Committee in Solidarity with Central America and the Caribbean. It was a far-left organisation sponsored by the Socialist Workers Party – a Trotskyist group advocating socialist revolution, particularly in developing countries. CISCAC was well to the left of the campus Labor Club. Penberthy thought the club 'a bunch of apologists' for the economic rationalist innovations of the Hawke–Keating government.

The issue at the time was US president Ronald Reagan's funding of the Contras in Nicaragua, in their armed opposition to the Sandinista government. Penberthy persuaded Wong to join CISCAC, but she was never as involved as he was. 'I threw myself into it headlong,' he says. His chief activity was organising the sale of Nicaraguan coffee at markets throughout Adelaide to raise money for the Sandinistas. He would ride his bike around the suburbs every Saturday, delivering the beans. He also distributed literature on campus. Penny was less committed – more an interested fellow traveller. 'I think she saw it as a fringe activity,' says Penberthy. He recollects Penny attending the monthly meetings of CIS-CAC at the Adelaide University Union. He thinks she was present on the day they built a Reagan piñata and encouraged students to give it a whack, though she was not there on the day he led an occupation of the BHP offices in Adelaide, protesting against the company's investments in South America. He remembers an argument at one meeting about whether Daniel Ortega, the Nicaraguan president, should have done an interview with *Playboy*, and whether they should pass a motion expressing disapproval. Penny was in favour of the motion.

To him, Penny Wong was fascinating. 'She was a very striking, very beautiful person, and I guess to someone like me, who had led a pretty culturally sheltered life, you know, she seemed very exotic and very worldly. I'd never met someone who knew what a laksa was or what hokkien noodles were, or who knew what the patriarchy was. We just sort of started going out together all the time, and she took me to all these fantastic cafés, and places like the Asian Gourmet at the Adelaide Central Market, and we'd just sit there for hours solving the world's problems.'

They were not involved sexually or romantically, but the friendship with Penberthy has endured. He says, 'I kid her every now and again about starting up CISCAC again, and she just laughs. I think she's a bit embarrassed by it all.' Penberthy is married to Kate Ellis, who was until her 2019 retirement the Labor member for Adelaide, and in the party's Right faction while Penny Wong is a member of the Left. Had events played out differently, and Wong's ambitions taken a different direction, Ellis and Wong could easily have found themselves rivals. If Wong were ever to move to the House of Representatives and make a bid for leadership, the natural electorate for her to contest would be the seat of Adelaide.

Wong claims that her politics have changed less than those of many other student politicians she mingled with at university. She has always, she says, been a social democrat – supporting government interventions in favour of social justice, but within the framework of a liberal democracy and capitalist economy. She remembers the conversation in which she told Penberthy that she was not a socialist. 'He said, "Really?" And I said, "Look, I think the market's got a place, and private property has a place."' Penberthy was apparently shocked at this contention.

By the end of their first year, both Penberthy and Wong were moving away from CISCAC. Penberthy describes his disenchantment as sudden. He woke up one morning and realised he no longer had the motivation to spend his weekend delivering coffee beans. He was becoming interested in journalism. He began writing for *On Dit*. Once he was a journalist, he says, 'My view suddenly became "Let's treat all the student politicians with a degree of contempt."'

Meanwhile, Penny Wong was making what Penberthy describes as a 'steely-eyed decision' to get involved in the mainstream. As he puts it, with a self-deprecatory dig at his younger self, 'She wanted to have an impact, rather than being involved in this really quite minute and bizarre conversation that CISCAC were having. I think at the end of that first year she decided it was time to stop hanging around with that ratbag Penberthy and get serious.'

Academically, Penny is remembered as studious. In first-year politics tutorials she was the one who had always done the reading, and always had a forthright view. Her own memory is different. She describes her first year as a bit of a mess. She did one semester of drama, following through on her school involvement, before concluding she was no good at it. She enrolled in Spanish as a substitute for Portuguese, but did not persist with it. Later, as her political involvement shifted up a gear, she made compromises. She claims she did enough study to get by, but not enough to excel. University life was different back then: it was possible to swot in the weeks before exams and pass well, while spending most of the semester attending political meetings or talking on the campus lawns.

Penny was learning at least as much outside the classroom as in it. In these years, the University of Adelaide punched above its weight in terms of its students' future contribution to public life. David Penberthy went on to be a newspaper editor and senior journalist. Also part of Penny's wider social circle were Annabel Crabb and Samantha Maiden, both of whom would also become prominent journalists. Wong remembers attending performances on campus by Shaun Micallef and Francis Greenslade, who had recently left the university, where together they had dominated the Theatre Guild. Others on campus included Christian Kerr, later a Liberal political staffer and then a journalist. Embryonic politicians included the future Australian Democrats leader Natasha Stott Despoja, who was at different times an ally and a rival of Penny Wong's, but broadly aligned with her in the battles over union control; Jack Snelling, later Labor treasurer of South Australia; Pat Conlon, then a mature-age law student, later a minister in the South Australian government; and Mark Butler, today shadow minister for climate change and energy in the federal parliament. Jay Weatherill, a future premier of South Australia, had graduated the year before Wong began her degree. Christopher Pyne overlapped her by one year. He was president of the University Liberal Club in 1987 and went on to be a minister in the Abbott, Turnbull and Morrison governments. Butler, Conlon and Weatherill would all prove vitally important to Penny Wong's future, but in her first couple of years at university, Butler and Conlon were acquaintances rather than friends, and she did not cross paths with Weatherill until 1989.

The legacy of Penny Wong's flirtation with CISCAC was membership of a broad left coalition on campus that included some Labor Party members, but also many who were not aligned with a party but were active on particular issues – such as opposition to apartheid in South Africa or environmental causes. It was the Hawke–Keating government's proposal to introduce a 'graduate tax' – a fee for higher education to be collected once graduates were earning – that brought this group together and bound them in a loose coalition called the Progressive Education Team. In 1988 it propelled them onto the streets in the largest student demonstrations since the Vietnam War.

Universities faced huge waiting lists but lacked the funds to expand. The federal budget was tight. Federal education minister John Dawkins established a committee, chaired by former New South Wales premier Neville Wran, to find a solution. Its report recommending the graduate tax was released in May 1988. The next week, an estimated 5000 students protested on the steps of Adelaide's Parliament House.[3] In the months that followed, there were sit-ins, attempts to storm the premier's office and more demonstrations. Penny Wong was in the midst of the protests. She had been to demonstrations before – when she was a teenager her mother had taken her to marches marking International Women's Day, for example – but these were the first political demonstrations she attended in her own right. The issue went to the heart of her family's story. She had been raised by a father whose life had been transformed by education. Her mother, who had completed her degree and social work qualifications as a single parent in a fee-free system, was another example.

In July 1988, Penny Wong succeeded in her first electoral campaign, being voted onto the Students' Association and the board of the Adelaide University Union as part of the Progressive Education ticket. Her candidate statement read:

> Back in '87 student politics didn't appear that important to me (the bar seemed like the place to be!). Then Mr Dawkins started talking about 'more students to the dollar' and fees and amalgamations were suddenly on the agenda. Some of these changes may be good, others not so good, but one thing we must not lose sight of is that it is OUR education that is being discussed. You have a right to be heard. I'm not interested in petty politicking – let's concentrate on the real issue: our education.[4]

Viewed from today's perspective, that call to arms is classic Wong – measured, almost fence-sitting, in its acknowledgement that some of the Dawkins-proposed changes might be worthwhile. It was also a little disingenuous. Penny Wong had never been one for hanging around the university bar, and she had always been interested in politics.

It was while handing out election material with other members of the Progressive Education group that she met Wendy Wakefield (no

relation to the founder of South Australia), who was active in campaigning against apartheid and in support of the African National Congress.
Wakefield was elected president of the Students' Association. She and
Penny Wong were to become lifelong friends. Wakefield remembers that
they first bonded over fried rice at the university refectory dedicated
to serving Asian-style food. Wong also met Anthea Howard, who was
elected education vice-president of the Association. She was a politics
student destined for a public service career specialising in environmental
management. By the beginning of 1989, the three women were sharing a house in the suburb of Prospect. The political battles of the next
few years were discussed over the kitchen table. They enjoyed cooking
for one another. Penny Wong's abilities in the kitchen were a revela-
tion. Wakefield remembers: 'It was the first time I had seen a prawn that
wasn't pink, a green prawn.' Wakefield became a vegetarian at one stage,
only to recant when faced with Penny's chicken curry.

Penny Wong's political rivals thought she was intimidating and
chilly. To her friends, though, she was 'great fun', though always with
an undertone of seriousness. It was clear to all of them that Penny Wong
was destined for great things – but not necessarily for politics. Wakefield says, 'I remember saying to her that I didn't know if she was going
to be a judge or a politician.'

*

In the same week that Penny Wong won her first election, the leader
of the federal opposition, John Howard, launched a new immigration
policy for the Liberal–National coalition. Called One Australia, it advocated the end of support for multiculturalism, which had been bipartisan
policy ever since the end of the White Australia policy. Howard's initiative followed a four-year debate on Asian immigration sparked largely
by the historian Geoffrey Blainey, who argued that Asian immigration
threatened Australia's 'social cohesion'.

During an interview on the John Laws radio program, and again
that evening on ABC Radio, Howard said the level of Asian immigration was too high. 'I do believe that if in the eyes of some in the

community it's too great, it would be in our immediate-term interest and supportive of social cohesion if it were slowed down a little, so the capacity of the community to absorb it was greater.'[5]

The Labor government exploited discomfort on Howard's frontbench by quickly introducing a parliamentary motion rejecting the use of race to select immigrants. Three Liberal MPs – Ian Macphee, Steele Hall and Philip Ruddock – defied their leader by crossing the floor. But Howard had support. The shadow finance minister, John Stone, insisted that Asian immigration had to be slowed, and the National Party leader, Ian Sinclair, warned against any 'undue build-up' of Asians.

Until this moment in Australian history, there is no compelling reason why Penny Wong's hatred of racism should have caused her to lean more to the Labor Party than to the Liberal Party. Anti-racism had for more than a decade been bipartisan – and a prominent feature of Liberal prime minister Malcolm Fraser's record. Going further into history, the Labor Party and the union movement had been at least as racist as their opponents. Jane Chapman's concern for social justice, and Penny's experience of poverty in a developing country, would probably always have driven her towards Labor, but this new policy made it almost inevitable. Howard's remarks, and his use of race for political purposes, meant that in her view the Liberal Party was not only historically wrong but also immoral.

Ask Penny Wong about her memories of John Howard's comments today and it is as though the temperature in the room has fallen ten degrees. Her head drops, her eyes harden, her speech slows. 'I will never forgive him,' she says, with intensity.

Howard's remarks legitimised the things the bigots were saying. They placed the future prime minister of her country on the same side as all those who had abused her and Toby over the years. She was used to discrimination – racist comments were made to her all too frequently in shops and on the street. But she remembers conversations from this period in which people who were supposedly friends assured her that, while she was 'OK', perhaps there were, after all, too many Asians.

Sometime during the Howard years, Toby, by then in his mid-teens, failed to come home from school as expected. Jane and Penny were frantic as the hours ticked by. Eventually he arrived, footsore and weeping. A group of young men had got on the bus and abused him for being Asian. The bus driver had stopped and made Toby get off. 'I remember thinking that this is what Howard was doing,' says Wong. 'He was talking to those people. Those racists, that bus driver.'

Two weeks after Howard announced the One Australia policy, Penny Wong joined the Australian Labor Party. This followed a conversation that has remained a touchstone of her political involvement.

Lois Boswell and her husband, Don Frater, are two of Penny Wong's oldest and closest friends. Today, they are both senior bureaucrats in the South Australian government. In 1988 they were still fairly new to Adelaide, self-exiled from New South Wales, where they had been involved in Young Labor. Moving to Adelaide was an impulsive decision. Frater had been working for Telecom, Boswell for the Federated Miscellaneous Workers' Union. For different reasons, both were feeling sour about their employment. They met for lunch one day and agreed it was time to move. Where to go? As Boswell retraces their reasoning, 'Can't move to Queensland, Bjelke-Petersen is in power. Can't move to Melbourne, we're from Sydney. Can't move to Hobart, it's too small. Can't move to Perth, it's too far away. Can't move to Darwin, it's too hot. Bugger it. Adelaide, here we come!'

When they arrived, in early 1987, their only contacts were other members of Young Labor, in particular Ian Hunter – a Flinders University science graduate active in campaigning for gay rights. He had founded the Flinders University Gay Society and helped found the state's AIDS Action Committee, as well as campaigning for South Australia to outlaw discrimination based on sexuality. Hunter welcomed Boswell with open arms and invited her to join him at Labor's state convention that year. Boswell recalls a young woman was onstage talking about the importance of moving Bubbles the dolphin from the entertainment park Marineland before it closed. 'In Sydney, they would have turned the microphones off,' she says. Later that night there was a division over a point in the rules, and all the combatants had a civilised cup of tea together afterwards. Boswell was in culture shock. For someone reared in the tough world of New South Wales Labor, politics Adelaide-style was hard to take seriously. 'I could hardly believe it.'

Soon after, she and Frater attended a sub-branch meeting in Adelaide dominated by the Centre Left. Boswell nominated for the position of president and set about doing what you would in Sydney: 'doorknocked everybody and rang people'. She notes, 'We found half . . . were residents at the homeless shelter. We turned up on the night and started challenging votes.' She lost 58–57, but she and Frater won two of the sub-branch's positions to the state convention. Soon, rumours were circulating that they had been brought over by the Left to take over the party. But 'we had just been taught in a different style of politics', she says.

So it was that in August 1988 Boswell was attending the state Labor convention at Adelaide Trades Hall, where one of the hot topics was the Wran proposal for a graduate tax. Boswell was opposed to student fees, but was also taking a pragmatic position: 'If we are going to end up with this thing anyway, how do we stop it from preventing poor people from going to university?'

It was a bitterly fought conference. The voting was delayed by a dispute over whether Young Labor could take part in its own right. After a vote, Young Labor members who did not also represent local branches were locked out.[6] The victims of this rude rebuff were outraged, and joined a gathering group of student protesters outside the conference. Among the students were Penny Wong and her friends from the Progressive Education Team.

There were two votes on the graduate tax. In the first, then premier and ALP national president John Bannon moved to support the tax. The delegates tied at 96-all.[7]

It was probably after this that Boswell stepped out to visit the protesters. Penny Wong stood out immediately. 'She was very striking and clearly had some sway with the people she was with.'

The two women fell into conversation. Fired up by the vote, Boswell told Wong she agreed with her stance on education. But what,

Boswell asked, was she doing outside demonstrating when she should be inside trying to influence the future of the party?

Penny Wong replied that she could not, on principle, join a party that was proposing to introduce fees for education. Boswell referenced the vote that had just taken place – a tie. It really mattered 'who was in the room'. Wong should be in the room. Being outside protesting was easy. Winning the debates that mattered was harder.

It turned into an extended conversation, with the central theme being that it was better – more sensible, more effective and braver – to be on the inside trying to bring about change, even if that meant compromise. Being outside protesting might mean you could stay pure, but you were also impotent. Boswell remembers, 'I pitched a whole lot of stuff with it. We talked about uranium, we talked about feminism. We talked about racism. It was all about values, but I was talking about these issues as a battle within the ALP between progressive and less-progressive politics. And if you wanted to really make a difference, you had to be inside the room having that battle.'

By the end of the conversation, Lois Boswell had signed up Penny Wong as a member of the ALP.

Later that day there was a second vote. The convention defied Bannon in a 106–81 vote against the graduate tax. It was written up at the time as a significant blow to the Hawke–Keating agenda, but it made no difference in the long run.[8] The graduate tax was introduced on New Year's Day 1989.

The irony, Wong says today, is that she now believes the policy rationale for what became known as the Higher Education Contribution Scheme (HECS) was correct. Her political experience, not least her time as a finance minister, has given her a deep understanding of revenue and husbanding limited resources. The tertiary system had to expand to give opportunities to students with fewer advantages than her. Provided the revenue raised from fees was reinvested in education, she now says, 'I think it was the right policy.'

Over the three decades that have passed since Penny Wong made that fundamental decision about what serious political involvement required, the phrase 'it matters who is in the room' has become something of a mantra between Wong and Boswell, often invoked when planning, strategising or rallying after a defeat. The words, or phrases reflecting the same sentiment, recur in Wong's speeches and public statements. They are used, often, as a justification for being in politics – including the compromises Wong has made in order to retain influence within the Australian Labor Party.

As Wong recounts, her decision to join the party was driven by a recognition that those such as Lois Boswell, Don Frater and others on the left of the Labor Party were 'people like me ... there was a comradeship or an affinity or a philosophical kind of alignment'. It felt like finding her home.

Frater and Boswell have been important backroom operatives in Labor politics ever since. They keep a low profile. The clippings file on each of them is thin, but they are occasionally referred to in the Adelaide press as a public-sector power couple. Frater is a deputy chief executive at SA Health. When Penny Wong was minister for climate change and water in the first Rudd government, Frater was her chief of staff. Boswell served as Jay Weatherill's deputy chief of staff when he was premier of South Australia, and after a stellar public-service career is now deputy chief executive at the Department of Human Services. The couple are known to be among Wong's key advisers.

Thanks to Boswell and Frater, by the time Penny Wong took up her position on the board of the Adelaide University Union she was a member of, and in regular touch with, the left wing of the Labor Party, and had redefined her involvement in student politics as part of the broader battle for control and influence over the party's future.

*

George Karzis knew and liked Penny Wong. In theory she was studying law alongside him – although his attendance record was poor. He remembers turning up to an exam on jurisprudence, and running into Penny, who 'politely but in disbelief' asked him if he was there for the exam. He confirmed it. 'Have you attended a single lecture?' she asked.

He said he had not, and she playfully whacked him on the shoulder. He managed to score a credit in the exam.

Karzis was the president of the University of Adelaide's Labor Club, and from the Right. After Julia Gillard left Adelaide, the club tore itself apart through factional rivalries, but in 1987 he reconstituted it. Karzis was a supporter of the graduate tax: as a working-class boy, he saw the tax as a means of opening the door to tertiary education to those with fewer social advantages. More broadly, he believed in the Hawke–Keating economic agenda.

Penny Wong had joined the campus Labor Club sometime in the first half of 1988 – before she joined the party proper. At first she was barely active. Now, armed with a broader sense of why campus politics mattered, she began to organise.

The Labor Club's annual general meeting was usually attended by only a couple of dozen people. In May 1989, it was packed. There were several disputes about voting rights, but in the end 114 people were deemed eligible to vote. Penny Wong ran on a ticket against Karzis with another Labor Club member, James Greentree, and Karzis was rolled. Greentree was elected president and Wong general secretary – but there was no doubt about who was really in charge. In the barrage of letters Karzis wrote to *On Dit* in the ensuing weeks, the new leadership team was dubbed the 'Wong–Greentree oligarchy'. Karzis claimed the club had fallen victim to 'the Progressive Left and its McCarthyist tactics'. He accused Progressive Left 'bouncers' of demanding voter ID only from Greek Australians and of intimidating others. 'The Progressive Left, led by James Greentree and Penny Wong, talks about democracy but denies members a vote ... Hail the new regime!'[9]

Greentree had a letter in the same edition describing the AGM as an 'ordinary event' where members had made their democratic decision. The only attendees who had been denied voting rights, he said, were Liberal Party members trying to make mischief. Meanwhile, the club was getting to work, hastening to organise a forum on uranium mining, with Richard Mills, a member of the ALP's Uranium Policy Review Committee, as the guest speaker.[10]

With this takeover, Penny Wong became one of the significant political operators on campus. Meanwhile, on the Adelaide University Union board, the battle with Andrew Hamilton and the medical students was getting underway.

Within the Labor Club, Andrew Lamb was an opponent of Wong's. He was further to the right than she was. But in the battle on the Union board, they were allies. Also on their side, more often than not, were Andrew Lamb's partner, Natasha Stott Despoja, and Penny Wong's housemates, Wendy Wakefield and Anthea Howard.

Underneath the petty wrangling with Hamilton over the presidency, there were important issues for young students to be negotiating. The student union managed a budget of $8.5 million, had a staff of more than 100 and held responsibility for three refectories, the bar, dozens of clubs and associations, *On Dit* and the Students' Association. Debate could move from compulsory student unionism, or renegotiating awards and unfair-dismissal cases, to whether the beer in the bar had a terrible aftertaste, and what could be done to correct this before Orientation Week.

At the beginning of 1990, Hamilton returned to focus on his study as he entered a new year. The Adelaide University Union presidency, which carried an honorarium, was meant to be a full-time position, and he claimed to be doing his presidential work on evenings and weekends. Penny Wong and her allies demanded a close accounting of how he spent his hours. They wanted him to keep a diary. They picked holes in his reports and criticised him for not following board directives.[11] The argy-bargy over Hamilton fed into a wider dispute about whether elected Adelaide University Union officials should be paid an honorarium. Those opposed to the professionalisation of student politics argued that money should be spent on services, such as refectories and sporting clubs, rather than on politics. It was in this context that Wong wrote her first article in *On Dit* – and the first thing she had published since her teenage poetry in the Scotch College magazine.

Shorn of the heat the disputes ignited at the time, the article is a nerdy yet eloquent statement of the objectives to which she was to devote her professional life. Today Wong says she does not remember writing it, but remarks that it could be run under her name today and would still reflect her views. She described political representation as being a service – indeed, one of the most important forms of service that can be provided to students or citizens.

> Australians have a tendency to damn all forms of political representation. How often do we hear people saying, 'Those bloody politicians, they're all the same'? Given the current leaning of our politicians, I'm not sure I'd disagree. However, there is a danger of equating the players with the game and throwing both in the rubbish bin. I have heard some extremely convincing criticisms of both our Prime Minister and the Leader of the Opposition. I have yet to hear any argument that could convince me that political representation is not a good thing ... Political representation is also a service, and the students at this university deserve competent and committed representation ... political representation with maximum consultation and participation of the wider student body must be a priority for any student organisation worth its salt. It is not an optional extra.[12]

Wong and her allies finally won the battle against Hamilton. It was in the second calendar year of his term, with just weeks to go. He was spending large amounts of time at hospitals. Finally, they got the numbers to move a motion of no-confidence in him, and he resigned on the morning of a meeting at which he would otherwise have been sacked.

Andrew Lamb took the presidency, with Wong's support. Recalling these events today, he says he believes Wong would have much preferred 'someone more left-wing'. However, he was a consensus candidate – someone the non-aligned board members would support.

To Lamb, it seemed that Penny Wong had arrived at the University of Adelaide fully formed. Her skills were formidable, her poise extraordinary. She was more emotional than she appears to be these days, he says, but a fearsome debater. 'A lot of people going into student politics sort of make their mistakes there. I don't remember Penny making mistakes or being foolish. She was always very thoughtful and considered,' he says.

Others recall that even in the most heated exchanges Wong would frequently show flashes of temper but never shouted. She also adopted the habit – which others soon followed – of referring to 'Mr Lamb' or 'Mr Hamilton' rather than using first names. Some thought it pompous. Others thought it showed that she was taking things seriously and wanted others to as well. She still does this today. Her opponents remark they know people are in trouble when she calls them 'Mr' or 'Ms'.

Remembering their battles, Wong and Hamilton agree – though in very different terms – about what was achieved. He thought she was practising on him, already focusing on a future political career. Wong denies that she was knowingly preparing for politics, but says that through this period she learned how to 'exercise influence and win, even when you don't have the numbers'. And it was great training for the Senate.

In the 1989 elections, for those taking up office in 1990, Wong helped organise a ticket that encompassed the broad left on campus. It supported Natasha Stott Despoja for women's officer, and David Penberthy and Steve Jackson as editors of *On Dit*. Wong ran for education vice-president of the Students' Association – an important position, particularly at a time of such disruption in education policy and campus amalgamations. The post had previously been held by Wong's housemate Anthea Howard. Even as the vote was held, Wong was widely understood within the organisation as 'meant to be' the next education vice-president. Most candidates on the ticket were successful, but Penny Wong was not, losing to Mel Yuan, an independent who had also been on the Union board.

Losing was a shock. The memory clearly still stings. Asked about it, Wong describes it as her 'first experience of the disloyalty and banality that can come from within my own party'. There had been a deal around the ticket, but the Right 'broke off and supported an independent against me. So it took the Liberals and the right wing of the Labor Party acting together to beat me.'

Mel Yuan remembers events differently. She says she won through old-fashioned retail politics. It was 'a war of wallpaper paste': whoever put up the most posters around campus won. She was also prepared to do what Penny Wong would not – go into lecture theatres and persuade students to get down to the ballot boxes and vote. 'There were no debates, there were no policy issues. This was Adelaide. It was just a matter of who did the best job of getting out there and getting people to vote.' As an independent, she worked closely with the Overseas Students' Association, and remembers 'those guys were amazing at turning people out to vote.' Independents on campus, she says, were a cross-section of 'Labor right, wet Libs, non-aligned centrists, party girls and guys. Our voting base came from across campus ... We could get people to come out and vote who traditionally didn't. I was an economics student and so had that base, who normally didn't vote ... Medical students had me on their ticket. Liberals had me on their ticket. We had candidates from every faculty on our ticket.'

Stott Despoja, too, was a strong campaigner – at that time 'friendly' to the Wong–Wakefield–Howard grouping, but later aligning herself more closely with the independents. She would front lecture halls of engineering students not known for their interest in politics and get them to the ballot box. 'They loved Natasha, those engineering boys,' recounts one contemporary.

Andrew Lamb describes the contention that the right of the Labor Club undermined Penny Wong as 'completely wrong, even if Penny believes it ... Mel Yuan got elected on the coattails of the tide of additional votes for the "Independents" faction that year.' Meanwhile, Karzis also denies an organised anti-Wong campaign. He says today that he still likes Wong. One of the reasons is because she has integrity. Her ruthlessness is never personal. He knew she was coming for him, and he remains awed by how successfully she did so.

Whatever the reasons for her loss, in this 'war of wallpaper paste' and lecture-hall bashing, Penny Wong failed, despite her proven abilities as an operator. She was formidable but not, at this stage, a good campaigner – and was also apparently outclassed on election strategy.

Wong acknowledges that she was not a natural 'retail politician'. Popular campaigning did not come easily to her. Partly it was her constant suspicion that her ethnicity would count against her. Partly it was her natural reserve and shyness. She has got better at it, but admits that even today it is not her 'natural game'. As her profile rises, increasing numbers of Labor MPs want her in their electorate come election time. She does her best to be there, but her colleagues observe that a day of campaigning will drain her, whereas others – the Anthony Albaneses and Bill Shortens of the world – are energised by it.

Education vice-president at the Adelaide University Union was the only elected office Penny Wong has ever contested and not won. It spelled the end of her close involvement in student politics. She continued to attend National Union of Students meetings, and was on the executive, but had no deep or long-term involvement. She did not run again for any campus positions. By now, she had moved on to bigger things.

4

BOLKUS LEFT

In the summer of early 1989, Penny Wong took a road trip. She was travelling with a group of fellow Young Labor members to a national conference in Melbourne. They must have taken the scenic route – via the Coorong and the Great Ocean Road – because they stopped overnight at a youth hostel in the South Australian coastal town of Beachport, near the Victorian border. Here, she attracted the attention of a young industrial officer at the Australian Workers' Union, Jay Weatherill. They both remember their walk along the Beachport jetty – proudly if underwhelmingly promoted, at 1.2 kilometres, as the second-longest in the state, stretching over the waters of Rivoli Bay.

Weatherill was four years older than Wong and had graduated from the University of Adelaide with degrees in Law and Economics in 1986. In some ways they could not have been more different. He was from a working-class background, the product of an unremarkable state school. Young Jay had been raised in the western suburbs of Adelaide. His father, George Weatherill, was an English-born migrant employed by the waterworks, as well as being a part-time wharfie and a shop steward. He worked out of the Port Adelaide depot of the waterworks and organised other waterside workers. He moved on to a job with the Australian Government Workers' Association (later part of the Miscellaneous Workers' Union), and acquired the nickname 'Bolshi George'. In 1986, when John Bannon was premier, he was elected to the upper house of the South Australian parliament. Jay Weatherill was already deeply involved in student politics and it was widely assumed he would at some stage follow his father into parliament. In fact, he was to surpass his father's career, serving as premier of South Australia for seven years, from October 2011 through to March 2018.

But on this day in Beachport, that was far in the future. Weatherill, like his father, was part of the Left faction of the Labor Party, which was locked out of power and influence within South Australian Labor by an alliance between the Centre Left and the Right. Given that Wong was being drawn into the Left, it is surprising that she and Weatherill had not met before this trip, but he is sure this was their first encounter. 'I'm certain. I would have remembered,' he says today. He was instantly smitten. There would have been important issues to discuss at the national conference they were due to attend – fees for higher education were being introduced that year, universities were amalgamating, the Hawke–Keating economic agenda was taking its grip – but today all Weatherill can remember about the conference is his pursuit of Penny Wong. 'I was attracted to her, and that was the main issue at conference for me. She was beautiful, immensely attractive.'

Soon after the conference they became a couple. It was not Penny Wong's first love affair. Those who knew her at university in 1987 and 1988 recall her dating a radical left-winger called Nick – usually referred to as 'Nick the environmentalist'. He has disappeared from history, and Wong, with a wince and a laugh, declines to give his surname. Jay Weatherill, however, was her first longstanding relationship. At this time, none of her contemporaries had any reason to think she was other than heterosexual.

By 1990 Weatherill and Wong had moved in together. Altogether their relationship lasted five years, of which four were spent living together. Over that time, they shared several townhouses and flats around the East Terrace area of Adelaide.

The relationship was formative for both of them. Weatherill credits Wong with 'knock[ing] me into shape', particularly on women's rights and feminism. He had come from a traditional family, his mother not working outside the home. 'I was a pretty unreconstructed bloke, and I would just make assumptions about the role of women. With Penny if I made any kind of mistake I was very quickly corrected ... it was tough but very rewarding. I was constantly being challenged.'

Wong says of Weatherill, 'I think he's actually the most talented politician of us all, of all our generation. He's smart and he's as determined as I am, but he has much better emotional intelligence than I do. He knows how to bring people with him much better than I do, or did back then. And I learned some of that from him.'

Weatherill remembers Wong as 'passionate and exciting' but, at the same time, intensely competitive and ambitious, and hyper-alert to any suggestion that she was not being taken seriously. 'She would have flashes of temper ... She's much more relaxed now.'

He accompanied her on some of her regular trips to Sabah to see her father and siblings. On one trip they met in Singapore and spent weeks travelling the length of the Malay Peninsula. It seemed to Weatherill that Wong got her sense of social justice and her feminism mostly from her mother. She resembled her father, though, in her reserve and reluctance to show too much public emotion, as well as in her methodical, logical thinking and organised habits.

Penny Wong's grandmother Lai was still alive at this time and in her mid-seventies. Weatherill met her but didn't come to know her well. She loomed large, though, in their conversations. Wong often referred to her as an exemplar of courage and strength. Weatherill also met Toby. He was 'a really charming, cool kind of guy' – easy to like. He would come and cook for them. By now, though, his drug problem was increasingly evident. 'Penny was constantly worried about him and spent a lot of time trying to help him.'

Many people remember Penny Wong at this time as oversensitive to any suggestion of racism or sexism. She could be oddly combative, sometimes taking offence for reasons that were not apparent to others in the room. But those who thought her sensitivity excessive didn't live in her skin. Her friends all share stories of being out with Penny and being surprised when suddenly somebody would hurl a racist taunt. She would shrug, they say, and dismiss it. She was used to it.

Jay Weatherill remembers that an issue between them was the depth of his connections within the Labor Party, thanks to his father.

She thought he was privileged in that way, and that she was at a disadvantage. He remembers taking her to a Labor lunch his father hosted
at Parliament House. They walked into a room of 'crusty old Labor
blokes'. As they passed by, one man looked at Wong and said in a stage
whisper to his dining companions, 'Don't mention the war.' She heard
it. According to Weatherill, it helped confirm her view that she would
have to work harder, and be tougher, if she was to make her way in
the party.

Today Jay Weatherill and Penny Wong remain good friends. They
have dealt with each other frequently over the years, both regarding
internal Labor Party and factional politics and while negotiating deals
of national importance, such as when Wong was the minister for water,
and Weatherill was South Australian premier, intent on cutting a good
deal for the state's irrigators. At the time of writing, Weatherill had just
been appointed to conduct a 'warts and all' review of Labor's 2019 election loss.[1] Long after they ceased to be a couple, Wong and Weatherill's
alliance continued as part of the drive to transform South Australian
Labor and build a platform for power.

*

There aren't many models for female political power in Australia. We
have trouble dealing with it. We seesaw between discomfort with women
seeking and exercising influence, and idealising them as somehow better
to and different from men. Then we punish them if they turn out to be,
after all, like other politicians – making the same kinds of compromises
and engaging in the same types of political warfare.

It's shocking to look back at the media coverage from the early part
of Penny Wong's parliamentary career. She was elected to the Senate in
2001 – less than two decades ago – yet the headlines show that it was
still permissible to belittle and trivialise female elected representatives.
Wong was billed as a 'lipstick warrior'.[2] Another headline proclaimed,
'Women come to the rescue', greeting the fact that more women from
both the major parties had been elected to the federal parliament, and
that for both parties, women were 'the standout performers'.[3]

Meanwhile, *The Advertiser* assured its readers that Penny Wong and her fellow Labor senator Linda Kirk were 'determined to be seen as serious politicians rather than "pretty faces"'.[4] Wong was frequently compared to Natasha Stott Despoja, who had been elected to the Senate in 1995 for the Australian Democrats. After all, they were both women.

None of this was unusual. Victorian premier Joan Kirner had to put up with cartoons showing her as a fat, harried housewife in a polka-dot dress. Carmen Lawrence, who was on the Labor frontbench when Penny Wong was elected, received similar treatment. South Australian Liberal senator Amanda Vanstone was regularly ridiculed for her weight.[5] In the years ahead there would be the denigration of Julia Gillard for being 'deliberately barren', for being Bob Brown's 'bitch', for being a 'witch' – and, of course, for her empty fruit bowl. 'Sexism is no better than racism,' Gillard was to say later.[6] But it isn't only about negative prejudice. The tendency is to hold women leaders to different standards – idealising them, then tearing them down.

Penny Wong is different and not different at the same time. Carol Johnson is a political scientist at the University of Adelaide. She has known Wong since she was a student, and subsequently became a friend, even though they disagree on some policy issues. Johnson has cited statements by Wong in her academic work, and Wong has quoted Johnson's extensive publications on the history of social democracy in some of her speeches.[7] Johnson describes Wong as part of the broadening of the Australian Labor Party from an organisation that understood tackling inequality as negotiating a better deal for white working men to one that practised a more complicated and ambitious politics – including seeking equality of opportunity across gender, race and sexuality.[8] Wong is both an advocate and a personification of this broadening. It is not an easy position.

But Wong is also a player in a Labor Party formed by its narrower history. In the past, socially conservative Catholics were a key part of its power base, and they remain important, particularly in her home state, South Australia. She is bound by party loyalty and both constrained and enabled by factional power plays. Labor Party factional politics is deeply

unappealing to most outsiders – perhaps particularly those who adore
Penny Wong and like to think of her as above the machinery of political
power. The truth is that it is not possible to understand the rise of Penny
Wong without seeing her as an accomplished and sometimes ruthless
player in those contests. Why should we expect different?

Labor's factions are usually mentioned with negative connotations.
The factions have a strong and sometimes determining influence on preselection of election candidates. Sometimes factional allegiance counts
more than talent. They also have a central influence over who gets frontbench positions and what policies are pursued. Both Kevin Rudd and
Julia Gillard have at different times described Labor's factions as out
of control, 'nonsense' and a 'cancer' on the party.[9] Perhaps it is only
possible to appreciate the positive side of factions by considering the
alternative. In some countries, political parties are mere flags of conve-
nience, while the real power is held by family or business dynasties. Or
internal contests for power are resolved by the jailing or killing of opponents. Just as political parties are part of an orderly democracy, party
factions are part of the machinery that enables large groups of people
with different views and multiple ambitions to work together. Factions
allow large and diverse parties to cohere. Through factions, the cats
are herded, power is distributed, preselections are contested and, when
we are lucky, policy is debated and honed. Sometimes, and for some
people, factions represent political positions. Sometimes they represent
nothing other than the advancement and containment of ambition and
allegiance. Minor parties, usually lacking formal factions but not factionalism, have trouble holding together and lasting. The Labor Party
persists largely because the factions are part of the managing of internal
power contests and policy disputes. The price is that sometimes the faction members hate one another more than they hate those on the other
side of politics.

In the 1990s there were three main factions within the ALP – the
Left, the Right and the Centre Left. Within each, there were subgroups
based on geography, personalities and the all-important union affilia-
tions and sponsorships. The federal Left faction was divided between

the so-called soft Left and hard Left. The Left faction within the South Australian branch was a small player in the national scheme of things but generally seen as aligned with the soft Left. This was the faction that Penny Wong had joined, driven by both personal conviction and by her affinity with individuals such as Jay Weatherill, Lois Boswell and Don Frater.

When Weatherill and Wong met, South Australian Labor had been through a period of disruption. In the Don Dunstan era, the internal machinations of the party had been dominated by a few towering figures – federal ministers Mick Young, Clyde Cameron and Senator Jim Toohey among them. They had mediated the power of the unions and managed the factional contests. When the Labor state government was trounced in 1979, after Dunstan's resignation, the party had to reassess and reflect.

Peter Duncan had been state attorney-general under Dunstan and was a federal minister then parliamentary secretary in the Hawke–Keating government. He had corralled a group of left-wing unions in South Australia and dominated the faction with the assistance of their votes. From 1979 until about 1984, he was highly successful: the Left dominated the state party. But every action has a reaction.

The South Australian Labor Party was different to its eastern siblings. In particular, it had not been through the split in the 1950s that scarred the party along the east coast. One of the effects of this in South Australia was that the Catholic conservatives had remained within the party, and they retained great influence. For them, Duncan was an obnoxious and dangerous figure. The Centre Left, meanwhile, was dominant – effectively the governing faction in the state. The premier, John Bannon, was allied with it, and so were federal representatives Mick Young and Senator Chris Schacht. From 1984, the Centre Left and the Right allied to lock the Left out of preselections, power and influence. The preselection of Jay Weatherill's father in 1986 was the last to be won by the Left, and that had been close-run. The Right would not deal with Duncan: he was considered abrasive and radical. Duncan himself seemed content with maintaining control of his faction rather than seeking meaningful influence within the larger party. Meanwhile, Senator Nick Bolkus, also of the Left, had entered federal parliament in 1981 – and he and Duncan did not get on.

Jay Weatherill was one of a group of nascent political leaders who were increasingly convinced that Duncan's stranglehold on the Left had to be challenged. They wanted the ability to cut deals with the Right – to have greater influence in a growing party. That wasn't possible under Duncan. In later years, when it began to get noticed, the media referred to this group as the 'Bolkus Left'. Today, Bolkus and all those involved regard the tag as a misnomer. Bolkus was the group's senior member, and provided contacts, mentorship and support, but he was not its leader. The initiative came from Weatherill and Wong's former university acquaintances Pat Conlon and Mark Butler. Also important was Ian Hunter, the gay rights campaigner from Flinders University who was working in Bolkus's office. Don Frater and Lois Boswell were also involved.

Penny Wong has loyal friends. In particular, she has loyal female friends. Long before she agreed to be interviewed for this book, they were monitoring its progress. As word got around that I had interviewed one person, the next would show in their response to questions that they were aware of what I had asked. An idea floated or a perception voiced to glean a response would be greeted at the next interview with a comment like 'I hear you think …' and a reply that showed the signs of workshopping behind the scenes.

When word got around that I had interviewed Nick Bolkus and Mark Butler, the message that came back through Penny Wong's female friends was that the men should not be allowed to get recognition for her political achievements. 'None of the men can claim credit for Penny Wong or her views,' I was told firmly by Lois Boswell. Perhaps it was this fear – that the men's voices might dominate this book – that helped Wong decide to agree to be interviewed.

To some extent, she need not have worried. Nick Bolkus agrees that he put opportunities in her way, but he does not take credit for her rise. In the late 1980s and early 1990s, Bolkus hosted barbeques at his home to nurture and cultivate a group of young Labor people 'who obviously had talent and were frozen out of most of the decision-making in the party'. They seemed to him to be the kind of people the party could not afford to ignore. By this stage he had stepped back from state factional contests to focus on his federal career; in 1988 he had become the minister for consumer affairs. Nevertheless, he supported the group's ambitions for the Left to wield greater influence, easing the path for Butler, Hunter, Weatherill and, a little later, Wong. He built connections between those in South Australia whom he regarded as 'the pragmatic Left' and their eastern state and national counterparts – the likes of Gerry Hand and Pete Steedman in Victoria. 'It was a model that was prepared to make deals and to compromise to get good policy out,' he recalls. That meant cutting deals with the Right.

Mark Butler was central to the group. An Arts/Law graduate, he was two years younger than Penny Wong. Butler is now shadow minister for climate change and energy, but for most of his career he was a union leader and a key factional powerbroker, vital to the internal manoeu-vrings of the party at a state and, increasingly, federal level. He became the secretary of the South Australian branch of the main Left union in South Australia, the Liquor, Hospitality and Miscellaneous Workers' Union (known as the Missos, pronounced *miss-ohs*) in 1996, and the following year was elected as president of the South Australian Labor Party – the youngest in its history.

Butler shared a house and was close friends with Pat Conlon, who had begun his working life as a roof tiler, storeman, timberhand and deckhand before working for the Missos and then enrolling at the University of Adelaide as a mature-age student. As the so-called Bolkus Left cohered, Conlon was working with Weatherill and Butler at the main Left law firm in town, Duncan & Hannon. Conlon went on to be elected to the lower house of the South Australian parliament in 1997, and became one of the most influential ministers in the Rann and Weatherill governments. If Butler was the quintessential backroom strategist, Conlon had the talent for reaching out, persuading and cutting deals.

Bolkus claims no credit for the faction that bore his name. Very soon, the young people had their own networks and connections on the east coast and were as helpful to him as he was to them. He does remember when Penny Wong and Jay Weatherill used to attend barbeques at his house. He talked to Wong about racism, and they shared their outrage about John Howard's One Australia policy. As the son of migrants, Bolkus sympathised with her experiences of discrimination.

Bolkus says today that he recognised 'natural political capacity' in Penny Wong and admired her frankness. 'I liked the fact that you could talk with Penny and she didn't feel shy about disagreeing with you. You could have an honest discussion with her and get insight into what people were really thinking. When you are in the federal cabinet, people don't always tell you the truth, but Penny was always ready to tell me what she thought.'

He did his best to put her in positions where her talent would be recognised – recommending her for work on party policy committees and the like. She soon needed no help from him. She was a success in all the roles she took on, 'She could read the play very well. Penny was not a person who would isolate herself with inept contributions. She could read who her opponents were and who her supporters were, and she knew how to handle herself in a political situation.' Before long, she was dominating the policy committees she served on at state and national conferences, and getting noticed across the party.

Today, asked about Nick Bolkus, both Penny Wong and Mark Butler speak with hesitation – almost embarrassment. They are no longer friends with him. By 2003, Bolkus was on his way out of parliament. The reason was what Bolkus saw at the time as a fundamental betrayal by Butler and Wong. She says she did what she thought was best for the party, and in any case it wasn't her decision.

But that was in the future. By the mid-1990s the Bolkus Left had routed Duncan and taken control of the Left in South Australia. By the end of the 1990s they had cut a deal with the Right to form what was dubbed 'The Machine' – an unassailable coalition that divided up preselections between them. This laid the path for the parliamentary careers of Jay Weatherill and Penny Wong – and later of Mark Butler and Ian Hunter. In the process they destroyed the Centre Left and the political careers attached to it. The resulting bitterness has lasted to the present day.

The Right faction was led by the secretary of the Shop, Distributive and Allied Employees' Association, Don Farrell, who also entered the Senate. South Australia is a small pond, and in most areas the differences between Left and Right were not enormous. Back in the 1990s, those topics on which they fundamentally disagreed – social issues including abortion and gay rights – did not seem as defining as they were later to become.

*

In 1993, at just twenty-four years of age, Penny Wong was deputy chair of the state Labor policy platform committee, and had successfully spearheaded a proposal for racial vilification legislation, making it illegal to abuse someone on the grounds of his or her race. At the July state party convention, she moved for it to be adopted as party policy. The Centre Left, led by state MP Ralph Clarke, argued against her on free-speech grounds. It got fiery. Clarke, who had just been made state president of the party, went head to head not only with Wong but also with the premier, Lynn Arnold, who was strongly in favour of the proposal. Wong conferred with Lois Boswell, who had observed that she probably didn't have the numbers to win. 'I remember Lois saying to me that I could decide how I handled it, but I could probably win it if I "did the personal thing" and told my own story.' For the first time in her political life, Penny Wong used her personal trauma for political ends. She told the story about the neighbour who had abused her as a child, and the racist graffiti on her driveway.

There is, she notes, always a cost to 'going personal'. In the heat of debate, Clarke stood up and said either 'two wrongs don't make a right' or 'two Wongs don't make it right' or 'two Wongs don't make a white'. Memories differ about which it was, but everyone remembers the uproar. Mark Butler recalls, 'It just blew the show up.' Penny Wong remembers hearing a collective intake of breath across Trades Hall. Then people booed and hissed, and cried out 'Racist!' The ruckus was reported in the next day's *Advertiser* – the first among thousands of times Penny Wong would be mentioned, and quoted, in a mainstream media publication.[10]

Opinions differ today about what Clarke meant. Weatherill and Butler both think he didn't mean to be personally offensive. He was harking back nearly half a century to when Labor leader Arthur Calwell had said 'two Wongs don't make a white' while arguing for the White Australia policy. He was trying to say the days had passed when people said such offensive things – and that therefore the legislation wasn't needed. Penny Wong agrees with Weatherill and Butler's interpretation. At first she claims she wasn't upset by the exchange. When pressed, she acknowledges that she was shocked her personal story had been used against her. But 'that's the risk you take', she says. Others remember differently. One person says she was 'glowing with rage'; others say she was in tears. But everyone agrees that, within minutes, she swept back into the debate with perfect aplomb, and won the day.

*

Through her university years, Penny Wong worked a handful of jobs. She was a care assistant for the disabled, and waitressed – 'very badly', she says – at private functions in the homes of Adelaide's wealthy.

Her first serious job began in her final years at university. She began doing paralegal work for the state branch of the Federated Furnishing Trade Society of Australasia, where Don Frater was an organiser. The union represented a wide range of occupations, from woodworkers and musical-instrument makers to sewing machinists and wickerworkers. (At that point Wong did not know enough about her family history to appreciate the symmetry, but she was also working for cabinetmakers – the trade of her great-great-great-grandfather Samuel Chapman.) Wong had taken on a lot. She appeared before the South Australian Industrial Relations Commission (IRC) on unfair-dismissal and wage-underpayment claims even before she had graduated. She recollects these experiences as 'terrifying, but good'. In her final year she had to take leave from the union job to finish her honours thesis, which was 'a bit of a disaster'. But by 1993 she had graduated and accepted a full-time position with the union while also studying for her Graduate Diploma in Legal Practice at the University of South Australia. Meanwhile, Don Frater had become the branch secretary, and the union was in the process of amalgamating with the Construction, Forestry, Mining and Energy Union (CFMEU).

In the words of one of her oldest friends, Wong is not 'a leaning-on-the-bar-having-a-few-beers kind of person'. Being a union organiser was the first time that she had dealt on a daily basis with ordinary working-class people. It was a shift of culture – but, as in every previous stage of her life, she adapted, learning the language and adopting the tone.

She remembers visiting one factory on a forty-degree day and seeing rows of migrant workers – mostly Vietnamese women – sitting at sewing machines under a corrugated iron roof. 'I thought, *Bloody hell, this is Adelaide.*' Her attempt to organise them into the union failed. The capital costs of entering the industry were low; the employers were fly-by-night operators who would close down and set up somewhere else at the slightest sign of being held to account. The women were desperate for the income and frightened of losing the work.

The job also gave her a direct experience of sex discrimination. The trades covered by the union were mostly male-dominated. The exception was the sewing machinists, who were nearly all women. They were also the only ones that did not have a trade-agreed rate of pay. Wong undertook a detailed identification of the work skills involved so as to establish a trade rate. The result was a brace of decisions by industrial relations courts and commissions reflecting enterprise agreements with local blind and furniture manufacturers.[11]

*

Most of those who knew Penny Wong at this time assumed that she was set on becoming a politician. By now it had become common for Labor Party figures to suggest she should consider a political career. Bolkus claims he raised the idea early in their friendship. Wong remembers a conversation in about 1994 with Terry Cameron – a member of the South Australian Legislative Council and the nephew of Whitlam government minister Clyde Cameron – in which he suggested she run for the South Australian upper house. She claims her reaction to Cameron's suggestion was horror. 'At that time it just seemed like a dreadful idea.' She felt the idea advancing on her, acquiring an air of inevitability. She needed to escape.

It was a bitter time for Labor in South Australia. With a landslide loss looming at the 1993 polls, Bannon quit as premier in September 1992, swamped by a tidal wave of fury at the collapse of the State Bank of South Australia and the resulting public debt. Successor Lynn Arnold's fifteen months in office ended in a crushing defeat. An opposition seat in the state upper house would have been an easy job, but also an obscure one for Penny Wong. This was also a difficult time for her on a personal level. In 1994 she ended her relationship with Jay Weatherill.

A few months after the break-up, Weatherill recalls, Wong arranged to see him to break the news 'before everyone else told me' that she was in a relationship with a woman. Weatherill was surprised. There had been no hint of Wong's attraction to women during their time together. But, looking back, he says, 'I think I found it easier than if she had been involved with another man.' Soon, Wong was bringing a female partner to Bolkus's barbeques. Bolkus says, 'I can't remember if anyone told me she was with a woman or if I just kind of noticed it. She never made a secret of it.'

Penny Wong is reluctant to talk about her sexuality. It is, as she says, deeply private; yet she will acknowledge it possesses a political dimension. One of the reasons she was uncertain about a political career was 'I think I was very frightened about being openly gay ... there was the Asian thing, and I had added this.' There was no model.

Today, she acknowledges, she *is* the model. And for that reason she talks about it.

Wong says she did not think of herself as exclusively gay until well after the relationship with Weatherill had ended. She says, 'If you'd asked me at the age of thirty, "Would you ever have a relationship with a man again?" I would probably have said, "If I fell in love with a man, yes." For me it is always about the person first. You fall in love with the person. It's different now because I've been in a long-term relationship with a woman for so long, but back then I didn't see it as rigid. I hope I have some empathy for those whose coming-out experience was really formative, but that wasn't my experience. I was who I was in most ways before I decided I was in love with a woman. I was formed much more by an awareness of race than sexuality.'

At the same time, some of her other supports were falling away. Lois Boswell and Don Frater had moved back to New South Wales. Her mother, Jane, had re-partnered and moved to Melbourne. A few years later, Toby also moved there, where he acted as a consultant to gastro-pubs wanting to redesign their menus. Shane Grant, who had gone to school with Penny and Toby, remembers catching up with him around this time and being shocked at his appearance. Cheap heroin was flooding into Melbourne, and Toby was in its grip.

As Penny Wong saw it, 'I just had to get out of Adelaide. It was a pressure cooker. And I didn't really know what I wanted to do, whether I wanted a political career. I could feel it all closing in on me. It was a very confusing time. I just needed to do something different.'

An opportunity presented itself. As the Federated Furnishing Trade Society of Australasia was absorbed further into the CFMEU, Penny Wong was drawn into that union's politics. She met the top CFMEU official, Michael O'Connor, a factional ally of Julia Gillard's in her unsuccessful 1993 attempt to gain preselection in Victoria. She also met Gavin Hillier, a leader of the union in New South Wales. Towards the end of 1994, he offered her a job in Sydney with the union's timber-working division. She quickly accepted.

She must have been packing her bags by the time of the October 1994 South Australian state Labor convention, which was a high point in the long campaign by the 'Bolkus Left' to seize control of the faction. A key issue was who would go into the party office representing the Left – Ian Hunter or a candidate backed by Peter Duncan. The long work of cultivating unions paid off. Duncan lost the vote, Hunter went on to become state Labor Party secretary and, as Mark Butler puts it,

'Peter Duncan just spat the chewy and left the faction.'

People who knew Penny Wong at that time remember her as cool, even chilling. She could be oddly combative, sometimes resorting to cutting words without provocation. She was also emotional, showing anger and sometimes tears. It would be wrong to describe her as brittle, because nobody thought for a moment she would break. Wong was formidably strong. For the most part, she had the ability to hide inner turmoil beneath an impenetrable exterior and use her intellect to dominate the room.

Adelaide in the mid-1990s could be an ugly place. Leadership of the far-Right National Action organisation had passed to a local man called Michael Brander, a Roman Catholic who had studied for the priesthood without completing his novitiate. Brander knew who Penny Wong was. Having opposed the racial vilification laws she had advocated at the state Labor convention in 1993, he led a protest that featured a poster with the words 'Stop the Asian invasion'. It showed a caricature of a Chinese man with buck teeth and slanting eyes, wearing a conical bamboo hat. More demonstrations followed. Over Easter 1994, protesters went on a rampage in Rundle Mall and held a rally against the 'Asianisation of Australia'.[12]

Penny Wong was always watchful. Racism could come from any corner in the midst of her ordinary life. Suddenly there would be a word, a casually flung phrase or, more rarely, outright abuse – all of it saying, 'You do not belong, you are not one of us.' And now she had added sexuality to the mix. Would the city of Adelaide – let alone the state, or the country – ever elect someone like her? And what would she be opening herself to if it did?

She turned twenty-six in November 1994. It had been six momentous years since she began dabbling in student politics. She was now recognised – whatever her own feelings on the topic – as a political talent for the future, and in her home state friends and allies were in control of the Left of the party.

But Penny Wong was moving away.

5

INTO THE WOODS

Penny Wong thought of herself as an environmentalist. If you had asked her in her university years about the roots of her political commitment, she would have talked about anti-racism and equality of opportunity – and the environment. One of her first substantial contributions as a Adelaide University Union board member was to devise an environmental policy for the union. In the wrangling with Andrew Hamilton and the medical students it got reduced to debates about whether staff could distinguish what bin to use for paper recycling, but behind the argy-bargy lay a political commitment.

Through the amalgamation of the Federated Furnishing Trade Society of Australasia with the Construction, Forestry, Mining and Energy Union, Wong was drawn into what is arguably Australia's oldest culture war – land use, and access to the resources that go with it. Battles over land use are almost impossible for the Australian Labor Party to navigate successfully, as they pitch working people whose incomes rely on resource industries against those dedicated to limiting those industries, or in some cases closing them down. The themes she encountered, of environment, identity and resources, were to recur throughout her political career, including in the 2019 election campaign.

January 1995 saw Penny Wong waving a placard outside Parliament House in Canberra as part of a blockade by the forestry industry. She was demonstrating for more Australian native forests to be opened for logging and woodchipping. Chris Schacht, a then senator who knew Wong from the Labor Party in Adelaide, saw her there 'among the megaphones and speaking to the rally' and recalls thinking that she was putting herself in a 'difficult position ... of opposing the Labor govern-ment's policies'. Other Labor parliamentarians also noted her presence. Penny Wong's enemies within the party have not forgotten that she was there. They still refer to it when questioning if she is the unsullied left-winger her fan club would like her to be. Is she a woman of principle, or pragmatism?

The blockade of Parliament House lasted for several days and was devastating for the Keating government. It was, as forest expert Judith Ajani has described it, the first public display of 'Howard's battlers' versus Keating's 'special interest elites'[1] – or the division between the insiders and the outsiders, as Mark Latham would later put it.[2] Prime Minister Keating was forced, day after day, to encounter crowds of bray-ing, horn-tooting demonstrators. His speechwriter and adviser Don Watson has recalled that it 'visibly diminished him ... They blew their horns and jeered him. Perhaps it was paranoia, but it felt as if the log-gers represented all that section of the community which wanted to be rid of the Keating government ... Truly it was like watching the strength drain away before our eyes.'[3]

So what was Penny Wong, environmentalist, doing there? Asked about the blockade today, she describes it as an example of what hap-pens when 'you allow the politics of identity and division to dominate a policy debate'. People adopt hardline positions that are not only about the facts. Environmental issues are often like this. They are tied up with how people see themselves. The politics becomes 'us and them', with both sides resistant to reason and persuasion. This is the enemy of good policy. In this sense, Penny Wong says, the forest wars were like more recent battles over climate-change policy. The interview in which she said this took place in late 2018 – but the same tendencies were part of the story behind the 2019 election defeat, which saw coal-mining communities in Queensland swing hard against Labor. Sandwiched between a fear of losing votes in the inner suburbs of southern cities and a fear of alienating the working people of Queensland, the party had been ambiguous about its attitude to the Adani coal mine and was punished for it.

There is a phrase that Penny Wong uses a lot. She used it when talking to journalist Greg Sheridan about her religion.[4] She used it in interviews for this book, when speaking of the challenge that confronts Australia in navigating between its alliance with the United States and its trading relationship with China. It is 'binary thinking'. She dismisses it as a kind of intellectual laziness. Few things are binary, she says; the world is complex. Environmental issues are almost never binary. Wong seeks to navigate the binaries and the complexities. She is a compromiser, a negotiator. But people who knew her well during this period would sometimes listen to her discuss the complexities, noting her caution and reserve, and tell her not to sit on the fence. 'You sit on the fence and you get your balls ripped off' was the crude advice of one close friend.

The forest wars had barely touched South Australia. The desert state had few native forests subject to logging, and instead was home to softwood plantations, which offered an important component of a long-term solution to the conflict over the woodchipping of native forests. But on the east coast of Australia and in Tasmania the issue was a determinant of federal political victories and losses. Graham Richardson, as minister for the environment in the Hawke government, had corralled environmentalist votes by protecting the Daintree Rainforest. The Keating government's mishandling of the issue damaged that legacy. Years later, Labor leader Mark Latham's 2004 pitch for power was wrecked by pictures of Tasmanian timber workers cheering Prime Minister John Howard.

In March 1991 Bob Hawke had announced legislation whereby the federal government would allow logging of native forests, provided state governments guaranteed that environmental obligations would be met. There was to be a process of forest assessments resulting in agreements identifying which areas were to be protected and which could be logged. By 1993 the process was stuck, frustrated by the Liberal governments that dominated the woodchipping states. With the exception of Queensland, no state government had yet invited the federal government to assess its native forests.

In late 1994, as Penny Wong prepared to move to New South Wales and work with the CFMEU, an enormous political row was brewing in Canberra between the minister for resources, David Beddall, who was close to the forestry industry, and the minister for the environment, Senator John Faulkner.

Each year, the federal government issued licences for the export of woodchips.[5] As resources minister, this was Beddall's responsibility. Faulkner, as environment minister, was meant to provide advice to feed into the decisions around these licences, to ensure the government met its environmental obligations. Faulkner and Beddall didn't get on.

Because of the stalled assessment process, Faulkner lacked information to work with. His office commissioned environmental groups to provide advice. The result, after much back and forth, was a list of 1297 coupes – about 30 per cent of the area proposed for logging – that Faulkner said should be protected.[6] It was an ambit claim. Faulkner was trying to delay logging long enough to allow for proper assessments, but the woodchipping industry was desperate to convince Japanese buyers that Australia was a reliable supplier. Buyers were fickle, and there was competition from Chile, the United States and South Africa. The forestry industry lobbying ramped up. On 20 December 1994 Beddall announced the new licences. Only eighty-five of the 1297 coupes identified by Faulkner's office would be protected. The wrangle between Faulkner and Beddall erupted onto the front pages of the nation's newspapers. Labor began to bleed green votes. There were environmentalist marches in the capital cities and a tent embassy on the lawns of Parliament House. A Newspoll showed that 80 per cent of Australians wanted an end to native forest woodchipping.

The New South Wales election was weeks away. The leader of the state opposition, Bob Carr, did everything he could to distance himself from the mess in Canberra, promising that, if he was elected, woodchipping native forests would stop. Two days after Beddall's announcement, Keating returned from holiday to try to sort out the mess. He made a statement blaming the woodchipping states' recalcitrance and threatened to ban all native forest woodchip exporting in regions that did not have a forest agreement in place by 2000. In late January 1995, he announced that another 509 coupes would be withdrawn from logging. That announcement was the spur for the blockade – a demonstration of power that had been months in preparation. The logging trucks descended on Canberra, and Penny Wong went with them.

Today, Wong justifies her participation by saying that the list of protected coupes identified by Faulkner and withdrawn from logging by Keating was 'stuffed up' by the public service. The CFMEU members' jobs were on the line, and 'because of the consequences for jobs in the immediate term, yes, I was there demonstrating'.

The solution to fights over forests, Wong says today, is 'non-binary'. You can't simply shut down the industry, because it means more logging in places such as Borneo, which is less sustainable because regulation there is less robust. The only way forward, then and now, is to arrive at a settlement between the different interests.

The attempt to put that thinking into practice, and reach a balance between jobs and environmental sustainability, was to dominate almost two years of her professional life.

Penny Wong's participation in the blockade had another consequence. Her work for the union movement – both in Adelaide and now in New South Wales – was bringing her into direct daily contact with working people for the first time in her life. As always, she was alert for prejudice. But outside Parliament House that January, she experienced the opposite. She was in a union t-shirt and surrounded by forest workers when a woman representing the far-right Citizens Electoral Council – anti-globalisation, implicitly racist and certainly anti-Semitic – began to hand out leaflets. The CFMEU members surrounding Penny took the papers, but she refused. 'I disagree with your views,' she told the woman. She recalls, 'There were five men around me. They didn't know me personally. I was the only Asian in sight and one of very few women. These were people from rural working communities. But when they heard what I said, they all handed the pamphlets back to the woman. They said, "If the union girl won't take them, I won't either."' It was, Wong remembers, 'a beautiful moment'. She took their gesture as one of profound acceptance and group solidarity. 'If you ask me what I learned about being a trade unionist, it was that. That solidarity, that trust.'

It must also have served as a small example of how someone like her – in so many ways an outsider to Labor traditions – might, after all, be able to exercise leadership.

*

Penny Wong's new boss within the CFMEU was Gavin Hillier, former secretary of the New South Wales branch of the Australian Timber Workers Union and, following the amalgamation, state secretary of the forestry division of the CFMEU. Hillier was central to the forest wars. He was also, within the CFMEU, often in opposition to the Victorian-based forestry division national secretary, Michael O'Connor, who was frequently aligned with the industry and vehemently critical of environmentalists. O'Connor has been described by Paul Keating as a 'Labor rat' who should be 'excommunicated'[7] for his role in jointly organising, with the forestry industry, the blockade of Parliament House; by Mark Latham as a 'sellout' for rallying the CFMEU Tasmanian timber workers to support John Howard;[8] and by Julia Gillard as her 'closest confidant' and most committed supporter.[9]

Hillier, on the other hand, was a subtle operator. Wong recalls that when Beddall announced the woodchip licences Hillier 'just closed his eyes and shook his head and said, "We're in for it," because he knew what would happen and what the reaction would be. There was enormous outrage across the country. People wanted to know why we were exporting woodchips to Japan from our beautiful Eden forest. And that was quite legitimate.'

Hillier argued that the blockade was necessary to get Labor to pay attention to the workers' interests, and not be captured by the greenies.[10] But he, unlike O'Connor, was prepared to deal with the environmentalists. An ABC documentary in the lead-up to the 1995 New South Wales state election caught Hillier cheerfully telling green activists that he, like them, was a 'feral' – and that he had sabotaged vehicles belonging to the bosses and non-union contractors in his time. 'You guys probably got

blamed for it,' he chortled.[11] He and the environmentalists compared
notes on the difficulties of dealing with their 'electorates' – his members committed to continuing old-growth logging, and theirs refusing
to contemplate any result other than closing down the industry.

Gavin Hillier was an unlikely friend for Penny Wong, the Scotch
College girl from Adelaide. He was a former tiler from Wagga Wagga
who had become a timber worker, then a union official, after his father
was made redundant. The ex-boxer was an Elvis Presley enthusiast.
Wong recalls him as a 'rough diamond' with missing teeth and huge
hands. He wore thick gold rings that he never took off: 'I think he just
got bigger and bigger and the rings stayed on.' But Hillier was also, in
her estimation, an 'extraordinary political leader' because he saw that
the industry could not win the forest wars in the long term. He wanted
to protect his members' interests by making sure environmental policy was accompanied by industry policy, including good redundancy
and retraining opportunities. Wong thinks he recruited her because 'he
could see what was to come' and wanted her negotiating skills, which
she was already known for within the union. Despite their differences,
they were similar in rejecting binary thinking. They both believed in
compromise and cutting a deal.

Immediately after the Parliament House blockade, the leading
conservation groups formed a delegation to see the New South Wales
leader of the opposition, Bob Carr. The conservation groups, while
disappointed in the Keating government, were aware that forestry
policy had to be implemented by state governments, since they had
responsibility for land use. They had high hopes about Carr, given
his historically strong position on the environment and his December
promise to end woodchipping in the state's native forests. After that
meeting, Carr tasked frontbench MPs Kim Yeadon, later to be minister
for land and water conservation, and Craig Knowles, a trusted adviser
and later to be the minister for planning, with devising 'a forest policy
that meets the needs of the industry and the conservationist aspirations, especially with regard to the South East Forests'.[12] It must have
seemed like mission impossible.

Yeadon remembers that about six weeks before polling day Hillier came to see him. Hillier said he believed Carr could win the election and that if he did he would implement the National Forest Policy Statement. He wanted an industry assistance package for retraining and redundancy for workers who would leave. He also wanted money to help the timber-milling industry re-tool to process plantation and regrowth logs in place of native old-growth forest logs. In short, Hillier wanted a 'seat at the table' for the CFMEU. He brought Penny Wong with him and introduced her to Yeadon as the CFMEU's chief negotiator.

The result, Yeadon recalls, was a raft of long and tense meetings in Parliament House. The environmentalists – groups such as the North East Forest Alliance, the South East Forest Alliance and the Total Environment Centre – were in one room. Most of them wanted to hold Carr to his promise to end logging in old-growth forests. In the other room were Penny Wong and the CFMEU, intent on protecting the interests of their members. The MPs and their staff moved between the rooms. The positions seemed irreconcilable, and time was short. It was clear that failing to resolve the forest issue would probably doom Carr's attempt to win government: Labor would lose either the environment vote or the votes of workers. It was the classic Labor Party dilemma. On one occasion, Yeadon remembers, he and members of staff ran down the road to buy pizzas in order to keep the negotiators at the table instead of allowing them to go home for dinner.

Yeadon was immediately impressed by Penny Wong. She emerged, he says, as a clear thinker and formidable negotiator, constantly clearing the thicket of disagreement to find a way through. Yeadon says today that Hillier was the 'catalyst' for the agreement that was reached – acceptance of limits on old-growth logging, together with an industry assistance package. In negotiating this, Wong was a key player.

The result was a forestry policy that fell short of Carr's promise to end all old-growth logging but shifted the industry towards plantation and regrowth. Carr committed to a string of new national parks, but also to a guaranteed supply of sawlogs for the industry, and money to refit mills for plantation timber. There would be $60 million for

industry restructuring and to provide retraining and redundancy packages. Carr announced all this with Hillier and the environmental groups
at his side. In his speech, he singled out Hillier as 'one of the finest
unionists in the state'.[13]

Gavin Hillier paid a price for cutting a deal with the hated greenies. Wong remembers he would not let her go with him to a meeting
of timber workers in Eden just after the policy was announced. He
feared for his own and his staff's safety. Arriving on site alone, he was
bombarded with eggs and rotten fruit. He told the workers that the
deal meant their future was guaranteed, so long as Labor won. If Carr
lost, old-growth logging would still be in decline and they would get
nothing. ACTU secretary Bill Kelty swung in behind Hillier, calling for
plantations to 'double and triple the number of forests in this country'
while old-growth forests were protected. Kelty topped Carr's assessment, describing Hillier as 'one of the great trade union officials in this
country'.[14]

Labor won the New South Wales election by one seat. The environmental vote was key. The deal in which Penny Wong had been a
negotiator – an environmental policy with a strong industry policy to
go with it – had helped bring about a change of government.

The challenge of implementation remained. In all the forest areas of
the state, coupe by coupe, decisions had to be made about what should
be preserved and what freed for harvest. According to Yeadon, it was
Hillier who suggested that Wong should transfer to his office to drive
the process. Hillier wanted someone he trusted on Yeadon's staff, and
Yeadon was easily convinced. Wong had to be persuaded. Yeadon recalls
that she told him she wanted to return to South Australia and seek preselection. Wong believes she would have said this later, during her time
working for him. She says when he recruited her, she still hadn't settled
on a political career.

Yeadon persuaded her to give him twelve months. It turned out to
be closer to a year and a half. She was his principal policy adviser, dealing
with a wide range of issues but with the implementation of the forestry
policy her main task.

It was high-level, difficult policy work with many stakeholders. Given Labor's narrow majority, the environmentalists feared the government might fall before patches of forest could be protected. They were pushing for areas to be locked up as quickly as possible, and the maximum amount of land preserved. On the other side, the forestry industry wanted guaranteed access and secure supply. The north-east forests were assessed in a process described internally as 'quick and dirty'. In all this, Wong was at the centre of negotiations, a crucial person in the minister's office. The environmentalists found her frustrating – a roadblock in their campaign to hold Carr to his promises. Judith Ajani has described the negotiations as clever tactics, in which Carr neutralised the environmentalists by involving them in 'years of grinding meetings with the bureaucrats, industry and unions in Sydney ... it compromised and distracted the environmentalists and left them with little energy for public campaigning'.[15] Yeadon, on the other hand, thought Penny Wong was invaluable, and today he says it was thanks to Hillier and the industry assistance package he argued for that New South Wales had a 'relatively peaceful' implementation of the twenty-year Regional Forest Agreements, which covered the management as well as the conservation of native forests. Without Hiller, and Wong as his frontline negotiator, Yeadon says, 'Yes, reform would have been undertaken, but it would not have produced the millions of acreage of national parks nor an improved industry. Just as importantly, it spared a lot of workers and businesses severe economic hardship.'

The New South Wales policy, together with other Regional Forest Agreements, became the largest natural resource-planning process ever undertaken in Australia. Some thought the 'forest wars' were settled – but that was optimistic. Carr doubled the area of protected public forests in New South Wales, and crucial zones were safeguarded. Yet the area of public native forests available for logging fell only 4 per cent. According to Ajani, the inventory work resulted in the identification of more native forests, which explains 'this seeming miracle'.[16] Meanwhile, at the time of writing, the Regional Forest Agreements are up for renegotiation, and environmentalists argue that the original estimates of sustainable yields were too generous.

The work in Yeadon's office was Penny Wong's first involvement in the intricate day-by-day grind of policy implementation. The contentious nature of the issue also required political strategy – keeping everyone onside.

The process left her cynical about the environmental movement. In the end, she says, they 'couldn't deliver ... We delivered our part. We halved the quota, we agreed to the moratorium, we agreed to the national parks. But they had to go through a process compartment by compartment and they couldn't agree internally, because compromise is not part of their make-up ... because basically their position internally is that there should be no timber industry.' As well, she points out, if the timber industry in Australia ends, logging will move elsewhere – to regions with less regulation. Closing down the forestry industry in Australia is only progressive policy if you ignore the international impact.

History unrecorded disappears. The environmentalists wrote books about the battle for the forests. So too did the politicians. The working people did not. Gavin Hillier was difficult to track down in research for this book. The CFMEU under its current leadership was either unable or unwilling to provide contact details. The number Yeadon had for Hillier had long since been disconnected. The man once described as the finest unionist in the country had disappeared from the public eye.

Hillier had returned to his home town of Wagga Wagga. Over the years he made a couple of appearances in local media – once, wearing his trademark Elvis Presley shirt, in an ABC vox pop on train services in Wagga, and again in a 2018 newspaper story about his collection of Presley memorabilia. He was shown clutching a guitar and surrounded by posters and vinyl records. The piece made no reference to his union past.[17]

Penny Wong got a call when he passed away on 5 December 2018, aged seventy-two. The funeral notices carried the legend 'He will be Rockin' and Rollin' with Elvis', and asked people attending the memorial service to wear bright colours 'in honour of Gavin's memory and his quirky dress sense'.[18] Bill Kelty read a eulogy and described him as an unsung hero. Kelty also reminded Yeadon that Hillier had always predicted that Penny Wong would 'go places'.[19]

When Wong told me Gavin Hillier had died, she cried.

Meanwhile, the lessons learned and the attitudes adopted during her involvement in the forest wars were to endure. There was the need for negotiation. There was the shunning of what she describes as 'binary thinking'. There was the view of environmentalists as 'unable to deliver' and unable to compromise. All of these battlelines, issues and attitudes were to resonate when she was the minister for climate change and water, dealing with what Kevin Rudd famously declared 'the greatest moral, economic and social issue of our time'.[20]

*

In the second half of 1995, early in her time in Yeadon's office, Penny Wong met Dascia Bennett, a woman eight years her senior. Bennett had been working with an NGO involved in timber industry restructuring before moving into the superannuation sector, but they didn't meet through work. Rather, the connection was made through a network of former South Australians. Bennett was a country girl from the north of the state. She had married young to Mark Weckert, a farmer from the town of Brinkworth, about two hours north of Adelaide, and together they had moved to Grass Patch in Western Australia, where they established a broadacre wheat-and-sheep farm. They had two children, Rohan and Courtney. Bennett was a member of the National Party. She ran, under her married name of Dascia Weckert, in the third position on the ticket for the upper house of the Western Australian parliament at the 1993 election. Yet she claims that when she met Penny Wong she discovered that their core values were not so far apart. Today, she describes her early politics as 'agrarian socialism', with a concern for community at their core. This, she says, she shared with Wong.

Bennett's marriage to Mark Weckert had broken up amicably in 1994. She had moved back to South Australia with the children, then to New South Wales, for a job. She had never thought of herself as gay, but when Wong invited her out on a date she was open to the idea, if a little nervous. 'It took me a little by surprise, I suppose,' says Bennett today. Soon she felt 'really very comfortable'. Those first dates were 'fascinating, layered, not one-dimensional, because she was so smart and interesting and vibrant ... I remember thinking she was someone who was going to go far in politics, and I wanted to be part of that journey.' Once again, the language of love – food – was central: 'She was just amazing; she could cook beautifully and I was good with wine, so I think we complemented each other.'

Bennett's children, then in primary school, adjusted easily to Wong. Once the two women were cooking together while the children watched television; the Sydney Gay and Lesbian Mardi Gras was on, and Rohan looked up and asked, 'Are you two gay?' Penny responded quickly, 'Yes, we are.' And that was that. Bennett says, 'Kids of that age don't have any preconceived ideas in their heads. They respond to love, respect and boundaries. They thought Penny was just a wonderful person that came into my life and made Mum happy.'

Soon the four were a family. Bennett and her children were living in Coogee. Wong was 'a real star in New South Wales', and Bennett's career was also progressing. Their mutual busyness meant it was difficult to see enough of each other. Around mid-1996 they had a conversation in which Penny made it clear that she regarded the relationship as serious. When there were children involved, she said, one should not muck around but be prepared to commit. 'She said she thought she should move in, so she did.'

It was a happy time for both women, but not without shadows. Bennett remembers walking with Penny when two young white men turned and spat at them, spewing anti-Asian abuse. 'I don't want to repeat the language they used. I was a country girl. I wanted to go and throttle them, but Penny held me back.' It was always there, says Bennett, 'the presence of that prejudice. It was awful, for someone like her, who is so brilliant and articulate and smart. To be seen as lesser is just intolerable.'

Toby Wong used to visit them. Bennett describes the connection between Toby and Penny as 'very close, a connection you could sense in the room'. He taught Rohan and Courtney to cook. He bought them a milkshake maker because, he said, 'all children need a milkshake maker'. She recalls, 'Toby was a very creative young man and blessed with amazing skills.' It was clear that he struggled with drug addiction and depression, but 'he was in and out of dealing with those challenges. I never saw the darkness. I just saw a lovely man.' Meanwhile the children's father, Mark, and Penny also got on. 'He would visit the kids, and he and Penny would sit around drinking red wine and gently prodding me and teasing me.'

Several people take credit for bringing Penny Wong back to South Australia to seek preselection for the Senate. Nick Bolkus and Pat Conlon remember flying over to Sydney to talk to her. She was keen right away, they say, but concerned to know whether they were genuine: was it a real possibility? Mark Butler, too, remembers a lunch with Wong near the Macquarie Street government offices in which the idea was discussed. Again, her main concern was whether the opportunity was tangible enough for her to abandon her career in New South Wales.

Butler and the other members of the so-called Bolkus Left were in a strong position to persuade her. The new Machine was in place, and the party in South Australia was operating in a stable and professional fashion. They were in the midst of generational change at state and federal levels. The Left could only expect to get one senator preselected in South Australia for the next federal election, and South Australia – a 'small show' in the context of the federal party – could only expect to get one minister in a federal Labor cabinet. Penny was clearly the leading contender, says Butler. It was obvious that if she entered parliament she would become a senior player. He was able to assure her she would be the Left candidate for the Senate, and if preselected would be placed in a winnable position on the ticket.

Everyone involved assumed that she should contest the Senate rather than the House of Representatives. Looking back, Butler says that he saw her as more naturally oriented to the Senate. She was 'better suited to the policy and committee work of the Senate than the daily electorate work of a House of Representatives seat'. As well, although nobody remembers an explicit discussion along these lines, there was a perception that a gay Asian woman would be challenged in winning a popular vote for the lower house.

Wong herself was always clear that she would run for the Senate. She feared the impact of racial prejudice. In the lower house this could cost the party a seat. 'If people don't like Asians, then no matter how you perform and how good your policies are, you just do the maths. If one in twenty people change their vote just on that issue, that's 5 per cent, and that could lose you the seat. I wasn't prepared to risk that for the party, or to put myself through it.'

Dascia Bennett was not surprised when Penny Wong raised the idea of a return to Adelaide. She says she knew that her partner 'was something really special. She was clearly going to do something extraordinary. And why not do that in South Australia, the state of Don Dunstan, the home of good social policies? That was our journey, and it was a very shared journey.'

Bennett became an active member of the Labor Party. She gave up her job to follow Wong back to Adelaide. She enrolled to study at Flinders University, and threw herself into the social and political occasions involved in preparing for preselection.

Wong acknowledges that Bennett was vital to her success. Bennett, she says, is an extrovert, 'unlike me', and was 'good with the working-class blokes'. Bennett says the two of them would rarely disagree on policy, but would sometimes disagree on the right approach. Penny Wong was always cautious, always able to see both sides. 'You sit on the fence and you'll get nowhere,' Dascia would tell her. 'Sometimes you have to give it a red-hot go.'

'Penny and I were a good balance for each other,' Bennett says. 'She is more a policy generator and into the detail of policy. I can do that, but she probably needed a partner who could go to the barbeque or be at the bar and do the fundraiser and talk to the union boys.'

Meanwhile, there was a natural job for Penny Wong. Adelaide is a small town, and the law firm that served the left-wing unions, Duncan & Hannon, drew nascent Labor left-wingers like iron filings to a magnet. Jay Weatherill had worked there, as had Pat Conlon and Mark Butler. At the time Wong joined the firm, one of her colleagues, Anthony Durkin, was sharing a house with Weatherill. He had moved in when she moved out, two years before. It was a close-knit, almost claustrophobic, circle. Wong had returned to the heart of the internecine world of Adelaide Labor.

The then senior partner of Duncan & Hannon, Peter Hannon and his wife had met Penny through Weatherill, and through their Labor Party involvement. Hannon had floated the prospect of a job with Wong just before she moved to New South Wales. When Wong rang to tell Hannon's wife, Karen, that she was coming back to South Australia, Peter was happy to hear the news, and quick to offer her a job. First, he thought she would deal well with the 'esoteric' and often difficult area of industrial law at a time when the parameters of employment awards were being tested by the Howard government's new industrial laws. Second, he was always keen to build connections with key unions. Her background with the CFMEU and the Missos could only help. 'It was good PR,' he recalls. He knew she wanted a political career. He had employed a few people who had gone on to become politicians. He and Wong struck a deal that while working for him she would be 'fully on board' and focused, but when the time came for her to concentrate on politics she would tell him and leave with no hard feelings.

She didn't disappoint. In addition to her intellect, he says, she had a 'calm and considered approach' and was able to quickly get across factual and legal complexity. Many people who want to be politicians do not make good lawyers, observes Hannon. 'They are big-picture people, but Penny Wong could be both big-picture and appreciate the detail,' he says. 'She was really excellent that way.'

Few of the matters she was involved in during her time at the firm were significant, in the sense that they were heard in the junior courts and set no legal precedents, but each had importance for the people involved, and many of them were difficult. They serve as a reminder that, while factional union powerbrokers were negotiating over her preselection, Wong was dealing with the 'real' work of the unions – advocacy on behalf of ordinary working people. Before the Workers Compensation Appeal Tribunal, she argued – successfully – for an aged-care nursing assistant. The woman had made a stress claim after her employer pushed to get rid of older staff.[21] She represented eleven workers made redundant from an aged-care home[22] and a metal polisher whose workers compensation payments for carpal tunnel syndrome had been halted.[23] Another case concerned a nurse working for the Royal Flying Doctor Service, the issue being whether a new enterprise agreement designed to cover health workers applied.[24] Then there was a raft of unfair dismissals, an injured carpenter in dispute with the WorkCover authority about how much he was to be paid[25] and a worker in a hospital with an injured back.[26] Added to this was a dispute about whether a builder's meal allowance should be included in the wages used to assess a workers compensation claim[27] and the case of a childcare worker who lost a finger in a slammed door.[28] Hannon says the published judgements are only a fraction of the work she did. In workers compensation, only about 1 per cent of matters reach judgement; the others are settled. Penny Wong was a formidable negotiator. Her tenacity led to better settlements.

Working at the firm was rewarding, remembers Anthony Durkin, who is now at the Bar. There was a sense of purpose and camaraderie. 'You felt part of a movement, you felt part of a group of people who were committed to doing the right thing. On the other side was the dark side, and we were on the light side, on the side of the powerless.'

Durkin had known Penny Wong for years. He, too, had been involved in student politics at university, though he was some years ahead of her. Meeting her again when she returned to Adelaide in late 1996, he was struck by her 'undercurrent of seriousness'. She could be fun – she had a ready and hearty laugh – but nevertheless it was the professionalism that left the greatest impression. Sometimes they had to handle each other's files when one of them was on leave or unavailable. If Wong had been involved in his matters, he would get the file back with meticulous handwritten notes bringing him up to speed: 'It was evident the clients had been in good hands.'

It was Wong's work for the firm that resulted in one of the first articles mentioning her in the mainstream media. *The Advertiser* reported on 9 March 1998 that a bus driver she had represented had won a landmark case before the full Industrial Relations Court of South Australia.

Former soldier Barry Leddy had been classified as a part-time worker but was paid for more than thirty-eight hours a week by the State Transport Authority. The court found that he was entitled to full-time pay and conditions. Towards the end of the article, Wong is quoted: 'These drivers were Clayton's part-timers. The department can't have its cake and eat it too.'[29]

Nine weeks later, *The Advertiser* used her name again – this time in a report that she had been selected as the Left faction's candidate for the Labor Party Senate ticket. The Machine – the Left and the Right in their power-sharing agreement – was splitting the positions between them. Linda Kirk was the Right candidate. That meant that if the Machine had its way with preselections, the 'marginalised Centre Left' sitting senator Chris Schacht would be relegated to an almost unwinnable spot. (The other sitting senator, Rosemary Crowley, did not seek preselection and supported Wong to replace her.)[30]

But the battle wasn't quite over, and it was about to get dirty.

In the meantime, Penny Wong switched jobs. Mark Butler had become secretary of the Miscellaneous Workers' Union at the end of 1996 and president of the South Australian branch of the Labor Party the year after. It was a crucial time for the unions. In light of the new industrial laws, the Missos needed a dedicated legal officer. In late 1999, Butler offered Wong the job.

Peter Hannon was sorry to lose her. She left at an inconvenient time – on the eve of a large and complex Australian Education Union state industrial case – but he recognised that she was adhering to her deal. 'The stars were aligning for her politically, and it was a natural job for her to move to.'

The close-fought work continued, but this time with the additional challenge of a need to define the boundaries and implications of the new industrial laws. There was an action before the full Industrial Relations Court about the cessation of night-shift penalties,[31] another about the entitlement of Buttercup Bakeries staff to take industrial action,[32] and a third about the rights of contract cleaners who were sacked when their company lost a contract and immediately rehired by another, related company.[33] Then there was the school groundsman and whether he should be paid an 'on call' allowance,[34] a dispute about the correct wage for qualified childcare workers,[35] and a case concerning a dealer at the Adelaide Casino who had developed depression following his return to work after an injury – this in the context of the casino trying to negotiate Australian Workplace Agreements with its staff. Another case, in which Wong represented a glass cutter who had not been paid overtime, resulted in a resonant passage in the judgement of the South Australian Industrial Relations Court:

> An award is an exercise in public lawmaking; it has the force of legislation because it is legislation ... No one can contract out of an award, and any attempt to do so is illegal and unenforceable in the courts. It is remarkable how often this court has urged upon it the submission that it should not apply the provisions of an award because the parties are said to have agreed to something different. The only challenge in the exercise lies in penetrating the thicket of words in which this basically untenable argument is camouflaged.
>
> The present trends towards enterprise bargaining do not alter this principle at all.[36]

The glass cutter got his overtime, plus interest. Meanwhile, the judgement was an eloquent statement of the main issues that the Labor Party was to contest in the years ahead – an attack on collective bargaining, and ultimately the WorkChoices legislation.

The federal election in which Penny Wong was elected to the Senate was held in late 2001. Because of the way the Senate works, she did not take up her seat until the middle of the following year. Right up until then she was doing this work: dealing with the nitty-gritty of the wider struggle, the local implications of changes taking place on the national stage.

She was representing the all-too-often-forgotten basis and justification for union power – the worker.

6

CHOSEN

When Wong and her new family returned to Adelaide, they began to attend church on an occasional basis. Dascia had what Penny Wong describes today as 'a nice sort of Christian faith. Not into the formality but just a sense of God.' It was something they shared. The church they attended, the Blackwood Uniting Church in the Adelaide Hills, brought Wong full circle with her Australian ancestry: her grandparents had been married there when it was Methodist.

The minister was the mother of one of Courtney's schoolfriends. When she met Dascia and Penny for the first time, she encouraged them to come to a service. 'We've dealt with all the homophobia,' she assured them. Through this minister, and through her relationship with Dascia and her children, Penny's inchoate sense of God began to find a form of expression that felt fitting. Soon, she wanted a ritual – not a confirmation, but an affirmation of faith. On a Sunday morning, as part of a normal service, and after preparatory discussions about faith, Penny Wong was baptised.

Pressed on what she believes – is God a creator, for example, and what about the problem of evil – she resists. Wong seems cool and logical to the outside world (indeed, this is one of the reasons she is seen as a natural leader) but she is, she says, primarily driven by emotion. She describes her faith as instinctive and emotional, not intellectual. 'You can tie me up, ask me a hundred questions to which I don't have a clear theological answer. I just have a sense that God is there, and I want to continue to have some sort of relationship with Him, or Her.'

She quotes John Shelby Spong: 'There are different paths to God. I find God through Jesus of Nazareth but others find God in other ways.'

Her father had remarried a devout born-again Christian. In that household, prayer was frequent: grace was said at meals, and regular appeals were made to God. Penny never found the evangelical style of faith appealing. But she liked the 'incredibly moving' quiet of the practice of faith at the Uniting Church, the sense of grace and mystery. She would not, she says, go to any place of worship where she did not feel accepted. The anti-gay rhetoric in some religious communities is 'sad'. The Uniting Church is where she found her spiritual home.

Today, she is an irregular attendee at her local Uniting Church. She prays in quiet moments. 'I don't think of God as a power to go to with a shopping list. I think more of asking for the patience or the courage to cope. For me, it's more of asking that he walk with me.'[1]

Those who have met the family say they see the influence of both parents in Penny Wong. Both Francis Wong and Jane Chapman are fiercely intelligent, but otherwise almost opposites. She has her father's reserve and well-organised habits, her mother's expressiveness. People who work closely with Penny see her in tears. 'They are strong tears,' says one former staffer. 'You don't ever think for a moment they are weak.'

*

Penny Wong had returned to the incestuous world of Adelaide Labor factional politics as the presumptive candidate for the Left in the Senate, but preselection was not guaranteed. There was still campaigning to be done. The preselections that took place in 1999 in preparation for the next federal election marked a fundamental shift within the state party as the power-sharing deal between Left and Right, brokered by Mark Butler on the Left and Don Farrell on the Right, took hold at the expense of the Centre Left. But the Centre Left had one last punch before it died.

Preselections for election candidates were decided by delegates to the state convention. The unions appointed half the delegates, with

individual unions' voting power decided in proportion to their membership. Amalgamations with the liquor and baking trade unions had made
the Missos, where Penny now worked, one of the strongest unions in the
state. Farrell, meanwhile, was secretary of the enormous Shop, Distributive and Allied Employees' Association, which was a power base for the
Right, and deeply conservative on social issues – including gay rights.

The other 50 per cent of the preselection vote was determined by
the sub-branches and other affiliated groups – the ordinary membership
of the party. In the lead-up to the power-sharing deal, Left and Right
were jockeying for position and influence to strengthen their negotiating positions. This led to one of the most outrageous exercises in branch
stacking in the history of the Australian Labor Party – which is saying
something. Branch stacking – or 'vigorous recruitment exercises', as the
operatives prefer to call it – was part of politics as normal within Labor,
but even in that context what happened was breathtakingly filthy.
Gary Johns, who had been a minister in the Keating government, later
described it as a 'veritable stacking spree'.[2] Had the stacking succeeded,
Penny Wong would have been one of the beneficiaries, together with the
other bright young candidates – Jay Weatherill and Pat Conlon – who
were the hope of the Left in its bid for increased power in the party of
government after the next state election, due by 2002.

How much did she know about what her party colleagues were up to?

The deadline for new members to join if they were to be allowed to
vote for convention delegates was 26 February 1999. On that single day,
2000 new memberships were lodged and paid for, by about ten people.
According to the paperwork, most had been signed up on the Australia
Day holiday, a month before.

The stack almost doubled the state party membership. Sub-branches
were flooded with new members who were strangers to the existing
ones. Seats made newly marginal by an electoral boundary redistribution were at the centre of this frantic activity. Some quadrupled their
memberships overnight, swollen by recruits from both Left and Right.
The police investigated allegations made in the remote town of Coober
Pedy by Indigenous residents who said they had been signed up without

their consent. A report was sent to the South Australian Director of Public Prosecutions, but no charges were laid.[3] Ramsay, the seat of the state opposition leader, Mike Rann – later to be premier – was also among those stacked, probably by his own Right faction in order to protect him.

In the wake of this flood of new members, the non-aligned and Centre Left MPs went door-knocking in their branches and, as they had suspected, found many people who didn't know they were now members of the Labor Party. The party's rules said that new members had to be nominated and accepted by the sub-branch to which they were affiliated; clearly, the rules had not been followed. The cost of the new memberships was $42,000, which, as Labor politician Ralph Clarke later remarked, 'means that the entire SA branch could be purchased for less than $100,000'.[4]

Clarke, a former party president and Centre Left state MP, was one of the victims of the stack. It had been Clarke who opposed Penny Wong in the state conference debate on racial vilification legislation six years before. He was an effective parliamentarian, but scandals in his personal life had left him vulnerable, and now the Machine was moving against him. He was fighting for his political life.

He and other Centre Left members challenged the memberships with a complaint to the party's state executive – which closed ranks. Wong was on the state executive at the time.

Ian Hunter, a foundation member of what had previously been known as the Bolkus Left, and now state branch secretary, defended the sudden boost in party membership. It was all within the rules, he said. 'Whenever you try and put a restrictive rule on this sort of thing around the country people try and get around it ... rather than encourage people to break the rules, we will try to keep our rules as simple as possible,' he said.[5] Don Farrell described the 'rumblings' as 'all a pretty normal part of the preselection process' and predicted that any resulting tensions would soon settle.[6] He was wrong.

There was a disputes procedure within the party, but instead of following that process, the state executive passed a motion declaring the new memberships valid, and followed up by making plans to call a special convention to confirm that validity retrospectively.

Clarke and his fellows complained to the national executive of the party. The leader, Kim Beazley, was reported to be concerned – but the numbers on the national executive were dominated by the Right and Left.[7] By July 1999, both state and national executives made it clear there would be no investigation.

Ralph Clarke took the only remaining course open to him and launched a Supreme Court action against his own party, seeking injunctions to stop the special convention and prevent the preselections going ahead. It was the first time action of this sort had been taken.[8] Conventional wisdom at the time was that party rules were internal matters and not subject to court review.

Yet on 27 July 1999 the Supreme Court ruled in Clarke's favour. It would decide whether the 2000 new members had been signed up in accordance with the rules and, in the meantime, the preselection round was frozen. The state conference, scheduled for October, was postponed, and all the candidates for preselection were placed in limbo – including Penny Wong.

Asked about the branch stacking today, everyone is predictably coy. Off the record, some of the main operatives admit it was a 'bad look' but insist that 'everyone was doing it'. Even Clarke is on the record as admitting to contributing to a slush fund known as 'Labor of Love' to pay for memberships and shore up the Centre Left faction in the 1980s.[9] The problem, these people claim, was that it just got a bit out of hand.

What about Penny Wong? Those who were around at the time say that she and Jay Weatherill were not directly involved and 'very clean'. One of her enemies says, 'She is far too high and mighty ever to dirty her hands with a stack.' Others, more friendly, assert that she and Weatherill were deliberately kept out of the 'dirty business'. It was the factional operatives – Butler and Farrell – who were assumed to be chiefly responsible.

Butler admits some responsibility. 'There was a generational change happening at state and federal level and, you know, there's no question

that it sort of got out of control.' The party was 'shooting for state government and there was a generational change needed in federal caucus'.
It was time to remake the branch, and 'we had a strong incentive to
make sure that we had the numbers to do that ... there was a strong
motivation for effective recruitment.'

The resulting controversy, he acknowledges, was damaging and
embarrassing. The court decided against the party because the state
executive had not dealt properly with Ralph Clarke's complaint. Asked
whose fault that was, Butler says, 'Well, I guess mine, to a degree. The
leadership of the two big groups, Left and Right, I guess.'

Butler absolves Penny Wong of any responsibility. She was not on
the committee that managed the party's response to Clarke's complaint.

Non-aligned Labor MP John Hill later chaired an investigation
into the stack, which recommended changes to the party's rules on
recruitment. Penny Wong sat on that committee. It recommended new
measures to ensure the bona fides of members, and that full membership
rights should only be confirmed after three years – removing some of
the incentive for stacking. The investigation found that a single individual was responsible for signing up almost half the new members – but
the report never revealed who that was, and when interviewed for this
book Hill claimed not to be able to remember. Wong, too, claimed not
to know.[10]

Penny Wong says today that she was aware of the recruiting drive.
She remembers signing up her family and friends. But, she claims, she
had no idea of the extent or the egregious nature of the stack. She
believes Clarke was right to take the party to court: 'It was a good lesson for us.' The fact that the rules are subject to court challenge remains
a good discipline on the party, she says, and the rule changes that followed the episode were beneficial.

What is the difference, in her view, between a recruiting exercise
and a branch stack? 'It's in the eye of the beholder,' she says, with not
a hint of a smile.

The Australia Day stack, as it is remembered, was an embarrassment on the road to a long period of success and stability for the South

Australian Labor Party. There is little doubt that the Machine resulted in talented politicians being selected at state and federal level. There was a generational change that has helped form the modern party. Penny Wong was preselected for the Senate. Jay Weatherill entered state parliament. Pat Conlon was preselected and became a highly successful state minister. In time, Mark Butler entered federal parliament, and he is now a frontbencher. On the Right, Don Farrell was elected to the Senate in 2007. Most Australians wouldn't recognise his name, but he is a factional powerbroker and was a shadow minister of state, as well as being one of the 'faceless men' who engineered the overthrow of Kevin Rudd and the ascension of Julia Gillard to the nation's highest office. At state level, Labor won power in 2002 with Mike Rann at the helm. He was succeeded by Weatherill, to make the longest-serving South Australian Labor government. The party was remade, and the power and influence of the Left increased. Meanwhile, the Centre Left disappeared. The South Australian machinations were one of the foundation stones of the current form of the Labor Party at state and federal level.

But back in 1999 Penny Wong had to get preselected without the additional numbers the stack might have provided. 'I doorknocked a lot of members and phoned a lot of people,' she says. She and Dascia Bennett worked as a political team to get a broader union base to support her. When the state convention was finally held, in April 2000, Wong led the preselection vote with 36.4 per cent of the ballot. Linda Kirk, the Right's candidate, was next in line, with 33 per cent. The casualty was Chris Schacht – a sitting senator and former federal minister, who lost narrowly, by three votes. Schacht was part of the Centre Left, and the Machine's verdict was that he had had his day. He was relegated to third position on the ticket – a humiliation and, thanks to the popularity of Natasha Stott Despoja as the lead candidate for the Australian Democrats, almost certainly an unwinnable spot.

When the ticket was announced, with Wong in first place and Schacht in third, she told a reporter that Schacht had been 'one of the big men of the SA party ... but every party must continue to reassess itself'.[11]

A few weeks later, typically well organised, Wong applied to revoke her Malaysian citizenship. The revocation was granted in July 2001.[12] Years later, when the dual citizenship of some parliamentarians came to light, Wong frustrated journalists by refusing to release the documents proving her claim that she held only one nationality. For a while, the media included her on lists of parliamentarians whose status under the constitution was in doubt. In fact, her eligibility was always crystal clear.[13]

Today, Left operatives are unrepentant about the casualties of the deal that saw Penny Wong preselected. The Centre Left, they say, was a faction without a purpose. It had to go. But the execution was ruthless. Wong, the young upstart, had knocked off one of the established figures of the party.

Schacht was devastated, and not prepared to give up easily. He remembers going to Penny Wong some months after the vote to ask for her campaign help. The only way he had a chance of winning, he said, was if she helped him with a large campaigning effort. He was prepared to put aside any bad feelings and asked her to do the same. They should get out and tour the state, particularly rural areas, he suggested. 'I remember going to her and saying … we have to campaign, and we have to go around the state. She made the comment to me, "Chris, I don't think I could do that. People in the country have strange views about Asian people. I don't think it's wise for me to do that." I said, "Penny, you have to face that issue one day. The only way to do it is to see people face to face."'

Wong was not convinced, and there was no separate campaigning effort for the Senate team, which did not help Schacht. Today he thinks she was not so much unwilling as 'very shy. She is very clever. She might be the cleverest person in parliament from South Australia. But you put her into a community arrangement, ask her to go down and meet the waterside workers in a couple of pubs at Port Adelaide, or go and talk to the Country Women's Association in Naracoorte, she won't be in it.'

Schacht admits he is hardly an impartial observer, but he says that Wong, despite her popularity within the party, has not been a vote winner in South Australia. Since the 2001 election, when she was placed first on the ticket, the party has often not done well in the state Senate race. It is a difficult claim to assess. The Senate voting system is complicated, and mainly about votes for party groupings rather than individuals. In South Australia, in the time Wong has been a candidate, the Democrats, then Nick Xenophon and his team (now Centre Alliance) and Family First have stolen votes from the major parties. How much of Labor's poor showing can be attributed to Penny Wong? It's hard to say, but the trend is perhaps a small corrective to those in her fan club who believe she would be outstandingly popular if she moved to the House of Representatives. There is so far little evidence that she attracts votes outside a left-wing demographic.

As for the wider issue of popular campaigning, everyone acknowledges that Wong has got better at it, but she says of herself, 'I am an introvert.' She criticises herself for not doing what Bolkus did for her – making an effort to reach out to and socialise with young Labor talent coming through.

*

Sometime around 1999, during the manoeuvring over preselections, Mark Butler invited Penny Wong out to a night of karaoke. It wasn't her thing, but he persuaded her. Needless to say, she didn't sing. But it must have been a friendly occasion, conducive to openness. Some time during the night they reflected on the rift between Bolkus and Duncan, and what it had cost the Left before they took action. 'We must never let that happen to us,' Wong said to Butler. They must never allow any dysfunction in their personal relationship to become a political dysfunction. 'If we have disagreements in the future, let's resolve them,' she said to him. He agreed. They could not fall out, he said, for the sake of the faction and the party.

This agreement has held. Mark Butler describes himself as a 'huge fan' of Penny Wong. She says of him, 'Mark's a friend, a colleague. What sets him apart is both his intellect and that he puts the collective – the party – ahead of himself. We've been through many transitions and many fights and many disagreements together. And he has been very supportive and very loyal to me ... We trust each other. We don't always agree. But we've dealt with those disagreements properly ... now I am senior to Mark, but he has more weight factionally than me. He uses his power thoughtfully, and that's good because some people use their factional power unthinkingly.'

One of the parts of the Machine deal was that Mark Butler would at some stage be given the safe seat of Port Adelaide. He entered parliament in 2007 – the election Kevin Rudd won. He is currently shadow minister for climate change – the portfolio that Penny Wong held in the first Rudd government.

Meanwhile, in the current opposition, Butler and Wong's longstanding alliance is one of the most powerful and effective in the party. She is leader of Labor in the Senate, the deputy manager of opposition business in the lower house. She is shadow minister for foreign affairs, and he has the portfolios of climate change and energy.

The influence of both South Australia and the Left faction is greater today than it was when Penny Wong sought preselection, and this is largely the legacy of the generational change Butler and Wong helped engineer. Their political alliance will be important to the future of the parliamentary party.

*

It seemed to Chris Schacht that Penny Wong was unreasonably sensitive to 'the race issue'. Easy to say. Race, and racism, was an inescapable dimension of her political and personal life, not something she could escape. Politically, her non-Anglo ethnicity could easily have both defined and constrained her. She was the first Asian-born woman elected to the Australian parliament; at no previous time in the nation's history could someone like Penny Wong have emerged. Yet the decision to run for the Senate was a combination of her belief that she was not a natural retail politician and her fear of racism. Penny Wong's fan club sometimes talks about her as though, because she is 'different', she exists above or outside the dirty business of politics. The circumstances of her preselection, the factional battles of which she was a beneficiary, give the lie to that. She is a politician, in all senses of the word. Of course she is. And yet she *is* different.

Sometimes, racism posed a risk to her personal safety. In August 1998 Wong organised and led a large rally in Adelaide, including a march and a candlelight demonstration of solidarity against racism. In the days before the event, she took a frantic phone call from Toby. His drug use, work in hospitality and social circles meant he had connections to the darker side of Adelaide. He had heard a rumour that National Action – the militant white supremist group founded by neo-Nazi Jim Saleam and, at that time, led by Adelaidean Michael Brander – was going to 'take her out' at the rally. The organisers took the threat seriously enough to make plans ensuring Penny would always be in the middle of a protective group, difficult to reach or target.

It is an example of her steely resolve that she went. On the day of the march, about half a dozen National Action members turned up, but police reported no clashes.[14]

Race is the undercurrent, the backdrop, the topic that Australia is not comfortable discussing. The topic that, in Howard's time, could turn elections and was at the centre of the 2001 election campaign.

In August 2001 the Norwegian freighter *MV Tampa*, carrying 433 refugees plucked from a distressed Indonesian fishing boat, was denied permission to enter Australian waters. The same day, the Howard government introduced the Border Protection Bill 2001 into the House of Representatives. The asylum seekers were taken to the island of Nauru for their refugee status to be assessed. This marked the beginning of a series of measures that became known as the Pacific Solution.

When the *Tampa* crisis broke, Labor leader Kim Beazley initially supported the government, saying that the last thing the country needed was a 'carping opposition'. Two days later, when SAS troops were aboard the *Tampa* and Howard introduced legislation giving his government the retrospective power to turn back boats, Beazley decided to oppose the bill – in the full knowledge that this stance might cost him the election. The legislation was defeated in the Senate on the votes of Labor, the minor parties and independents – but subsequent border protection legislation was passed with Labor's support. In the days that followed, the other elements of the policy that has been part of Australian politics ever since were gradually cobbled together, including the excision of islands from the Australian migration zone, detention centres on Manus Island and Nauru, and use of the navy to turn back boats.

A few weeks later, the September 11 attacks on the World Trade Center in New York sent the world into cataclysm. Terrorism, racism and border security became conflated in the Australian public's mind. This led to Howard's famous election promise, splashed on posters and leaflets: 'We will decide who comes to this country and the circumstances in which they come.'

In October, at the tail end of the election campaign, senior Howard government ministers alleged that asylum seekers on a boat foundering on its way to Australia had thrown their children overboard to force a rescue. Days later, the government was re-elected with an increased majority. Howard had won a third term, fuelled by One Nation votes returning to the Liberal Party.

After the election, a Senate select committee found that the 'children overboard' incident was a fabrication. No child had been thrown overboard, and the government had known this before polling day. Howard's election win was what journalists David Marr and Marilyn Wilkinson were later to describe as his 'dark victory'.[15]

The 2001 election was devastating for the Labor Party. It created internal division, pitting progressives against the Right. It 'knocked us off balance for a long time', John Olenich, then Penny Wong's soon-to-be-staffer, recalls. The 'true believers' of the Left hungered for power, but could hardly stomach caving to Howard's agenda.

During the election, Penny had managed the campaign for the marginal Adelaide seat of Hindmarsh on behalf of local candidate Steve Georganas – a member of the Bolkus Left. Hindmarsh was one of the seats Labor had to win if it was to form government. Georganas suddenly became reluctant to doorknock, which he normally loved. When Wong quizzed him on why, he told her that electors were saying they thought asylum seekers should be shot. This was his community. He had lived in the electorate all his life. He was himself the child of Greek migrants. It was 'awful', he recalls today, to see the electorate manipulated on race.

Wong says that at this time she rejected the idea that there were 'pull' factors bringing asylum seekers to Australia. As she saw it then, it was all 'push' – desperate people running for their lives. She was therefore among those wanting a softer, more compassionate approach.

Her view today has shifted. She says that as leader of Labor in the Senate and as a shadow minister for foreign affairs, she has had security briefings that have led her to conclude her earlier views were wrong. There are 'pull' factors that encourage people to get into leaky boats and come to Australia. Government policy can't afford to encourage people smuggling. Given the sheer number of people in the world on the move and seeking a better life, policy has to be tough.

The problem with the 2001 election, she says, is that Howard fused a challenging policy issue with xenophobia and racism. The legacy, she says, is that 'the Left reacts to the race issue, and doesn't want to deal with the border security issue, so everyone gets locked in'.

So what does a good policy look like? What role will she play in this as shadow foreign minister – and perhaps one day the minister?

She shares a vision that has been proposed ever since the Fraser government was dealing with the influx of refugees from the Vietnam War – the much-touted but little enacted 'regional solution'. 'The core of it is better regional arrangements, removing the incentive for movement from transit countries, but that is difficult,' she says. She adds that she thinks 'we can't have indefinite detention in the way you have had on Nauru and Manus Island'.

And in the absence of the chimerical regional solution, does she support boat turnbacks and mandatory detention? 'I support the current Labor policy,' she says. 'It's not comfortable coming to that view. It's much easier not to.'

That policy emphasises 'strong borders, offshore processing, regional resettlement and turnbacks when safe to do so because we know it saves lives at sea'. It also talks of 'negotiating third-country resettlement options' to end indefinite detention on Nauru and Manus – and that includes accepting New Zealand's standing offer to resettle refugees. It commits Labor to increasing Australia's humanitarian intake of refugees, ending temporary protection visas and funding the work of the United Nations High Commissioner for Refugees.[16] While it opposes the use of Nauru and Manus for indefinite detention, it describes them as 'temporary regional processing centres' and is silent on whether they would remain open. It is also silent on the fate, under a Labor government, of any future *Tampa*, or of any boats that evade detection and reach Australia's shores.

In 2001, the senators elected from South Australia were, in order: Robert Hill for the Liberal Party, Penny Wong for Labor, Jeannie Ferris for the Liberals, Linda Kirk for Labor, Grant Chapman for the Liberals and Natasha Stott Despoja for the Australian Democrats. Stott Despoja took the seat that Chris Schacht had desperately hoped to win, by a margin of 1 per cent, or a few thousand votes. To this day, Schacht believes a proper Senate campaign in the rural areas could have made the difference and secured him another term.

Georganas, meanwhile, did not win Hindmarsh, despite a spirited campaign managed by Penny Wong. He lost the contest by less than 2 per cent of the vote – a situation almost unchanged from the previous time he had contested it, in 1998. In the context of a *Tampa*-driven defeat for Labor, it wasn't a bad result.

The same could not be said for Kim Beazley. This was the second election he had lost against John Howard. The implications of that, and the manner of Howard's victory, were to infect Penny Wong's first term in parliament.

7

A NEW VOICE

O n election day 2001, Toby Wong turned thirty. Ten days later, he died. The death notices described it as a 'tragic accident'. It was not for another eight years that Penny Wong publicly shared the truth: Toby's death was by suicide.[1]

'We will miss you Tobe,' said one death notice. Another, 'fun and free, your gentle heart and kind spirit will live with us always'.[2]

In the weeks and months before his death, during the campaign that brought her into federal parliament, Penny had been one of her brother's main confidantes. He was living in Melbourne and she in Adelaide, but there were long, intimate and challenging phone calls between them as she tried to comfort him, to talk him into a better place.

Her friends remember the memorial service. They remember the weight of the grief, almost unbearable. They remember Penny reading the eulogy – which she will not share today, because it is too personal. Her friends remember her saying that she felt she had been given twice her brother's strength: that he was a softer person than she and did not have as many defences. He had found it harder coming to Australia, and the world had not been kind to him.

Her parents were at the service, along with all the Chapman aunts and many family friends. Remembering it, Wong says she was struck by how well her parents supported each other, and what decent people they were. Love persisted even after divorce. Another who was present describes Penny as seeming to accept the burden of the grief. She gave the impression of carrying her family – being the navigator of their differences, and the 'captain of the ship in the waters of grief'. Penny, this friend remarks, always steps forward, taking and shouldering responsibility rather than running from it or crumbling under the weight.

But she must have wished to crumble.

The topic of Toby's death cannot be broached without causing further pain to the Chapman and Wong families. It is the topic that Penny Wong was most concerned by when approached about this book. She is fiercely protective of her parents. She will not say more about the loss of her brother.

She saved her public tribute to Toby for her maiden speech, delivered in the Senate on 21 August 2002. Penny had tried to draft the speech in Adelaide but couldn't focus. She is a slow writer – the kind who has to be happy with each sentence before moving on, rather than throwing words down and then tidying them up. She flew to Canberra, shut herself away in her parliamentary office and wrote the speech over an intense three days. Then she went to see the Labor leader in the Senate, John Faulkner, to warn him that she was going to 'go hard on race'.

Not all of the connections would have been clear to her listeners. She was new to the parliament, and few members knew her personally. Those outside her immediate circle didn't know that Toby's death was suicide – although it was implicit in what she said – or that she blamed racism, in part, for his death. But in Penny's mind it was all linked: the election they had just been through, Toby being thrown off a bus after being racially abused, his phone call warning her about National Action wanting to 'take her out' – all the things that had happened to him, and to her, since they arrived in Australia. Penny did not think of herself as damaged by her childhood trauma, although some of her friends, noting her hyper-vigilance to racial discrimination, thought her more affected than she was inclined to admit. In her mind, she had learned to cope by developing a tough exterior. Toby, though, had been gentler, more vulnerable.

It was this personal context underlying her words that made her speech extraordinary. She was told later that the leader of the government in the Senate, Robert Hill, had leant over to John Faulkner and told him it was not appropriate for a maiden speech to be so angry, so explicit in its targets. The convention was to speak of one's electorate, perhaps gesture towards social justice or universal values, and keep it civil.

Sharryn Jackson had been elected as the Labor member for the Western Australian seat of Hasluck at the 2001 election. As the assistant state secretary of the Miscellaneous Workers' Union, she and Penny had been in each other's orbit for a while, without having met. On this day, Jackson walked across to the Senate to hear Penny speak. By the end, she was in tears. The two women embraced, and have been friends ever since.

Jackson, too, had been devastated by the changing mood in the electorate around race. She had doorknocked and heard her electors using language she could barely stomach. 'Being in a marginal seat, it was very hard to confront people all the time on asylum-seeker issues. It was an awful election, very distressing.' Yet here was Penny Wong – the first Asian-born woman ever to sit in the Australian parliament, and one of very few Asians ever to do so.

Standing in the red Senate chamber, Penny looked younger than her thirty-three years. She had yet to adopt her current work uniform of slacks, well-cut jackets, immaculate haircut and simple shirts. She wore a maroon jacket over a black dress, a white necklace and simple pearl earrings. There was little sign of the accomplished, acid-tongued parliamentarian of more recent times. She read from her script, and as she began, her delivery was flat and fast, betraying her nerves.[3] Her theme was compassion – and its absence.

She began by talking about Poh Poh, her beloved grandmother. 'That her granddaughter is here today would have been a source of pride but also probably some consternation to her. How much the world can change in two generations,' she began. This family history, she said, was why she believed that compassion lay at the heart 'of any truly civilised society'. Compassion was the 'underlying principle, that core value at the heart of our collective consciousness. If not compassion, then what? Economic efficiency? Or the imposition of some subjective moral code, defined by some and imposed on the many?' To call for compassion was not political correctness, nor weakness, she said.

It is to assert that those with power should act with compassion for those who have less, and that the experience of those who are marginalised cannot be bypassed, ignored or minimised as it so often is. Compassion is what underscores our relationships with one another, and it is compassion which enables us to come to a place of community even in our diversity. Yet this country in recent times has been sadly lacking in compassion.

And then she went for it. Referencing Pauline Hanson's maiden speech – delivered in the same building six years earlier, in which she had talked of Australia being 'swamped by Asians' – Wong said that she feared Australia was instead 'in danger of being swamped by prejudice'. She called for 'us' to reclaim the phrase 'one nation': 'I seek a nation that is truly one nation. One in which all Australians can share regardless of race, or gender, or other attribute, and regardless of where they live, and where difference is not a basis for exclusion. We do not live in such a country. We are not yet truly one nation. But it is the task of political leaders to build one.'

She spoke about the economy and social opportunity – of the need to ensure that globalisation benefited both rich and poor, and of her father's transformative experience as a Colombo scholar. She spoke, at some length, about educational inequality, including in the suburbs of Adelaide. But finally, and most powerfully, she turned again to race, and to the role it had played in the election:

Let us speak openly and honestly about race in this country, about what last year's election signified and about where we are now. Let us speak openly about the damage that has been done … In recent years there has been much preaching from the current prime minister about political correctness – that we have had too much of it. Instead, now we have a climate in which someone who speaks out about injustice, prejudice or discrimination is dismissed as simply being politically correct. Compassion has been delegitimised – instead it is seen as elitism.

She talked of Samuel Chapman and his journey on the *Cygnet*, and then about the racial abuse she had suffered in the schoolyard. 'It used to lead me to wonder, how long do you have to be here and how much do you have to love this country before you are accepted?'

Then, in the most powerful passage of the speech, she set her sights on Howard. She had by now apparently conquered her nerves: her delivery was controlled, her words slow and forceful. She was still clutching her script: from time to time she looked up. There was a sign of what was to become the trademark Wong glare.

> Never forget that it was this current prime minister who called for a reduction in Asian immigration in 1988 ... The Prime Minister premised his arguments on the grounds of social cohesion. You have to ask what effect his own comments had on social cohesion. I know how it felt for me and my family and many like us during this time.

When Pauline Hanson gave her maiden speech, Howard had defended her. 'What sort of message does this send to our community? That it is acceptable to rail against people who look different? That these sorts of comments are no different from any other sort of political commentary? Leadership was called for, not to deny freedom of speech but to assert the harm in what she said. Leadership was called for, but it was not provided.'

She spoke of the Howard government's reaction to native title, including Howard's use of a map of Australia on television to provoke fear that backyards were going to be claimed. Then she turned to the *Tampa* and the election just past:

> Who can forget that most enduring image of last year's election campaign, that photograph of the Prime Minister, in sober black and white, attempting to look statesmanlike, with the slogan, 'We will decide who comes to this country and the circumstances in which they come'? This is the statement which epitomises Prime Minister Howard's vision for this country. This is the core of what he offered

us at the last election. It is a statement of self-evident fact. It is not
a policy statement. Of course we decide who comes to this country.
So why say it? The only reason that you would is if you wanted to
strike a chord of discord or if you wanted to foster division.

On the Children Overboard affair and the government's failure to
correct the record, she was scathing. 'There may be some who will say
I am being too critical. I ask them this: When has your prime minister,
John Howard, done or said something that made you feel proud to be
Australian? When can you point to a time when he exercised his lead-
ership to bring Australians together?'

Most Australians were good-hearted, she said. The main things that
undermined social cohesion were economic inequality and poor political leadership: 'People don't share if they do not have a fair share. They
will not listen if they are not listened to.' There had to be work to create
a fair community. Australia must never again go down the path it had
taken during the 2001 election, when the fault lines in society were used
'for base political purposes'.

She moved on to thank those who had put her into parliament,
mentioning Mark Butler, Pat Conlon, Ian Hunter and Jay Weatherill, as
well as Nick Bolkus – who was sitting beside her as she gave the speech,
gazing up with avuncular pride. She mentioned the unions that had
supported her preselection.

Finally, she came to Toby. She coughed, clearing her throat. Her voice
broke. Toby had, she told the parliament, 'turned thirty on the day I was
elected to this place, and died ten days later ... Your life and death ensure
that I shall never forget what it is like for those who are truly marginalised.'

She finished with thanks to 'Dascia, Courtney and Rohan' – her
partner and stepchildren, saying that without their love and support she
'would never have considered standing for preselection'.[4]

After the speech, Jackson remembers walking back to the House of
Representatives. People were remarking that Penny Wong was in the
wrong house – meaning that she was leadership material. 'But it was a
hard and sad state of affairs in Australia at that time, that the thought of

a gay Asian woman being elected to the House of Representatives was just not something that was going to happen,' Jackson recalls.

Politics had always been an option for Penny Wong. Nevertheless, the last sentence of her speech crediting Dascia was true. It was Dascia who had helped to encourage Penny to be brave – not to sit on the fence, not to let the bastards win, not to permit other people's prejudice to limit her potential. Yet, even as she delivered these words, the relationship was in trouble. A few months later, it ended. They had been together for seven years, during which time Bennett's children had grown into teenagers.

Theirs had been both a personal and a political partnership. Bennett was known and liked in Adelaide Labor circles. She had thrown herself into the party and its aims. Today both women acknowledge that it was she who helped Penny win over key unions to support her preselection. It was she who would enthusiastically greet union members at social occasions, who would lean on the bar with them and have a beer. She helped Penny to overcome the campaigning disadvantages of her naturally introverted nature.

Bennett had abandoned her career to accompany Wong back to Adelaide. At first, finances had been stretched – Wong was the main income earner, and on a lower salary as an industrial lawyer than she had been as a political adviser in Sydney. Bennett worked part-time as a consultant for the Australian Student Traineeship Foundation, and had returned to study a Bachelor in Public Policy and Political Science at Flinders University. After she graduated in 1998, Bennett began a career in the superannuation and financial services industry, working her way up.

Often, when politicians' relationships break up, their former partner is left bitter. They gave all the support in the early years, only to be left without proper acknowledgement. This is not the case for Bennett and Wong. Today Bennett is the chief executive of Super SA – the fund that covers the state's public sector employees. She is at the peak of her career, an industry leader and one of the most senior executives in her home state. Yet, interviewed for this book, she described helping Penny to achieve preselection as one of the proudest accomplishments of her life.

Why did the relationship not endure? Wong will say nothing about this. Bennett, too, is sparing when discussing it. As her career took off and Penny began flying back and forth to Canberra, it was hard to stay connected. 'I suppose our relationship just came to a point where we decided that she was going to go that way, and I was going to go another.'

They remain friends. Today Penny's current partner, Sophie Allouache, and Dascia sometimes sit and drink red wine and gently heckle Penny, just as Mark Weckert and Penny used to prod and tease Dascia at the beginning of their relationship.

Penny Wong is good at family. When blended families break up, it can be a breach or an expansion. Penny and Dascia made it an expansion. They put family first. So far as possible out of the public eye, they gave priority to friendship and the care and emotional wellbeing of the children. They did all this without any of the social and legal structures that would have supported them in naming what they had – and still have today – as a family. Rohan and Courtney, now adults, regard Penny as their stepmother, and consider Alexandra and Hannah, the daughters of Penny and Sophie, as siblings. When Courtney married in 2016, three people stood up to give her away – her father, her mother and her stepmother, Penny Wong.

Back in 2002, the hurt and loneliness must have been uppermost. Penny Wong had achieved political success but was weighed down with grief and the end of a relationship. She was revolted and threatened by the election just past – a reminder of the side of Australia that would always reject her. Now her career lay in Parliament House, that cloistered environment both at the heart of national life and profoundly removed from it. Interviewed a few months after her maiden speech, she described parliament as like a spaceship: 'It's a very enclosed and high-pressure environment. I'd expected that, but not to the extent that it is.'[5]

Asked about all this today, and how she felt, the only comment Penny Wong makes is all the more powerful for its patent and characteristic understatement. 'It was a very hard time.'

*

Penny Wong entered the Australian parliament as a Left, gay, Asian, South Australian woman. Every adjective signalled the likelihood that she would be marginalised – seen as a special case, attended to only when representing the issues those descriptors suggest. She was also one of the most junior members of a party that had been defeated in three consecutive elections. That Penny Wong transcended the adjectives to become one of the most senior politicians in the land, and to today hold a key leadership role in the Albanese shadow ministry, was no accident. Nor was it only because of her undoubted ability. It was also the result of a clear-eyed, hard-headed strategy and campaign, accompanied by competitiveness and, when required, ruthlessness.

She made an impression in her first two years, emerging as a penetrating cross-examiner in Senate committees, and taking the lead in negotiating Labor Party rule changes that guaranteed more women would enter parliament. Three other extraordinary things happened. She made what she describes today as the worst mistake of her political career. She betrayed one of her chief patrons and, hardest of all, she voted to ban same-sex marriage.

All this was part of her advancement.

John Faulkner remembers Penny Wong's arrival as a 'breath of fresh air ... a lot about her was very different to your average garden variety of senator'. She struck him as articulate and capable – 'one of those people who can turn their hands to anything: make a speech on policy, go on a committee and make a contribution'. He began sending opportunities her way.

Faulkner is too loyal a party man to say it, but he was presiding over a low point in the Senate Labor team. In years past, some of the Hawke–Keating government's best performers had come from that house. Senators John Button, Gareth Evans and Peter Walsh had been high-profile government ministers of intellectual ability and strong policy agendas. In 2002 most Australians would have been challenged to name a member of the Labor Senate team, and the party's main strength was in the House of Representatives. Faulkner thought the Senate committee system was the perfect place for Wong to fulfil what she made clear was her ambition – to cut her teeth on a range of issues and wrestle with serious policy. She asked him to consider her for appointment to committees that dealt with the difficult and unglamorous stuff, such as finance and public administration. She resisted being put on those that dealt with social policy because, she says, 'that's where they put the girls'. Instead, 'I threw myself into learning about the financial system and the economy ... I wasn't going to be a person who did a lot of social policy. I made that decision absolutely consciously.'

She had employed as her senior adviser John Olenich, who was later adviser to Australia's permanent mission to the United Nations. After the 2019 election, he resigned that post to return to Penny Wong's staff. When he first met her, he was a young Labor Party member who had come up through student politics in South Australia and gravitated towards Penny Wong and Jay Weatherill because they were, as he recalls, 'these exciting new figures on the scene. You know, they were smart, they were charismatic, and they had a lot of substance. Adelaide is a place with a lot of pride in its tradition – the state of Don Dunstan. And people saw Penny Wong and Jay Weatherill as the inheritors of that tradition.' Olenich was convenor of the state's Young Labor Left factional wing and had been active in student Labor politics at both the University of Adelaide and the University of South Australia. There had been very little Labor Left presence on these campuses when Olenich and his friends began their work, but he ended by being elected president of the University of South Australia Students Association and head of the National Organisation of Labor Students. It was evidence of superb organising and strategic capabilities, and Penny Wong noticed.

Olenich had been recruited to work with Wong as a 'jack of all trades' when she was managing the campaign for the marginal seat of Hindmarsh in 2001. Afterwards, she asked him to join her staff when she took up her Senate position. 'I was quite stunned because of course she was a rising star and everyone wanted to be in her orbit. And I didn't hesitate.' Like her, Olenich is gay. He also came from an immigrant family. 'I thought she represented a future vision of Australia: assured, capable, diverse. Her own identity was metaphorical – herself an immigrant but also having roots back to proclamation – she expressed the progression to a more contemporary Australia. She clearly had the makings of an iconic Labor figure, and could give voice and visibility to a significant part of the community who had never seen themselves represented in Australian politics.'

Olenich and Wong – supported with advice from friends and political allies such as Lois Boswell and Don Frater – set about transcending the adjectives that threatened to limit her career. They had an exemplar of what not to do in Senator Natasha Stott Despoja, Penny Wong's foil and the woman who had out-campaigned her at University of Adelaide Students' Association elections eleven years before. Stott Despoja had been elected as a senator in 1995 and entered parliament on a wave of media enthusiasm. The media profiles were effusive, and focused on style over substance, routinely mentioning her Doc Martens, her attractiveness and her youth. She became leader of the Australian Democrats in April 2001, but by the time Penny Wong entered parliament she was on the way down – forced to resign as leader in a party-room revolt. Stott Despoja retired from parliament in 2008 when her term expired. Penny Wong deliberately set a different course. As Olenich puts it today, 'There were lessons there for us. We had great respect for Natasha – she was ethical, thoughtful, had awesome political gifts and was a pioneer in many ways. But we saw the way her depiction as the voice of youth unfortunately limited her reach; self-evidently you can only be the youth candidate for so long.'

Very early, in the weeks before Wong's maiden speech, she and Olenich were debating 'how to deal with the sexuality issue'. The discussion was about how to get it out of the way, rather than devising a plan to advocate on gay rights. As part of her determination not to be marginalised, Penny had decided to shun personal media, although it was an easy way to raise her profile. She recalls, 'I knew I could get a lot of soft media if I talked about myself and my relationships, and I made a political decision to avoid that and not to do it ... it was not the kind of lift I wanted.' Nevertheless, Olenich felt it was important to make some sort of public declaration in a way that she could control. He recalls her protesting that she had never been in the closet and therefore could hardly 'come out', but in the end he persuaded her. They decided to talk to an old connection – Penny Wong's acquaintance from university days, Samantha Maiden – who was now a political reporter at the Adelaide *Advertiser*.

The result was a profile of Wong and the other new Labor South Australian senator, Linda Kirk. Maiden made 'difference' a theme of the piece. She began by recapping the sexist 'lipstick warrior' headlines that had accompanied their election – a reminder, as she put it, that women in politics were 'still regarded as colourful exotica'. The article moved smoothly on to state that 'difference had always been a part of [Wong's] life' before summarising her family history. There followed a single internally contradictory sentence that has, ever since, been referred to as Penny Wong's 'coming out': 'In Labor circles, it is also well known Senator Wong is gay, a fact she would prefer to leave as a private matter.'

A non sequitur followed. 'It was not an issue during her preselection to Labor's highest ranks.'[6]

The tactic worked. Penny Wong's sexuality was simultaneously 'out' yet also dismissed as defining. A few weeks later, Maiden was writing about Penny Wong again, but this time there was no pussyfooting around the personal. Wong, Maiden wrote, had emerged as a 'future star' and a 'key dealmaker'.

The context was affirmative action within the party. Simon Crean had replaced Kim Beazley as Labor leader in the wake of the 2001 election defeat. He made reforming the party one of his priorities, and now there was to be a special conference on party rules. The main issue was a hotly contested proposal to dilute unions' influence by reducing their quota of delegate representatives. Crean was successful. The so-called 50:50 rule was adopted, providing for equal numbers of delegates for trade unions and ordinary party members. It was a more substantial change than any previously advocated by a federal leader since Gough Whitlam.[7] Another item on the agenda was the anti-stacking rule changes resulting from the Ralph Clarke affair. Penny Wong had had a role in devising those, but now she was involved on a different front.

Labor had adopted an affirmative action rule in 1994 that committed the party to preselecting women for at least 35 per cent of winnable seats by 2002. Now that date had arrived, and the rule was up for revision. The Left wanted a commitment to 50 per cent preselected women in winnable seats by 2012, and Penny Wong and Sharryn Jackson had been appointed to negotiate on the change.

Jackson remembers, 'The blokes were all focused on the union power issue. We didn't get much media at all.' They were junior parliamentarians – virtual unknowns. Nobody gave them a chance.

Undaunted, months before the October 2002 conference they set about gathering support from the state delegates, starting at the top. Penny contacted Queensland premier Peter Beattie, who became one of the first to back the rule change. She approached Geoff Gallop, premier of Western Australia, who opposed it – which, says Wong, means she has never been a fan of his. 'One remembers these things.'

There was hostility and support across the factions. Wong remembers briefing one 'very senior member of the parliamentary Left' and being shouted at and told the proposal was ridiculous. 'I said to him, "You misunderstand why I am here. I am not consulting you. I am telling you where we are at."' Her relations with this colleague – many years her senior in the parliament – have never recovered.

Wong was the expert negotiator with the factional chiefs. Jackson concentrated on organising women across the party. Wong was 'incredibly considered, very patient and very sensible' in explaining how the change would work in practice, recalls Jackson. A winnable seat was defined as having a margin of 5 per cent or less. She assured the men of the party that there were many ways the change could happen without threatening those of talent among them.

On the day of the conference, Jackson and former Victorian premier Joan Kirner had organised a showy, sequinned, purple-clad female marching band, armed with arrows pointing up to indicate a growth in female political representation. It caused a stir, but they still didn't have the numbers. Then, on the conference floor, there was a shift: the remnants of the Centre Left split on the issue. Now it was impossible to

predict how the vote would go. Faced with possible defeat, the Right
was suddenly interested in negotiating. Crean indicated he would back
a watered-down proposal for a 40:40 split between the genders, with the
remaining 20 per cent unallocated. Wong was thrust into backroom talks
with the senior men of the Right, including Senator Robert Ray. According to one observer, the discussions began with Ray dismissive, but in the
end the deal for female candidates in 40 per cent of winnable seats by
2012 was voted through unanimously. Wong, Samantha Maiden wrote,
had 'blazed a trail for women MPs' and emerged as 'a politician to watch'
after just a few months in parliament. Nick Bolkus was quoted saying
that Penny Wong would definitely be a minister and 'I think she will be
one of the best ministers to come out of South Australia.'[8]

By 2003 Penny Wong was using her cross-examination skills in Senate Estimates, grilling public servants on the details of funding for the
environment and the issue of permits for land clearing in Queensland.
Because she was a junior member, the outcomes of her questioning were
contained in media releases by the relevant shadow minister, Kelvin
Thomson,[9] but her work was acknowledged and drew attention within
the party. Later that year she became the leading questioner as part
of a Senate select committee inquiring into ministerial discretion in
migration matters. Labor had accused the minister for immigration,
Philip Ruddock, of granting visas in exchange for electoral donations,
including one by a Filipino businessman, Dante Tan, who had been
given a business visa and then Australian citizenship despite being a
fugitive in the Philippines. Tan had contributed money to Ruddock's
2001 re-election campaign. There was a 'black hole' in accountability, the committee report concluded.[10] Meanwhile, in South Australia
Penny Wong concentrated on two popular and pressing local issues – the
Howard government's proposal to site a nuclear waste dump in the state,
and the condition of the lower Murray River, on which Adelaide depends
for its water supply. Olenich worked hard at getting her statements into
the local media, and soon *The Advertiser* was running her articles on its
opinion page. She was finding her feet and building her profile.

*

On 2 December 2003 Simon Crean resigned the Labor leadership after senior party figures told him he had lost his colleagues' support – the result of months of undermining by Kim Beazley's supporters. In the ballot to replace him, Mark Latham defeated Beazley: forty-seven votes to forty-five.

Penny Wong voted for Mark Latham.

Asked about this today, she puts her head in her hands and bends over with a groan.

In 2019, with Mark Latham representing One Nation in the New South Wales parliament and a long history of misogynistic public statements behind him, it is almost impossible to understand how Penny Wong, the feminist anti-racist, could have supported him.

John Olenich remembers the thinking in her office at the time. They respected Beazley, but Latham showed signs of being able to set the debate. 'At that point we had been on the back foot for a long time, constantly wedged ... Latham seemed like someone who could actually win and take the fight to Howard. Obviously time has shown that to be a huge misjudgement and one we learned from.'

Penny had read some of Latham's considerable work. She didn't agree with all of it, but she thought he had correctly diagnosed Labor's challenge. She says today: 'Class, as a marker of identity and as a driver of voting behaviour, was being weakened ... Labor needed to grapple with those issues, and he seemed to be doing that ... It's hard now to think back without being tinged by the way he has unravelled since. But there was a brilliance to him.'

She was far from alone in that view. At the time, Latham seemed to offer hope for a Labor Party repeatedly wrong-footed by John Howard. He had written impressive books on progressive policy.[11] In the 2002 Menzies Lecture, he had offered a penetrating diagnosis of how Howard had managed to fracture Labor's support base – the alliance between the working class and educated progressives that had held since Whitlam. The modern political spectrum, he argued, was best understood as a struggle between insiders and outsiders, 'the abstract values of the powerful centre versus the pragmatic beliefs of those who feel

disenfranchised by social change'. He talked about how identity politics
was trumping the politics of class: 'People see their place in society as a
reflection of their access to information and public influence.'[12] It was
a powerful and prescient analysis, made before Trump, before Brexit.

Wong had not worked directly with Latham, and didn't know
him well. The Left had split on the issue of leadership. Julia Gillard
and the 'soft Left' – with which the South Australian Left was usually
allied – backed first Crean, then Latham; the 'hard Left', led by Anthony
Albanese, consistently backed Beazley.

Albanese remembers the leadership ballot as one of the few occasions on which he rang people 'pleading with them to vote in a certain
way' on a leadership issue. He had grown up with Latham in New South
Wales Labor, and knew him well. He thought Latham unfit to lead the
party on character grounds. Penny Wong was not one of those Albanese rang. He assumed, correctly, that she would vote along factional
lines with the soft Left. But he did ring Mark Butler, her factional ally.

Butler was in a supermarket checkout queue when he took the call.
He recalls, 'Albo was frantic ... He was saying, "What the fuck are you
doing? He'll win, and it's a fucking disaster," and I said, "He won't win,
nobody is saying he'll win." And Albo said, "He'll win." Albo is the best
vote counter.'

Butler says today that 'smart people', including Nick Bolkus and
Laurie Brereton, were arguing that Beazley's supporters should not be
easily rewarded for their campaign to undermine Crean's leadership.
They had convinced people that Latham would not win, and that Beazley would be the leader – but a strong vote for Latham would teach
them a lesson. This, he now thinks, was calculated and 'Machiavellian'.

Butler doesn't recall giving Wong any advice, although he is sure
they would have discussed it. 'My view was she should make up her own
mind.' Sharryn Jackson, on the other hand, remembers detailed conversations with Penny about the leadership. They talked long into the night
in their parliamentary offices. Jackson supported Beazley as a fellow
Western Australian and a potentially fine prime minister. Latham, on
the other hand, 'had this element of ruthlessness about him that I wasn't

comfortable with'. Penny was not convinced. 'I think she genuinely felt that we couldn't go back to Beazley, that he could not defeat Howard ... Penny and I agree on a lot of things but we have disagreed on a lot of leadership issues,' Jackson says.

The deciding factor for Penny Wong was that Julia Gillard, a leader of the parliamentary soft Left, was rallying other Left women to support Latham. In the end, Penny followed her lead. Today she describes her support for Mark Latham as 'one of the worst mistakes of my political career'.

*

In the dry, sometimes claustrophobic near city-state of Adelaide, it can be all too easy to obey the dictum of Sun Tzu and Al Pacino: keep your friends close and your enemies closer. Within Labor factional circles, you don't have much choice.

Nick Bolkus remains an integral part of Adelaide life. He entertains in the coffee shops of Hutt Street, greeted regularly by former constituents and friends, the very image of the respected Greek senior. Penny Wong runs into him sometimes at Labor Party functions, and they are civil to each other – but that's as far as it goes. Despite the fact that she rose within the sub-faction that carried his name, despite his early promotion of her and his pride in her advance, the two are not friends. In early 2004 she – in collaboration with Mark Butler and Jay Weatherill – was part of a piece of ruthless internal party politics that ended Bolkus's career.

Today all the participants shift uneasily when asked about this rift. *The Advertiser* has written it up as one of 'South Australia's 10 most poisonous political feuds'.[13] The main players can't avoid one another. They get by, it seems, by not talking about it.

In March 2003 Nick Bolkus announced that he wanted to seek another six-year term at the 2004 election, assuming that he would again be preselected as part of the Machine deal between Left and Right. This would have capped his 23-year-long parliamentary career. Bolkus assumed that his experience, seniority and record of nurturing talent

within the party gave him the right to depart parliament at a time of
his choosing. Within the Left it was understood that he planned to
retire mid-term, in the expectation that his position would be taken up
by Pat Conlon, then a minister in South Australia's Rann government.
Conlon was close to Bolkus. So was Mark Butler. Conlon and Butler
had shared a house and an office back in university days. Now, Conlon
put both Butler and Bolkus on notice that he wanted a federal parliamentary career.

Bolkus claims he consulted Mark Butler before making his
announcement. If so, Butler does not remember it. To Bolkus's former
protégés, and to his enemies within the party, it seemed as though he
was taking his Senate position for granted. Meanwhile, Conlon was an
important state minister at a time when Labor was in minority government. The faction didn't want to lose him from state parliament.

The opposition to Bolkus and concerns about Conlon's move came
together in a wave of opposition to Bolkus's preselection. Bolkus claims
his one-time protégés never confided their concerns or made it clear to
him that he had lost their support. Instead, he went through a process
of 'slow water torture' in which they froze him out: 'Gradually I had to
piece it all together.' At the time, the betrayal was excruciating.

In all this, Penny Wong's opinion, and the need to protect her
emerging career, was crucial.

Conlon was not inclined by either temperament or ambition to be a
backroom operator or part of anyone's support team. If he went into federal parliament, it was expected that he would want a frontbench position.
The South Australian Left could only expect one frontbench position –
either Wong or Conlon, not both. Given Conlon's deep cross-factional
connections with the powerful men of the party, there was no guarantee
that Wong would win the inevitable battle. Even without this competition, Penny Wong and Pat Conlon did not get on. Having them both in
the Senate was a recipe for instability.

Today Mark Butler says that if Conlon had indicated his interest
earlier, things might have been different. Perhaps he would have been
preselected instead of Penny Wong – although that would have raised

issues with affirmative action quotas. But by this time, the faction had already chosen Wong as part of its path to power, and she was doing well.

She must have thought it a bit rich for Conlon to expect to muscle in now. Her opinion was asked, and she made her position very clear. As well, Butler made what he thought was the only sensible political decision – no matter how difficult it was for him personally. He was backing Penny Wong.

Bolkus was vulnerable. He had got caught up in allegations involving Dante Tan – the same Filipino businessman who had featured in the cash-for-visas scandal on which Penny Wong had been pursuing immigration minister Philip Ruddock. Bolkus had taken nearly $10,000 as a political donation from an associate of Tan's and not declared it, instead making a donation in his own name to the campaign for the marginal seat of Hindmarsh at the 2001 election – the campaign Penny Wong had managed.

The scandal blew up in parliament in June 2003, with Bolkus accused of 'laundering' the money into a Labor account. Bolkus said that the donation had been for raffle tickets. He had met Tan and one of his associates to discuss his visa issues. Bolkus declined to give any immigration advice, and then, 'He wanted to make a donation. I said, "Well, we're running a raffle." [I] had the books with me at the time, so he said, "I'll buy some tickets." So, fair enough, I thought, maybe a grand. He bought close to $10,000 worth.'[14]

Questioned by journalists, both Penny Wong and Hindmarsh candidate Steve Georganas reportedly said they couldn't remember the raffle. Wong commented, 'I recall being told we did raffles, but didn't have any involvement at the time.'[15]

In June the South Australian branch of the party announced it would make a 'correction' in Australian Electoral Commission records, amending to note that the generous donation was from Tan, and Bolkus apologised for not correctly reporting it. Investigations by both the SA Police and the Commissioner of State Taxation followed, and by early 2004 Bolkus had been cleared. He later successfully sued newspapers for suggesting he had behaved improperly.[16]

But the damage had been done to his political standing. In June 2004, after it became clear that his faction was not going to back him, he announced he would retire from parliament after the election due later that year.

The move against such a senior Labor figure split the South Australian Left. Pat Conlon, one of the earliest and most important members of what had been known as the Bolkus Left, considered leaving the faction – which he eventually did, though years later. Butler and Conlon had been close, but this strained the friendship – although Butler says they have since overcome their disagreements and remain friends.

Interviewed for this book in early 2018, Bolkus took care to deny that Penny Wong had any involvement in, or knowledge of, the Tan donation. He was not quite so careful with his words in the interview he gave for the National Library of Australia's oral history project in 2010. There, he said he had taken the money as a result of Penny Wong as campaign manager 'desperately needing money to win that seat' – though he did not claim she knew about Tan. He told the National Library interviewers:

> Now I came back to Adelaide, they ran the raffle, there were witnesses there. It's just that a couple of the critical people who wanted to get me out of politics had memory lapses. People like Steve Georganas, for instance, he was there holding the hat, but he couldn't remember being there when everyone else could remember Steve being there. So I think the sort of treachery of some of my former colleagues made it much worse than it was ever going to be.

The scandal, he said, had been used against him when it came to his preselection, and he blamed Wong squarely. 'I think Penny Wong, for instance, may have been worried that if Pat Conlon had come to Canberra he would take her position on the frontbench. So she was a major opponent.'[17]

With Bolkus out of the way, the Left instead backed Anne McEwen for the Senate vacancy. Today Butler says this was largely because she had a 'warm, close and personal relationship with Penny'. Anne and Penny had known each other since their student days at the University of Adelaide. Butler says it was felt she would be a 'good support' for Penny, rather than a rival. And that is how it worked out. McEwen was elected to the Senate in 2004 and went on to be chief whip while Wong was the government's leader in the Senate. Conlon, meanwhile, continued as a senior minister in the Rann and Weatherill state governments until his retirement from parliament in 2014. Bolkus left parliament at the expiry of his term in 2005.

Today, Bolkus claims he holds no grudges against Penny Wong and Mark Butler. At the time, he felt they had betrayed him. Now, he thinks they made the right decision. 'My time was over. They were right,' he says.

After he left parliament he went into business with Ian Smith, the husband of Natasha Stott Despoja, and former political foe Alexander Downer. They launched a lobbying firm, Bespoke Approach. Bolkus has been chief fundraiser for the Labor Party, a lobbyist for businesses that require government-approved developments, and a director on numerous company boards.

But the events surrounding Bolkus's demise still rankle in Adelaide Labor. Steve Georganas had worked for Bolkus in the mid-1990s. There is no doubt, he says, that 'Penny wouldn't be where she is without Nick, and nor would I. He was a great mentor to us both ... He could see things in Mark and Penny well before they got into the parliament.'

Georganas, like Bolkus, is from a Greek background. During his early years in the party, Georganas says, 'Nick was special for us ... to have a cabinet minister of Greek descent was pretty big ... He'd have Whitlam coming to our Greek events, which was unheard of, a prime minister going to an ethnic event.'

When Butler and Penny Wong moved against Bolkus, says Georganas, it was a 'very sad time'. Meanwhile, he was worried about his own preselection. He felt he had to support them. For a period, his own relationship with Bolkus was fractured, but he says they are 'all right' now. 'He understands I really had nothing to do with it.'

Georganas says today that he does remember the raffle. He says he drew it, and even remembers who won.

So were Penny Wong and Mark Butler right to move on Nick Bolkus?

Georganas pauses. He is worried about getting into trouble, counting himself a friend of both Bolkus and Wong. 'It would have been nice to see Nick go in his own time,' he says carefully. 'He had earned that right.'

Asked about this history, Penny Wong is defensive. 'I'm not going to talk to you a lot about this, I would just say two things. In that and in other things ... I was motivated by what I thought was the right thing for the group and for the party.' It is difficult, she acknowledges, to fall out with former allies and friends. 'I am quite emotional. That emotion is probably what drives me. But I try to make political decisions on a judgement of what I think is right. It wasn't about whether I liked [Nick Bolkus] or not.'

She also denies responsibility for the choice over Bolkus's preselection. It is true, she says, that her opinion was asked, and she gave it – but in the end she did not have a vote. 'The decision ultimately had to be made by those people who were responsible for the majority of votes inside the Left. And that was not me. It has always interested me – on a number of issues – how much power people think I have.'

What she says is true, but also disingenuous. One of the main issues was protecting her position. Nobody else who was involved doubts that her opinion – and her encouragement to Mark Butler to make tough decisions – were crucial to what happened. And, while it may have been for the good of the party, it was also important to her own political career.

Asked whether the relationships have been repaired, Wong is uncertain. She saw Nick Bolkus a few evenings before our interview. They were polite to each other. Told that Bolkus said that she and Butler made the right decision in 2003, she is taken by surprise. 'That is a nice thing for him to say.'

*

From the beginning of 2004, after navigating her first eighteen months in parliament, Wong made a determined effort to lift her profile and develop her media skills. Dealing with the media was the part of the job that she found hardest, but if she was to become a minister, it was important to show she could perform in the media. The priority was to build her profile beyond what she was already known for – her Senate committee cross-examinations skills and backroom policy smarts. She worked hard over several months, practising speaking more concisely, learning to appear less of a 'turgid intellectual'.

An important opportunity – and a marker of how much she developed as a media performer over this year – was the ABC Sunday morning television program *Insiders*. At that stage it included a regular item at the end of the program called 'The Adjournment Debate', the name a nod to the parliamentary procedure by which members are entitled to raise any matter they wish. In this segment, a backbencher from either side of politics was given a fifty-second piece to camera, giving their take on a topic of the day.

The first time Penny Wong appeared, in February 2004, she was shown walking around the internal courtyards of Parliament House. She was a stilted performer, her speech sing-song, her gestures stagey. She returned to the themes of her maiden speech, saying that John Howard's election motto, 'For all of us', came with the small print that it did not apply to those dependent on Medicare or public schools. 'The Howard government thinks like the membership of one of those exclusive clubs – certain people need not apply,' she said.[18]

Her next performance, just a few weeks later, was more accomplished. She emerged from the emergency department of an Adelaide hospital and spoke to camera with a critique of the recently announced Extended Medicare Safety Net. It was not so much a safety net as a 'safety pin to hold together the fraying threads of the health system until after the election'.[19]

Wong appeared again after tax cuts were announced in the May federal budget. She strode through a childcare centre full of children at play and said that childcare workers – as well as nurses and teachers – were among 'Howard's forgotten people': denied a pay rise and overlooked in the budget provisions. She pointed to the camera. 'Chances are he's forgotten you too.'[20]

Olenich comments that Wong always wanted to be a policy reformer, rather than a celebrity. 'But she knew she would never make an impact without a public profile.' Over time, he says, she learned to show 'her authentic self, and the warmth and sass her friends knew her for. It was partly an intellectual exercise for her, learning to adapt to an unnatural setting.'

Penny Wong's final performance on *Insiders* for 2004, in the lead-up to the election campaign, was shot inside Adelaide Central Market. She walked between market stands and talked about 'big issues', including climate change and dental care, and accused the Howard government of attempting to 'buy its way back into power'. Now, she was calm, confident and likeable in front of the camera. In particular, she had learned to use her face to convey meaning and emotion. There were her dimples, when appealing to the good sense of her audience – and those eyebrows, raised when skewering the Howard government.[21]

She had found herself as a public performer, and become the Penny Wong the public sees today.

8

STAYING IN THE ROOM

In August 2004, Penny Wong made one of the most painful moves of her political career. She voted in favour of legislation that banned same-sex marriage. Those who hero-worship Penny Wong, who identify her chiefly with the successful reform of the marriage laws in 2017, or who remember her tears when the postal survey result favouring the legalisation of same-sex marriage was announced, are often puzzled by this part of her history. Some condemn her as a hypocrite. The Greens' Christine Milne cites this episode as evidence that Penny Wong is 'just a machine Labor politician', prepared to compromise principles in the interests of her political career and her pursuit of a frontbench position. Penny Wong's stance hurt those in the gay community who looked to her as a role model, says Milne. What was she doing?

Penny Wong was openly gay. That alone was a political statement. Yet, in 2004, there was no sense in which she could legitimately have been tagged as a campaigner for gay rights, at least in the public sense. Even within the Labor Party, she was not the leading voice, although she supported reform behind the scenes. By the early 2000s a group of gay-rights activists with the party had begun to organise what eventually became Rainbow Labor – now an officially recognised policy caucus of the party in most states. John Olenich, Penny Wong's key staffer, was centrally involved, and Wong supported his involvement from a distance. According to Olenich, most in the party simply didn't want to be bothered with gay rights. 'People in the party were supportive in the sense that they were not against us ... but it was so far from the front of mind, and indeed it was seen by many as unhelpful in the Howard culture-war era … There just wasn't the political capacity to take that issue head on in those days.'

The Labor parliamentarian who had made the most headway on gay rights was the leader of the 'hard Left', Anthony Albanese, for whom the issue had been a personal crusade since entering parliament in 1996. Albanese introduced a private member's bill in 1998 that would ensure federal equality for same-sex couples under superannuation law. He was to try nine more times over the next decade without success, until the Rudd government in 2007 saw the bill passed into law. Today Albanese remembers that when he first spoke on the bill in caucus in 1998 'people shifted in their seats uncomfortably, because it was not the thing for people to go into the caucus and talk about sexuality. It just wasn't a mainstream issue … People were saying, "Why are you raising this?"' He heard on the grapevine that people were saying they hadn't realised 'that Albo was gay … They couldn't understand why I would be raising it otherwise, whereas in fact I have always thought it was easier for someone who wasn't gay to pursue this issue than [for] people who are.'

Penny Wong was not yet in parliament, and Albanese did not know her well. Nevertheless, he remembers her being 'generally supportive' in party forums. He says she understood the strategic nature of the change he was pushing for. Even those opposed to equality on the basis of sexuality could be convinced by the argument that people should be able to allocate their money to their partner if they wished. 'It was an issue that appealed to individualism as well as collectivism, so it was a good place to start,' he says.

Until this time, advances on gay rights had been achieved mainly by state Labor governments. Homosexuality had been decriminalised: firstly by South Australia in the 1970s with other states following – Tasmania last, in 1997. From 1994, some states had begun to recognise same-sex couples on the same basis as de-facto heterosexual relationships when it came to wills, licence fees and state superannuation. Little had been done at the federal level, and progress stopped decisively with the election of the Howard government in 1996. Howard's aspiration of making Australians 'relaxed and comfortable' meant reasserting the centrality of Christian values, including traditional heterosexual families.[1]

Before Howard, same-sex marriage was barely on the political agenda. Albanese recalls that in all his years of activism on the issue 'nobody had ever rung me saying they wanted to get married and asking for the law to change. It just wasn't an issue.' Howard changed that. In May 2004, the government introduced a bill to change the *Marriage Act 1961 (Cth)*, which until then had not defined marriage. The key amendment would insert words mandating that marriage be recognised exclusively as a union between 'a man and a woman'. The bill would also prevent the recognition of same-sex marriages lawfully entered into in foreign jurisdictions.

It was another example of 'wedge politics': dividing progressive Labor voters from socially conservative and Catholic supporters. It was also designed to cause mayhem within the Labor Party. In South Australia, for example, Don Farrell, from the socially conservative Right, was vehemently opposed to same-sex marriage.

With weeks to go until the election, Labor announced that it would support the Howard amendments, but would also commit to reforming all federal laws that affected de facto relationships, to make sure that same-sex couples were treated equally. The announcement was effectively made by shadow attorney-general Nicola Roxon without caucus consent, and backed by Latham. The caucus agreement had been to pass the amendment in the lower house, then refer it off to a Senate Committee.[2]

In June, there was an anguished caucus meeting. Carmen Lawrence spoke against the amendments but also urged her colleagues not to 'confuse politics and principle'. Marriage, she said, was only about property. She argued unsuccessfully for a conscience vote on the issue. Penny Wong recalls the meeting. She had accepted that with Roxon and Latham having already committed the party, there was no changing direction. 'I figured, we have five years to make this change, and it's not going to happen now. So I have to do a few things in this meeting to set it up for change in the future, and one of them is to make people feel ashamed of themselves. That sounds harsh, but I wanted to make them understand what they were doing. So I gave a speech about my parents being married under the White Australia policy, and how in the 1950s in the USA some states would have banned their marriage, and how nobody in that room would consider discriminating in that way, or against a disabled person marrying, or people of different ages. But because it's about gays, we are doing it. And I considered that speech an investment in shaping hearts and minds.'

This, she says, was the first step in a considered strategy. Marriage was 'totemic' so would come last. First was to remove other kinds of discrimination against gay couples.

As is the way in Canberra, some of her speech leaked to the media – but bled of its power. She was reported as having compared banning same-sex marriage to the 1950s laws against interracial marriage in the United States.[3]

Caucus backed the compromise deal. Penny Wong, according to Olenich, had front of mind the 2001 election and the *Tampa* affair that dominated it. 'She was scarred by that, as all of us were. I think she was determined not to let Howard weaponise anti-gay sentiment to win an election as he had done with anti-immigrant sentiment. She wanted to head that off at the pass.'

The amendment to the *Marriage Act* passed the lower house on 24 June, and came before the Senate on 12 August. Natasha Stott Despoja gave a passionate speech attacking both Labor and the government, noting that she was the only senator from South Australia opposing the legislation. Labor was adopting a small-target strategy, she said. 'If they are wanting another three years on the opposition benches, their continual kowtowing to the government's agenda will ensure it.'[4]

Penny Wong's speech picked up on the *Tampa* theme. The bill should be seen in the context of Howard's history of using division, particularly attacks on asylum seekers, for political advantage, she said. 'The prime minister would happily make lesbian and gay Australians the asylum seekers of this election. He would dearly love this to be the new Pacific Solution,' she said. She believed that the legislation would have minimal real effect. 'It reaffirms the existing common law and statutory definition of marriage. It does not change the legal definition.' It was a 'dog whistle: an appeal to people by implication rather than explicit meaning ... Nobody has a monopoly on commitment and love, nobody has the right to judge the worth of another person's relationships.' It was an odd speech – made in the knowledge that she was going to vote for the bill, yet avoiding saying she supported it.

Wong voted with her party, in favour of the changes that explicitly removed her own right to marry. There were only six votes against – those of the Greens and the Democrats.

Parliament rose that night, and Penny Wong flew home to Adelaide for the weekend. She had an appointment to catch up with a friend – the University of Adelaide political scientist Carol Johnson and her female partner. They were going to see a film and have dinner.

Wong and Johnson had known each other since Penny was involved in student politics and Johnson was a junior politics lecturer at the University of Adelaide. As the years went by, they had become friends. Johnson had developed a speciality in writing about the Labor Party and progressive policy, including gay rights. She had followed the debates over the *Marriage Act* amendments closely and had read Penny Wong's speech. 'Naturally, I was keen to talk about it,' she recalls.

Johnson says that Wong swore her to secrecy about their conversation that night. She was in pain and needed to confide in a context where she would not be accused of breaching party solidarity. When approached to be interviewed for this book, Johnson asked Wong if she could be released from the promise of secrecy. She wanted to put her recollections on the record to scotch any suggestion that Penny Wong was once in favour of discrimination against same-sex marriage.

That night Penny Wong had been in anguish. She told Johnson she was in an impossible position, that she felt she had done the best she could. 'Basically she felt bound by party policy, and that leaving the party wasn't really an option because what would it achieve?'

Wong told Johnson that evening that she would commit herself to changing Labor Party policy on same-sex marriage. Having spent her first years in parliament working hard not to be dismissed as 'the gay candidate', she would now step up and make the issue her own.

Johnson thought the Labor Party didn't fully understand what it had done to Wong in forcing her to choose between her personal beliefs – her very identity – and her political allegiances. 'I don't think it would have occurred to most of her colleagues just how difficult it was to ask this woman to basically vote for her own oppression ... Penny was prepared to do that because she knew that if the law was ever going to change, you need to work with the major parties ... that it was a longer-term political project. But it was incredibly difficult and distressing to her.'

Today, asked about her vote for the banning of same-sex marriage in 2004, Penny Wong is defensive and combative. I asked about the Liberal MPs who crossed the floor in 1988 to oppose Howard's discriminatory immigration policy. Did they do the right thing?

'Of course they did,' she said.

So should she have crossed the floor in 2004?

It is, of course, an unfair comparison. The Liberal Party rules, in theory at least, allow parliamentarians a free vote – though the reality is that there is a heavy political cost to crossing the floor. Labor's rules make national conference and caucus decisions binding on MPs. If Penny Wong had crossed the floor to vote with the Democrats and Greens against the changes to the *Marriage Act*, she could have been expelled from the party. At the very least, her rise would have come to an abrupt halt. She certainly would not have made the frontbench so quickly, if at all.

In any case, she says, the comparison is false on principle. Howard's immigration policy in 1988 was a fundamental change both to his party's policy and to the history of bipartisanship on immigration in Australia. The changes to the *Marriage Act* were merely a restatement of the status quo – a political tactic.

And then she displayed her trademark lawyer combativeness. 'With all due respect,' she said, 'I'm a little tired of slogans from people who've done nothing very much to achieve equality in this country. I have had to put myself on the line. I had a decision to make at that time that I could either resign in a blaze of glory or I could stay and fight. And I did make that decision in 2004 – that I would make sure that we changed the party platform one day, and that ultimately we would change the country.'

It is tempting to think that Penny Wong is applying hindsight. Was she really as committed, and as strategic, as she claims today?

A number of sources confirm that from that date on Wong involved herself actively in building the momentum for change within the party, while publicly continuing to support existing policy. Her key staffers were increasingly involved in Rainbow Labor with her urging and encouragement. The long process of winning hearts and minds had begun, and she was integral to it. In the years ahead, Penny Wong was accused by gay activists of betraying their cause. Within the party, nobody regarded her that way.

In 2004, Wong chose to stay 'in the room' – to compromise herself personally and on principle in the interests of remaining part of the conversation, part of long-term change. In the years that followed there were twenty-three bills dealing with marriage equality or the recognition of same-sex marriages introduced into federal parliament, most of them sponsored by minor parties. Four came to a vote, three in the Senate.[5] Ironically, Howard's attempt at wedge politics had made same-sex marriage a parliamentary issue. It was almost constantly before the parliament from then until 2017, when marriage equality was finally achieved.

In November 2008, Wong again voted against marriage equality when both major parties in the Senate voted down a Greens amendment to Rudd government laws removing other kinds of discrimination against same-sex couples. She absented herself for two other Greens-sponsored votes in February 2010 and July 2011. Through all this time, she kept her loyalty to the party. She trod a difficult line in her public statements, avoiding explicitly supporting marriage discrimination but not openly opposing Labor policy. That was until, thanks largely to her work and persistence, the party platform changed in 2011.

*

For the first few months as leader of the opposition, Mark Latham seemed to be vindicating the judgement of his supporters. Until March 2004 Labor had a strong lead in the opinion polls, and Howard seemed rattled. But as the year wore on the polls began to turn. Howard announced the October election date in August. The contest, he said, would be about who voters could trust.[6] Despite the government's own record of dishonesty over the Children Overboard affair, it was a message designed to exploit voter concerns about Latham's character – a persistent feature of the campaign. Yet for much of the campaign the polls showed the contest was too close to call. On election eve it was far from clear, even to senior political journalists, that Labor was beaten.

Meanwhile, Penny Wong was once again managing the campaign for the marginal seat of Hindmarsh. The sitting Liberal member, Christine Gallus, had retired, and returning Labor candidate Steve Georganas was up against a first-time contender, thirty-year-old Liberal political staffer Simon Birmingham. Once again, this was a seat Labor needed to win if it was to form government.

Hindmarsh was a sprawling electorate, taking in the largely working-class western suburbs of Adelaide as well as the wealthier beachside suburbs. It also had one of the oldest populations of any electorate in the country, meaning health and aged care were key issues. Wong, always a shrewd strategist, directed that everyone in the electorate over the age of sixty-five should receive direct mail on Labor's Medicare Gold policy, under which the party promised to end waiting lists and subsume all hospital costs for those aged over seventy-five. She dispatched Georganas to do targeted doorknocking of older constituents.

In the last week Wong insisted that Georganas make phone calls to voters who had been identified as undecided. He remembers, 'She sat me down and put a whip to me and made me ring a thousand of them.' He had completed the task by the Thursday evening before election day. After a six-week campaign, he was exhausted. On Friday he was thinking of the campaign as effectively over when Wong gave him another list of 240 swinging voters and told him to call them. Fighting exhaustion, he complied. He was on the phone until nine o'clock on the Friday night, by which time he was so tired he could barely speak.

It made all the difference. Georganas won the seat by just 108 votes (two-party-preferred). Without Wong forcing him to make those calls, he believes, he would not have been in parliament. (His opponent, Simon Birmingham, would enter the Senate in 2007.)

But the campaign for Hindmarsh was a rare bright spot in a devastating national loss for Labor. The party had gone backwards, losing a net four seats in the lower house. A few days later, it became clear that when the new senators took up their positions in July 2005 Howard would also have control of the upper house – the first time since Malcolm Fraser's prime ministership that a government would have control of both houses.

One of the lower-house seats lost was Hasluck, held by Penny's closest friend in parliament, Sharryn Jackson. The two women, in their late-night discussions when Latham and Beazley were vying for the leadership, had talked about whether Latham would be good for marginal-seat holders such as Jackson. Penny had been wrong. Latham had proven a disaster – the first Labor opposition leader for nearly a century to make no headway against a government in his first election. Penny was, says Jackson, 'devastated', politically and personally, by the scale of the defeat.

Yet Latham was good for Penny Wong. As he considered his frontbench after the election, he wrote in his diary that his 'first priority [is] to promote progressive young women such as Penny Wong and Tanya Plibersek. All the talented Labor women are in the Left.'[7] On 22 October it was announced that Penny Wong would join the Labor frontbench. Given she had been in parliament for just over two years, it was a considerable promotion. Her hard work on policy, her impressive fierceness in the Senate, her deal-making abilities and the building of her public profile had all paid off.

Her elevation made the international media. Agence France-Presse described her as 'the first openly gay member of a national leadership team'.[8] In Sabah, the local media called Penny Wong's father. Francis fondly recounted how he and Penny had climbed Mount Kinabalu together, and said how proud his mother would be if she were still alive. 'I want to say, "Well done, Penny, I am very proud of you."'[9] The Chinese media reported that the country once known for the White Australia policy now had a woman of Chinese ethnicity rising through the political ranks.[10]

Locally, the response was not universally rapturous. News Limited columnist Andrew Bolt described the new Latham frontbench as a 'disaster', incorporating the 'gay rights activist Penny Wong and Israel basher Tanya Plibersek'.[11] His descriptor was insultingly dismissive, but also unintentionally ironic, given the compromises Wong had made on gay rights just weeks before. Former Labor politician Stephen Loosley described Wong as 'excellent new talent' but said she and the other new frontbenchers were 'effectively on probation' and would have to face new levels of scrutiny and accountability.[12]

A few days later, it was announced that Penny Wong would take on the shadow portfolio for corporate governance and responsibility, and for employment and workforce participation. She was interviewed by a journalist from *The Australian*, and asked a question that she would never forget. 'He asked me how an Asian lesbian could represent the people of Adelaide's northern suburbs. I was actually lost for words. It was so unexpected and so personally aggressive ... You know, that was just an example of the little indignities, the way in which people just undermine you.' She reflected that she should have responded, 'How can John Howard represent women?' but she didn't think of that quickly enough.

The resulting article, headlined 'Gay senator prepared for when it gets personal', started by reassuring readers that 'Canberra's only openly gay frontbencher is well prepared for the potential personal abuse that comes with political office'. Without apparent irony, it quoted her as saying that she preferred not to bring her personal life into the public spotlight.[13]

In January 2005, after weeks of leadership speculation and bouts of pancreatitis, Mark Latham suddenly announced his resignation from the leadership, and from federal parliament. The resulting contest for the Labor Party leadership shaped up between Kim Beazley and Kevin Rudd. At the last minute Rudd withdrew because it became clear that he would not win.

Penny Wong was key in Rudd's decision to withdraw. It was when she announced her support for Beazley that the fall of the numbers became clear, and Rudd's defeat became a certainty. Julia Gillard had also been doing the numbers. Wong's declaration helped to scupper that attempt as well.[14] Wong said at the time that she regarded Gillard as 'one of our star performers' but that a steady hand was needed at the wheel: 'I have simply come to the conclusion that Kim Beazley is the leader that can unite the party.'[15] Having backed Latham in 2003, Wong from that date on put a high value on leadership stability. She stayed loyal to Beazley and, in particular, to his deputy, Jenny Macklin, for as long as it was an option.

Wong claims today that the potential for rivalry between Kevin Rudd and Julia Gillard was already apparent to her in 2005. In that context, she judged that Beazley and Macklin were the more stable leadership team. She thought Rudd was 'brilliant ... he had an extraordinary vision, was extraordinarily bright and had an ambitious and progressive agenda'. Nevertheless, in 2005 she did what she could to swing the numbers against him by declaring for Beazley publicly.

Beazley left Penny Wong in her two shadow portfolios – corporate governance and responsibility bracketed with employment and workforce participation. The latter, in particular, was important. Now with control of the Senate, Howard planned radical changes to welfare and working conditions, including the weakening of unfair-dismissal laws. With hindsight, it is clear that Howard gifted the Labor Party the perfect issue: deregulation of the industrial relations system. Latham was later to describe the defeat of 2004 as the darkness before the 'false dawn' of the Rudd Labor government.[16] Howard had repeatedly divided Labor with his wedge politics; now his changes to workplace rights united the party's traditional supporters in opposition to his government.

In early 2005, though, none of this was clear. The Labor Party was in an agony of self-flagellation and reflection. Beazley might have represented stability, but he had also repeatedly failed to beat Howard. There was an aura around Howard, as though he would never be defeated. For a career politician such as Penny Wong, the election defeat was a heavy and seemingly defining blow. Would she always be in opposition? Had the excoriating compromise been for nothing? There were meetings of Labor Party insiders, including Wong, Carmen Lawrence, Lindsay Tanner, John Cain and ACTU head Sharan Burrow, at which everyone agonised over, as one participant put it, 'where in the fuck do we go from here?'

In the meantime, Wong made the most of her frontbench position. Her corporate governance portfolio meant she was at the forefront of Labor's campaign against James Hardie, the asbestos manufacturer, and its meagre compensation for asbestosis and mesothelioma victims. On Senate committees she attacked the Australian Securities and Investment Commission's decision not to prosecute Steve Vizard, the Telstra director accused of insider trading. Meanwhile, she was taking every opportunity to talk to the media. Olenich remembers a punishing routine: he would rise at four in the morning, collect the papers from a service station on the way to work and try to spot opportunities in the day's headlines for Penny to make a statement, then write briefing notes for her to read as soon as she arrived at the office. When parliament was sitting, she began to do what is known in the bizarre world of Canberra media as 'the doors', the heavily stage-managed ritual in which a politician wanting to get media pretends to be walking into Parliament House so they can be approached by journalists gathered for the purpose. Penny Wong was now a comfortable performer, adept with the one-liner and confident in handling questions.

Employment and workforce participation were at the centre of national debate. The government's Welfare to Work program increased the number of people required to look for and accept work, and targeted parents caring for young children, people with disabilities, older jobseekers and the long-term unemployed. Welfare became conditional on the idea of mutual obligation: jobseekers were expected to work for the dole, do voluntary work or undertake training, education or an apprenticeship. Elements of the policy, particularly Work for the Dole, had been in place for years, but the 2005 federal budget changed parenting payments so that single parents with children older than eight were no longer eligible for the parenting payment, and restricted new claims for disability support.[17] WorkChoices, meanwhile, was to remove unfair-dismissal laws for companies below a certain size, curtail the right to strike, and privilege individual workplace agreements over union collective bargaining.

Wong and Olenich together agreed on an angle of attack. Howard's message – that welfare should come with a requirement to seek employment – was electorally appealing. They decided not to combat it directly but rather to question whether jobseekers were receiving the support they needed to get off welfare. Olenich recalls: 'At that point, the labour market was very tight – many of those that were on income support had been for a long time, and it was clear that existing interventions weren't really working. Genuine investment in capacity was needed. All our work with the sector and all the research showed – as does common sense – that it was not enough to make people look for a job, they needed to have the skills those jobs demanded.'

The day after the 2005 budget, Wong 'did the doors' and told the media that 1.4 million welfare recipients would have to fight for 136,000 training and support places, and that only one in seven parents about to be subjected to welfare cuts would have access to support to find a job. 'What this shows is the government is not interested in training and support. What it's interested in is moving people from one welfare payment to a lower welfare payment. This package is not about welfare to work, it's about welfare cuts,' she said.

She kept hammering the themes in regular media releases – sometimes several in a week – throughout 2005 and 2006. Olenich recalls that, in accordance with protocol, he would ring Beazley's office when Penny was 'doing the doors' to get the agreed talking points for the day. At first he got a puzzled response. Why was Penny doing all this? What were they up to? Olenich's reply was that nobody from the Labor Senate team was taking the battle up to Howard directly in the media.

Increasingly, this became recognised as Penny's role. She discussed the finer points of what had emerged in the often long and under-reported wrangling before Senate Estimates, distilling it into soundbites: that parents would be forced to take a job even if the effective return was only $25 a week; that the government had deemed homeless people not 'exceptionally vulnerable' and would therefore deny them income support if they were penalised for non-compliance with jobseeking tests.[18]

In late 2006 she gave a speech at her alma mater, the University of Adelaide, on the topic of values and politics. She used it to bring her by now well-worn rhetoric on racism together with a condemnation of Howard's workforce policies and the idea of mutual obligation in welfare. She attacked Howard for his response to race riots at Cronulla in Sydney in 2005. Howard had said he didn't like 'hyphenated Australians'; in this, she said, he had once again set citizens against one another:

A hyphenated Australian, presumably being someone who might describe themselves as a Greek-Australian or a Chinese-Australian, or in this context presumably a Lebanese- or Muslim-Australian, is cast in contrast to an 'Australian'. Just what a non-hyphenated Australian is, is not articulated. But it doesn't need to be in order for this statement to serve its political purpose. The assumption that most of us would immediately make, and the context of the racial conflict that drove the Cronulla riots, is that the non-hyphenated Australian is the white Australian. And that this is the type of Australian that the prime minister likes.

She acknowledged the concerns that Howard was speaking to – the fears of difference: 'We are more connected to the world, and we feel more exposed.' Unity, she said, did not come from sameness but from 'a sense of belonging – of being part of a greater whole ... and unity can encompass difference'. There was an agreed framework of values within which diversity could be embraced. The debate should be about the elements of that framework.

Howard speaks of the spirit of a fair go, while putting in place
industrial relations laws that strip away rights and remove conditions. He speaks of compassion for those in need while cutting the
incomes of some of the most vulnerable Australian families by pushing many people with a disability and sole parents onto the dole.
He speaks of tolerance, then attacks hyphenated Australians. His
hypocrisy is breathtaking.

Australian values are not the possession of any politician. They are
not held under lock and key in the prime minister's office. They are
the heart of our nation. They are the unwritten rules that ordinary
Australians live by. They speak to the New World's passion for democracy and justice; they acknowledge the lessons of our past. When a
politician talks to you about values, ask them not to express their values in words but in their actions. Better still, ask them to express your
values in the decisions they make every day in your name.[19]

The culmination of Penny Wong's work on welfare policy was a
discussion paper, released in November 2006. Titled *Reward for Effort:
Meeting the Participation Challenge*, it was classic Wong: both careful
and clever in its politics. The aim, Olenich recalls, was to 'move the ball
forward, but be very, very cautious about it'. The risk was that Labor
would be seen as reckless – as a friend of so-called welfare cheats.

The paper opened with an acceptance of the principle that 'people
should work if they can' and adopted the government mantra that the
best form of welfare was a job. Labor wanted to 'bring obligation and
opportunity together', it was stated, 'Participation is good for people ...
People need to feel that they are contributing, like they are helping
others and that they can rely on themselves and their loved ones to get
through life. Work is one of those essential things, like family, that gives
meaning to our lives.' The argument then zeroed in on what Wong had
detected as the weakness in the Howard government package – the
measures designed to increase workforce participation. The chapters
that followed included an analysis of the Australian labour market,
accusing the government of failing to invest in developing the skills of

the workforce, and of the jobless in particular. The paper analysed the impact of the policy changes on those who found work but went backwards in terms of total income. At ninety-six pages, it was detailed and wonkish, but delivered with a powerful spin and a saleable political message. Wong told the media upon its release that her focus was on 'making better use of mutual obligation'.[20] Labor committed to redefining mutual obligation so it would include capacity building, education and training. Labor would invest in that.

The reception for this detailed policy work was muted, because the media were distracted by yet another leadership convulsion in the Australian Labor Party. Just ten days after *Reward for Effort* was released, Kevin Rudd and Julia Gillard challenged Kim Beazley and Jenny Macklin for the leadership and deputy leadership. Gillard had become convinced that Beazley could not beat Howard and, recognising that she didn't have enough support to contest the leadership herself, had thrown in her lot with Rudd, mounting the challenge as his deputy. 'I worried that the fire to succeed was not burning strongly enough in [Beazley],' she wrote in her memoir. 'My fear was that in the final ballot-box judgement of Australians, Kim would not be chosen.' Rudd, she judged, would be the 'embodiment of safe change' and thus acceptable to the Australian people. With the wisdom of hindsight, she asked, 'Was I wrong in my judgement of Kim Beazley in 2006? I fear I may have been.'[21]

In this contest, Wong was one of Beazley and Macklin's most vocal supporters. Macklin, especially, had been a mentor and, as an 'encyclopaedia of knowledge' on welfare policies, had helped her in those first days in her shadow portfolios. Today, Wong describes Macklin as one of the party's best policy thinkers. It was to her, more than Beazley, that Wong felt personal loyalty. Macklin had no leadership ambitions, so she and Beazley represented a safe team. Meanwhile, she barely knew Kevin Rudd. She regarded him as a risk. Gillard had persuaded her to back Latham as the exciting and untested candidate in 2003 – a decision everyone involved now bitterly regretted. Wong was determined not to make a similar mistake.

An atmosphere of dread prevailed in Wong's office over the weekend preceding the leadership spill as it became clear that Rudd and Gillard had the numbers. On Monday 4 December, Rudd won against Beazley by forty-nine votes to thirty-nine. Macklin withdrew, allowing Julia Gillard to be elected deputy leader unopposed. For some days, Wong was unsure whether she would be punished. She was mentioned in a media report of the first Rudd press conference as 'glumly observing the new regime' from the sidelines.[22]

Several credit John Faulkner with persuading Kevin Rudd to keep Penny Wong on the frontbench. An insider says that Faulkner 'explained to Rudd, who didn't have the foggiest idea of how the Senate worked, that we needed to keep on Penny … That she was one of the heavy hitters, and we needed that, particularly with Howard trying to get all this contentious legislation through.' A full week after the spill, it was confirmed that Penny Wong would not only retain her two existing portfolios, but would acquire another – public administration and accountability.

It was a portfolio in search of a definition, but for that reason filled with opportunity.

But first came an indication of what life under the new leadership regime would be like. Just before Christmas, utterly exhausted by a difficult year, Penny Wong and her staff were attending the wedding of a colleague in Vietnam. Rudd called. The holiday, Wong told her staff, would have to be interrupted. Rudd wanted policy papers on each of their portfolios within twenty-four hours. There was no question of pushing back. She and her staff took to their hotel rooms and wrote the papers over a frantic, sleepless twelve hours. So far as they know, Rudd never read the results.

*

On their return to Australia, Wong and Olenich sat down to plan her approach to the new job. It was, as Olenich remembers, a 'wet-cement moment – an election year'. With the hard work on workforce and welfare policy already done, the new portfolio allowed Wong to range far and wide, needling the Howard government.

From early 2007 until the election campaign began in October, Penny Wong hammered the government on ministerial accountability as a series of minor scandals engulfed Howard's frontbench. She and Rudd zeroed in on the amount of taxpayer money being spent on advertising in this election year and promised that Labor would introduce new rules to stop the rorting.[23] She 'did the doors' to embarrass Centrelink over the case of Matthew Pearce, a young leukaemia sufferer who had been denied the disability support pension. Wong and the man's local member, Kim Wilkie, launched a petition to support him, forcing the government to back down. This was the face of Howard's 'extreme welfare measures' and gave the lie to the claim it looked after 'the battlers', said Wong.[24]

As the election approached, she dabbled in populism. In May 2007 she issued a media release asking why John Howard's office had spent almost $200,000 on 'posh chairs' for cabinet. Attached to the media release were extracts from the Officeworks catalogue, showing much cheaper chairs. 'It would have been a lot quicker and cheaper if the PM's staff hired a ute and drove down to Officeworks in Fyshwick or Braddon,' the release said. The chairs, like their occupants, had 'passed their use-by date', but in the meantime 'the Byron High Back leather chair with one-touch gas-lift height adjustment is a good choice at $99 a pop'.[25]

The next day, doing the doors, Wong described Howard as 'Lord of the ads', saying that his pre-election advertising was 'the biggest epic since *Lord of the Rings*'.[26] Two days later she shifted genres, using the thirtieth anniversary of the first *Star Wars* movie to attack Howard's taxpayer-funded election advertising: 'George Lucas' efforts have been dwarfed by John Howard's taxpayer-funded re-election advertising epic. A key difference is that people can choose whether they want to watch *Star Wars*.'[27]

The next month she was attacking assistant treasurer Peter Dutton for spending more than $10,000 a day on a trip to the United States. 'Peter Dutton seems to be more interested in living the life of a supermodel than getting results for working Australians,' she said. 'Who does he think he is? Linda Evangelista?' The comment made front-page headlines.[28]

But by far her most successful media hit was what jokingly became known as the cash-for-canapés affair. Penny Wong's office was combing through the costs to taxpayers of Howard's decision to live at Kirribilli House, rather than at the Lodge in Canberra. They found out that in June 2007 he had used Kirribilli as the venue for a Liberal Party fund-raiser. Attendees had paid more than $8000 each, and there had been no charge to the Liberal Party for the venue. Howard claimed that the food had been paid for by the party. Wong went through the figures. The cost of food had been just $9.46 a head. In the Senate, she ridiculed this. 'You would struggle to pay less at your local pub for a fisherman's basket and a pint of beer.'[29]

Meanwhile, in the House of Representatives, Anthony Albanese asserted, 'The only way that the food at Kirribilli could have cost $9.46 a head was if guests leaned over the fence ... and fished it directly out of Sydney Harbour.'[30]

It was the kind of story that seized the popular imagination, and it ran and ran through the weeks ahead. Penny Wong, policy nerd, had emerged as one of the opposition's most successful attack dogs, able to translate dry work on the figures into political hits.

A few weeks later, it was announced that Penny Wong would be the spokesperson for the 2007 Labor election campaign. Any suggestion that she might be sidelined for supporting Beazley had long since been forgotten. The media reported that the 'popular and eloquent South Australian senator' had become a key member of 'Team Rudd'.[31]

Wong remembers taking the call from Tim Gartrell, the Labor Party national secretary, in which he suggested she should take on the role. As usual, she was nervous about prejudice and its effect on Labor's pros-pects. She recalls, 'So Gartrell rings me, and says he was wondering if I would be campaign spokesperson. And I said, "But Tim, I'm an Asian lesbian. How will that play?" He laughed and said, "You have no idea how much we need that demographic."'

It was a 'huge jump' in responsibility. Today she credits Gartrell for giving her the opportunity that propelled her onto the frontbench in a Labor government.

She spent most of the campaign in the Sydney office. The day would begin early, with strategy meetings, after which she would do morning radio, pressing whatever had been decided as the message of the day. Her secondary role was to 'take the poison, to do the difficult things ... to protect the leader and allow him to stay on message'. If there was a delicate issue or a negative story, she would try to get out and deal with it before Rudd's first media encounter of the day.

Wong was chosen by the ABC's Mark Colvin to represent Labor in a regular weekly spot on the Radio National *PM* program, debating policy against Liberal Marise Payne. She appeared on *Insiders* – not in the fifty-second 'Adjournment Debate' segment but as the main event, in an interview with the presenter, Barrie Cassidy.[32] The Wong who emerges from these transcripts is more accomplished than the wooden, nerdish media performer of early appearances. She laughs, she pivots, she skewers. She would never be, as one of her colleagues put it, 'warm and cuddly'. Hers was a different kind of charisma. But Penny Wong, as an attack dog and a spokesperson for the campaign, was dangerous to the government and a tonic for Labor.

Wong says it was from this campaign, and from working closely with Gartrell, that she learned about political framing and came to understand that winning elections was not, whatever she might wish, about rational debate, but rather about 'which frame wins ... which understanding of the issues wins'. She also learned a vital lesson. It was not enough to hate what Howard was doing to the country in order to beat him. Hate had to be set to one side. 'It's a characteristic of Left politics that we think our emotional response to an issue or a person is enough, and it's not. It really isn't. So I learned that you have to take people with you. Just because you really hate patriarchy, it's not going to make patriarchy go away.'

In the decade since Howard had come to power, 'we had fought him with all of the emotional energy associated with our view. We had fought him out of hatred of what he was doing to the country and what he was doing to race politics in Australia ... and what we had to realise was that we were not going to get others to think like that. We had to find another way to get them to not vote for him. And WorkChoices was critical because it broke the idea of the Howard battlers. We were able to frame him with it, saying that he wasn't really on the battlers' side after all.'

Rudd came to power thanks to an effective alliance between between Labor and the trades unions, fighting against WorkChoices. Rudd presented himself as a safe change – a 'fiscal conservative', his main points of difference from Howard being opposition to WorkChoices and a commitment to action on climate change.[33] On both issues, Labor was able to frame Howard as out of touch. Rudd described Howard as running a government 'full of climate-change sceptics' and followed up by continuously rolling out initiatives to address climate change, in the midst of a nationwide drought that helped drive the issue to the forefront of public concern.

Penny Wong's most prominent public role was at the wonkish end of policy – a continuing assault on government accountability and waste. With the shadow minister for finance, Lindsay Tanner, she announced commitments to cut ministerial staff numbers by 30 per cent, to reduce spending on media monitoring, and to reduce 'abuse of government advertising' by requiring that all advertising campaigns over $250,000 be vetted by the auditor-general or their delegate.[34] She appealed to the Westminster traditions of public service independence and neutrality. If elected, she said, Labor would not purge the senior ranks of the public service, and would adopt a code of conduct to reinforce the principle of ministerial responsibility – which, she argued, had been compromised under the Coalition.[35]

As campaign spokesperson, she dealt with the dirty stuff – such as tangling with the Liberals' Andrew Robb over fake documents distributed in the seat of Lindsay, asserting that Muslims wanted people to vote for Labor. She accused senior Liberals of being involved, and called on Howard to 'front up and disclose all that he knows and all that the Liberal Party knew about this scandalous affair'.[36]

Meanwhile, behind the scenes, she was part of the preparation for government. This was quiet work. The polls gave them every hope of success, but they were careful to keep it low-key, aware of the risks of hubris.

Labor mounted an effective election campaign in 2007, Penny Wong contends, because after fighting the prime minister in successive elections 'with all our disgust, all our passion, all our hatred for what he was doing to the country', in 2007 'we stopped trying to make people hate Howard. That was important. People were not going to follow us into that.' Instead, 'we framed him as WorkChoices, we framed him as at the end of his tether.' This she learned from Gartrell. It was a lesson of lasting importance.

Gartrell, says Wong, was an amazingly good campaigner. When the referendum for marriage equality began in 2017, he was 'the obvious person to run it'. She realised that either same-sex marriage could be framed as a departure from tradition, contrary to how most Australians lived, or it could be framed as about love and commitment. 'I learned that, the importance of framing, from him. It was a very important lesson.'

On election day, 24 November 2007, Labor won in a landslide. The following Monday, *The Advertiser* predicted that Penny Wong was about to become South Australia's most powerful political figure.

The portfolios were announced at the end of that week. Penny Wong was to be the minister for climate change and water. It was not an area in which she had had any previous involvement, other than as part of shadow cabinet. As one of her first duties she was to accompany Rudd to Bali, where Australia would at long last sign the Kyoto Protocol on climate change. It was an enormous promotion, and a hugely challenging set of portfolios.

The story of Penny Wong's elevation was again international news. Sabah's chief minister told his citizens that her appointment was a great honour for their state. All Malaysians should aspire to be as successful as Penny Wong.[37] The British *Daily Telegraph*'s first paragraph proclaimed that 'a former rock star and a lesbian barrister' were among the ministers of the new Australian government.[38] The 'rock star' was, of course, Peter Garrett, formerly of Midnight Oil, who had been recruited by Mark Latham in 2004. The more serious journalists noted that Garrett had been given the environment portfolio but not climate change.

Other media noted that Penny Wong was the first ethnic Chinese, and the first lesbian, to be a cabinet minister.

Journalist Annabel Crabb penned a ditty about the new cabinet:

The Ruddbot, from the captain's deck, proclaimed his final crew:
There's Gillard who's so good at jobs she took not one but two!
And Garrett (who when told the news was sure he'd heard it wrong:
He'd kept the name but lost the game to canny Penny Wong).[39]

Political commentator Mungo MacCallum described Penny Wong as a symbol of fundamental change in Australian politics. 'A year ago, did you imagine that the Prime Minister would be sending an openly gay woman of Chinese ancestry to Bali, to ratify the Kyoto Protocol on Australia's behalf?'[40]

Just five years before, Wong had been one of the most junior members of the Labor Party in parliament – highly intelligent, yet sometimes a stiff media performer, always on the alert for moves to demean her, always vigilant for victimisation and prejudice. Now she was carrying two of the most important and challenging portfolios in the new government, loaded with all the symbolic baggage and expectation that her difference – female, lesbian and Asian – brought with it.

In the new year, *The Advertiser* ran a profile of her headlined 'Minister for saving the world'. The lede read, 'Political powerhouse Penny Wong has had an incredible rise – but can she save the world?'[41] The answer, of course, was no.

9

PENNY WONG FAILS TO SAVE THE WORLD (PART 1: WATER)

T he fifth interview with Penny Wong for this book took place at her Adelaide electorate office in early March 2019. It was a little more than two months before the federal election, which was expected to bring Labor to power and restore Wong, as leader of the government in the Senate, to the position of third-most-senior politician in the land. So it was fitting to speak about 2007, the previous time that Labor was preparing to form government. Like today, the country was in the grip of a punishing drought. The Murray–Darling Basin was in crisis, with millions of native fish dying from lack of oxygen in polluted, saline water weeks before our interview. Like today, action on climate change was an important, potentially defining, political issue.

Penny Wong was twelve years older. There were lines around her eyes, and her hair, black in 2007, had turned pepper-and-salt. She was a mother. She was also a veteran of the long, sad farce of the Rudd–Gillard leadership battles and all the disappointed dreams.

The Rudd and Gillard governments have been characterised by journalist and historian Paul Kelly as over-promising and under-delivering – as offering the lesson that Australia's political system is failing to deliver the results the nation needs. They are, he suggests, an exemplar of the dilemma in Western democracies: the political decision-makers' inability to address the problems of their nations. The causes of this, he says, are deep-seated and of longstanding: 'The business of politics is ... decoupled from the interests of Australia and its citizens.' There is a malaise in political decision-making, he says. Reform is nit-picked by the media and attacked by oppositions. An inability to build consensus has eroded the capacity for change. The political dialogue is debased: 'A country that cannot recognise its problems is far from finding a solution.'[1] His judgement on Labor in government is harsh. In saying it under-delivered, he puts to one side, perhaps too easily, the reforms and initiatives – disability insurance, school funding, demand-driven higher education, the apology to the Stolen Generations, the Royal Commission into Institutional Responses to Child Sexual Abuse, a contribution to international action on climate change, the legislation that established the Murray–Darling Basin Plan and putting a price on carbon. The latter came late, which made it relatively easy for the Abbott government to dismantle it. But Kelly's judgement is also surely correct in its thrust. The political scientist Rod Tiffen distils this history: 'Any policy achievements of the Rudd–Gillard governments pale before the political carnage they inflicted on themselves.'[2]

Writes Kelly, 'The Rudd–Gillard–Rudd era saw Labor buckle in government ... Neither of its prime ministers nor Labor as an institution was able to hold the line and assert sustained policy authority over a period of years.'[3] That conclusion is hard to argue with, and in that story Penny Wong was an actor.

Wong was a cabinet minister. She can't be absolved of her share of responsibility for the government's failures. Nor is she entirely to blame. The problems she dealt with had deep and tangled historical roots. There was the long, drawn-out farce of a dysfunctional cabinet. There was the Liberal Party's hard turn to the right. There was the Greens, not prepared to give Labor an even break. Indeed, 'the counterfactual', as she would put it, suggests some things might have been worse if she hadn't been there, and others might have been better if her advice had been heeded at key points.

In previous interviews I had asked Penny Wong about the machinations between Kevin Rudd and Julia Gillard. She said that she had read or seen only sparingly the many books and documentaries about those years – the ones by journalists, the memoirs of Kevin Rudd, Julia Gillard, Wayne Swan, Greg Combet, Peter Garrett, Bob Carr and the rest.[4] It was too painful. She couldn't bear it. She said she is the kind of person who tends to look forward, rather than back. I remarked that this is a characteristic of an activist, and she liked that.

I asked her what, given her fierce protection of her family's privacy, it would be possible to say in this book about her present partner, Sophie Allouache. She bridled. 'Well, she's lovely,' she said, as though that closed the topic. Then: 'We've been together for twelve years. We have two children and a mortgage. What more do people need to know?'

So how did she meet Sophie?

'I'm not going to go there,' she said.

Not even in general terms? Through mutual friends? Online?

'Oh no, not online. Nothing like that.' She relented. 'Well, we both did a lot of yoga.' And then she laughed. 'Is that a lesbian thing to say?'

I had met Sophie Allouache in the foyer of Penny Wong's office. She shook my hand and, when asked, confirmed emphatically what Penny had already told me – that she was not prepared to be interviewed for this book. I had also seen Penny and Sophie's youngest daughter, Hannah, on a day when the family juggle meant she was being cared for in the office for a few hours. Penny was reading her a picture book when I arrived.

Sophie Allouache, Wong has said, is 'the calmest and most grounded person I know'.[5] They met in late 2006, were separated for a while when Sophie travelled, and became a couple in 2007. Their relationship was formed with foreknowledge of the impending burden of government. 'Poor Sophie,' sighed Wong.

Allouache, seven years younger than Wong, has a French father and an English mother. Like Wong, she was involved in student politics at the University of Adelaide – part of the next generation of campaigners against the abolition of compulsory student unionism. She was women's officer in 1997 and Students' Association president the year after that. Wong remarks, 'She is not at all a public person, so it's strange in one way she was Students' Association president. But she says she liked the work.' Allouache graduated with a Bachelor of Arts in 2000, worked as a volunteer coordinator with women's services in South Australia and then managed a women's information and referral service.

At the beginning of 2009 she joined the South Australian Department of Health and worked on Aboriginal early childhood health projects. Today she works part-time in the Department of Human Services and is the main carer for their children.

Penny Wong's friends say that her family is crucial to her. It keeps her sane and grounds her. She protects them from public scrutiny for their sake, but also for her own. These relationships are a retreat from public life. Hence the staunch refusal to allow any interviews with Allouache. 'That's not going to happen,' said Wong when I first asked. As a result, Sophie Allouache remains an enigma. She is also a pioneer, in her way. When Penny Wong went to Government House in 2007 to be sworn in as a minister, Allouache was there – the first time a same-sex partner had been in that position. Her story, too, has become in part a political issue. But Allouache does not want a public life, and Wong is happy for it to remain that way.

*

Today, Penny Wong agrees that it was a mistake for her to have been given both the portfolios of water and climate change. Either alone would have been challenging; managing both as well as she wanted to was a near-impossible task. Both involved policy problems with lots of costs, no easy solutions and many traps. Like the battle over the forests in her early career, the issues were environmental but also economic, and enmeshed in ideology and identity. Her big promotion from junior shadow minister to such high-profile, key portfolios was evidence of Rudd's regard for her ability. She had been, with John Faulkner and Robert Ray, part of the team preparing for government while Rudd focused on campaigning. She had impressed. But Wong, only thirty-nine and in parliament for five years, was also lacking the clout to insist on the support of her fellow cabinet ministers, or to sway cabinet on her own. She had never been a minister.[6]

Rudd had announced during the campaign that he would choose his own ministry rather than heeding the Labor tradition of selection by caucus, in which ministers were effectively chosen by the factions.[7]

The fact that he loaded Wong up with two such difficult portfolios is, in hindsight, perhaps further evidence of his well-documented shortcomings as a manager of government business and of people. Of course, he intended to be closely involved himself, particularly with climate change – the defining issue of the election campaign.

Wong says that she pushed back against Rudd's urging that she take both portfolios. She thinks now that she should have pushed back harder. But she is also nothing if not ambitious. Her friends say she never runs from responsibility. Rather, she is only too ready to step forward and take it on.

Climate change was to become central to the government's trajectory and to Rudd's fate. It was a drawn-out agony – strong evidence for Kelly's assertion that Rudd crumbled in government.

And then there was water. In 2007, as in 2019, the most pressing issue was the health of the nation's food bowl – the Murray–Darling Basin.

In 2018, the Murray–Darling Basin Royal Commission was set up in Penny Wong's home state of South Australia. It reported in early 2019, during the period in which Wong was being interviewed for this book. The appointed commissioner, Bret Walker SC, wrote in his report that the ten years from 2008 had been a time of 'outstanding idealism and ... egregious shortcomings', with the health of the river system now desperately bad. It was a record, he said, that could only leave a sour taste. In this assessment he excoriated the Abbott government, but also the period when Labor was in government.[8]

Meanwhile, since Wong held the ministry it has become clear that water is most likely being stolen by irrigators in upstream states, with regulators apparently compliant or uncaring. There are inquiries into allegations in three states and at Commonwealth level, as well as prosecution proceedings in New South Wales and Queensland.[9] The evidence before the South Australian royal commission included claims of state government corruption, systemic problems with regulatory authorities and a collapse of public confidence in the system.

In 2007, in the tenth year of what became known as the Millennium Drought, the visible crisis in the Murray–Darling Basin was due to the condition of the wetlands of the Coorong and the complex of lower lakes where the river reaches the sea. The mouth of the Murray had silted over. The soils were acidifying; the Coorong was increasingly saline. In May 2008 an expert scientific panel stated that the Murray's southern reaches were almost beyond recovery, with wetlands dried up and native fish populations wiped out. Similar problems were occurring right along the river system, but the publicity to which Penny Wong was forced to respond in her home state concerned the Lower Lakes. The only way to save the Lower Murray was to reduce water use by farmers – but that would bring ruin to rural communities. Wong was reported to be taking expert advice. She resisted releasing it. The media speculated that this was because the news was too bad to be easily digested.[10] She later told a Senate committee that the advice revealed there were 'no easy options, only hard choices ... there is simply not enough water in the system to do everything we want and my view is that ... we have to give priority to Adelaide's water supply and that of other towns which rely on the river.'[11]

In August the following year, she was booed by protesters at a demonstration at Goolwa, the South Australian town at the mouth of the Murray, because she had declined an invitation to speak. The demonstration observed a two-minute silence for a river system that was dying. Senators Nick Xenophon and Sarah Hanson-Young criticised Wong for claiming that no extra water could be found upstream to save the lakes. 'I say, Penny, "Look harder,"' said Xenophon.[12] Easy to say.

The crisis in the Lower Lakes was, in Penny Wong's first year as the minister for water, as visible, divisive and urgent as the Darling River fish kills in 2019. So what did Penny Wong do about the state of the Murray–Darling Basin?

*

Water connects people. Rivers are often referred to as arteries. The metaphor is a cliché, yet exactly right for the Murray–Darling. The first settlers thought Australia must have an inland sea because all the rivers ran towards the centre. Instead, they found this water system. As Europeans pushed inland, it became a means of transport. On the eve of Federation, irrigation began. Since then, the Murray–Darling system has been a lifeline and a drain, with capillaries running to and fro, carrying water to crops, cities and gardens, and discharging wastes to the sea. It makes a large part of Australian life possible.

More than this, in the lexicon of the imagination on which nations are built, the basin's rivers carry myths and meaning. They connect the Dreaming stories of the first human occupants. Most of the indigenous peoples who lived in the Murray–Darling Basin shared the story of the great Murray cod – *ponde* in the language of the Lower Murray – that carved the river's course before being speared by Ngurunderi in the Lower Lakes.

The European myths are also powerful – archetypal, even. European settlers dreamed of gardens in the wilderness, and growing fruit in the desert. It was these dreams that led to astonishing changes to the landscape, and the dominance of the irrigation engineer. Today the Murray–Darling system is not only a collection of rivers. Rather, it is one of the most heavily plumbed river basins in the world.[13] The Murray–Darling Basin Authority has schematic maps of the system that show it as pipes, with weirs and storages and taps that enable the precise management of water flowing along the river. For decades the engineers were heroes – creators of the gardens in the desert.

Water not only connects. In Australia it also divides. Under the agreements made at Federation, the power to manage the Murray River belongs with the states through which it flows. South Australia is at the end of a long, dysfunctional chain of cause-and-effect over which it has hardly any control, yet Adelaide depends on the Murray for more than half its water supply. The federal government has authority only as the states agree to give it. When it comes to the Murray–Darling, all the federal government has to negotiate with is moral suasion, a chequebook and a limited amount of power flowing from constitutional obligations to enforce international environmental treaties.

The crises that Penny Wong faced on assuming the portfolio had a long history.

In the 1980s, with Labor governments in power federally and in South Australia, New South Wales and Victoria, the basin states met to formalise what became the Murray–Darling Basin Agreement, which established an intergovernmental structure with a ministerial council drawn from each state to manage the use of water from the basin. It was already clear that the volume of water being taken from the system was unsustainable, but little progress was made towards addressing this.

History shows that progress towards better management systems for the river happens only when there is a visible crisis. In the early 1990s, a blue-green algal bloom infected more than 1000 kilometres of the river system. The shock of the river turning toxic made clear to everyone that the water in it had been drastically over-allocated. A few years later, in 1995, a cap was put on water extractions, although it was often honoured in the breach, and was constantly disputed between the states.

Then came the Millennium Drought. Inflows to the river system were at record lows – less than half of the previous record low. The stress on the river was obvious, and water allocations were cut. In September 2004, the Howard government began a program that allowed for a formal return of water to the river system for environmental purposes. New legislation, the *Water Act 2007 (Cth)*, was passed by federal parliament with bipartisan support. The Act relied for its constitutional validity on the Commonwealth government's powers to ensure compliance with international environmental treaties. For the first time, legislation governing Australia's largest river system rested on environmental outcomes, not on social or economic grounds. The Howard government created a new body, the Murray–Darling Basin Authority, to oversee water resource planning, and created a Commonwealth Environmental Water Holder to manage this vital resource for the environment.

Commissioner Bret Walker later described the *Water Act* as a 'pivot' in the history of the river. He proclaimed his 'admiring praise' for the Act, together with his pessimism about whether its objects and purposes – which are to enable the sustainable management of the river system in the national interest, while protecting the environment – would ever be achieved.[14] In its dying days, the Howard government – with Malcolm Turnbull as the minister for the environment and water resources – tried to quicken the pace of reform against intransigence from the states. Despite the new legislation, they were dragging the chain on undertaking the necessary reforms and the work to give it effect.

Enter Penny Wong.

By the time the Rudd government came to power, the gum trees along the sides of the river were dying. Water allocations had been cut across the basin states; there were fears that the big cities would run out of drinking water. Desalination plants were planned by state governments. Meanwhile, in the basin, cotton production fell away entirely, and Australia began to import most of its rice.

When Penny Wong said that there simply wasn't enough water in the system, this was the hard reality. It wasn't an easy political message to deliver. She says today that she always assumed the Millennium Drought was not *just* a drought – that, thanks to climate change, there would be even less water in the years ahead. She had holidayed to Goolwa, on the Coorong, during university camping trips. She had seen firsthand the impact of increased salinity and reduced water flows. 'I brought a South Australian perspective to the issue,' she says. Her top priority, she maintains, was to simply buy water for the environment – spending federal money on purchasing entitlements from willing sellers and sending the water downstream.

The main way the purposes of the *Water Act* were to be achieved – and the immediate task of the Murray–Darling Basin Authority – was to use the best available science (a legal requirement) to develop a whole-of-basin plan incorporating every aquifer and irrigation channel across the basin. It was to be the first ever comprehensive audit of the basin, and it was meant to lead to an understanding of how much water could be taken on a sustainable basis. It was a massive research undertaking, with huge economic implications. The plan was to set a sustainable diversion limit of water that could be taken for agriculture and other human needs. Clearly, there would be reductions in water allocation.

Livelihoods would be affected, futures compromised and townships hit. As Wong knew, there were no easy answers. Throughout her period as minister, the research work leading to compilation of the plan bubbled away, a potent but sleeping political issue – keenly appreciated in rural basin communities but largely neglected and not understood by city-based media and many politicians. The draft Murray–Darling Basin Plan was due to be released in 2010.

There was a fair degree of bipartisanship between Labor and the previous government on water policy, although neither side would admit it. John Howard had set aside $10 billion to address the over-allocation of water. The main policy difference Labor took to the election was the addition of a national urban water and desalination program, with subsidies and incentives for rainwater collection and the use of greywater. More controversially, Labor also promised to bring forward $400 million of the $10 billion to start buying back Murray–Darling basin water.[15]

The bureaucrats who worked on the Howard government program remember two things about the transition to power. First, there was a comprehensive review of the Howard government program for implementing the *Water Act*. This review was run from inside Rudd's office by Terry Moran, secretary of the Department of the Prime Minister and Cabinet. The perception among many of the public service workers involved was that Moran had reservations about the idea of the Commonwealth getting involved in water. Only after the review was complete could Penny Wong announce her program. It largely adopted the Howard agenda, but brought forward water buybacks, and added money for urban stormwater programs. Inevitably, there was a change of name. The Howard government's Living Murray program became, under Labor, Water for the Future.

Second, even before agreement had been reached with the states, Wong prioritised the buying back of water for the environment. This had always been part of the plan, but under Wong it got a giant push. In February 2008 she put $50 million on the table to purchase water in the Murray–Darling basin. 'It is the first time in the nation's history that the Commonwealth government has directly purchased water, so we're not waiting for agreement from the states to make that water purchase, because we understand the river needs it,' she said at the time.[16]

'The message was "Get on and do it,"' remembers one senior bureaucrat. '"Don't wait. Just do it." It was the main difference between the governments, that sense of urgency about it.'

Penny Wong says that the water portfolio quickly taught her new priorities. The policy was complicated and the politics almost impossible to manage, but there were also problems with implementation. She was not well prepared, as a first-time minister, to deal with this. 'Politicians tend to assume that the challenges are all to do with politics and policy. They tend to miss the third – implementation – because they are not trained for it. I sort of assumed that the public service would just get on and do things,' she says. In charge of the new, high-profile portfolio of climate change, she was working with some of the best bureaucrats in the system, who flocked to help achieve progress in this area of vital importance. But, Wong says, in the Department of the Environment, Water, Heritage and the Arts (today part of the Department of Environment and Energy), years of neglect by the Howard government had left 'good people' in need of greater ministerial guidance. She fell into the habit of sending back briefing notes with extensive annotations and holding meetings with water bureaucrats at 'the next level down' to guarantee the implementation of policy in ways she had not expected would be necessary.

Unsurprisingly, the bureaucrats who were there at the time remember it differently. Penny Wong brought in a new secretary, Robyn Kruk, in 2009, but the staff below Kruk were left largely unchanged – although some individuals were made aware that Wong was trying to get rid of them. Today these people nevertheless describe Wong as having been a good minister. 'But she could be very cutting,' says one.

Meanwhile, the architecture of the *Water Act* was in place but the states had yet to agree to refer their authority over water allocation to the Commonwealth. Howard had written to all state and territory leaders in January 2007, asking them to cooperate with a new system of management devised by the Commonwealth. New South Wales, Queensland and South Australia indicated they would comply, but Victoria refused, insisting that the state should not be worse off under any deal. Wong says today she was keenly aware of her lack of power – yet the Murray–Darling Basin Plan would come to nothing unless she could get the states on board. It was another example of her needing to persuade when she lacked the power to compel.

The negotiations came to a head in Adelaide in March 2008, first at a meeting of the Murray–Darling Basin ministerial council, then at meeting of the Council of Australian Governments (COAG), held at the Adelaide Convention Centre. The commentators were pessimistic about what could be achieved. Political analyst Dean Jaensch remarked that Penny Wong had no real ammunition 'to fight what is clearly a political war ... Queensland, New South Wales and Victoria will continue to raid the basin for whatever they want, and South Australia, at the end of the system, can whistle in the wind'.[17]

On 27 March, in the final hours of the COAG meeting, journalists were told to gather at 1.30 pm for a media conference. It was expected a deal would be announced. They were left idle as the media conference was repeatedly delayed. Reporters texted contacts inside the meeting, only to be told there was no progress and there might be no deal to announce. Kevin Rudd was in one room with the premiers, Penny Wong in the other with federal and state water officials. Messages were run from one room to the other. Rudd needed to return to Canberra for a foreign policy announcement. Time was running out.[18]

Wong was, sources told reporters, 'amazing to watch' as she negotiated her way through the conflicting arguments.[19] It was Penny at her best – chairing a debate, bridging the gap between different positions, moving the players from intransigence towards a deal. But, in the last hours and when hope seemed lost, she effectively sidelined the bureaucrats, stepped forward and did the deal with the premiers herself. It was a hard piece of pragmatic politics, but it broke the deadlock. Today, Penny Wong credits Kevin Rudd with the breakthrough, but at the time he gave her the credit. 'She did fantastic work, and her shuttle diplomacy between the states played a key role in reaching the outcome,' he told reporters once the deal was done.[20]

Perhaps. But the hard fact was that it was the Commonwealth chequebook that did the trick. Victoria was brought on board with a $1 billion sweetener – journalists wrote it up as a bribe[21] – in funding for the second stage of the Foodbowl Modernisation Project. Stage one of this program had recently been criticised by the state's auditor-general. It was funding to update irrigation infrastructure – sealing irrigation channels and building more-efficient methods of delivering water to crops. In theory, it would save 200 billion litres of water, of which half would be returned to the river. Even at that time – and certainly later on – it was recognised that the figures on how much water such programs would save were dubious, and that it was a very expensive way to save water.

The deal established the Murray–Darling Basin Authority as the single body responsible for the overarching management of the basin. The Commonwealth minister would approve the basin plan, including a new cap on the amount of water to be used. Within this structure, states would continue to manage allocations in accord with the plan.

Penny Wong was interviewed by Tony Jones on the ABC's current-affairs program *Lateline* in the weeks after the deal. Why was it, he asked, that taxpayer money had been spent on the dubious Foodbowl program? She dodged the question. It was the program's first stage that had been criticised. 'We didn't fund stage one. My focus is on stage two.' Jones went on to raise rumours that water was being siphoned off through unauthorised channels in the upstream states. She told him that compliance had to be managed by the states and assured him that the Murray–Darling Basin Plan would address any such problems.

Finally, he asked her if the deal would be enough. Her plan – a modification of what Howard had been trying to achieve – was to be implemented over ten years. Did the Murray–Darling have that long? Water scientists were calling on COAG to ditch the deal and instead approach the state of the Murray in a manner that reflected the reality: a national crisis. Much more was needed, and urgently, they warned.[22]

But Penny Wong had cut a deal – the political skill with which she was familiar. And in this interview she demonstrated one of her defining political traits: the reverence for the negotiated solution and the compromise necessary to achieve progress.

Challenged on the funding for the Foodbowl program today, Wong arcs up. 'We got – for the first time in a hundred years – that intergovernmental agreement. That was a big achievement. I was at that COAG. We nutted that out and that was critical. And yes, you're right. We allocated dollars to irrigation infrastructure. The difficulty with all of this is that where you want to get to requires so much agreement, and action from state governments. It's very, very difficult. And the only thing you can use is the power of the purse.'

Wong's compromise was significant because every independent inquiry that has examined spending on irrigation infrastructure, including those conducted by the Productivity Commission, state auditor-generals and the Australian National Audit Office, has concluded that it is largely a waste of taxpayer money – an expensive and ineffectual way to save the river.[23] When water is used inefficiently, it seeps back into the river system, meaning not all of it is lost to the environment. A 'saving' by preventing that seepage is not necessarily a saving at all. The maps of the basin represent it like a bathtub – as though all flows can be precisely measured. The reality is very different. As well, spending on more-efficient irrigation infrastructure benefits individual irrigators at taxpayer expense, and the figures on the water savings they achieve are sometimes proclaimed with great confidence but in fact are highly dubious. Some 'efficiency' schemes have worked, largely by helping communities make their own assessments of sustainability. But, for the most part, money would be better spent in simply buying back water for the environment.[24]

Doling out federal money to irrigation communities is a short-term political fix. Wong secured the deal with the states largely by opening the chequebook for spending that, she says today, she knew was probably not the best way to help the river but was politically necessary.

Top: Penny Wong was born in the Malaysian city of Kota Kinabalu. Here she is as a child, several years before moving to Coromandel Valley in the Adelaide Hills at age eight.

Bottom: Francis Wong and Jane Chapman, Penny's parents, with Penny and her brother, Toby, circa 1972.

Top left: At Coromandel Valley Primary, Penny was the only Asian student in her class and was bullied regularly. She learned to guard her internal life fiercely and to show a tough face to the world.

Top right: Penny was school captain at the elite Scotch College in Adelaide in 1985. She is pictured here with co-captain Peter Ker.

Bottom: Family has always been important to Penny, shown here as a teen with Francis (second from the left); his wife, Loris (far right); and other children of the family.

Top: Penny Wong was Australia's first Asian female senator. In her maiden speech on 21 August 2002, she delivered a rousing condemnation of John Howard's use of race as a political issue, marking her out as a politician with leadership potential.

Bottom: Governor-General Quentin Bryce congratulated Penny Wong during a ministerial swearing-in ceremony at Canberra's Government House.

Top left: Penny Wong's elevation to climate change minister meant she was suddenly big news. Just a week later, the media described her as the star of the 2007 UN Climate Change Conference in Bali.

Top right: As water minister, Penny Wong joined Prime Minister Kevin Rudd at Casuarina Sands on 28 May 2008 to announce the purchase of almost 240 gigalitres of water rights: the single largest purchase of water for the environment in Australia's history.

Bottom: Baby Alexandra was born on 11 December 2011 to new parents Penny Wong and her partner, Sophie Allouache.

Top: In their home city of Adelaide, Julia Gillard holds Alexandra before the Labor state convention on 27 October 2012. Sophie Allouache stands on Penny's left, while Jay Weatherill, South Australian premier, stands behind Gillard.

Middle: Penny Wong is known as a formidable questioner in Senate Estimates hearings. Public servants and advisers

have reported being daunted by the prospect of appearing in front of her on such occasions.

Bottom: As Leader of the Opposition in the Senate, Penny can be a fiery interlocutor. Speaking in December 2018 on the Sex Discrimination Bill to protect LGBTIQA students, she excoriated finance minister Mathias Cormann across the chamber.

For years, Penny Wong campaigned for marriage equality, at first within the Labor Party, and then in public during the marriage equality postal survey. She is speaking here on the steps of Parliament House in Adelaide at a rally in September 2017.

Top: When the result of the postal survey was released on 15 November 2017, Penny Wong could not hold back tears. This moment became one of the most widely published images of the historic day. Senators Pat Dodson (left) and Sam Dastyari (behind Wong) and others comforted her and draped her in the rainbow flag.

Middle: Penny Wong celebrates the survey result with her second daughter, Hannah, on 15 November 2017.

Bottom: A long-time supporter and friend of Anthony Albanese (middle), Penny Wong was one of the first to congratulate him when he was elected leader during a Labor caucus meeting on 30 May 2019, replacing Bill Shorten (right).

As the shadow minister for foreign affairs, Penny Wong is a key player in the Labor cabinet and a vital voice as Australia negotiates the Asian Century. She may yet be foreign minister.

In April 2008 she announced $12.9 billion of spending over ten years, including $5.8 billion on 'efficiency' measures and $3.1 billion for water buybacks. The remainder was to be spent on urban water, including desalination, rainwater and greywater initiatives.[25]

Wong says today that she tried to resist allocating too much funding to the so-called efficiency measures. She attempted to ensure that strict criteria were set before money was handed out – but reviews since then suggest they were not strict enough. The Murray–Darling Basin Royal Commission found that the various 'efficiency' schemes involved a lack of disclosure on who had received funding, for what purpose and how much water had been returned to the Commonwealth as a result. The most reliable and effective way to help the river, the royal commission report stated, was water buybacks.[26] Figures from the Parliamentary Library and from Wong herself tend to support her account. They show that the theoretical savings from infrastructure spending didn't really begin until 2010 – when she was nearly at the end of her tenure as minister.[27]

Penny Wong did buy water. It is the first thing she says when asked about her time as portfolio minister: 'I bought a lot of water.' She pushed ahead with a program of buybacks from willing sellers, inviting tenders despite vehement opposition. The administration of this was complex – working through, with the public servants, the catchment areas, valleys and plains where buybacks would be most effective and where the increased environmental flows would be of most use. They were working with inadequate information. The Basin Plan, intended to inform such decisions in the long term, had not yet been developed. Penny Wong was moving fast, with urgency, not prepared to wait. In September 2008 – less than a year after the election – it was announced that the Commonwealth and New South Wales would buy the vast Toorale cotton station at a cost of $24 million, with up to 20 billion litres of water to be returned to the Darling River. It was a colossal figure at the time, and remains one of the largest single water buybacks in dollar terms. The local farmers claimed it would devastate the Bourke region. It was 'anti-rural', they felt, and a 'sop to the green movement'. They feared the hollowing out of their communities. Toorale Station was a significant local employer.

Another reason for controversy was that there was a heritage-listed dam that stopped the water getting into the Darling River.[28]

Right across the basin states, the water buybacks were enormously controversial. Rural communities blamed them for what they said was a Swiss-cheese effect, creating holes in the system of irrigation. Wong was accused of hastening the collapse of rural communities, ending whole industries. She was burned in effigy at demonstrations in Griffith. But every inquiry since has concluded that buying back water was the right thing to do to work towards the sustainable management of the river.

In 2011, the Australian National Audit Office examined the water buybacks Penny Wong oversaw. The report commented that the water buybacks had begun four years before the Basin Plan that was intended to establish how much water was needed for the environment. The information needed to decide what water was to be purchased, how much to pay and how to allocate the water to the environment was far from perfect. This was the largest water entitlement purchasing initiative ever undertaken in Australia, and unique in the world, and it was being done in a hurry. Nevertheless, the audit office gave Wong's initiative a fairly clean bill of health. Decisions had been made on the best available information. Procedures and guidelines had been developed on the run, but were mainly fit for purpose. There was room for improvement in the procedures, but no reason to think the decision-making process lacked integrity.[29]

Meanwhile, the Productivity Commission, the government's main independent research and advisory body, has determined that irrigators' fears about water buybacks are largely unfounded. Farmers adjust to lower water allocations. There is no proportional relationship between reductions in water and farm production. If more water had been recovered through buybacks and the proceeds used to support the affected communities, spending on health, education and aged care could have generated more than twice the number of permanent jobs as the same amount spent on irrigation infrastructure.[30] So much for the evidence – but water politics is irresolvable for a good reason. It reflects a world of pain. Across the Murray–Darling Basin, the pace of change for farmers and rural communities is hard for the city-based to understand – out of proportion to anything urban Australians have had to endure. The irrigation system is under strain. Increasingly, family farms are disappearing. Towns have faded as mechanisation replaces rural labourers. Mixed crops – rice and dairy – are giving way to corporate-owned industrial cotton and nut farms. With the advent of the drought of 2018–19, the dairy industry in the basin collapsed and is unlikely to survive. Fourth-generation farms are unable to keep going after just one year of drought.

It is all to easy for the affected communities to blame all these problems on water buybacks – and Penny Wong copped much of that blame. But the issue goes deeper. It is about rural Australia, and the failure of politics and political processes over a couple of generations to meet the needs of these Australian communities. Wong was the first and is so far the only federal water minister to buy such large amounts of water for the environment. From 2007 until 2010, when she lost the portfolio, the federal government purchased 770 gigalitres of water allocations for the environment. Another 311 gigalitres were bought in 2011, and, given that the process was established on her watch, that can also be counted as her legacy.[31]

When the Abbott government came to power in 2013, water buybacks all but halted and infrastructure spending took off. Just 3 gigalitres were bought in the 2014–15 period. In 2015 Minister for Water Barnaby Joyce introduced a 1500-gigalitre cap on water buybacks – a figure that was already more than halfway reached due to water purchased under Penny Wong. The cap meant that the emphasis would shift to doling out money for infrastructure and 'efficiency' measures. In the years since then, the highest level of buybacks was in 2016–17, when just 32 gigalitres was purchased. The shift to 'efficiency measures' rather than water buybacks was pure politics – and not supported by the evidence. But the politics were just too hard.

At the time of writing, there are calls for Joyce's buybacks to be investigated. The Greens, Centre Alliance and the Shooters, Fishers and Farmers Party are agitating for a royal commission.[32]

In late 2018 and early 2019, in the teeth of the drought and the eve of the election, water politics once again went feral. Allegations were raised in the media that Barnaby Joyce during his time as minister had paid $200 million – well above market price – in 2017 including to a company that had been associated with the minister for energy, Angus Taylor, without a proper tender and when there was good reason to doubt the water purchased would actually reach the river, because banks that trap it had not been removed. (There was no implication that Taylor improperly influenced the purchase.) Faced with calls for a royal commission, Joyce insisted that Labor's period in office also be examined. After all, he stated, it was Penny Wong who had begun water buybacks.[33] At one stage, in a bizarre interview on ABC Radio, he responded to questions by simply shouting 'Labor, Labor Labor, Labor'.[34]

Behind the scenes, Wong's office organised for the record to be scoured to see if there was any vulnerability for her. The conclusion was that Wong's work would stand up to scrutiny and political attack.

Penny Wong is quick to talk about Barnaby Joyce's shortcomings but avoids speaking directly about another hard truth. The problems around plummeting buybacks and dubious infrastructure spending set in under the Gillard minority government, after Wong had left the portfolio. The Gillard government depended on rural independents Tony Windsor and Rob Oakeshott for its hold on power. On water buybacks, Windsor was a sceptic.

In September 2010, three weeks after the election, Tony Burke replaced Penny Wong as the minister for water. A month later, in October 2010, a guide to the proposed draft Murray–Darling Basin Plan – a document that was brewing throughout Penny Wong's time as water minister – was released. The research that lay behind it had been internationally peer-reviewed. It was comprehensive, scientifically based, transparent. Today, it remains the best available document for determining how to sustain the river system.

The figures should not have come as a shock. The previous May, Wong had warned that there would be 'very tough' cuts in water usage. 'Everyone is going to feel some pain. We are undergoing a major change,' she said.[35] In fact, communities were ill-prepared for the nature of the report's findings. There were near-hysterical reactions at community consultation meetings. Copies of the plan were burned among signs asking, 'Is Hitler reborn?'. The president of the Victorian Farmers Federation said the plan proposed a 'legislated drought'.[36] The report recommended cuts of between 27 and 37 per cent of the water drawn for irrigation, with some rivers targeted for cuts up to 45 per cent. This would return an extra 3000 to 4000 gigalitres to the environment.

The government apparently had no strategy to deal with the political consequences and the controversy.

Under the plan, the figures for water returns were conservative – towards the lower end of what the scientists thought could be supported. Yet, almost immediately, Burke backed away from the guide and the detailed scientific data it represented. He told parliament he had sought legal advice on the meaning of the *Water Act* and whether more attention should be paid to social and economic factors in addition to environmental ones – even though the constitutional basis for the Act rested on caring for the environment. In December 2010 the chair of the Murray–Darling Basin Authority, Mike Taylor, resigned, under pressure from Burke to compromise environmental outcomes for social and economic objectives. Taylor was replaced by Craig Knowles, Penny Wong's old acquaintance from her union days in New South Wales. He continued the process of backpedalling and became actively hostile to the proposed plan. At a community meeting in Narrabri, Knowles said it was 'no secret' he had a 'poor opinion' of the plan, that he did not have a 'high degree of ownership' of it and that it was 'time to move on'.[37]

Within a year, the guide and the plan it outlined had become politically irrelevant. By April 2011 a process of negotiation had begun, focused on determining a new, lower amount to be recovered for the environment. The figure arrived at – 2750 gigalitres a year to be returned to the environment – was not scientifically backed, but it was judged to be politically saleable.

The Basin Plan, as the revised plan became known, was legislated by Labor in 2012. None of the scientists who reviewed the figures regarded it as consistent with the evidence of what was needed, even if the likely impact of climate change was ignored. The Wentworth Group of Concerned Scientists, an independent action and lobby group on the Murray–Darling Basin, described the plan as a document that 'manipulates science in an attempt to engineer a pre-determined political outcome'.[38]

Later, when Craig Knowles left the Murray–Darling Basin Authority in 2015, he criticised the focus on water buybacks and the scepticism about spending on water efficiency under Wong's tenure as minister. Knowles claimed the 'singular focus' on buybacks had been 'a flawed solution that missed the point' – the 'early reform agenda' had failed to 'properly consider' the value of water 'efficiency' projects. Even then, he was speaking in the face of the evidence.[39] And later still, in 2018, Penny Wong's water buyback program was being described as a disastrous 'unguided missile' by an irrigation representative. Tony Burke, he claimed, had recognised the 'devastation' she had caused.[40] This was in the context of upstream states threatening to walk away from the Murray–Darling Basin Plan entirely unless water allocated to the environment was clawed back for use by their irrigators. As Senate leader, Wong said that unless the government addressed allegations made about water theft and corruption, Labor would not support such changes. Trust in the plan had to be rebuilt, she said.[41]

The Murray–Darling Basin Royal Commission found that the Basin Plan adopted by Labor was likely in breach of the *Water Act* because it employed a 'triple bottom line' approach – putting social and economic concerns on an equal basis with protecting the environment when deciding how much water could be taken from the river. The royal commission had been opposed by the federal government, and current and former Murray–Darling Basin Authority and CSIRO staff had been prevented from giving evidence. Burke, too, left it until just weeks before Bret Walker reported to write a letter defending himself, when it was clear that the finding might be made that he had acted illegally.

Penny Wong was still in cabinet, though no longer in this portfolio, while all this went on. So what did she think of these events?

Consistent with her pledge not to reveal cabinet discussions or criticise Labor colleagues during these interviews, she refuses to respond. 'I'm not going to tell you what was said in cabinet, or what I said.'

I put it to her that Labor crumbled. She shakes her head and remains silent. Then she says, 'This puts me in a difficult position. I think the state royal commission demonstrates the problems with water policy.'

But it is not simple, she says. 'Some would argue that the kind of compromise in the plan that was criticised by the royal commission was required in order to keep New South Wales in: that perhaps they would have walked away if we had pressed ahead with my approach. And I was in a lot of conflict with the sector. Perhaps those who have a different political view of the world would say I was too confrontationist. Or too pure.'

She prefers to talk about Barnaby Joyce and what happened under the Abbott and Turnbull governments. Joyce, she says, trashed the river.

Famously, in November 2016, Barnaby Joyce wrote a letter to Ian Hunter, once of the Bolkus Left and by 2016 South Australian Minister for Water and the River Murray, in which he backtracked on 450 gigalitres of water promised to the state as a result of the 'efficiency' measures. He was effectively announcing that he planned to ignore even the weakened plan.[42] Shortly after the letter was delivered there was a ministerial council meeting in Adelaide. Hunter and Joyce were among a group that went for dinner at Rigoni's Bistro in the CBD. The royal commission report later described the dinner: 'The South Australian minister made his and perhaps the then state government's views known to his interstate and Commonwealth colleagues in unambiguous terms, with Minister Hunter apparently telling Minister Joyce, in colloquial terms, to leave the jurisdiction.'[43]

The Adelaide media were less circumspect. They reported that Hunter had told Joyce, and Victorian Minister for Water Lisa Neville, to fuck off.[44]

Just over twelve months later, amid the media attention, Penny Wong's former partner, South Australian premier Jay Weatherill, announced the royal commission.

The trajectory of the Murray–Darling Basin Plan, said commissioner Walker, was 'a story of cynical disregard … to the lasting discredit of all those who manipulated the processes to this end'.

Wong says she agrees with much of the royal commission report, and its analysis of where things have gone wrong, but that Bret Walker is a purist. It is not politically realistic to suggest that no account be taken of the social and political impact of reduced irrigation allowances. She doesn't accuse Walker of lacking an understanding of *praxis* – practical political action – but she implies it nonetheless. He is an excellent lawyer, she thinks; just not a politician. The former minister for water says she put priority on buybacks because 'it was clear to me it was the cheapest and fastest way to try and reduce what has been taken out of the river … That's just instinct.'

Commissioner Walker's most scathing criticisms concern what happened after Wong left the portfolio. But the period of her tenure doesn't escape criticism. In particular, Walker asks why the release of the Murray–Darling Basin draft plan came as such a surprise to the affected communities, making it easier for lobbyists to push for it to be dropped. Why was there no preparation, no communications campaign leading up to the release? His criticism is aimed mainly at the Murray–Darling Basin Authority – but it can also be read as a criticism of Wong. Is this another example of her shortcomings as a 'retail politician'? Should she have been out in the irrigation communities visiting the farmers, talking up the future?

Wong agrees more communication about the reforms would have been better, but what, after all, could she have said? 'The hard reality that no amount of communication is going to fix that. For some of these industries and some of these communities it doesn't matter what policy you have in place, there's not going to be sufficient water for business as usual.' Penny Wong did notch up other achievements in her time as the minister for water. One of the Labor additions to the Howard government's programs was money for urban infrastructure, in the form of subsidies for water tanks and other means of capturing stormwater – all part of the preparation for climate change. There is little doubt that, as a result, urban Australia is marginally better prepared for climate change than it might otherwise have been.

*

For most of the first ten years of the twenty-first century, the mouth of the Murray was kept open by dredging machines – sometimes two at a time – working to move sand and maintain a minimal flow to the Coorong, preventing it from warming, stagnating and dying. In 2010 the drought ended and dredging was stopped. The Murray flowed again to the sea.

Five years later, with the start of the current drought, the dredging continued. Today, two dredges remove sand daily to keep the river connected to the sea.

In February 2019, Penny Wong and Tony Burke issued a joint media release – she as Leader of the Opposition in the Senate and he as Shadow Minister for Environment and Water. They announced that if Labor won government it would repeal the 1500-gigalitre cap on water buybacks introduced by Barnaby Joyce. They cited the 'dire warnings' from the Productivity Commission review and the royal commission. 'As we get closer to the period where the Murray–Darling Basin Plan will be due for review … we need to make sure our options are open to recover water. By removing the cap on buybacks Labor is removing [a] legislative barrier to providing more water for the basin, if that is what is needed.'[45]

Wong and Burke were apparently united, preparing for power and another go at saving the basin. It was clear that, with the nation again in the grip of drought, water politics was about to blow up. It was an election issue, with rural independents gaining votes by calling for the entire plan to be abandoned and reset.

If Penny Wong had her time as the minister for water over again?

She says, 'I think counterfactuals in retrospect are so self-serving.'

But she would agree to take on only one portfolio, climate change or water – not both. And if she had water, she would keep a closer eye on the implementation.

She says she feels the Rudd government achieved a lot between 2007 and 2010. But today 'it's disappointing to see, nine years on, where the country is'. The recent fish kill, she said when interviewed in early 2019, weeks before the election, was an example of a 'crisis that can be used' to spur 'what we do next'.

She was speaking on the assumption that Labor would get that opportunity after the election. Those expectations were dashed.

Looking back on Penny Wong's record in the portfolio, it is clear that much, much more was needed to save the Murray–Darling Basin and the river. Perhaps a different kind of minister – a bolder vision-ary, someone less cautious – would have pushed harder, achieved more. Though it is likely that if she had taken any more water back for the environment the entire agreement between the states and the Common-wealth would have come undone. More likely, without her careful work in cutting a deal with the states, her balancing of what she thought was right with a preparedness to dole out cash, nothing would have been done at all.

The reality is that a better result was not politically possible with-out a long-term strategy for managing change in rural communities. Neither side of politics has composed such strategies. Wong, on her own, could hardly have done so in her three years as minister, given that Labor showed no sign of having developed appropriate policies in opposition. The development of good policy for a fast-changing rural Australia should be the work of decades, and the failure to do so is, likewise, a generational failure. The results extend beyond irrigation communities. This is the malaise that affects coal-mining and power-generation communities, farming communities, all those asked to bear the heaviest burden of change.

Once these rural communities were at the heart of Australian life and identity – storied and balladed, proud of their role in feeding and powering the nation. They were at the heart of the history of the Austra-lian Labor Party – founded by striking pastoral workers in Barcaldine, Queensland. Now, rural Australians have become what Mark Latham in his better days would have termed outsiders – deprived of voice, alienated, cynical. After decades in which they have been offered no hope, they are now resistant to hope and therefore resistant to political messaging.

When Labor left power, things got worse. Cynical politics thrives in communities without hope.

Maryanne Slattery is a senior researcher at the Australia Institute and a former director at the Murray–Darling Basin Authority. She was a witness before the Murray–Darling Basin Royal Commission, and describes Wong's time in the portfolio as 'good compared to what came after'. She says that if a criticism could be made of Penny Wong's time, it is that probably the rush to buybacks led to the Commonwealth paying too much for water, sometimes where the water flow was of dubious reliability. But after Wong left the portfolio, Labor crumbled. Then, after the change of government, it got much worse, with maladministration, malfeasance and 'dodgy deals'.

Water politics cost both Labor and the Coalition heavily at the 2019 election. Labor was easily characterised as being out of touch with rural communities, and the National Party lost three seats amid anger over drought, water allocations and the Murray–Darling Basin Plan. Those seats were picked up by minor parties and independents – those not burdened with the hard responsibilities that come with being a party of government.

After the 2019 election, National MP David Littleproud was reappointed the minister for water resources. In his first public statement, he vowed an investigation into the 'purity' of the water market and promised Murray–Darling Basin communities he would equip them with the tools to 'recover and restructure'. At the time of writing, there are as yet no details as to how he proposes to do this.[46] Meanwhile, the calls for a royal commission grow, and the agreements between Commonwealth and states, essential to the implementation of the *Water Act*, are fragile, vulnerable to populist politics in communities deprived of story, voice and dreams.

Is it true that the political processes in Australia are no longer capable of meeting the needs of the people? This question underlies Penny

Wong's time as the minister for water and the dilemmas she faced. It is also one that underlies a review of her entire parliamentary career, and her future in the wake of the 2019 election defeat.

10

PENNY WONG FAILS TO SAVE THE WORLD (PART 2: CLIMATE CHANGE)

O ne image of Penny Wong has fixed in the minds of journalists who reported on the United Nations Climate Change Conference – the Copenhagen Summit – in December 2009. She was with Kevin Rudd, holding a media conference in the early hours of the morning after all-night negotiations in a windowless room. The process had been, at best, only a partial success, and a devastating disappointment to Rudd, who had hitched many of his hopes for change on this event. Penny was swaying on her feet. She had snatched minutes of sleep on a blow-up mattress in a corner of the conference centre. The journalists thought she might faint. They stopped their questioning long enough to offer her a chair, which she declined.

Penny Wong spent two long years and eight long months as the minister for climate change. The portfolio was about the exercise and limitations of government power, and the shifting dynamics of geopolitics. It was a portfolio that involved the tide of human history and the future of the planet – that focused on the 'greatest moral challenge of our generation', according to Kevin Rudd. And all of this was winnowed through the limitations of human capacity.

At its most basic, there was the need to sleep – at least sometimes. There was the need, in the maelstrom, to find time to think. Time to think is a scarce asset in government and under the pressure of the media cycle. Yet thinking time, says Wong, allows you to 'settle yourself ... to determine what is urgent, and what is important. To be creative and think laterally, creatively, about how to get around obstacles.' Kevin Rudd, she believes, did not give himself enough of it. 'Woven through those needs, those limitations on the doable, there are the other weaknesses of human beings – their egos, ambitions, capacities for greatness and for panic – the future of the planet tangling on the wreckage of politics as usual.

During Penny Wong's time as minister, climate change became the most toxic issue in Australian politics. It was crucial in the demise of both Kevin Rudd and Malcolm Turnbull as leaders of their parties. It went on to be a key factor in the second rise of Rudd, the defeat of Julia Gillard by Tony Abbott, and the second fall of Malcolm Turnbull – this time as prime minister.

Because climate-change policy was so determining of the political trajectory of the Labor government, just what happened and why during Penny Wong's time as minister has been reported, chewed over and analysed by many both inside and outside parliament. Climate-change policy features prominently in the memoirs, often self-justifying, of Labor's Kevin Rudd, Julia Gillard, Wayne Swan and Greg Combet, and the Greens' Christine Milne. Each gives a very different view of who said what and who was to blame. Penny Wong emerges well from both Gillard's and Rudd's accounts, although they are poisonous about each other and agree on little else.[1] There have been journalistic accounts as well, including Sarah Ferguson and Patricia Drum's *The Killing Season* and Paul Kelly's *Triumph and Demise*.[2]

How could a policy begun with so much idealism and high hope end in a train wreck for Labor and for Australian action on climate change? Today, Australia is the only nation in the world to have abolished a climate-change framework that included a price on carbon and legally binding emissions reduction targets. As Mark Butler wrote in his book *Climate Wars*, 'we are also pretty much the only major advanced economy where carbon pollution levels are rising rather than coming down'. Australia is in the first rank of carbon polluters, with the highest rate per capita of carbon pollution output in the world.[3]

Penny Wong acknowledges there was trauma involved in having worked so hard for such a paltry outcome. When asked to revisit those years for these interviews, her distress was obvious. 'I get very distressed talking about it.'

*

The climate change ministry was an enormous promotion for Wong. She had not had much to do with climate-change policy in opposition, and climate action was a centrepiece of Rudd's agenda. Days after the end of the election campaign, she was in the thick of it – attending the United Nations Climate Change Conference in Nusa Dua, Bali. Her adviser John Olenich remembers the rush to pack and get on the plane, and then the sudden realisation of the changes that came with being in government – being greeted by the ambassador at the airport, Wong being whipped away to briefings and high-level meetings.

As she departed for Bali, the new Department of Climate Change was being composed in a tearing hurry. It was to sit within Rudd's own portfolio, the Department of the Prime Minister and Cabinet, making Wong, in this area, effectively his assistant. She was operating in a policy area that Rudd had made clear he intended to dominate. This positioning was emblematic of the anomaly in Wong's status. She was, as Mark Butler puts it today, a 'junior senior' minister: junior in the sense that she had been in parliament just over five years, had never been a minister and lacked the clout within cabinet to command support; senior in the sense that she carried two of the most important portfolios, was widely recognised for her ability, and had been important to Labor's victory in her role as 2007 campaign spokesperson.

An optimistic outlook may have been a factor in Rudd's appointment of Wong to two very difficult portfolios in climate and water. Few foresaw quite how challenging the reforms on climate would prove. Brendan Nelson was leader of the opposition, and there was bipartisanship on taking action to reduce carbon emissions. Tony Abbott had considered contesting the Liberal Party leadership after the election but withdrew when it was clear he didn't have the numbers; nobody anticipated the formidable political foe he would become.

In Bali, Rudd was greeted as a hero. His first act as prime minister had been to ratify the Kyoto Protocol, the international agreement that committed countries to reduce greenhouse gas emissions. Australia, along with the United States, had been one of only two developed nations not to have signed.

Rudd addressed the conference on 12 December and repeated that climate change was 'one of the greatest moral, economic and environmental challenges of our age'. He stated that Australia was 'ready to assume its responsibility, both at home and in the complex negotiations which lie ahead across the community of nations.'[4] The speech was greeted with a standing ovation. 'The mood of the conference, at least for a time, grew almost euphoric,' Rudd recalls in his memoir.[5]

But, days after his address, the rift between developed and developing nations became apparent. It seemed the whole process towards devising a successor to the Kyoto Protocol, including a road map and a timetable towards reaching agreement by 2009, might fall apart. Rudd directed Wong to try to convince developing countries to drop their demand for the inclusion of an emissions target for developed countries in favour of a commitment to attend the next round of talks, scheduled for Copenhagen in 2009. It was more important to get a commitment of attendance from all countries than it was to push for targets.

Penny Wong called a press conference – the biggest of her career so far. Australia was world news. The media crammed into the courtyard of a hotel. The preparation had been intense; Penny was absorbing briefings on the run. Olenich was nervous.

He needn't have been. The media conference took over twenty minutes. In the humidity and under hot lights, everyone was swimming in sweat – except Penny Wong. One journalist asked how she managed not to perspire. She told him she was – just more quietly.

The Australian reported 'a remarkable performance ... she calmly managed one of the toughest baptisms of fire possible for a young new minister'. She had repaid Rudd's faith in her.[6]

Penny Wong had a reputation with some in parliament for being 'dour, detail-obsessed and dogged, willing to dig and claw her way relentlessly in pursuit of whatever rodent she has been sooled onto'.[7]

Now she had emerged as something else entirely: a charismatic negotiator. A future leader.

As time ran out, Wong was invited to chair a dialogue in a bid to
rescue the deal. The bureaucrats who watched her in action describe her
performance that day as 'breathtaking'. 'She took hold of that meeting
and did an absolutely textbook job on them, defining the issues, keeping
them in line, pushing and pushing,' said one. Wong briefed the media
in the final hours that an agreement looked unlikely. Just ninety minutes later, it was announced that at the last minute the United States had
caved in and agreed to support the 'Bali roadmap' – a series of measures
to take the world to Copenhagen.

On the way home, Wong, Olenich and their team crossed the hot
tarmac at Denpasar Airport to board a Qantas flight that had been
delayed just for them. Ahead they saw Indonesian president Susilo Bam-
bang Yudhoyono, just as he saw Penny. She had made a mark by chairing
the dialogue at the meeting. On that tarmac, Yudhoyono turned and
nodded to Wong in an unmistakable gesture of respect. Olenich recalls,
'It was arresting. We went straight from a junior shadow ministry basically scrapping for attention to the leader of the fourth most populous
country in the world paying her that acknowledgement.'

'Move over, Kevin Rudd. You may be running the country, but
Penny Wong is running the world,' wrote News Limited journalist
Glenn Milne, reflecting on her performance. She had emerged from
the 'almost subterranean' shadow portfolio of public accountability to
being a star with an international profile.[8]

Before Bali, there had been some anxiety about working for Wong
among the senior bureaucrats, several of whom were to be shifted to
the new department. She was not an unknown quantity to them. One
remembers when he was first quizzed by her at a Senate Estimates hearing in 2002. He returned to his department and asked about the 'very
bright young lawyer' who was new to the Senate. Over the years Wong
had developed a reputation in these hearings as someone for whom you
needed to prepare. 'If I knew she was on the team, I'd be swotting the
night before and nervous at breakfast,' remembers one. Now, having

watched her performance in Bali, and seen her sop up their rapid brief-ings, they were reassured, and impressed.

Some of these same bureaucrats noticed a more disturbing issue in the months ahead. Wong had a strong reputation as a negotiator, but they were taken aback by her combative approach in international discussions. It emerged not only when she was dealing with a clear opponent – which is rare in international diplomacy – but also when negotiating with people broadly in sympathy with her position. They found it puzzling. Discussing it among themselves, they assumed it was her union training – a 'take down the bosses', no-prisoners approach. As the months went by, their regard for Wong increased. She won their respect as decent, well motivated and 'in the top deck' intellectually. This combativeness, however, remained. 'At times it made her a very poor negotiator,' one says. Some wonder how events might have been differ-ent if Penny Wong were less aggressive with others in the parliament.

Meanwhile, amid all the optimism and hype following the Bali conference, Wong and Rudd were being cautious. Australia would not set a target for reduction in carbon emissions, they told journalists, until the government had reviewed the results of the Garnaut Climate Change Review.

Before the 2007 election, as part of Rudd's positioning, Labor had used the fact that it was in power in all states and territories to get COAG to appoint economist Ross Garnaut to study the impacts of climate change on the Australian economy and advise on the best response. After the election, the new government's policy development process and the Garnaut review ran in tandem. From Garnaut flowed an interim report, a discussion paper, a draft report and then a final report in September 2008. From the government came a Green Paper, Treasury modelling, a White Paper and then the release of new measures and changes. The early idealism was accompanied with great caution and meticulous pol-icy development over more than a year.

As for the politics, after Bali it was all downhill.

*

There she was, sitting behind Kevin Rudd, in that windowless room.

'Opposite us was US President Barack Obama, flanked by Secretary Hillary Clinton,' Wong has recalled. 'To my right was President Luiz Inácio Lula da Silva of Brazil, with Dilma Rousseff behind him, German chancellor Angela Merkel, Swedish prime minister Fredrik Reinfeldt, and French president Nicolas Sarkozy. Also spread around the room were British prime minister Gordon Brown, Indian environment minister Jairam Ramesh, Chinese negotiator He Yafei, South African president Jacob Zuma and Mexican president Felipe Calderón. Next to me sat the Bangladeshi delegation, whose prime minister made an impassioned plea for action in the late hours of that night. I thought to myself, *this room could do anything. The combined political, economic and strategic power assembled here could deliver transformational change.* But it failed to do so.'[9]

Another image from the months before. Penny Wong, in tears, in the second half of 2009, as she is trying to negotiate passage of the Carbon Pollution Reduction Scheme (CPRS) through the parliament. Rudd has sent her to see if she can cut a deal with the opposition. Labor does not have the numbers in the Senate.

Wong goes to see Julia Gillard, because she doesn't know what Rudd wants her to do. Should she cut a deal, or crash the negotiations so that Labor can call an election on the issue and get a renewed mandate?

The account of that meeting is from Gillard's memoir.[10] Wong says it is 'not inaccurate'. But she also claims, 'I knew what I was trying to do. I was trying to get a deal.'

Then, another image, this from April 2010. Rudd is being pressured by a key cabinet subcommittee – Strategic Priorities and Budget, better known as the Gang of Four – to drop the CPRS, because it has become a political liability. The decision about whether to include it in the federal budget has to be made now. Gillard and the treasurer, Wayne Swan, on Rudd's account, insist it must go. Rudd rings Penny Wong, who is in Honolulu, on her way back to Australia. He discovers that Gillard and Swan have kept her in the dark about their plans to ditch the policy. Rudd will rail in 2018: 'This was outrageous, given she was the minister responsible ... Penny argued passionately against the proposition ... Penny was in tears on the other end of the phone. I could hear it, even over a bad line, as I sat on the edge of my desk, with the other three sitting in the burnt orange lounge chairs in the middle of the office.'

On that call, Wong gives her leader some prescient advice. Alone of the senior people advising him, she calls the politics correctly. Has he considered, she asks, the impact of a decision to drop the CPRS on him personally? 'PM, if the funding line is removed [from the federal budget] then the immediate conclusion of the public and the commentariat would be that we no longer cared about climate change.' Rudd concludes, 'Of course, Penny proved to be absolutely right, once again.'[11]

But Penny Wong loses out. The CPRS is dropped from the federal budget. Rudd's standing in the opinion polls dives, and within weeks Julia Gillard replaces him as leader.

So how did it all go wrong?

*

After returning from Bali, Penny Wong used a speech to the Australian Industry Group to outline the framework for a national emissions reduction scheme. Olenich had worked on the speech while Wong was overseas, talking to her frequently by phone. It was a key piece of positioning, and began stirringly:

> Future generations will look back on us all and ask what we did. With the prospect of sea levels encroaching upon our mostly coastal population, they will ask why it took so long to act. Seeing our river systems die before our very eyes, they will ask how this was allowed to happen. With our knowledge that climate change puts our food and water supplies at risk, they will hold us accountable.[12]

The scheme under development would have a cap-and-trade emissions reduction framework. A cap would be placed on the total amount of emissions allowed. Tradeable permits, with the number tied to the cap, would be issued to polluters. Companies would have a choice – either reduce pollution or buy permits, whichever was cheaper for them.

The proposed CPRS was one of the most comprehensive systems in the world – covering three-quarters of Australian emissions and all six Kyoto greenhouse gases – and was being introduced in the world's most carbon-intensive economy.[13]

The ambition was obscured by disputes over the target for total emissions reduction, which would govern the number and price of permits, and over how much assistance industry and households should receive to help them adjust. On these issues, Rudd and Wong were cautious. The intent, Rudd told Garnaut, was to get a scheme up and running, then seek a mandate at the 2010 election for stronger action.[14] At first Rudd and Wong set the target for reductions at just 5 per cent below 2000 levels, with an increase up to 15 per cent if there was an international agreement for action at Copenhagen in December 2009.

The Green Paper that outlined these plans was released on 16 July 2008. Wong had worked on it throughout the winter break. It committed to using all the funds raised from an emissions trading scheme (ETS) to compensate households and business. Those industries hit hardest would get a specified number of free permits.

A profile of Wong published around this time pondered:

So how do you usher in a huge and complex economic reform in just 18 months – one that is going to result in higher prices for much of what we consume – without causing excessive political pain at a time when anxiety over living costs is palpable? Most people would turn to jelly. Yet Senator Wong, difficult to read, often mechanical in her delivery and apparently unrelenting in her pursuit of detail, appears calm.[15]

The modesty of the emission reduction targets and the levels of assistance to industry meant that, once the White Paper was released in December 2008, the scheme came under attack from all sides. The environmental movement and the Greens wanted more ambitious targets and little or no compensation for industry. Business was prepared to accept change but sought more compensation. Meanwhile, Garnaut regarded the amount of compensation the government was proposing to pay industry as unjustified. He went public. 'Never in the history of public finance has so much been given without public purpose, by so many to so few.'[16] Given his reputation, Garnaut's criticism carried weight.

Today Penny Wong includes Ross Garnaut in her critique of why action on climate change ultimately failed. His advice was good: 'The Garnaut report is impressive. Nothing I say about him should be seen as a criticism of his work.' But 'there was a little bit too much of his ego associated with this … he decided if we didn't do what he said he was going to criticise us. I think he gave grist to the forces of darkness … I think he should have looked at the nation, and what was needed. And what was needed was people standing behind the prime minister to deliver a major reform.'

She adds, 'This sort of change is hard, really hard. If you go back through the history of our country and the big reforms, they're all hard-fought. And they have to involve compromise. Unfortunately we had too many fundamentalists on both sides.'

Given the size of the reform, it is extraordinary in retrospect that the original plan was to introduce it so quickly – by July 2010. The CPRS was not only about the environment. Introducing an ETS would touch every home and business in the land. It was, Penny Wong said at the time and maintains today, the biggest restructuring of the Australian economy since the Hawke–Keating moves to float the dollar, dismantle tariffs and open Australia's financial system to the world. It was huge.

With it came risks. The new department, and Treasury, were working overtime on the implications. She recalls, 'We had to make sure we had a policy that didn't have unintended consequences. Those risks were throughout it. Are you going to have this massive crash in the energy sector? Are you going to impinge on exports? Will polluting companies just move offshore, and we lose those jobs? All that had to be worked through, and compensation for adjustment was part of the assessment of those risks.'

By early 2009, it was clear that the scheme was sinking under the weight of criticism from all sides. Wong met with Rudd and successfully urged him to renegotiate with business and environmentalists. She and her chief of staff, Don Frater, brand new in the job, flew to Noosa to see the president of the Business Council of Australia, Greig Gailey, who was on holiday there. At the same time, she was roping together a coalition of the more moderate environmentalist groups, trying to garner support for the government's plans from both sides of the debate.

Meanwhile, the effects of the global financial crisis were hitting the nation. This would have provided an excuse for the scheme to be dropped. Instead, Rudd held firm but announced a one-year delay in implementation, with a low fixed price of $10 per tonne to remain on carbon until mid-2012. The government also raised the reduction target. If the world came to an agreement on climate action at Copenhagen, Australia might aim for up to 25 per cent. Other changes included a $4 billion increase in compensation to business, now amounting to $7.3 billion.

Both Rudd and Wong thought – and still think – that changes on the scale of the CPRS needed bipartisan agreement. Business needed certainty that the scheme would not be unpicked with a change of government. Alongside this, both decided early not to continue to engage with the Greens. Wong considered this an appropriate decision. She thought the Greens were positioning themselves as more morally pure than Labor. They were not willing to do the work and undertake the compromises needed to achieve reform.

In theory, the opposition supported action on climate change. As the 2007 election had approached, Howard had announced that he, too, would introduce an ETS – in 2011. He was later to admit that this was not a matter of principle but a political response to a 'perfect storm' of record levels of public concern, the drought and Rudd's position on the issue.[17] Nevertheless, both sides of politics had, at least in theory, committed to action.

Brendan Nelson, who had become opposition leader following Howard's defeat, lost the leadership to Malcolm Turnbull in September 2008.

Turnbull was strongly in favour of action on climate change, but in reality bipartisanship support was weak. The Coalition was deeply split between climate-change sceptics and those who supported action. Turnbull was vulnerable.

The CPRS legislation came before the parliament for the first time in June 2009, and was defeated in the Senate with the Greens and the independents voting with the Coalition. In an attempt to paper over the divisions, the Coalition had decided to oppose the legislation this time around and consider its position on the bills' second presentation.

The stakes were higher when the legislation came before the parliament the second time, in October. If the bills were rejected, Rudd would have the trigger for a double dissolution election – having resoundingly won a climate change election less than two years before.

Rudd sent Wong to negotiate a compromise with the opposition. Turnbull was keen for it to happen. He hoped to get the credit for making the scheme more business-friendly.[18] Rudd, on the other hand, was according to some always sceptical about whether an agreement would be possible. Perhaps this was the reason for Penny Wong's confusion over what he wanted her to achieve – a deal, or a crashing of the deal so Labor could win another climate-change election. At first, Wong's negotiating partner was Greg Hunt MP. It was hopeless, she says. His idea of negotiating was to 'tell me why I was wrong ... I said to Turnbull, "Give me someone else."' That someone else was Ian Macfarlane, who had been the minister for industry, tourism and resources under Howard. Penny Wong and Ian Macfarlane made an odd couple: he a right-wing Queenslander and she a left-wing Adelaide feminist. As negotiators, though, they worked well together – both of them combative but straightforward. The media reported that they came to trust each other (although he declined to be interviewed for this book).

In November, with the bills again before the parliament, they met every day, as she remembers it, 'working it through sector by sector, gas by gas'. Meanwhile, Turnbull had been weakened by missteps in the Utegate affair. Turnbull had alleged that Rudd had acted improperly in seeking financial assistance for a Queensland car dealer. Turnbull had based his allegations on a leak from a Treasury official, Godwin Grech, who turned out to be a fabricator who had forged an apparently incriminating email. The affair damaged Turnbull. A leadership challenge was brewing.[19]

Meanwhile, against expectations, Penny Wong and Ian Macfarlane had struck a deal. The resulting CPRS legislation passed in the House of Representatives on 16 November, and came before the Senate the next day. On 20 November Abbott publicly declared he did not support the deal Macfarlane had negotiated, and seven days later he announced he would call for a leadership spill if Turnbull didn't quit.

The Senate debate began on Monday 23 November. Today Penny Wong thinks this was a turning point – a moment when a better outcome might have been achieved. She recalls, 'I was saying to people that time was running out, that we had to make the Senate sit, that we had to get enough of [Turnbull's] senators to vote for a motion to say we sit until we finish, over the weekend if necessary. And it didn't happen. I remember coming out of the chamber on the Thursday and saying, "Are we going to sit over the weekend?" and the decision had been made that we wouldn't.' Why? She won't say, beyond, 'Some people didn't want to do that.'

On Tuesday 1 December, Tony Abbott won a leadership spill against Malcolm Turnbull by one vote. Overnight, the party's policy on the ETS changed. The next day, Wednesday 2 December, the Coalition, the Greens and the independents combined to vote down the CPRS.

This, as it turned out, was the key vote in which the Greens' position might have made a difference. The government needed the independents and other crossbenchers as well as the Greens to pass legislation. In the earlier vote, the Greens' opposition to the legislation had borne no consequence. Even if they had voted with the government, it wouldn't have been enough. But this time it was known that some Liberal senators were considering crossing the floor to vote with Labor. The leader of the Greens' negotiating team at the time, Christine Milne, recollects, 'I didn't know how it would turn out. I thought the legislation might pass.'

As it turned out, two Liberal senators – Judith Troeth and Susan Boyce – did cross the floor. Had the Greens voted for the CPRS this time, the legislation would have passed.

Ross Garnaut comments today that it is one thing for the Greens to exercise a protest vote when it has only symbolic value. This was the vote that mattered and, despite his criticisms of the CPRS, 'it would have been better to have it than not'.

If the Greens had voted with the government in 2009, Australia would have had the CPRS since 2011. Quite possibly, Kevin Rudd would have remained prime minister, at least until the end of his term, and therefore Labor probably would have won the 2010 election outright. When a change of government came, it would have been much harder for Abbott to unpick a scheme already settled in its operation. Today, we would probably still be arguing about whether the targets in the CPRS were too modest – but at least the mechanism for action on climate change would be in place. The Greens' vote scuppered that.

Milne, though, is today unrepentant. She says that even if she had known that Troeth and Boyce would cross the floor, it would not have changed the Greens' position.

With the legislation rejected a second time, Kevin Rudd had been handed the trigger for a double dissolution election. John Faulkner and others were strongly in favour of the calling of an election. The party wargamed and prepared over summer. A study indicated that Labor would win – though perhaps not increase its majority. The figures also showed that public support for action on climate change was fast decreasing. The lengthy policy development process – with so many reports, papers and alterations, together with the continual attacks from the opposition and industry – had eroded support. The Labor national secretary, Karl Bitar, advised Rudd that if he was going to fight an election on the issue, it would need to be soon.[20]

Penny Wong, consistent with her pledge not to reveal cabinet discussions, even when others have done so, will not say what her position was, but others say she pushed hard to go to an election.

In the meantime, there was Copenhagen.

Wong left for the fifteenth Conference of the Parties to the United Nations Framework Convention on Climate Change at Copenhagen days after the parliamentary vote. She was joined by Rudd on 15 December. The conference was held in what David Marr was later to describe as the 'big bland Bella Centre',[21] eight kilometres from Copenhagen's city centre, or, as Rudd put it, 'the middle of nowhere'.[22] It was freezing outside.

Wong says she approached Copenhagen with some optimism. Her previous dealings with world leaders, including China's, had left her 'able to see what the contours of an agreement might be' – but it was clear to her very shortly after she arrived that the Chinese were not going to play ball. China and India pushed back against the Western nations of the world and their pronouncements on what should be done about climate change. The world order was changing, and China was asserting its newly acquired status as a superpower. Copenhagen was one of the places where this battle for China to be taken seriously – as a rule-maker, not only a rule-taker – played out.

By the time Kevin Rudd arrived, along with the other heads of government, the conference was deadlocked. The images beamed to the world were of chaos on the floor of the conference, with endless bickering and procedural motions. A team of developing nations had come together under China and India's leadership to block agreement.

Penny Wong and Kevin Rudd retreated with other national leaders to that windowless room. Away from the conference floor, and at the invitation of the Danish prime minister, they led a negotiating group of twenty-five countries from developed and developing nations, aiming to reach some resolution. As Rudd tells it, 'To say the surroundings were unprepossessing would be an understatement. It was a celebration of Scandinavian minimalist design. That's an elegant way of saying the room was small, airless and uncomfortable.' He and Penny Wong were to be in the room for most of the next twenty-seven hours.[23]

Painstakingly, they worked through a rough draft of an agreement, focusing on areas of disagreement – chiefly around reducing greenhouse gas emissions to the extent necessary to keep temperature rises below 2 degrees Celsius by the end of the century, and the size and timetable for a global fund to help developing nations adapt. Time was limited. So were political will and physical energy.

On that first day they continued until 3.00 a.m., when Rudd went to snatch a few hours' sleep. Penny Wong had no such luxury. She managed a little sleep on the air mattress in the corner, then took over from him and worked through the night until Rudd returned at 8.00 am, and they worked together until 1.00 the following morning. Obama joined them mid-morning the following day, rolled up his shirtsleeves and got to work. They kept trying to reach a point of compromise, strung between low-lying nations such as Bangladesh, which wanted the limit to be 1.5 degrees Celsius, and those like China and India, which baulked at 2 degrees. Rudd suggested the deliberately vague wording 'below 2 degrees centigrade', which left open the actual limit. The debate rolled on into that night. Eventually, they reached a 'landing point', in Rudd's words – the first time in the process that both developed and developing countries agreed to cuts in greenhouse gas emissions.[24]

Wong recalls Rudd as 'wonderful ... extraordinary, outstanding' at this meeting – as was Obama. 'When you're involved in politics a lot, inspiration comes sporadically. But I think they both had moments in that horrible room that were really impressive.'

Finally, at 1.00 am on the morning of the 19th, they had the text of what became known as the Copenhagen Accord. Wong and Rudd snatched an hour's sleep, then faced the media, Wong swaying on her feet.

But the chaos and the political positioning on the conference floor continued. The accord was not adopted as an officially approved resolution. It therefore had no legal status. Progress had been made in that windowless room, but so far as the world was concerned, Copenhagen had failed. In Australia, it lent credence to the view that the nation would be moving too far and too fast ahead of the rest of the world if the CPRS were passed.

Kevin Rudd recalls that even before the conference was over he was taking calls from Karl Bitar and fellow New South Wales 'machine man' Mark Arbib. In 'full panic mode', Arbib demanded that Rudd use the failure of Copenhagen to drop the CPRS back home, 'lest it kill us politically'. Rudd records, 'I told him to calm down and fuck off.'[25]

In hindsight, the Copenhagen Accord represented significant progress, even though it was not formally adopted. Its main tenets – the figure of 2 degrees; shared responsibility between both developing and developed countries; and an international system of measurement, reporting and verification – were the basis for the agreement reached at the Paris conference in 2015.

Penny Wong and Kevin Rudd had pushed themselves to the limits of physical endurance. They had done everything possible. Back in Australia, they got little credit.

Wong was interviewed just before she flew out of Copenhagen. She admitted she was disappointed, but added, 'What we need is to keep pressing on. This has never been easy.' Meanwhile, Tony Abbott was proclaiming that Copenhagen was a 'dud' and that the government should not bother reintroducing the ETS. Some in Labor, including Julia Gillard and Wayne Swan, were beginning to agree.[26]

Wong remembers meeting Christine Milne at some stage during that frantic, sleep-deprived time in the Bella Centre. She says Milne was shocked to find that no agreement would be reached. Others remember Milne taking briefings from the bureaucrats with the Australian team, and her face collapsing in horror as she realised Copenhagen, far from being the game-changer she had expected, might well fall apart. She had thought the world would move, and that meant Australia would be forced to move too. She had expected Copenhagen to reveal that Labor's CPRS was too modest, not bold enough to merit support. Wong says she told Milne, 'This is hard, Christine. Big reform is hard.' She spoke about how it entailed compromise. 'I think she maybe realised that what I was saying was right, and maybe that caused a shift in attitude.'

Milne says she doesn't recall the conversation but Wong's account accords with her state of mind at the time. Yet nothing, she insists, would have convinced her, then or now, that Labor's CPRS scheme was worthy of support.

*

Common to all the accounts of the fate of the Rudd government – except his own – is the perception that the prime minister was in a bad way after Copenhagen. Some describe it as close to a breakdown. He had panic attacks at meetings, became unable to make decisions, and the business of government bogged down.[27] Climate-change policy, in particular, drifted.

The vital decision was whether to go to a double dissolution election.

In their memoirs, both Gillard and Rudd describe – with different emphases – a key meeting in January 2010 on the verandah of Kirribilli House. Rudd writes that Gillard told him she could not support going to an election, and that they had to dump the CPRS package. This weighed heavily with him. Gillard says she advised this course of action because she considered him unfit for an election campaign, but did not tell him so. Paul Kelly, having interviewed them both, deems this 'one of their decisive encounters – complex, psychological and prone to contested interpretations'. He concludes, 'It is false to think Gillard vetoed an election, because there is no evidence Rudd wanted an early election.'[28] In the end, in Penny Wong's words, the decision not to go to a double dissolution was made 'by not making a decision'.

In Wong's view, this was the second turning point, after the failure to make the Senate sit until the legislation was passed. Once it became clear that there would be no election, she felt adrift. 'I'm not a bad politician, but I couldn't figure out what the way forward was once we knew we weren't going to a double dissolution.'

But she says that in some ways Gillard may have been right. 'I'm not sure Kevin was up for a campaign. And she's the deputy leader of the party and she has a role, and that's her call. That's a hard call to make. I didn't agree with that at the time. We should have gone to an election, and Kevin agrees with that now. But I don't discount Julia's view. Kevin was in a difficult place at the time. What is unknowable is whether he would have been in better shape if he felt he had the team around him and everyone saying, "We have to do this and we're behind you."'

In February, Kevin Rudd was considering delaying the CPRS and asked Karl Bitar to brief him on how to manage the retreat. Bitar commissioned focus groups and reported back that it was important to manage the timing and justification or it would do great damage to Rudd's standing.[29] Wong knew nothing of this at the time, but John Olenich remembers that they were both aware that Gillard and others were mounting a campaign for the policy to be dropped. Wong remembers at some stage in this period Bitar distributing polling figures that showed the CPRS had become an electoral liability. She says she responded, 'Has anyone polled how bad it would be if the prime minister stands for nothing?'

Meanwhile, Wong flew to Hobart to talk to Christine Milne, who had spent the summer preparing a Greens negotiating position, based around the idea of a fixed carbon price for two years at $23 a tonne – effectively a carbon tax – which would then segue into an Emissions Trading Scheme in which industry would pay for carbon permits and carbon emissions would be capped.[30] Milne says she got the idea of a fixed price as a starting point from Ross Garnaut. Milne recalls that she and Bob Brown were 'shocked when [Wong] rejected the scheme outright, saying she would not even take it to the prime minister for discussion'. Milne now believes this was because Labor had already decided to abandon the scheme.[31] Wong disagrees. On her account, the Greens' position was not politically realistic. As for Milne's account of their dealings, Wong says she doesn't remember refusing to take the Greens' position to Rudd, and doubts that she would have said this: 'It's not my style.' Nevertheless, Milne has repeated this claim in a number of interviews, including for this book, in her memoir, and in interviews for Paddy Manning's *Inside the Greens*.[32]

Wong believes that in this period Rudd had not decided to abandon the CPRS, but was searching for a fix that did not exist. He called for more papers and more analysis. She wanted him to face up to the battle. His focus had turned to health and hospitals. He would not. Meanwhile, Gillard was 'implacable' in wanting the CPRS dropped. Wong remembers, 'It was difficult between us ... I've given a lot of thought to what I might have done differently through all this time, but by this stage, given that I didn't have the backing of the deputy prime minister and the treasurer, it was pretty hard for me to hold the line. It was hard for Kevin for the same reasons.'

The issue came to a head at a meeting of the so-called Gang of Four – the cabinet's Strategic Priorities and Budget Committee – on 21 April. Gillard and Swan insisted that Rudd drop the CPRS in the context of finalising the federl budget. This was the moment when Rudd rang Wong in Honolulu, who gave him the advice that turned out to be 'exactly right' – that backing away from the CPRS would be disastrous for his personal standing. Nevertheless, he made what in his memoir he admits was one of the worst mistakes of his political career: he agreed to drop it from the budget. Labor would delay the scheme until the end of 2012, and then proceed only if there was international progress.

Rudd claims that he would have reopened the discussion at the full meeting of cabinet the following week but that option was closed down by a leak. On 27 April, journalist Lenore Taylor broke the news that the CPRS had been dropped.[33] Rudd blames Gillard for that leak, seeing it as designed to damage him.[34] Gillard describes it as damaging but is silent on its source. Wong, meanwhile, says, 'I still get stressed when I remember that day. Lenore had the whole box and dice. She knew the lot.'

Like all good journalists, Taylor will not reveal her source, but she says today there was no single source for the leak. She heard a version of events and tried to check it out. Some whom she would have expected to know if a decision had been taken in fact knew nothing, making her think what she had heard must be wrong. It took her days to be confident enough of the story to publish.

Kevin Rudd portrays the Lenore Taylor story as what locked in the decision to drop the CPRS. Penny Wong disagrees. 'I think I knew I'd lost before it leaked. The leak was an awful political problem ... it was a bad decision by the government that had been leaked in a way that maximised the damage. Once you have a shift like that and it leaks and it comes out without any explanation, it's catastrophic.'

The impact on Rudd's popularity ratings was immediate. His moral authority never recovered.

*

The move on Kevin Rudd by Julia Gillard and her supporters in June 2010 blew up fast out of a groundswell of panic and personal animosity, fuelled by factional powerbrokers and made possible by Rudd's reduced standing.[35] Doing the numbers for Gillard were the powerbrokers of the Right, prominent among them Senator Don Farrell – one side of the Machine power-sharing deal in South Australia. It was a revolt fomented not chiefly in cabinet but in the caucus, with backbenchers nervous about their seats.

Mark Butler, at this time a backbencher and the parliamentary secretary for health, had heard the rumbles. The plotters were saying that Julia Gillard was more competent than Kevin Rudd, that the government was adrift and change was needed, that marginal seats would otherwise be at risk. Butler knew more about what was brewing than some cabinet ministers, who found out for the first time that the move was on when it broke on *ABC News* on the evening of 23 June.

Meanwhile, Wong had been trying to show support for Rudd, even as she struggled to justify the decision, which she had so vehemently opposed, to drop the CPRS.[36] As late as 19 June, quizzed by a journalist on whether there was a move against the prime minister, she denied it. She said the claim 'couldn't be further from the truth ... we are absolutely focused and united behind Kevin.'[37]

Wong says there were problems with Kevin Rudd's prime ministership but they have been exaggerated by those who deposed him to justify their actions. 'People make things "more binary" than they really were,' she says. Rudd was doing too much. He had a tendency, when things became difficult, to become paralysed, or simply move on to the next issue rather than dealing with the difficulty. It was, she thinks, a symptom of being emotionally overwhelmed. 'I learned from that. You can't allow yourself to become paralysed when things become difficult ... And all these brilliant people who were advising him: they might criticise him now, but at the time none of them came up with anything except telling him to retreat ... What was their great strategy? Something which killed a prime minister and massively damaged the government.'

She thinks it a failure of cabinet that the problems with Rudd were not managed. Frank conversations should have been had with the prime minister about what needed to change, and about his deputy's ambitions and the need to restrain them. Those conversations never happened. 'I carry my share of the blame for that,' she says. Butler, though, excuses her. Her position as the 'senior junior' meant that it was not her place to have those discussions. Rather, it should have been Gillard herself, Swan and the other senior ministers.

Rudd claims in his memoir that Gillard 'despised' Wong. He writes, 'From Julia's perspective, "Wong", as she routinely referred to her, was an "inner-city leftie" who just didn't understand the real world.'[38] Gillard, in her memoir, describes herself as 'among Penny Wong's supporters' and an admirer of her 'abilities and cool head'.[39]

Wong herself regards her relationship with both Rudd and Gillard at that time as mainly good. Gillard was not a friend but, despite their disagreements over the CPRS and the difficulties that caused, their relationship was 'professional and courteous'. If Gillard despised her, she never saw any signs of it.

But she agrees with Anthony Albanese that the leadership change of June 2010 'destroyed two Labor prime ministers'. Rudd had his problems, but his policy analysis was 'brilliant'. Gillard should have been a 'great prime minister, she should have won another election and gone on after that. She is one of the best politicians I know.' But the manner of her ascension to the prime ministership destroyed her credibility and propelled her to the position before she was ready for it.

On the evening of 23 June, after the challenge became breaking news on the ABC, Mark Butler and Penny Wong were besieged in their parliamentary offices. All the ordinary rules about where television cameras were allowed to go in Parliament House were disregarded as the press gallery tried to make up for having been ambushed by the imminent challenge. There were cameras stationed at the end of the corridor in the ministerial wing.

Nobody got much sleep that night. Butler and Wong spent a lot of the time together. Albanese came in and out, also spending time with Rudd.

He and Butler worked the phones for the embattled incumbent, trying to bring numbers his way. None of them – Butler, Wong and Albanese – thought the move to depose Rudd was a good idea.

Sometime late at night, Butler and Albanese raised their eyes from the telephones. It was clear that Gillard had the numbers. They were powerless. They could not stop what was going to happen.

Butler and Wong conferred. Wong says now, 'We realised this was happening. It was a crock for the party. So what do we do, how do we best deal with this?' Butler remembers that they talked about whether a statement in support of Rudd would make a difference, and concluded it was too late. 'We moved on to talk about how the next several hours would unfold, and what we could do to minimise the damage to the party. And we thought that making the switch to Julia, making it clear that it was a decisive switch, was probably the right thing to do.'

As the sun rose on a new day, Butler contacted the other members of the South Australian Left in caucus to tell them his thinking. The South Australian Left would vote for Julia Gillard.

Rudd records that at about this time Albanese visited him in his office and told him, 'You're fucked. And I don't think you should run.'[40]

There was no vote. Tears streaming down his face, Kevin Rudd announced at the party meeting on 24 June that he would not put Labor through the trauma of a caucus ballot, and resigned as leader in favour of Julia Gillard.

Four days later, Gillard announced her new cabinet. Penny Wong retained her portfolios of water and climate change. The day after that, Wong was on a plane bound for Rome. The Major Economies Forum on Energy and Climate – held in the Abruzzi regional centre of L'Aquila, which had been struck by a deadly earthquake only three months earlier – brought together the relevant ministers from the United States, China, India, Europe and Brazil to advance the agenda on international action ahead of the UN Climate Change Conference in Mexico that November.

Meanwhile, Julia Gillard announced that a price on carbon was one of her priorities, but that there needed to be community consensus to achieve it, and this might take years. She announced a citizens' assembly to discuss the issue and was ridiculed in the media for the apparent lack of political will and leadership that implied. Penny Wong held the line, echoing her leader's words. The Liberal Party and the Greens were to blame for the defeat of the CPRS, she said. She dodged and weaved, backing the prime minister as best she could.

Julia Gillard called the election for 21 August 2010. The result, after a difficult campaign beset by damaging leaks usually seen as coming from Rudd, was a hung parliament – the first in seventy years. During the seventeen days it took for Gillard to strike a deal with the Greens and the independents, Penny Wong suddenly had time on her hands. Gillard recalls ringing her one morning and discovering that she was roasting spices – 'making a complex meal from scratch to release her energies and fill in the time'.[41]

The deal was done when independents Tony Windsor and Rob Oakeshott declared for the Gillard government. In the new ministry, Penny Wong was to be the minister for finance. Greg Combet was to replace her in the climate change portfolio. It was rumoured that Penny Wong lost the portfolio at the request of the Greens. Sarah Hanson-Young told the media that the minority government would mark a 'new era' and that the minister for climate change needed to be 'more consultative and a better communicator' than the 'abrasive and dismissive' Penny Wong.[42] Other reports said that although Wong had been one of Labor's most promising parliamentarians she had failed to 'cut through' in the climate change portfolio.[43]

Wong says she asked for the change of job and recommended Combet as her replacement. Partly this was because she wanted to try something new, especially after such a difficult two and a half years in the portfolio. Partly it was because if action on climate change was to advance under the minority government, '[We] had to have ostensibly a fresh start. The Greens had to have a different face, and I didn't think I would be the right person.'

Greg Combet, Julia Gillard and Christine Milne went on to cut a deal that allowed for the introduction of an ETS with a fixed price on

1 July 2012. The negotiations were gruelling, affecting Combet's already failing health. At every stage, Combet thought the most likely outcome was that the Greens would walk from the negotiations. Milne agrees that almost happened.[44] Nevertheless, Combet developed a 'constructive and friendly working relationship' with her.[45]

Milne says today that she still believes the amount of assistance given to industry in the deal she brokered with Combet was far too high. The Greens agreed to it reluctantly, to get legislation through. As for the emissions reduction targets, on which they could not agree, the issue was defused by concurrence on setting up a Climate Change Authority of independent experts who would recommend the future target and therefore the cap when the scheme moved from a fixed price to one set by the market. In other words, a mechanism was agreed to put off the difficult issue of targets – and on industry assistance the Greens crumbled, bargaining in return for the establishment of a Clean Energy Finance Corporation (CEFC) and the Australian Renewable Energy Agency (ARENA).

Wong, meanwhile, says today that the policy negotiated between the Greens and Combet was basically the same as the one she and Rudd had tried to get through the parliament, but this second scheme included more compensation delivered faster to the energy sector. The other main differences were the CEFC and ARENA, and some of the assistance for industry was brought forward.

All of which raises the question of whether it might have been possible to cut a deal with the Greens in 2008, when Rudd and Wong first attempted to introduce the CPRS. Could a different negotiator have achieved this outcome earlier?

The Greens have copped a lot of flak from the Labor Party for voting with the Coalition to defeat the CPRS in 2009. Butler, for example, describes it as 'inexplicable ... an appalling tactical decision' and says Milne is 'hopelessly inaccurate' when she claims the Gillard scheme was better. He suggests that the Greens simply realised their error and chose not to repeat it a second time around.[46]

Garnaut believes it 'might have been better' if Wong and Rudd had at least talked to the Greens, setting up a second option if agreement with the Coalition could not be struck. Other observers suggest that had talks been held with the Greens, it might have been possible to play them and the Coalition's negotiators off against each other, increasing the pressure on the opposition to cut a deal acceptable to business.

Penny Wong does not agree. In her view, the Greens of ten years ago were incapable of compromise, and it was only 'when reality hit' Christine Milne in Copenhagen that their attitude changed. 'Then they copped it. They copped precisely the same scheme with a bit of money thrown at renewables, which was fine and I supported that. But the fundamental problem is the Greens have a kind of shallow view about the economy and economic players. They just dismiss any proposition that is about economic transition as being somehow about giving money to the big polluters. There is no kind of reality about what a transformation of this kind of scale means for industry.'

Labor faithful scorn the Greens, seeing them as stealing votes on the left. In kind, many Greens despise Labor. Christine Milne says that Labor had come to love power for its own sake. She describes Wong as a machine party politician, prepared to make any compromise to advance her career. When Wong talks about the Greens, there is a noticeable tone of contempt that goes beyond party positions. The Greens offend her foundational commitment to political life – the need to exercise the discipline, hard work, compromise and responsibility that go with being 'in the room' in a party that aspires to form government. In the view of many Labor people, including Wong, the Greens were cynically pursuing their own electoral advantage in 2009 – needing to appear on higher moral ground than Labor to maintain their hold on the left-wing vote.

Combet agrees that negotiating with the Greens would have been impossible in 2009. In his memoir, he notes:

This still makes me furious … How different would Australian climate-change policy have been if the Greens had acted responsibly in 2009? A carbon price would have been entrenched as a lasting reform … The Greens' answer to this charge is that Rudd preferred to negotiate with Turnbull, not them. That's true. But Labor had little alternative given the economic foolishness and the uncompromising nature of the Greens' position in 2009.[47]

Gillard, too, criticises Rudd for not engaging with the Greens in 2009 but, in one of her few concessions to him, says, 'The Greens would have voted the same way no matter what Kevin did. They wanted to look purer than Labor in the eyes of environmentally aware voters.'[48]

Could Penny Wong and Kevin Rudd have struck a deal with the Greens, either in 2009 or in early 2010? It is, as Penny Wong is fond of saying, a counterfactual. And those, she believes, are self-indulgent when entertained in retrospect.

*

What would Penny Wong do differently, if she had her time again and the benefit of hindsight?

The turning points, she says, were the decision not to make the Senate sit in November 2009 until the legislation was through, and the failure to call a double dissolution election. She concedes that setting a 25 per cent target, conditional on international action, might have been smarter in the first draft of the scheme. It would have made no difference in implementation, given the failure of Copenhagen, but would have blunted the environmentalists' attacks.

She agrees that communications with the public about the progress towards the CPRS were poor, and that public support for action on climate change was allowed to wither away. 'I could have communicated better ... I think that I had too much work – such a heavy load of policy work. It was very hard to find headspace for communications strategy ... I didn't make mistakes with the media the way others did, but I wasn't particularly retail.'

Ideally, such a communications strategy would have been a whole-of-cabinet effort, in which all ministers, including 'some of our better retail politicians', would have been engaged. But she lacked the seniority to impose that. And 'Rudd had too much on. We needed Swan and

Gillard to be more frontline.' But by the end of 2009, they were her main opponents on climate-change action within the cabinet.

It has been suggested by some that in retrospect it would have been better to move very quickly after the 2007 election, while public support was high, the policy at least theoretically bipartisan and business primed for change. Perhaps, the critics suggest, a narrower scheme embracing fewer industries, based on Howard's nascent moves, should have been introduced, then improved over time.[49] Wong disagrees. 'I have a lot of faults, but I can work through policy detail and formulation pretty bloody fast, and we could not have moved faster while making sure that we weren't going to tank the economy or have unintended consequences. I don't think we did anything wrong at all in terms of the policy development and I don't believe we could have done it any faster.'

The emissions reduction scheme introduced by the Gillard minority government became the focus of Tony Abbott's attacks. It was persuasively dubbed a 'great big new tax'. Gillard, in what she admits was one of her largest political errors, aided the attack by agreeing that the scheme could be described as a tax – making it possible for her to be accused of breaking an earlier commitment not to introduce one. Abbott declared the 2013 election would be a referendum on the 'carbon tax'.[50] After his victory, Abbott moved to repeal the ETS as one of his first actions in government. Labor and the crossbenchers blocked the legislation in the Senate, but when the new Senate sat in July 2014, it passed.

Meanwhile, Penny Wong had emerged from the leadership coup with the respect of all sides. She was no longer a 'junior senior' but unquestionably at the centre of Labor's leadership team.

Mark Butler remarks that one of the things that earned her respect was the way she dealt with the April 2010 decision to dump the CPRS. A different kind of politician, he says, would have resigned, or grown bitter and begun to leak. She did neither. She plugged on, doing her best to maintain the appearance of unity. In Christine Milne's eyes, this is evidence of her ambition. In the eyes of Penny Wong's colleagues, it is evidence of her principle, her decency, her commitment to the party and her cool head. She stayed in the room.

But that was behind the scenes. In public, Wong was attacked for being stilted in her communications and blamed for the failure of the policy.[51] Paul Keating's former speechwriter Don Watson, promoting his book on plain English, claimed her 'dead language' and management speak were so bad he couldn't bear to listen to her.[52]

In the maelstrom of April 2009, with despair about international action, panic in the party about the political cost, and Kevin Rudd losing his touch, Penny Wong was the only person advising the prime minister to hold fast to the policy and push on, the only one to warn him that dropping the CPRS would be disastrous. History shows it was extraordinarily good political judgement.

11

A WOMAN OF GOVERNMENT

P enny Wong rose to speak four days after her forty-second birthday and a little under three months after a bruising 2010 election outcome that resulted in Labor under Julia Gillard forming a minority government. Wong's first grey hairs were becoming apparent.

She had been invited to deliver the annual John Button Memorial Lecture, an opportunity to make a statement of purpose and lay out a vision. Her words that day were not only a public intervention but also, most likely, a bit of self-talk – a salve for her wounds and a reminder of what she believed. They were a justification for the political compromises she had made, and a recommitment to carrying on.

It is also possible to read her speech as an answer to the accusations from Christine Milne and others on the left that she was nothing more than a machine politician, consistently prepared to compromise principle for the sake of power.

Her theme was the discipline imposed by being a member of a party that sought to form government. Underlying the speech were familiar parts of her longstanding intellectual architecture. Although it is not explicitly stated, there is the commitment to 'staying in the room' and to seeking compromise in the pursuit of progress. Also implicit is the commitment to *praxis* – practical political action in the quest for change.

To this she added a third term, which today is among those her staff refer to as 'Wongisms': frequently used phrases, verbal tics. It is the word 'counterfactual'.

Penny Wong may well say counterfactuals in retrospect are self-indulgent, but when she looks forward, she takes a more positive view. Talking to her staff as they try to navigate their way around a difficult political problem, she encourages them to use the concept as an analytical tool. Before deciding on a course of action, she will say, 'Consider the counterfactual.' What would happen if the other course were chosen?

It was this kind of thinking that had enabled her to respond to Karl Bitar's polling figures showing the CPRS was a liability with the comment, 'Has anyone polled how bad it would be if the prime minister stands for nothing?' and to see clearly, in the awful pressure and panic of April 2009, what the impact on the government of dropping the CPRS would be.

In the John Button speech, she imagined the counterfactual of an Australian Labor Party not dedicated to forming government, with all the persuasion and compromise that involved. The Labor values were summed up as 'A fair go. A just society. A strong economy.' She referred to the trend of which she was both advocate and personification – the broadening of Labor's understanding of social equity from male white workers to something more inclusive. It was an ongoing project, she said. 'A fair go in 1960 would look less so today. A just society today, I hope, would look more inclusive than one in 1960.'

The Labor values were 'both subjective and dynamic ... inherently contestable', and resisted strict definition. But they demonstrated 'an understanding of the relationship between the ... community and the experience of the individual. A community that marginalises is not strong. Exclusion does not equate to unity. Equality has little relevance if it does not manifest as opportunity. And prosperity must be created to be shared.'

She spoke of the Whitlam Labor government: its social reforms but also its 'cautionary tale for progressives ... public confidence in a government's economic credentials is essential'. She spoke of the economic reforms of Hawke and Keating. 'The manner in which those reforms were delivered is instructive for Labor today. The drive to reform is not easy, but the benefits of positioning the economy and the country for long terms are pivotal. Worthy reform will always have critics and is almost always resisted.'

The economy, she said, was central to progressive politics. It was 'a reminder of the uniqueness of both Labor's position on the political field, and of our platform ... Those that view themselves on our left do not see the economy as their responsibility; those to our right do not see the economy as an enabler of opportunity.'

Then she returned to the place of Labor in Australian politics. It was a challenging time for the party. 'A low primary vote is a problem. A primary vote that is eroding from the left and the right is a more complex problem.' She continued:

The Labor project is to marry a mandate to govern with progressive values and economic responsibility. No other party or movement replicates this in Australia. This unique position brings with it two aspects of political character. The first is that we seek to form government. We cannot simply appeal to those who already agree with us, nor dismiss any who do not.

... We do not simply seek a Senate quota, nor to target a particular seat. We seek to govern Australia for all Australians. We never have the luxury of only playing to a narrow audience. We have to build agreement. We have to persuade. This involves far more than compromise, although some would airily define it as such. It demands both courage to hold firm, and the capacity to convince. It is not easy.

She concluded with the counterfactual. What would Australia be like if the Australian Labor Party had never formed government?

I'd ask those who criticise to contemplate an Australia without Labor governments. An Australia without a party committed to governing for progressive change. An Australia without universal health care, where someone's income, not injury determined the level of care they received. An Australia not brave enough to recognise those whose land we inhabit, not big-hearted enough to apologise to those we have harmed. An Australia where workers' rights extend no further than the minimum wage, and the most basic of conditions. An Australia where the opportunity embodied in tertiary education remained beyond the reach of those most in need. An Australia where gender and race can overshadow ability. An Australia where parochial interests drove economic decision-making, where we failed to open our eyes to the region and the world beyond our shores.[1]

It is complicated to be Penny Wong. She is dedicated to the Australian Labor Party, a true believer in the values she outlined in the John Button lecture. At the same time she is an artefact of its progress, and of a changing Australia. She both moulds and has been moulded by the party, the country and its limitations and strengths. She is an exemplar of a question of the times – do political processes work? Is it possible for someone of integrity and ability to make a difference? Does politics still work? There was no previous time in Australian history when a gay Asian woman could have risen so high in politics, and yet she is committed to maintaining solidarity in a party that includes social conservatives. It means that, as well as embodying change, she was destined to disappoint those who expected her to act as though outside or above party politics.

Five months before the John Button lecture, in July 2010, as the Labor Party approached the election, Wong had come under sustained attack from the gay community after an appearance on Channel Ten's *Meet the Press*. It began well: most of the discussion had been about the election campaign, and her portfolio responsibilities of climate change and water. That night there was to be an election debate between Julia Gillard and Tony Abbott. It coincided with the finale of the reality-television program *MasterChef*, and the timing of the debate's airing had been altered so the two didn't clash. Wong told the audience she liked to cook and would watch the debate, then switch 'straight to *MasterChef*'.

At the end of the program, the focus turned to questions sent in by viewers. One queried her support for the Labor Party's opposition to same-sex marriage. In a relatively unguarded moment, Penny Wong came as close as she ever had to expressly supporting Labor Party policy against same-sex marriage – rather than speaking in generalities about party solidarity, as she usually did. She talked about how Labor had removed discrimination against same-sex couples under many different pieces of legislation. The Rudd government had delivered on the moves agreed at the time of the 2004 *Marriage Act* debate, and same-sex couples were now treated equally in superannuation, social security, health care and many other areas of law. In total, more than eighty pieces of legislation had been changed. But, she said, 'On the issue of marriage, I think the reality is there is a cultural, religious and historical view around that we have to respect.' She claimed she respected the Labor Party view of marriage being between a man and a woman. 'I am part of a party and I support the party's policies.'[2]

Before that night's *MasterChef* contestants had assembled their ingredients, Penny Wong was at the centre of a social media storm that rapidly broke into the mainstream press. The spokesman for the group Australian Marriage Equality, Alex Greenwich, called her a hypocrite. It was once the 'cultural, religious and historical view' that women should not be members of parliament, that Asians should not be allowed into Australia and that lesbians should not exist, 'yet thankfully all that changed, allowing people like Penny Wong to contribute to Australian society at the highest level', he said.[3] Bob Brown, the leader of the Greens, said her words had 'horrified' him. 'To somehow excuse discrimination ... on the basis of culture or heritage ... Are we going to bring back in hanging?'[4]

The next night, Penny Wong kept a scheduled appearance with the ABC's *Q&A* television program, appearing on a panel that included Malcolm Turnbull and Christine Milne, as well as former Labor minister Graham Richardson. Milne and Wong tangled over the Greens having voted down the CPRS. Milne argued that the scheme was too 'browned down'. Wong responded, 'Oh, give us a break ... it's not economically effective to shut down the electricity sector and disrupt security of supply, Christine.' The panellists all talked over one another. Richardson posited that the previous evening's *MasterChef* had been more interesting than the 'very boring' leaders' debate.

Penny Wong knew that after the controversy of her *Meet the Press* appearance she would be asked about gay rights. Earlier that day she had talked to Lois Boswell, who had warned her that almost anything she said would 'blow the whole show up'. Boswell was referring to the behind-the-scenes preparations for that year's South Australian Labor Party convention. Negotiations and lobbying with the socially conservative unions of the Right had been taking place for months. One false step now could scupper the effort.

The inevitable question came towards the end of the show, from audience member Danielle Raffaele. 'Penny, you say that you support your party's decision to be against gay marriage, even though you are gay yourself. How can you sit idly back and allow yourself to remain silent about the obvious inequality that you are kept in?'

The audience erupted in applause.

Penny Wong turned to the chair, Tony Jones, and *sotto voce* warned him that her answer might take a while. Then she launched into a mini-speech.

She said that when she had entered the parliament she had thought 'very carefully about how to handle being Asian and gay and in the parliament, because it hadn't been done before'. She had decided to be open about who she was, and never shy away from it, and to 'try to be dignified, even when it might be difficult ... part of the reason I did that was I thought it was very important to show that you should never be ashamed of who you are, even when there are people who would try to make you be'.

She went on to talk about the work that she, Anthony Albanese, Tanya Plibersek and others were doing to 'improve the party's position' on gay rights, and the legislative changes achieved during the Rudd government. 'These are things that make a real difference to people's lives ... Now, I accept that you and some other people in the community would like us to have a different position in terms of marriage. That isn't the position in the party but what I would say to you is do take a moment to consider what we have tried to do, what we have advocated for and what we have delivered for gay and lesbian Australians.'

The round of muted applause was interrupted by Christine Milne denouncing Labor's 'lack of leadership' on the issue. Gillard should be allowing a conscience vote on same-sex legislation sponsored by the Greens and then before the parliament, she said.

Tony Jones batted that back to Penny Wong, who said she didn't agree with conscience votes. 'If we'd had conscience votes in the Labor Party on a range of issues ... there are many reforms which would not have been achieved. I have a view that you join a team, you're part of the team, and that's the way ... we operate.'

Jones threw it back to the audience, and a man asked why, if Malcolm Turnbull could disagree with his party's policy on climate change, Penny Wong couldn't disagree with her party on same-sex marriage. At that point, to everyone's surprise, Graham Richardson interrupted with a fierce defence of Penny Wong. As a senior figure of the party, he knew something of what was going on behind the scenes.

'Look, I'm amazed somewhat by these questions, really ... There are a lot of people in the Labor Party who don't agree with this stuff. At the moment there's nowhere near a majority, but there will be. There will be over time because Penny will work for it and it will get up in the end. But give her a break, for God's sake. She's part of a caucus. There's a whole lot of them. She doesn't run the government, she's a part of it ... There's a thing called cabinet solidarity ... and if she wants to break it she gets nowhere. You'll lose someone who fights for your cause. That, my friends, is dumb. Big-time dumb.'

While he spoke, Penny Wong sipped water and kept her eyes down. It was an example of that ability she had developed in school. To stay still and calm, even when emotions were raging.

Since Wong had voted in favour of Howard's changes to the *Marriage Act* in 2004, the party platform had been modified to support the removal of discrimination against same-sex couples under federal laws.

This had been opposed by some, but figures on the Right had been gradually persuaded to come on board. One of them was Joe Ludwig, of the Queensland Right. Wong recalls, 'He was a lawyer. He told me he went back to first principles. "Is this discrimination? Yes. Is it justified? No." ... It was an example of how that very traditional Labor notion of fairness sometimes overcomes people's personal prejudice.'

When Labor came to government in 2007, the platform was implemented. Labor kept the promise it had made in 2004 to remove legal discrimination against gay couples. Same-sex couples were now equal to heterosexual couples under Medicare, social security and superannuation legislation. The next step in the strategy was meant to be recognition of civil unions. Rudd had discussed this policy publicly, but in 2009 had acted to hose down debate on the issue at the national conference. At this stage, Rudd was personally opposed to same-sex marriage.

Meanwhile, Penny Wong and the members of Rainbow Labor – including, later on, her deputy chief of staff, Tom Mooney – worked to engage gay party members across the factions. John Olenich, her former staffer, had also been involved in Rainbow Labor. As he puts it today, Rainbow Labor, with Penny's staff centrally involved, had gradually changed the position in the party. In 2004, there hadn't been the capacity to take the issue head on but, says Olenich, Rainbow Labor had 'gradually chipped away and helped give Penny the political space to push the platform forward'. As Graham Richardson told the *Q&A* audience, it was generally thought that the numbers in Labor were still nowhere near a majority in favour of same-sex marriage, and even civil unions were likely to be opposed. But things were changing in surprising ways.

Gillard had declared herself opposed to same-sex marriage. This was widely understood as a condition of her alliance with Don Farrell, socially conservative leader of the South Australian Right faction, and one of the so-called 'faceless men' who had engineered her challenge against Kevin Rudd. Wong says today she had 'no insight and no direct knowledge' of such a deal, but she remembers talking about Gillard's stance with her own mother, Jane Chapman. 'Mum isn't involved in the detail of politics, but she said something very shrewd. She said it was a problem for Gillard because it was inexplicable. People would not understand how an atheist and a single woman in a de facto relationship could hold those views ... It added to that idea that she was somehow not authentic.'

In late 2010 the issue became part of the campaign of leaks – generally seen as being from Kevin Rudd or his supporters – that undermined Gillard's leadership. One revealed that Rudd had agreed privately with 'key Left faction leaders' to back same-sex civil unions, and that he had also intended to grant Labor MPs a conscience vote on same-sex marriage.[5] The next day, under pressure, Gillard announced that the Labor Party national conference scheduled for 2012 would be brought forward by more than six months, to December 2011, to allow for a full-blown debate over the party's policy differences.

But in the meantime there was the South Australian Labor convention, which took place just three weeks after Penny Wong gave the John Button Memorial Lecture. Wong had warned Gillard weeks before that at this conference she would publicly support a change to the party platform. This she could do in consistency with party rules because it was, as Kevin Rudd helpfully noted, 'within the formal processes of the Australian Labor Party'.[6] In Wong's judgement and that of her allies, there was now for the first time the 'political space' to move forward. If she had done it previously, she would have lost, and damaged herself in the process.

At the convention, as the most senior South Australian member, she held Julia Gillard's proxy. Knowing that she couldn't use it on this issue, she gave it to Don Farrell. That meant her opponents had an extra vote.

A motion called on the Labor national conference to amend the party's platform to support same-sex marriage. Farrell gave an incendiary speech. Recognising same-sex marriage would destroy the government, he said. It would mean the party had been 'hijacked' by the Greens. 'The Greens are running a bowl of issues up and trying to wedge the Labor Party.' The din while he spoke distorted the audio on the recordings. There were loud calls of 'Shame!' on both sides.

Then Wong rose to her feet. Her speech was just over 800 words long, but in terms of the party's internal politics it was seismic. Not only was she, after six years of publicly backing party policy, 'coming out' in favour of changing the party platform, she was also opposing the prime minister, Julia Gillard – who was already under attack on multiple fronts, from Abbott and also from Rudd.

Wong referred to her own experiences of racial discrimination and her reasons for joining the party. 'In the Labor Party, I saw the capacity to turn principle into action. I was not interested in simply criticising. I was not interested in simply talking about change. I wanted to be part of delivering it.'

She appealed to the party's tradition of fairness – the history of advocating for equality, from ending the White Australia policy to land rights and laws against racial and sex discrimination:

> Delegates, there has been some commentary which has confused my position of not commenting publicly on this issue with my position on the actual issue itself ... talking about change is not the same as delivering it. And delivering change is not the same thing as seeking headlines. There are some, including in the Greens political party, who would have Australians believe that the only test of one's commitment to equality is how loudly you criticise and how much you shout. Commitment to equality is also present when you deliver change as part of a party of government. And commitment to equality is also there when you seek to persuade and not only to condemn. And the commitment to equality does not recede because so many of us respect the principles of solidarity – the same principles which have helped deliver so much change over so many years.[7]

There was a standing ovation.

She did not expect to win the vote, although she judged she could move the issue forward. But when the motion was put it passed 90–88. The Right had split, and Don Farrell – the godfather of the Right and

Julia Gillard's numbers man – had been humiliated on the floor of the conference.

Wong remembers, 'I asked people, "How did we win this? How did that happen?"'

People directed her to the secretary of one of the unions usually allied with Farrell's socially conservative Shoppies, who had corralled his votes in her support. She went over. 'I said, "Thank you," and I asked him why. And he kind of shrugged and said, "It's my daughter." I nearly cried. And I thought, *This is why we will win. Because if you love someone, how can you tolerate them being treated that way?*

This was the first Labor state conference to support a change to the national platform on same-sex marriage. It was a precursor to the national conference, an indication that Gillard might face defeat on the issue in a year's time.

*

Eight months later, once again, Wong's personal and political lives intersected. In August she announced that her partner, Sophie Allouache, was pregnant. Under South Australian law, the couple had been prevented from seeking an IVF donor locally. Instead they had used sperm from a friend and undergone IVF in New South Wales. The baby was due in December – the same month in which the Labor national conference would debate same-sex marriage.

Wong had agonised over whether to make a public announcement of the pregnancy. But, on advice, she accepted the impossibility of keeping it secret, and knew that, in the context of the impending party debate, trying to do so would only make the invasive publicity worse. Getting the news out early was best. Her office released a brief statement on 9 August 2011 that stated the biological father was known to them. His identity would also be known to the child, but they would otherwise keep private the details of the pregnancy. 'Like any expecting parents, the prospect of welcoming this child into our lives fills us both with joy,' the statement said, and asked the media to respect their privacy.[8]

Fat chance. In newsrooms across the world, journalists immediately began scrabbling for the few public images of Sophie Allouache and Penny Wong together – one at the Canberra Midwinter Ball the previous year, another from when Wong was sworn into the Rudd ministry. Radio talkback lines ran hot. Television news went into overdrive; the ABC's *The Drum* even devoted a segment to the pregnancy.

It seemed that everyone had an opinion. New South Wales Christian Democratic MP Fred Nile said the conception should not have happened and should not have been made public: 'It just promotes their lesbian lifestyle and trying to make it natural when it's unnatural.'[9] Julia Gillard congratulated the couple and was, inevitably, asked whether it was fair that they could not marry. She responded that the 'strongly held views' in the party would be debated at the national conference and protested that she was a long-term friend of Wong and happy for her.[10] Sarah Hanson-Young said it was 'wonderful news'. South Australian premier Jay Weatherill – referred to in news reports as Penny Wong's former partner – said that Wong and Allouache were 'a lovely couple' and would make wonderful parents. New South Wales Liberal senator Concetta Fierravanti-Wells asserted that children were entitled to both a father and a mother. Terri Kelleher of the Australian Family Association told Channel Seven 'they can be good parents but neither of them can be a good father'.[11] A columnist based in the Middle East wrote about the pregnancy for an Arabic newspaper published in London and opined, 'Here, I thank God we are backwards.'[12]

At a media conference on the day of her announcement, Wong tried to talk about the business of government – recently released monthly financial statements – but inevitably ended up answering questions about the pregnancy. 'I think I've made it clear how I want to handle this,' she said, and maintained that line.

Meanwhile, hate mail began to flow into her office and dominate her social media feeds. The many congratulations on Twitter – some from people saying they wanted to have Wong's baby – were balanced by the poison. Miranda Devine published a strange opinion piece saying that the pregnancy was a cause of 'private celebration' but should not be publicly celebrated. 'The unorthodox situation of a lesbian artificially inseminated with the sperm of a male "acquaintance" we are supposed to laud as if it were the Second Coming, the wonderful precursor of what *The New York Times* once lauded as the "post-marital" future … it is politically incorrect to say so but the ideal situation for a child is to be brought up in an intact family with a father and a mother.'[13] The comedian and 'professional homosexual' Tom Ballard posted a thirteen-minute YouTube video in response to Devine, titled 'Miranda Devine: what the f&*k are you talking about?'[14] It went viral.

By 15 August, six days after the announcement, her office having withstood the most intense pressure, Penny Wong was again being interviewed on the Australian economy and whether she thought the federal budget would return to an increasingly chimerical surplus.[15] Behind the scenes, the couple continued to get some hate mail. That continues to the present day, as does homophobia on Twitter.

*

In her memoir *My Story*, Julia Gillard describes same-sex marriage as 'the most explosive' issue at the 2011 national party conference. She claims that, despite what Kevin Rudd was saying publicly at the time, she was personally in favour of civil unions; she had only helped put a lid on the debate at the national conference in 2009 'at Kevin's request'. She argues that her position is not that same-sex marriage is too radical, but rather that it is not radical enough. Marriage itself is an archaic institution. 'While my own reasoning and position were undoubtedly idiosyncratic, I nevertheless created the space for Labor to have the debate and resolve it.'

This is indisputable. By bringing the national conference forward, Gillard allowed it to be a genuine debate and airing of divisions rather than the stage-managed display of unity that would have been necessary had it been held closer to the 2013 election.

But, as the conference approached, it became clear that Gillard was likely to face a humiliating defeat on the issue. The party's two most prominent gay politicians – Penny Wong from the Left and Andrew

Barr, the Australian Capital Territory deputy chief minister, from the Right – were to move and second the motion that the party policy on same-sex marriage be changed. Michelle Grattan, doyen of the press gallery, described it as a 'pincer movement' with Gillard in its grip.

Gillard had staged a tactical retreat. Realising she would likely lose the substantive motion, she was appealing for enough support for a compromise motion – to allow Labor MPs a conscience vote when the issue came before the parliament. Grattan said: 'Losing the conscience vote would be a disaster for Ms Gillard, who has put her authority on the line over it.'[16] Penny Wong and most of the Left would oppose the conscience vote.

On the Friday before the key vote, Gillard appealed to factional leaders and senior cabinet ministers – including Anthony Albanese, the parliamentary party's longest-standing campaigner for gay rights, and by now a close ally of Penny Wong. They agreed to help her save face by backing a conscience vote.

The motion came before conference on 3 December, a Saturday, and the second day of the gathering. Ardent speeches were given on both sides. Joe de Bruyn, national president of the Shoppies, protested that 'since the dawn of humanity' marriage had been the union of a man and a woman.[17] Senator Doug Cameron roared, 'Prime Minister, you are wrong. Ministers, you are wrong.'[18]

Wong's speech struck the same notes as at the South Australian conference a year before. She said Labor's current platform 'makes it clear that not all Australians are equal'.

> If instead lesser rights were proposed on the basis of race or age or class or any other attribute, there would not be a person in this hall who would countenance it. But until now our party has accepted it and we should accept it no longer … So do not treat us differently. Do not ask us any longer to accept our relations being treated as lesser. Less worthy, less valued, simply because of the gender of our partner … There is nothing so persistent as the aspiration for equality.[19]

She knew, when delivering this speech, that the battle on changing the platform was won. They had the numbers.

The Australian Labor Party voted on the voices to change the platform in favour of legal same-sex marriage. While the numbers were not counted, it was clearly an overwhelming victory. Along with the core of Left support were dozens of Right delegates who thought the time for change had come.[20]

The issue was now whether Labor MPs would be allowed a conscience vote when the issue came before parliament – and Julia Gillard's attempts to save face.

In a compromise brokered behind closed doors, a motion was passed 208–184 allowing MPs a conscience vote when legislation for same-sex marriage came before the parliament. Apart from saving the dignity of the prime minister, many – including Albanese – were convinced to back this policy due to the knowledge that otherwise some Labor parliamentarians would cross the floor, meaning they would be expelled from the party. Labor MPs from marginal seats with high numbers of religiously conservative migrants protested they couldn't sell the issue in their electorates; Labor would lose seats at the next election.

The vote was close enough to mean that while Gillard was saved from an embarrassing defeat, the limits of her authority were exposed. She now led a party with a policy on same-sex marriage that she did not support.

Penny Wong was gracious in partial victory. Asked whether Gillard's leadership had been damaged, she said no, and that instead it showed 'something about the measure of the woman that she is willing to allow this forum of the conference to do what it wanted to do, which is to have a full and frank debate. I think all of us are very grateful for that.'[21] It took Graham Richardson, the senior powerbroker who had come to Penny Wong's defence on Q&A months before, to outline what the stakes had been. Had Gillard been defeated, she would have been 'finished, and God knows who would be leading a bunch of defeated demoralised ministers in a headlong burst to the cliff'. Meanwhile, said Richardson, Penny Wong was 'the belle of the ball'.[22]

That night, Wong attended a celebration of what she later described as an historic change. She didn't stay long. She went out for a quiet dinner.

In February 2012, when Labor MP Stephen Jones brought a private member's bill on legalising same-sex marriage before the House of Representatives, it was defeated 98–42. Tony Abbott had refused to grant his party a conscience vote. Turnbull declared that if there had been a conscience vote, he would have voted in favour – but he maintained party solidarity, and the Coalition voted unanimously against the bill. Thirty-eight Labor parliamentarians had voted in favour and twenty-six, including Gillard, against.[23] The Greens brought forward another bill that year. It lapsed without a vote. Labor senators Carol Brown, Trish Crossin, Gavin Marshall and Louise Pratt tried again in September 2012. The bill was defeated 41–26 in the Senate, with eleven Labor parliamentarians voting against. During the debate, Liberal senator Cory Bernardi said that if same-sex marriage was allowed, the next step might be sexual relations between humans and animals.[24] The head of a Christian lobby group, Jim Wallace, said gay lifestyles were more dangerous to health than smoking. Asked what she made of this comment in an interview with Emma Alberici, Penny Wong said, 'I think it only has to be said to be demonstrated to be ridiculous.'[25] They went on to discuss the government's attempt to achieve a surplus.

In 2013, Sarah Hanson-Young made two attempts to introduce a bill on same-sex marriage. One lapsed without a vote; the other was defeated 44–28, with twelve Labor senators voting against.

In May Wong again joined a Q&A panel, this one including Joe Hockey, then the shadow treasurer. An audience member asked how Hockey could claim that all Australians were equal and yet vote against same-sex marriage. He said he thought that having a mother and a father was best for a child.

Penny Wong responded, 'When you say those things, Joe, what you're saying, [to] not just me but people like me, is that the most important thing in our lives, which is the people we love, is somehow less good, less valued.'

Tony Jones asked, 'Is it hurtful?'

'Of course it is, but I know what my family is worth.'[26]

It was, as one commentator put it, a moment of 'remarkable grace and honesty ... from her heart, unconstrained by the need to follow whatever script was issued that day from head office'.[27]

After Tony Abbott took government in September 2013, there were eight more attempts up until mid-2015. All of them lapsed.

The issue was deadlocked. Either the Liberal Party had to grant a conscience vote or Labor had to disallow one. Until then, same-sex marriage would remain illegal.

*

On Sunday, 11 December 2011, eight days after the change in Labor Party platform and nine days before her due date, Sophie Allouache gave birth to a girl at the Women's and Children's Hospital in North Adelaide. Three days later, on the Wednesday, the birth was announced and a single image of the family released to the media. The statement again asked for their privacy to be respected.

They named the baby Alexandra, Sophie's middle name. Sophie had not wanted to know the child's gender before birth, so they had also picked out other names – 'all Old Testament', Penny Wong remarks. Had Alexandra been a boy, she would have been called Benjamin. As is the tradition in Chinese families, Francis Wong, the child's grandfather, chose the Chinese middle names. Tian, which means 'heaven', is a generational name. Alexandra's other name is Chen, which translates roughly as 'dawn' or 'morning light'.

Penny Wong took a month off after the birth. When her office issued the birth announcement, Penny and Sophie were experiencing all the sleep-deprived joy and stress of first-time parenthood. They were paranoid about co-sleeping, having read up on the risks of suffocation – but Alexandra would not sleep alone. Wong recalls, 'After the first two nights I thought, *If we don't do something, Sophie is going to die.* So I worked out if I slept on the living-room floor without a pillow, there would be nothing for her to suffocate under. And I just lay her on my chest and then she would sleep.'

Alexandra has grown to be a bright, assertive and emotionally intense child, says Wong. Parenthood is the most difficult job she has ever held. Most parents would say that, but given the other jobs she has done, for Penny Wong it is quite a statement.

'Kids are wonderful. They are the best thing in your life. You hear people say that, but it's actually true. It's a joyful, moving and humbling experience. But there is nothing in your life where you make so many mistakes so often. And that's OK. None of us are perfect.

'You have the care of these kids, not just in a real physical way, but you are trying to foster their spirits and their identity and give them safety but also joy and stimulation and develop who they are. It's beautiful and miraculous and it operates at so many levels.'

Today, Sophie is the primary caregiver for their children. Penny tries to compensate for being so often away by phoning and texting the children daily with 'lots of emojis'. At the time of writing Alexandra is seven years old, almost eight. She has taken to composing letters to her friends, and checks the mailbox daily. Penny has started writing her letters as well.

It was when Alexandra told Penny that she should be proud of her public profile that the attitude to this biography, for a while at least, began to shift from reluctant partial cooperation to something more positive.

But, as the 2019 election approached, Alexandra told her mother that she didn't want the Australian Labor Party to win. She knew what it would mean: more absence. Wong told me this in our last interview before the election. I commented that it must be hard, knowing your daughter didn't want you to win when every other part of your being was focused on achieving victory.

'That's hard,' she agreed.

*

By the time Wong returned to work in February 2012, after Alexandra's birth and a brief summer holiday, the Canberra press gallery was again in a fever of leadership speculation. Kevin Rudd, now foreign minister, was said to be considering mounting a challenge to Gillard. It was one of the first things Wong was asked about by the media, along with the mining tax and the perpetually receding surplus.

The ministers supporting Gillard had changed tack. They were now urged to talk openly about Rudd's shortcomings. Simon Crean had been on radio accusing his former leader of not being a team player, stating that Rudd had to accept he couldn't be prime minister again. Gillard's office had encouraged him to speak, but he went in harder than Gillard had intended.[28]

Penny Wong told the media that she had made a New Year's resolution. She wouldn't engage in any comment or speculation on leadership matters.[29] She was forced to break that resolution only three days later, insisting that Julia Gillard was the right person to lead the party and had her full support.[30] Meanwhile, Gillard presented her with a little cardigan she had knitted for baby Alexandra over the summer break. Gillard had also knitted two squares for a campaign blanket that was auctioned off to raise funds for the party.[31] In knitting, too, the personal tangled with the political.

Wong continued her attempts to bat away leadership questions throughout February. She was, commented one journalist, 'a rock in the stormy seas engulfing the Gillard government'.[32] It seemed that every day brought another leak. First, it was revealed that Julia Gillard's staff had drafted a speech for her to give on becoming leader long before, on her own account, she had contemplated any such move. Then a video of a furious, foul-mouthed Kevin Rudd appeared on YouTube. Rudd thought Gillard's office leaked it. Gillard maintains she had no idea where it came from.[33]

On 22 February, Rudd, who was in Washington, announced his resignation as the minister for foreign affairs, citing Crean's attack and making it clear he was preparing for a leadership challenge. Gillard announced that a spill would be held at 10.00 am on Monday 27 February.

The announcement led to the ministers who backed Gillard unleashing another storm of Rudd criticism. For months, they had held back in the interests of party solidarity; now they were given carte blanche.

Deputy prime minister Wayne Swan damned Rudd as 'dysfunctional';
Tony Burke said that 'the stories ... of the chaos, of the temperament,
of the inability to have decisions made – they are not stories'. Nicola
Roxon declared she could not work with Rudd again; Stephen Conroy
said that Rudd had harboured 'contempt' for his colleagues, the parliament and the public. It was an awful, devastatingly destructive public
lashing. It did Gillard no good. On the morning of the leadership spill
Newspoll showed that, among the public, Rudd was ahead of Gillard
as preferred leader by a factor of almost two to one.

Amid this public bloodletting, Penny Wong was restrained. The
leadership ballot, she said, was about 'resolving this issue once and for
all'. She would be backing Gillard. 'I think she is the best person to lead
the party, the government and the nation.' She baulked at joining in
the river of vitriol against Rudd. 'I am not someone who gets into the
details of personality and other issues,' she told ABC Radio. 'I served
Kevin Rudd loyally as a cabinet minister. I now serve in Prime Minister
Gillard's cabinet. I have made the judgement very clearly that the right
person to lead the country is Prime Minister Gillard.'[34] The following
day, she called on Rudd to give up his leadership aspirations if defeated.
The only way the party could recover from the damaging stoush was if
the leadership vote resolved the issue.[35]

The vote was 71–31 in Gillard's favour – but Rudd had won almost
a third of the caucus. The leadership issue was far from resolved. Meanwhile, the thwarted challenger moved to the backbench, and the Gillard
government lurched on, dipping ever lower in the polls.

*

As the minister for finance in the last three years of the Labor government, Penny Wong was central to its economic decision-making.
Finance minister is usually a backroom job, devoid of glamour. She
was described as a 'Dr No' figure, her role being to restrain the spending programs of other ministers.[36] In public she was often understudy
to the treasurer – initially Wayne Swan and, in the government's dying
days, Chris Bowen. Having been criticised for wooden communications

on climate policy, she now appeared most often on the heavy current-affairs programs – doing long set-piece interviews with the ABC's Emma Alberici or Leigh Sales. These encounters were a measure of changes in public life since she had first been dismissed as a 'lipstick warrior' upon entering the Australian parliament. There were senior women on both sides of the desk – both at the top of their game, both playing hard.

But Don Watson would have found little in her media appearances to rebut his view of her as a purveyor of dead political language. Certain rhetorical tricks had become trademark Penny Wong. 'Let me just say this,' she would often begin a response. Or 'What I would say is …' Or 'The point is …' All were ways of reframing a question to suit the government's narrative. There was another verbal tic she developed during this time, and continues to use today. When praising a colleague, she will describe them as 'the best of our generation'. She used it in the interviews for this book regarding Jay Weatherill, who she described as the best politician 'of our generation'. She used it after the 2019 election when endorsing Albanese for leader of the party – he was 'the outstanding parliamentarian of our generation'.[37] It is a powerful form of words in isolation. Once you are aware that it is also a Wong formula, it loses some of its impact.

As finance minister, underlying her rhetoric was the hard fact that she was often sent out to do a tough interview when the treasurer was unwilling. As well, despite her power and senior position, Wong was navigating conundrums she had inherited – the mining tax, the carbon tax (as it became known under Gillard) and, most of all, the government's firm promise that it would deliver a surplus in the wake of its big spending to ward off a recession during the global financial crisis. The surplus became a retreating chimera and was never achieved. For most of this time it was clear that the Labor government was on the way out, a victim of self-inflicted damage. It was a miserable time and a tough job. In Wong's public appearances there were not many jokes and very few smiles, except ones of incredulity or contempt when talking about the opposition.

In 2010 the treasurer, Wayne Swan, and new prime minister Julia Gillard had announced that the government would return to surplus by 2013. They based this on a Treasury forecast that turned out to be wrong. It was predicated on an optimistic prediction of how tax revenues would rebound as the country recovered from the global financial crisis. Despite Labor's success in avoiding recession through stimulus and spending, recovery was sluggish. Nevertheless, long before Penny Wong took on the finance portfolio, the government had harnessed its economic credentials to the promise, and even as figures flowed in through 2011 and 2012 that suggested a surplus was unachievable, Gillard and her cabinet continued to talk about it in absolute terms. 'Failure is not an option,' Gillard said. Wong echoed this sentiment, including it in her John Button speech and in many other public appearances.

In December 2012, Wayne Swan finally abandoned the ambition of a budget surplus in 2013, saying that it would now be achieved in the 2015–16 financial year. The continued commitment to a surplus had always been a political rather than an economic necessity. The economy was strong, with low unemployment, low interest rates and steady growth, but the promises made by Gillard and Swan – and repeated by Wong – meant that Labor's credibility was undermined. Postponing the surplus in the lead-up to the 2013 election played directly into opposition leader Tony Abbott's narrative. Labor could not be trusted with the nation's economy.

Today Wong says the mistake was in making 'a political commitment out of a forecast' and then retreating from it too late. She says she became aware of the sluggishness of revenue only through the budget processes in 2011. At that stage, the government should either have made much deeper cuts to deliver the surplus or abandoned the promise, doing its best to explain the reasons why.

Wong also inherited the mining tax, which had become a fiasco. The mining industry felt it had not been adequately consulted and had mounted a scarifying campaign against the tax in Rudd's last days as leader. In their respective memoirs, Rudd blames Swan, and Swan blames the mining industry, Treasury, Rudd and, to a lesser extent, himself.[38] Paul Kelly's verdict is that 'Labor got the timing, the design and the politics wrong'. As treasurer, Swan had not adequately consulted, but Rudd had also failed to pay sufficient attention. 'The whole saga is an irrefutable instance of a decision-making shambles,' Kelly concludes. In his opinion, if Rudd had got the tax right, he would probably have been able to lead Labor to victory in 2010 despite the damage done by his retreat on climate change.[39]

By the time Gillard took over the leadership in June 2010, the issue was inflicting mortal damage on the government. One of her first acts was to defuse it. She and Swan negotiated with the big mining companies. They needed a fix, and needed it fast. The government was in a weak position. The mining industry effectively co-authored the revised tax model. It was based on optimistic forecasts of commodity prices, which meant it was modelled to raise only a little less than the original. That proved too good to be true. Commodity prices fell, and the design of the tax meant that it raised almost no revenue. Nevertheless, the forecasts in 2010 meant Labor regained some credibility, and was able to maintain the bold predictions of surplus in the election campaign.[40]

The mining tax saga, she says today, highlights the 'stupidity' of the decision to drop the CPRS. 'So we are going to get rid of a price on carbon that we have said for years is the most important thing, and instead introduce a tax that nobody has ever heard of and doesn't understand the reasons for? Not great political strategy.'

The deal done by Gillard and Swan had to be made in a hurry 'because we were bleeding', but she remembers that after the election, when the mining tax revenue figures were released, the shadow assistant treasurer and shadow minister for financial services, Mathias Cormann, mocked her across the Senate chamber, saying that only Labor could design a tax that didn't deliver any money. She felt the sting in his words.

In this environment – shackled to the promise of surplus, with revenues constantly dropping below forecasts and a mining tax not worthy of the name – the government still delivered reforms. Minister for Families, Community Services and Indigenous Affairs Jenny Macklin steered through means testing of family tax benefits and of the private health insurance rebate, as well as a paid parental leave scheme. There were extra family benefits, a Schoolkids' Bonus, aged-care spending and income tax reforms to help low-income earners. Gillard also pursued two reforms – her attempt to set her own stamp on the government. These were the National Disability Insurance Scheme and a new model for school funding that arose out of the Review to Achieve Educational Excellence in Australian Schools, commonly known as the Gonski report.

The government committed to offset all new spending with savings. Getting the savings was largely Wong's job. This is where she became 'Dr No'.

Ministers remember her as the chief cross-examiner at Expenditure Review Committee meetings. They learned to dread these encounters. Wayne Swan recalls, 'Penny Wong did more than anyone to ensure we achieved [offsetting of new spending]. Ministers by this stage had become ashen-faced at the mere mention of the Expenditure Review Committee meetings . . . it was not uncommon to ask ministers presenting a spending proposal to also provide the offsetting saving. Sometimes, ruthlessly, we accepted the saving proposal but then didn't approve the spending proposal.'[41] Allan Behm was at this stage chief of staff to Greg Combet, the minister for energy and climate change, and thus working on the implementation of the climate-change package that had been negotiated with the Greens. The detail was complex. There was the management of the carbon accounting and carbon credits regime; there had to be compensation packages for low-income households, with social-security implications. There were plans for methane capture from tips and numerous other measures. All of it had cost implications. Penny Wong was involved in meetings with multiple ministers, nutting out the detail. She was, Behm remembers, 'so completely professional' in managing the pressures on the budget while recognising the priority the government was giving to action on climate change. 'Swan might have committed to the surplus, but it was Penny who had to try and deliver it. She would ask the right questions and exert discipline. People could come along and say, you know, "We're going to need X, Y and Z to be able to do A, B and C." And she would test every demand, and quite trenchantly. I mean, she's a formidable arguer.'

It wasn't enough. The 2010–11 federal budget, compiled before Penny Wong became finance minister, forecast a $41 billion deficit that ended up at $48 billion. The next year, when she was in the job, the deficit was predicted to be $23 billion but the outcome was $44 billion. For the 2012–13 financial year, Labor forecast a surplus of $1.5 billion that became a $19 billion deficit. For 2013–14, its last year in government and after Swan had admitted the surplus could not be achieved that year, Labor forecast a deficit of $18 billion that was quickly revised upwards, to $30 billion.[42] When Kevin Rudd resumed the leadership and Chris Bowen replaced Swan as treasurer, one of the first things they did was to hold a mini-budget that deferred the return-to-surplus promise by yet another year.

Throughout this, Penny Wong held the line, echoing Gillard and Swan, and later Bowen. In March 2012 she was promising that the mining tax would raise enough money to cover the government's promises, insisting that all the variables had been factored in.[43] After Swan's December 2012 admission that the surplus timetable could not be met, she fronted ABC journalist Chris Uhlmann to face a barrage of difficult questions. 'The key to this decision today is responsible economic management,' she said. 'The key to this decision today is jobs and growth ... What we can be absolutely trusted on is we will always be ... the party that puts growth and jobs first. And the evidence is the way we have managed the economy in the face of the worst global downturn since the Great Depression.'[44]

And in the wake of the May 2013 federal budget, it was Wong who fronted Emma Alberici on *Lateline* to explain the deficit. Why had Labor not taken a more cautious approach when it was clear revenue was not coming in, asked Alberici.

Wong did the best job she could with a terrible hand. 'Well, making a couple of points. The first is this, that we actually did take a more conservative approach, but what has occurred is an even bigger hit to revenues than was anticipated. And this is not a conspiracy ... what we've seen is the largest write-down of revenue for a very long time.'[45]

It was punishing stuff, awful to listen to and, while she does not admit this, awful to have to deliver. By now, everyone knew the government was in its dying days. The only question was the scale of the impending defeat.

*

By 2013 both the architects of the Machine power-sharing deal within South Australian Labor were in federal parliament: Don Farrell, of the Right, as a senator, and Mark Butler, of the Left, as member for the lower-house seat of Port Adelaide. Butler had entered parliament in 2007. The allocation of this safe seat to him was one of the Machine's benefits to the Left.

As the 2013 election approached, a factional brawl erupted in South Australia. It tested the limits of the Machine deal, and pitched Penny Wong against Don Farrell. In some ways, this wasn't a surprise: they had been circling each other for years – in so many ways opposites, other than in their shared commitment to the party.

Farrell came from a family steeped in Catholic values. If South Australia Labor had split in the 1950s, his family would probably have been with the Democratic Labor Party. He was also a parliamentary secretary – junior to Wong in terms of party position but more senior in factional terms. His support had been important to Gillard when she replaced Rudd as prime minister. This was generally thought to be the reason why Gillard opposed same-sex marriage – as part of a backroom deal made with Farrell. Though he had virtually no public profile, within the party he was a key powerbroker, and had been Wong's antagonist in the push to change the South Australian Labor Party position on same-sex marriage.

In late 2012 he moved on her again. Had he been successful, Penny Wong probably would not be in the parliament today.

At the South Australian state Labor conference in October 2012, the Right's Joe de Bruyn, a vehement opponent of same-sex marriage, organised the votes to unseat Penny Wong from the number-one position on the Senate ticket, in favour of Farrell. Farrell won the top spot easily: 112–83. This was evidence of Farrell's power, but also showed that Wong had her enemies within the state party, with the remnants of the Centre Left as well as the Right voting against her. Why was Gillard happy to have Don Farrell in the number-one spot?

Wong says today, coyly, 'You would have to ask Julia Gillard.'

After the conference, Gillard told the media that Penny Wong was 'an incredibly important member of my team' but refused to say whether she thought Wong should lead the ticket.[46] These comments, made in the same month as her notorious speech attacking Tony Abbott's misogyny, allowed for the opposition's Christopher Pyne to accuse Gillard of hypocrisy – of failing to support other women.[47]

At the time, these factional maneouvrings weren't seen as a bid to end Penny Wong's career. Labor expected to win at least two South Australian Senate spots, so second place on the ticket was presumed safe. But it was a humiliation.

Anthony Albanese was furious on Penny Wong's behalf. They had grown closer over the years. In his view, she had had to overcome immense barriers as a left-wing Asian lesbian woman, and she had done so without asking any special favours. She was also an individual of 'courage, character, policy depth', with the right combination of pragmatism and principle. 'If she was a straight white man she would still be outstanding.' In his view, it was 'absurd' for the low-profile Farrell to be placed above Penny Wong, the minister for finance, on the Senate ticket. 'There shouldn't have been any argument over it,' he says today.

Albanese went to see the prime minister. He recalls, 'It was one of the few arguments I ever had with Julia. She asked me to back off, basically, and I told her I wouldn't be doing that ... In my view it was just absurd, and it wasn't about Julia or Rudd or leadership or anything else. It was about the Labor Party having to be mature and sensible. You had this outstanding public figure versus Farrell, who is a good person but very much a backroom figure.'

Albanese says that his advocacy was not at Penny Wong's urging. 'She wasn't asking me to do anything. Far from it. It was my decision and my call to do it ... I thought people would back off, but everyone doubled down, so I doubled down.' He threatened to take the issue to the national executive and seek an intervention to reverse the decision. It wasn't necessary. In October 2012, a few days after the ticket was announced, Farrell backed down and announced he would give up the number-one spot to Penny Wong out of concern that the issue was damaging the party.[48]

Most thought this dispute was largely about form and protocol. But Chris Schacht, whose political career had been ended by Penny Wong's rise years before, remembers thinking that Don Farrell might have made a serious mistake. Schacht had made a hobby out of analysing the vote for the Senate – partly because of his conviction that Wong was not a vote-winner. He thought it was quite possible Labor would not get two seats. He was right.

Gillard began 2013 by announcing the election date almost nine months in advance. Leadership rumblings began again early in the year as the government dived in the polls – there were rumours that Kevin Rudd was again planning to challenge Julia Gillard for the prime ministership. In March, Simon Crean called a leadership challenge, hoping to flush Rudd out. Gillard called a spill but, in the absence of a challenge from Rudd or anyone else, was re-elected unopposed. Penny Wong, as the numbers were counted for the spill that didn't happen, was reckoned as one of those sticking with Gillard.

But by June, in the aftermath of a federal budget that Penny Wong was sent out on the media trail to support, the government's standing in the opinion polls had collapsed again. Labor was headed for a wipeout. The polls indicated that Kevin Rudd had a better chance of winning public support than Julia Gillard. Rudd declared to those urging him to challenge that he would do so only if key cabinet ministers were to prepared to announce they would back him. The ministers he nominated included Penny Wong, Bill Shorten, Greg Combet and Jenny Macklin.[49]

Penny Wong had been one of Julia Gillard's most public supporters, although behind the scenes their relationship was often difficult, due to their differences over the CPRS, same-sex marriage and, most recently, Don Farrell's attempt to secure the top place on the Senate ticket.

Mark Butler and Penny Wong talked about the leadership, as had been their habit over so many years, and as they had the last time the office of prime minister was in doubt, when Gillard replaced Rudd. Butler recalls, 'There were no angels in all that period. What people did to Kevin was incredibly stupid and did Julia no favours ultimately either. And now we were in that situation again, and we were trying to work out what to do.'

Many ministers – Swan, Conroy and others – were opposed to Rudd on personal grounds, not wanting to reward what they saw as his undermining and treachery. Others were opposed to Gillard because of what she had done to Rudd. But Butler and Wong were simply 'trying to work out the best thing'.

Butler says they both agreed that Gillard had been an excellent prime minister under extraordinary pressure. 'She kept things moving, she consulted, she gave ministers their head. There was no animus there in cabinet as there was about Kevin.' But Labor was headed for the kind of defeat that could see it out of power for a decade or more. The polls showed that it would lose 'really important people, the kind of people you need if you are going to have a chance at government any time in the future'. He says, 'There was no philosophical difference. It was not people backing Kevin because of his vision or Gillard because of her vision.' For all its disarray, the party did not have a deep ideological divide of the kind plaguing the Liberals.

Switching sides to Rudd was a difficult decision for them both – made not in the course of a single conversation but gradually, over several late-night talks from mid-June onwards. 'It was just, "What a fucking mess. How do we give ourselves some hope of winning this election?" ... We didn't sort of hold hands and leap over the cliff together. It was an iterative process in which we both reached the same conclusion at the same time.'

Penny Wong went to see Julia Gillard. Wong was in tears. She told Gillard she would be changing her support to Kevin Rudd, and begged her not to stand in the leadership spill the next day, saying it would be easier. Gillard responded, 'You mean easier for you, Penny.'[50] Gillard made it clear she would fight to the finish, but as she told author Mary Delahunty, it was after that conversation that Julia Gillard knew her prime ministership was over.[51]

Wong was repeatedly on the record as saying that Gillard was the best person to lead the party. Voting against her was both politically embarrassing and personally painful. Wong describes this as one of the worst – if not *the* worst – day she has had in politics. Nevertheless, on 26 June 2013 Kevin Rudd was elected leader of the Labor Party 57–45, with Wong one of his votes. She was the only woman in cabinet to desert Australia's first female prime minister.

Immediately after the vote, a collection of the ministers who had publicly disparaged Rudd stood and declared they would not serve in his cabinet. Swan resigned as treasurer and deputy leader, to be replaced by Chris Bowen as treasurer and Anthony Albanese as deputy. Stephen Conroy resigned as Leader of the Government in the Senate. Penny Wong was elected to replace him, unopposed. Her promotion was not a surprise. When Conroy had been appointed leader in the Senate in February 2013, her name had been mentioned as a possible alternative. She had chosen not to run – perhaps because of the demands of new motherhood.[52] She had been appointed as Conroy's deputy, and stepping up now was a natural move, particularly given her profile and ability. This made her the third most powerful person in the government, after Rudd and Albanese, and the first woman to lead the government in the Senate. Rudd commented in his memoir, apparently without rancour over her long support for Gillard, 'She was one of the stars of our side. And, unlike Conroy, she could hold her own in the parliament and in public as an accomplished public speaker.'[53]

Penny Wong walked out from the vote at Kevin Rudd's right shoulder, ready to greet the media.

Just over a month later, on 5 August, Kevin Rudd called the election for 7 September. Before the caretaker period began, Penny Wong made one last move. She organised federal funding for a program, pioneered in Victoria, that sought to foster a safe environment for LGBTQIA children at school. By the time Tony Abbott won government, the contracts – for an $8 million program over four years – had been signed. Years later, when Safe Schools was at the centre of the culture wars, Penny Wong was asked by author Benjamin Law if she had rushed the contracts through to force a commitment that the inevitable Abbott government would have to maintain. Law reported, 'She gives the faintest ghost of a smile. "Well, you could turn it around and say, 'Labor people believe a whole range of programs are important, and whatever we can do in the face of a hard-right prime minister to protect young people is not a bad thing.'"'[54]

The 2013 election campaign was regarded as shambolic by just about all the journalists who reported on it. Stories circulated that Rudd announced major policies on the run without consultation. Penny's university acquaintance Samantha Maiden wrote that the campaign trail was a 'voyage of the damned ... poor planning, exhausted staff, a siege mentality'.[55] Once again, Penny Wong was campaign spokesperson, largely based in Melbourne, at the campaign headquarters. Campaigning was being done 'on the fly' for the first three days, until she intervened and insisted on a campaign plan, which was composed in a telephone hook-up over three hours. 'It was adopted, but quickly became irrelevant as Mr Rudd and his travelling party of policy advisers changed destinations, announced unheard-of policies and conducted their own exclusive meetings.'[56]

One campaign blunder – the mistake most commentators saw as signifying the death knell of Labor's hopes – involved Penny Wong. On 29 August she, Rudd and Bowen fronted the media in Melbourne to claim that Treasury costings had identified a $10 billion hole in the savings announced by the opposition the previous day. They released minutes from Treasury, the Department of Finance and the Parliamentary Budget Office to back up the claim.

It blew up in their face when the relevant public servants came out later that day with a statement undercutting the claim. The figures had been done during the caretaker period, on the basis of material provided by the government, they said. 'At no stage prior to the caretaker period has either department costed opposition policies.' Laurie Oakes said Rudd, Wong and Bowen had used the public service 'in a bit of political trickery'.[57] Political journalist Tony Walker wrote, 'This is a debacle captured in the colourful language of one among many beleaguered supporters: "Holy shit, what have we done now?"'[58]

Today Wong acknowledges it was a 'bad mistake … a political disaster' to use public service figures in this way, but points out that the same thing has been done by the Coalition – including in the 2019 election campaign – without the same response from the bureaucrats. She also claims the costings proved correct.

Consistent with her reluctance to criticise others, Wong won't attribute blame for the election campaign. She takes her share of responsibility for the Treasury costings blunder, but as for the rest, she says, 'Yes, it wasn't the most functional campaign. It wasn't as good as the 2007 campaign but, when you have had two leadership changes and changes of key ministers, we were as professional as we could be. When you win, everybody wants to own it, and when you lose, everyone wants to distance themselves from it. People did their best. People make mistakes … There were things Kevin did which some were critical of. There were things Kevin did which helped us.' She believes switching to Kevin Rudd saved the party twenty seats, and left it in a position from which it could strike again at government.

A few days before the election, when Penny Wong was trying to 'keep the whole thing hanging together' at campaign headquarters, she was alerted that the polls for the South Australian Senate were looking particularly bad. Independent Nick Xenophon was attracting phenomenal levels of support. Labor's number-two spot on the ticket – Don Farrell's position – was at risk. There were appeals for her to come home and campaign. Unnamed sources from the Right warned the media that the Left 'would have to pay' if Don Farrell was unseated.[59] Too many people owed him their careers.

Penny Wong didn't respond to the threats and stayed in Melbourne.

She says today that the party probably needed her to go home and campaign – but it also needed her in Melbourne.

When the vote came in, Xenophon had scored a record 25.8 per cent of the primary vote, with the most ballots cast for a Senate candidate anywhere in the nation, beating Sarah Hanson-Young of the Greens. Penny Wong was the third senator, and the only Labor senator, elected from South Australia.

It was some days before it became clear that Farrell was out of parliament. Wong was quoted describing the result as 'unexpected and extremely disappointing'. However, she would not be drawn on whether she had any regrets about the Left's campaign to force Senator Farrell to give up his top Senate ticket position for her. 'No one was expecting this outcome when those issues were discussed,' she said.[60] Today she acknowledges that if Anthony Albanese had not saved her position on the ticket, her political career might have ended.

Chris Schacht blames the lack of campaigning squarely for the result. 'I asked them, "What are you doing out in the bush? Have you been to the industrial towns in Spencer Gulf? Are you campaigning?"' He says nobody listened. Instead, Don Farrell became the third Labor senator from South Australia to have his Senate career halted by the rise of Penny Wong.

The setback proved temporary. After the 2013 result, the party decided that it had to run fully fledged Senate campaigns in South Australia in future. At the 2016 election Farrell recontested for the Senate in the second position on the Labor ticket; the party mounted a strong campaign and he was re-elected, with Labor winning three Senate places, the third going to Alex Gallacher. Penny's friend, Anne McEwen, failed to make it. Nevertheless, it was the best result for the Labor South Australian Senate team for some time.[61]

The 2016 election was also the first in which voters had a choice of optional preferential voting below the line, without having to number every box on the ballot paper. Penny Wong, as the number-one candidate for Labor, got 17,899 personal first-preference votes, as well as her quota from the above the line Labor group vote. It was the second-highest personal vote of any South Australian Senate candidate – evidence of her growing profile. But she was well behind the populist frontrunner, Nick

Xenophon, who gained 25,777 personal first-preference votes.[62] Penny Wong was consciously anything but populist. During the 2016 campaign she said, 'Obviously Nick gets a lot of attention, but this election ultimately isn't about who gets attention, it is about what sort of country we want ... There is an open question as to what he's actually achieved. But as I say, I understand for people it's – you know, it's easy for a politician who tells you things you want to hear.'[63] That wasn't her way.

*

On 7 September 2013, Abbott and the Coalition won government with a majority of thirty seats and a swing of 3.6 percentage points. The Labor Party recorded its lowest two-party-preferred vote since 1996 and lowest primary vote since 1931. Kevin Rudd resigned as party leader and from the parliament.

Labor had to elect a new leader. Under rules introduced by Rudd, there was a new and very public process. The vote would be split between rank-and-file party members and the parliamentary party, with each group equally weighted. The process was to take two weeks and include two public debates. The candidates were former minister Bill Shorten and former deputy prime minister Anthony Albanese.

Penny Wong, as Leader of the Opposition in the Senate, announced that she would be backing Albanese but affirmed that both candidates would make 'outstanding Labor leaders'. Albanese had her vote because of his long-term support for women and 'he has the experience, the runs on the board, he's had some tough portfolios which he's handled really well. And he's also our best parliamentary performer ... I think [he] really lives his Labor values.'[64]

Albanese won nearly 60 per cent of the rank-and-file vote, but Bill Shorten won the leadership thanks to gaining more caucus votes.

The contest was conducted with extraordinary civility – any barbs well cloaked. Having made itself unelectable through a failure to govern itself, everyone was determined not to repeat the mistake. But, immediately after the vote, factional warfare broke out over front-bench positions, with a rift in the Right.

In a measure of her standing, there was no dispute about Penny Wong retaining her place as Labor's leader in the Senate. A few weeks later it was announced that she would be also become Shadow Minister for Trade and Investment.

In the wake of the 2019 election defeat, those around Penny Wong were inclined to recall this 2013 battle. Shorten had proved persistently unpopular with voters, particularly in Queensland, where he was remembered for his role in bringing down local boy Kevin Rudd. Penny Wong had been right to back Albanese in 2013, it was said. Perhaps if Albo had won, recent history would have turned out differently.

12

ARRIVAL

When, exactly, did Penny Wong become cool? When did she become, as Bill Shorten described her during the 2019 election campaign, 'the weapon' in Labor's journey to government?[1] The kind of person who has sandwiches named after her in hip inner-suburban cafés?

Certainly not during her early years in parliament. Her colleagues recognised her talents. When Kim Beazley embarrassed himself by not being able to name Labor's five South Australian senators, Penny Wong was one name he could recall. He covered up for forgetting the others by saying, 'Every now and again in politics you see a bright prospect emerging that is really a little bit special.'[2] Journalists regularly gave her high rankings in their end-of-year report cards for politicians, although they also criticised her for being excessively cautious and answering questions in bureaucratese.[3]

She was certainly not cool when she was the minister for water and climate change, embattled on all sides, including within her own party, and blamed along with Rudd and the Greens for the failures on climate-change action. Journalist Lenore Taylor profiled her under the heading 'The minister of cool' in 2009, but that was a reference to the portfolio of climate change, not to Wong herself, whom Taylor described as 'forensic, controlled, focused'.[4]

And certainly not when she was the minister for finance. It's hard to be cool in that job, particularly defending the surplus that never was, the mining tax that didn't work and the party that couldn't govern itself. In 2011 she made the list of Top 100 Most Admired Women in Australia, compiled from the votes of more than 1200 Australian women, but she didn't come close to the winner – Cathy Freeman – and was well behind Julia Gillard, actor Cate Blanchett, pop star Kylie Minogue and country singer Kasey Chambers.[5]

Perhaps she truly became cool when journalists began to comment on her eyebrows. In 2015 *BuzzFeed* put together a video of her eyebrow raises – usually the left, and usually in Senate Estimates.[6] *The Australian* described her eyebrows as 'a wonder, their movement a form of communication as whole and complex as semaphore, a single arch saying more than an entire harangue'.[7] *The Sydney Morning Herald* commented, 'The greatest interrogators extract their truths with nary more than a smile ... In this, Senator Penny Wong has emerged a master ... armed with a laser focus, quirked eyebrow, relaxed stance and unwavering dedication to her line of questioning.'[8] *The Guardian* writer Brigid Delaney imagined a movie version of Julia Gillard's prime ministership and suggested that Penny Wong should be played by that epitome of cool, k.d. lang. 'But k.d. is not Asian, I hear you say. Never mind ... she is evocative of the essence of P. Wong. The mood.'[9] In 2018, author and cartoonist Kaz Cooke suggested on Twitter that 'somebody should manufacture the Penny Wong Senate Estimates Committee Doll. When pressed, the doll raises an eyebrow and leans forward. Children can provide their own imaginative dialogue.'[10] Penny Wong's eyebrows provided content for dozens of social media gifs.

Opposition suited Penny Wong – if not her aspirations, then certainly her profile. Rather than having to explain complicated and contentious policy problems with no winners, she became the forensic, drily witty scourge of government, holding ministers to account and often making them look like fools. She was indeed the chief cross-examiner.

There was her testy exchange in the Senate with the Liberals' Ian Macdonald. He was interjecting continually while she spoke. He made a comment *sotto voce*, too quiet to be picked up by microphones or *Hansard* – but Wong heard it. She responded, 'You're not my type either, mate, don't worry about it.' The exchange went viral. The French website *Brut* described what Macdonald had done as an example of 'manterrupting'.[11] She tangled with the attorney-general, Senator George Brandis. She was interposing in a debate about his handling of the Sydney siege. He accused her of 'becoming hysterical' before telling her to 'just calm yourself'.[12] She tweeted to her followers, 'After being called shrill and hysterical by George Brandis, I'm off to my office for a cup of tea, a Bex and a lie down. #dinosaur #senateqt'

Then there was the time in Senate Estimates when she was cross-examining Brandis. She told him she was trying to 'square away' his answers. He leaned back expansively, twirling a pencil between his fingers. 'You mean reconcile,' he said. 'When you say square away, do you mean reconcile both answers?' Up went the Wong eyebrow, and she fired back, 'Are you going to be pompous the whole day, or only for this question?' That, too, went viral.[13] In 2017, after four years in opposition, she learned that a public relations firm had been hired to do role play with public servants and Department of Defence officials on how to manage appearances before her at Senate Estimates. She responded, 'I want to know who plays me.'[14]

When Brandis, an advocate for removing sections of the *Racial Discrimination Act*, declared, 'People do have a right to be bigots, you know,' she called out sarcastically, 'Yes, George, you go out there and defend the right to be bigoted.'[15] To him, she was a threat to freedom of speech, the 'high priestess of political correctness' in the grip of an 'unhealthy obsession' with Pauline Hanson.[16] To her, he was Gollum from *The Lord of the Rings*, in search of 'his Precious' – weakening the *Racial Discrimination Act* – while the government trashed legislation 'like a gang of orcs'.[17]

For left-wingers dismayed by the Coalition government, this stuff was gold, shared and gloated over. It was during this period that it became common to hear people ask why she wasn't the leader of the party, or even prime minister. Might she move to the lower house to contest the leadership? She continually batted away these suggestions, insisting she had no such ambition.

Within the parliamentary party she was one of few to emerge from the Rudd–Gillard–Rudd leadership traumas with her reputation enhanced. Unlike other ministers, she had never indulged in abuse and character assassination. She had held back from the demonising of Rudd when others sallied forth. Her relationship with Gillard was difficult – both over climate-change policy and same-sex marriage – but she had handled those disputes without ever allowing them to become personal. The internal politics of the Labor Party's decisions during government was not public knowledge until the brace of memoirs and journalistic accounts were published, but insiders knew that she alone of the leadership team had correctly called the political judgements around climate change. While she had switched from Rudd to Gillard, and from Gillard back to Rudd, she had done so reluctantly and with the interests of the party at heart.

Not everyone liked Penny Wong, and some in her own party dislike her. Some of her own Left faction thought she was too close to the Right – and increasingly during the opposition years, some of her strongest allies were from that faction. Her sharpness and aggression in caucus and shadow cabinet meetings continued to make her enemies. Despite this, she drew respect. Her internal enemies baited her with caution, even if they loved it when she bit.

Parliamentary gamesmanship was not her only contribution. In one of her first public appearances after the election of 2013, in a speech to the Chifley Research Centre on 3 November 2013, Penny Wong revisited the understanding of Labor values that she had spelt out in the John Button lecture. This time, the ideas were turned into the kind of speech a leader might give after a defeat – a rallying and a steadying of the troops. The Abbott government would, she said, be a secretive regime, for the few. Contesting its agenda would be a 'colossal task. But contest it we must. And, while we must learn the lessons of our loss, we do not have the time nor the space to indulge in blame. Now, we must both defend our legacy and we must be prepared to renew.' She added, 'My past experience of opposition is that it is nine-tenths discipline, one-tenth luck.'[18]

She moved on to display the discipline and make the most of the luck. Her public performances were highly controlled – not false, but also not entirely authentic. The internal life remained fiercely protected. As the political journalist Katharine Murphy commented:

> Labor's Senate leader enters political battle with a suit of armour, always composed, always perfectly prepared; she deploys a Boudicca-like character which is both real and curated public projection, to deliver what needs to be delivered ... If the Wong temper flares, if the eyebrow lifts, it's for a purpose, it's choreography, not impulse. Impulse is something that happens behind closed doors, never in the professional sphere, which is about reason, preparation and calculation.[19]

By now, she had a well-worn form of words for most situations. There was that Wong cliché 'the best of his generation'. She used it when talking about her mentor, John Faulkner, when he announced his retirement in 2014. He was, she said 'one of the outstanding parliamentarians of his generation'. In interviews, there were regular phrases 'let me say this', 'what I would say' or 'let me say two things'. But now, somehow, she had transcended the dead language. Penny Wong was cool. And she could also rise to oratory.

As leader of the party in the Senate, Penny Wong was central to Labor's strategy through the first and second terms of opposition. When the Abbott government delivered its first budget, she drove the strategy that saw it widely condemned as unfair. She denounced it as a triumph for the big end of town, and a 'vicious assault on middle Australia'; she told journalists it 'trashes decency and trashes democracy'.[20] She led the blocking of some of its most unpopular measures, including the Medicare co-payment, which was eventually dropped. It helped to permanently tarnish the government's reputation.

Until mid-2014, when the new senators took up their positions, Labor and the Greens combined to block repeal of the carbon tax. During this time, Greens leader Christine Milne found Penny Wong 'always polite and respectful. We worked well together during that period.' It marked a clear shift in attitude from Labor's time in government, when Wong had treated the Greens with contempt.

Outside the gladiatorial spectator sport of politics, Wong, as shadow minister for trade and investment, began to develop the strategic and intellectual agenda that, today, informs her approach to the shadow ministry of foreign affairs.

Much of this agenda brought her into conflict with members of her own faction. Penny Wong favoured free-trade agreements, despite those in the party and the union movement who argued they took away Australian jobs. She made speeches in which she described free trade as continuing in the tradition of the Hawke–Keating economic measures, and asserted that the best way to guarantee Australian jobs and prosperity in the long term is to open Australia to the world. In one of her early speeches as a shadow minister, she talked about socks and stents. Before the Hawke–Keating economic reforms, clothing and footwear industries had employed hundreds of thousands of Australians. Now, they hardly employed any. Socks could be made in developing countries where the wage rates for workers were less than $1 an hour. If Labor imposed a tariff to compete, poorer Australians would pay a lot more for clothing, and the nation would be locked into competing with the world's poorest countries on wages alone – 'a strategy of locking more Australians into jobs on the minimum wage'. This was not what a Labor government should do, she said. A more-progressive policy was for Australia to compete on skills-based initiatives and cutting-edge technologies. She gave as an example a company in Brisbane making and exporting endovascular stents – small woven tubes made by former clothing and footwear workers. Fewer were employed than had been on socks, but the jobs were sustainable and did not trap Australia into competing with the third world on price.

Wong advocated for a reduction of trade barriers in all countries. Kevin Rudd had been a prominent supporter of the World Trade Organization's Doha Round of negotiations, but by the time Wong became shadow trade minister talks had stagnated and were to be effectively abandoned in 2016. In that context, she said, while regional agreements could be positive, care had to be taken not to allow the world to become divided into overlapping trading blocs, each with different rules on labour rights and environmental protections. Some effort should be made to link the agreements, and she argued that Australia, as a member of both the Association of Southeast Asian Nations (ASEAN) and the Trans-Pacific Partnership, was ideally positioned to be a bridge.[21] In a speech in the lead-up to the 2015 United Nations Climate Change Conference, to be held in Paris, she compared the Doha Round with the difficulties of negotiating climate change: 'Nothing is agreed until everything is agreed and everyone must agree with everything.' The need for total consensus held things up. Regional agreements could help overcome the roadblocks, and linking them – which Australia was well placed to do – could lead to global progress.[22]

She also stood against those who demonised the rise of China. 'An ambitious free trade agreement between Australia and China is in the national interest,' she said. 'Some in our movement hanker for the days of protectionism, imagining that tariffs on imports support local jobs ... Protectionism is a false panacea ... Sitting on the sidelines while other countries negotiate trade agreements is also a false panacea. Refusing to enter trade agreements will allow our competitors to gain market share at Australia's expense.'[23]

She led Labor in supporting the China–Australia Free Trade Agreement in principle, but opposed the necessary ratification by the parliament until extra protections for Australian workers were built in. Tony Abbott accused Labor of 'economic sabotage' and refused to negotiate, but in 2015, after Malcolm Turnbull replaced Tony Abbott as prime minister, Penny Wong led intense negotiations with the trade minister, Andrew Robb, that resulted in a deal to pass the agreement with regulations to ensure employers tried to recruit Australian workers before seeking them overseas. The union movement remained unhappy. Bill Shorten fronted the media on the issue, but it was Penny Wong running the negotiations and standing up in caucus and shadow cabinet against representatives of the party's industrial base.[24] She took the same approach to the Trans-Pacific Partnership – approving trade agreements but arguing for improvements and negotiations over the detail – although this debate was overtaken by President Donald Trump's decision in 2017 to pull out, after a decade of negotiation. In June 2016 the ALP's trade policy was released to a cautious welcome by both business and unions. It included increasing the threshold for farmland sales to China, Japan and South Korea, and removing laws requiring foreign investments in agribusiness of more than $55 million to be screened by the Foreign Investment Review Board.

There were rumblings about Shorten's position as leader of the Labor Party, particularly after Turnbull had displaced the unpopular Abbott. In January 2016, Mark Butler was reported to be doing the numbers for Anthony Albanese.[25] Wong had supported Albanese against Shorten in the leadership ballot of 2013, but in the years since then she built her influence in Shorten's inner circle. Despite her previous backing for Albanese, and despite the rumours about her ally Butler, the media reported that she had become one of Shorten's central advisers. Wong's default position was that the party should support the leader, unless that had become clearly untenable. Shorten apparently trusted her.[26]

*

Many of those interviewed for this book who have spent substantial time in public with Penny Wong – in the street, in restaurants and at events – have a story about her being racially abused. It's shocking to hear these tales. It transforms her obvious achievements in overcoming prejudice from the abstract to the visceral. They contextualise her instinctive privacy and the armour she adopts. They explain, perhaps, her combativeness, as well as her response to Pauline Hanson, and to George Brandis's claim that people have the right to be bigots.

Typical is a story from the 2004 election campaign, when she was sitting outside a suburban Adelaide shopping centre with two young male Labor campaign workers. A woman – a complete stranger – yelled out a question. It was something like, 'How does a slanty-eyed slut like you get two guys?' The men were shocked into speechlessness, but Penny Wong had practice in dealing with this. She responded, coolly, 'Just lucky, I guess.'

There are other stories. The people driving past her in cars, windows down, hurling abuse, and once a can. Most of these experiences occurred before she was a recognisable face. Some have happened since, and are amplified by the slurs she receives on social media. Keyboard warriors bring with them homophobic abuse. In May 2013 she tweeted that she had received her 'first homophobic tweet of the day at 8am. Something incoherent about being a lesbian pie face.' The trail of replies contained more. 'Why do you think it makes you better than anyone else?' said one. Then there was a rape threat.

There was also support. Author and cartoonist Kaz Cooke wryly observed that Lesbian Pie Face would make a great name for a restaurant.[27]

The other reason Penny Wong's profile grew while in opposition was the momentum in the campaign for marriage equality. At first reluctantly, and then with increasing willingness and confidence, she became one of the faces of the movement. It was important politically. The Labor Party's 2011 change of platform, for which she had fought, was key. It represented the moment same-sex marriage became a mainstream political issue.[28]

It was also personally profound. Stepping into the spotlight on same-sex marriage was a decision to allow a collision between her politics and her personal life – the internal world that had been so heavily fortified against outsiders ever since she and Toby were embattled in the schoolyard. Penny Wong thought of herself as tough enough to withstand the homophobic and racial abuse she received but, as she told the parliament, many were not. In her maiden speech she had said that Toby's life and death would always serve to remind her 'what it is like for those who are truly marginalised'.[29] There was an echo of that in some of her speeches to the parliament as the issue of same-sex marriage came to a head in 2016 and 2017. For her, and for many others, hate speech was not an abstract thing, she said, but a daily lived reality.[30]

For many years her advocacy had been exercised in the back rooms of the party. That had changed in 2010, when she fought to modify the party platform on same-sex marriage at the South Australian state Labor

convention, and more dramatically in 2011, when Sophie Allouache's
first pregnancy coincided with the new platform at the national conference. As the momentum grew, she increasingly accepted that she was a
role model. Despite her shyness, her need for a refuge in family life and
any fear she may have held of the impact of abuse and prejudice, Penny
Wong, in the opposition years, began to step forward.

In March 2014 she took part in Sydney's Gay and Lesbian Mardi
Gras for the first time, appearing on the Rainbow Labor float with
Tanya Plibersek, Anthony Albanese and Sam Dastyari, in a red 'Love Is
Not a Crime' T-shirt. The week before the event she wrote an article for
The Guardian saying that there was a need for people like her, in positions of leadership, to 'speak out, be counted'.[31] On the nation's largest
annual street parade, Senator Penny Wong was sedate and obviously
less than comfortable amid the noise and flamboyance. 'It's much better when politicians don't dance,' she told reporters.[32] But she was there.

Early during her period in opposition, and a few weeks after her
forty-fifth birthday, Wong accepted an invitation to contribute to the
rolling series of events under the umbrella title Women of Letters. Prominent women were invited to read aloud a letter they had written on
a set topic. The occasion was not recorded, or shared on social media,
making it an oddly intimate public event, although some years later a
compilation was published in book form.

Penny Wong's topic was 'The time I changed my mind', and she
wrote a letter to her younger self. It was on her decision to enter politics,
and her ambivalence about public life. She revisited the elements of her
intellectual and political architecture – the importance of being in the
room and of practical action. The counterfactual made an appearance:
what would life have been like if she hadn't entered politics? She opened
by saying she thought about writing two letters; looking back, she wasn't
sure if she would advise herself to make a different career decision. So
one letter, she said, would 'encourage ... inspire and ... reassure'; the
other would 'scream and yell ... dissuade'.

The first letter would reassure her younger self that 'it will be all
right – more than all right ... it would remind me that who is in the

room matters … it would remind me … of how social change comes about – by changing hearts and minds, by deepening understanding, by working with others. Not by sitting on the sidelines.' This letter would also 'calm my fear that this life will destroy me. It would tell me that I can still love and live and nurture and heal. It would tell me that I will not lose myself. That I have not lost me.'

But the second letter would scream, 'Don't do it! Do you know what this country can do to strong women? To those who are pushy and presumptuous enough to stand up? You have no idea of the bile and vitriol coming your way.' That letter would tell her that there would be 'even more of the garden-variety "Go back to where you came from, you bloody Chink" abuse', and that there would also be 'homophobia – from those who can't decide if I hate men or if I want to be a man'. It would, she said, warn that 'there will be deep loneliness, not only because loved ones will be far away, but also because politics is the loneliest team sport'.

She moved on to muse that the 'notion of being a role model, which sits so uncomfortably with you today, matters not because of you but because it changes how others see themselves': 'It alters the limits others put on or take off their own aspirations. Because people can't be what they can't see … Don't worry about being gay. Most people will get over it, and those that don't will never change their mind, regardless of your competence.'

It is difficult not to read her final lines as a rallying cry not only to her younger self but to her contemporary one, gearing up for a battle of passion and principle, and the next episode in her journey to use politics to achieve change:

Knowing what I now know, I honestly cannot decide whether to warn you off or be supportive. Life and politics are always shaded by the myriad of counterfactuals, the endless what ifs, the possibility of another path. I don't know what I'm choosing between. So instead, here is a reminder of you, of who you are. You are not an artist. You are not a writer. But you do understand the power of imagination.

And the nation you imagine, the nation you hope for, is part of you. So, whatever you choose, do something that speaks to that part, to that hope, and you will never lose yourself.[33]

Early in her career, Wong had been determined not to be written off as 'the lesbian candidate' and had spent time and effort to make sure that didn't happen. Her journey from this to being prepared to put herself on the line over this issue began in 2004, with the excoriating vote for Howard's changes to the *Marriage Act*. That was when she promised herself, and her close friends such as Carol Johnson, that she would achieve change. It was a long journey. It had involved waiting, and strategising, to create the right political climate. Now the journey was nearing completion, and resolution.

*

Penny Wong was late one morning in early 2019 for an interview for this book. It was because of 'a dispute about fairy wings'. Her younger daughter, Hannah, was determined to wear a shirt with wings attached and 'it was in the dirty-clothes basket and it was filthy and I said, "You can't wear that." And so I had to look for the fairy wings we got for Christmas, which were somewhere in the back of the cupboard … It's hard because she is a gentle kid, and if you get angry with her she gets really upset, and it's …' She threw her hands over her face. 'It's, *arrrrgh.*'

Penny Wong and Sophie Allouache announced that they were pregnant with their second child in December 2014, with the baby due in April.

It had been a normal month in the life of the Labor opposition – a continuation of the hard work of holding the government to account and looking for political advantage. But it was also a momentous month for the world. China announced at the Asia-Pacific Economic Cooperation forum that it would agree to a peak in its greenhouse gas emissions in 2030, followed by a reduction. The commitment would be confirmed at the 2015 Paris Climate Change Conference, where the accord that Penny Wong and Kevin Rudd had helped formulate at Copenhagen was transformed into an international agreement to strive to keep global warming below 2 degrees Celsius by the end of the century. In 2014, Wong said the China announcement was a sign that the Abbott government was out of touch in its continuing poor record on climate-change action.[34]

A few days later, she was putting pressure on the Abbott government over broken promises regarding ABC funding, and successfully embarrassed defence minister David Johnston when, during a heated Senate debate, he claimed that the Adelaide-based Australian Submarine Corporation could not be trusted to build a canoe. 'He is a disgrace,' she said in the Senate. 'This is a man who has insulted thousands of hard-working Australians.'[35] Johnston was removed in a reshuffle a few weeks later.

The week after Johnston's gaffe, she was having a go at education minister Christopher Pyne after his bill to deregulate university fees was defeated by Labor and the crossbenchers in the Senate. 'Instead of trying to pretend he's Churchill, Christopher Pyne might actually try to go back to the drawing board and come up with a package that is more fair,' she said.[36]

Three days after that came the announcement of the pregnancy. She released the news in an interview with her hometown newspaper, *The Advertiser*. The baby, Wong said, had been conceived using the same IVF donor as Alexandra – a man known to the family but whose identity would remain private.

The announcement had effectively been made by three-year-old Alexandra. At the South Australian Labor convention in Adelaide in November, she had been sitting on the sidelines reading *The Gruffalo* over and over again to a baby. Wong came to check on her, and a friend said, 'She's just told everyone Mummy's got a baby in her tummy.'[37] Adelaide is efficient at nothing if not the spreading of gossip.

Reception of the news was far removed from the international media storm that had accompanied news of Alexandra's conception in 2011. This time there were only a handful of stories, most of them discussing Sophie's pregnancy along with the fact that South Australian Labor

MPs Kate Ellis and Amanda Rishworth were also expecting. A few days later, *Crikey* published its light-hearted annual awards list for politicians. Penny Wong was rated the third sexiest politician, behind Tanya Plibersek and the Greens' Larissa Waters. Sarah Hanson-Young was fourth. There was no mention of the impending birth.[38]

Hannah was born on Good Friday 2015. As with Alexandra, Francis Wong chose the Chinese middle names. Tian, the generational name, was shared with Alexandra. The second middle name was Hoong, which means 'rainbow'. Penny and Sophie chose the name Hannah because Penny liked it.

Once again, the birth came as the debate on same-sex marriage was heating up. The Labor Party was due to hold its national conference in July. Deputy leader Tanya Plibersek had announced she would be pushing for an end to the conscience vote on same-sex marriage, meaning that all Labor parliamentarians would be bound to vote for any future marriage equality bills before the parliament. The Coalition was split on the issue, and Tony Abbott was coming under pressure. Bill Shorten said he supported marriage equality but was against a binding vote. The media reported that the proposal would almost certainly be defeated. Other Labor MPs said they would cross the floor rather than vote to legalise same-sex marriage.[39]

Yet despite the political backdrop, this time around, the reception to her daughter's birth was muted. Penny announced it on Twitter, with a picture of Alexandra holding the newborn. The media commented that the photo was 'adorable', and moved on.[40] There was some hateful stuff on Twitter, but at nothing like the levels when Alexandra had been born. In just three years, the idea of a lesbian couple deciding to be mothers had moved from a scandal and a nationally divisive issue to a normal part of life. The country had moved.

But not all of it.

In June 2015, shortly after Penny Wong had returned to work after a month of parental leave, the Catholic Bishop of Port Pirie wrote to his parishioners saying that the children of same-sex partnerships would in future feel like a 'stolen generation'.[41] It made the national news. Penny

Wong later described the 'stolen generation' tag, which was picked up by others, as one of the most hurtful things ever said about her family.

In mid-2015, with Hannah in the first months of life and Labor's national conference approaching, it had become clear that the parliament could not, or would not, deliver on marriage equality until either Labor enforced a binding vote in accord with its platform or the Coalition allowed a conscience vote. Some were saying it was another example – along with climate change – of the Australian political system's inability to deliver good outcomes.

A lot had changed over the years Penny Wong had been a member of the Australian Labor Party. The Left faction, once relatively powerless, was growing in influence. Anthony Albanese had almost become leader in 2013. Mark Butler was now the party's national president. At the 2015 national conference, the Left would be on a near-equal footing with the Right. This was the result of many changes, but among them were the hard and dirty political work behind the scenes, the deals and the shaftings, some of which had involved Penny Wong. She was not outside or above politics. Penny Wong was, and had always been, absolutely and fundamentally *inside* politics and *of* politics. That was the choice she had made all those years ago. This was why what she did mattered, beyond the purely personal. That was why she had stepped into the spotlight on marriage equality.

In the lead-up to the July 2015 national conference in Melbourne, the Left faction was split on the issue of the conscience vote. The faction met privately on the morning of the vote, Sunday 26 July, in a final push to reach agreement. Albanese spoke emphatically in favour of a conscience vote. Then came Penny Wong. She said how rare it was for her to disagree with Albanese. She talked about how she had voted 'for my own discrimination' in 2004, because she believed in collectivism, and appealed for that spirit to prevail now. 'We are a party that stands together and fights together. We should stand together and fight together for equality before the law.' Some of the delegates were in tears.

The vote was conducted on the voices, and Penny Wong had a clear win. This victory meant that she was once again at risk of humiliating a

Labor leader – this time Bill Shorten – who had publicly backed a conscience vote.[42]

Penny Wong and Tanya Plibersek went to see him and negotiated
a face-saving compromise. The conscience vote would stay in place for
the rest of the parliamentary term, and the one after, but from 2019 all
Labor MPs would be obliged to vote for same-sex marriage in line with
the party platform. It was an intellectually inconsistent compromise –
suggesting that same-sex marriage was a matter of conscience for four
years but would then become an inalienable human right. In return,
Shorten was to make a public promise that within one hundred days
of a Labor government win he would introduce legislation to allow for
same-sex marriage.

Later that day, Penny Wong stood before the delegates at the conference. They all stood and applauded her – the room was so loud it
was a full minute before she could try to speak. The demonstration of
their support took her by surprise. Her jaw trembled. It seemed that
she might cry. But she rallied. 'Delegates, that was a very kind thing to
do,' she told them.

She reminded them of 2011, when the platform changed. 'I don't
think I have had a prouder day as a member of the Labor Party, and
I will be prouder still when we deliver marriage equality in law.' She
would like it sooner, she said, but 'this resolution does what we want,
which is to end the conscience vote, and you have the alternate Prime
Minister of Australia giving you the commitment of what a Labor government will do – one hundred days, a marriage equality bill. But I
want to win it sooner ... I want to win it in this parliament if we can.'

She challenged 'true liberals' to back same-sex marriage in the parliament: 'Marriage equality is a campaign of hope. It is a campaign of
justice and it is a campaign of equality. But most of all, delegates – and
this is why we will win – it is a campaign for those we love, for our partners, for our friends, our sisters, our brothers, our sons, our daughters.'[43]

Two weeks after the Labor Party conference, the Coalition party
room met to try to solve their impasse on the issue. Liberals in favour
of marriage equality – including Malcolm Turnbull – were furious

when Prime Minister Tony Abbott included the National Party, most of whom were opposed.

It was one of the most gruelling meetings in Coalition history. More than ninety parliamentarians spoke. The media were camped outside, marriage equality campaigners were glued to their televisions, and members of Australian Marriage Equality were on the telephones to the MPs and their influencers, armed with research, arguments and emotional support.

After six hours, Abbott emerged to face the media. He gave a long preamble, then announced that about two-thirds of his colleagues were against a free vote. Nevertheless, he had decided that the current term of parliament would be the last in which Liberal and National MPs would be bound to vote against same-sex marriage.

Right at the end of a long address, he said that in the next parliamentary term, same-sex marriage would be put to a public vote – a plebiscite. He gave no details – no idea of the timing or how the vote would be conducted. It was a way of managing the bitter divisions within the party. Penny Wong told marriage equality campaigners she was astounded by the lengths Abbott would go to in order to avoid a parliamentary vote in which, inevitably, some MPs would defy his authority and cross the floor.[44] As for the plan for a plebiscite, she described it to the media as 'a green light for hate speech ... We saw that Tony Abbott is a man who will fight tooth and nail to be yesterday's man.'[45]

One month later, Turnbull deposed Abbott as leader of the Liberal Party. He said the party needed to provide leadership that 'respects people's intelligence'. To become prime minister, he had needed the National Party to transfer the Coalition agreement to his leadership. The Nationals struck a hard bargain. Turnbull had to pledge, against his own principles, to stick to the Abbott plan for a plebiscite on same-sex marriage. He put it in writing. As Turnbull's numbers man, Simon Birmingham, put it later, the surrender on same-sex marriage was uniquely costly. 'That issue, more than any other, gave strength to Labor's narrative that Malcolm had capitulated to the Right. It didn't hurt immediately, but the symbolic power was huge.'[46]

Still, both sides of politics had now moved. Labor would enforce a pro-marriage equality vote. The Liberals would allow a conscience vote. The plebiscite was the conservatives' last hope – on an assumption that the public shared their views and would block change.

The 2016 election was a double dissolution called on the basis that the Senate had twice rejected government legislation to establish the Australian Building and Construction Commission, but was in fact fought mostly over jobs, the economy and the future of Medicare. It was to be an eight-week slog to election day and, once again, Penny Wong was campaign spokesperson. Marriage equality was a live issue. Turnbull said he would vote yes in any plebiscite. Shorten said that people's relationships shouldn't be 'submitted to a public opinion poll'.[47]

In June, at the height of the election campaign, Penny Wong delivered the Lionel Murphy Memorial Lecture, with marriage equality as her topic. She opened up about her experience of hate speech and the likely impact of a public vote.

For many gay and lesbian Australians, hate speech is not abstract. It's real. It's part of our everyday life. My Twitter feed already foretells the inevitable nature of an anti-equality campaign ...

As a public figure I'm pretty immune from the slings and arrows of public debate ... I am resilient enough to withstand it, but many are not ... I oppose a plebiscite because I do not want my relationship, my family, to be the subject of inquiry, of censure, of condemnation, by others. And I don't want other relationships, other families, to be targeted either.

Many same-sex couples don't hold hands on the street because they don't know what reaction they'll get. Some hide who they are for fear of the consequences at home, at work, at school ... Not one straight politician advocating a plebiscite on marriage equality knows what that is like – what it is like to live with the casual and deliberate prejudice that some still harbour.[48]

This was one of a collection of speeches and articles Penny Wong delivered during 2016 and 2017 in which she developed the case for marriage equality, and tackled the opposing arguments.[49] Sometimes, in the ones for the general public, she would speak mainly of love; in others, often for more specialised audiences, she talked history and philosophy. But the speeches all followed a similar trajectory. First, she placed the issue in the context of the long fight against discrimination. She compared homophobic policy to racial discrimination and laws of gender inequality – both now illegal.

Then she stepped through her opponents' main arguments. That marriage was immutable? That 'marriage just is', as Cory Bernardi had put it? History proved that untrue. Marriage existed long before Christian weddings were the norm, and at various times and locations, different groups of people had been excluded – slaves and prisoners, for example. In some places, marriage between those of different races had been banned. In parts of Australia, Aboriginal people had needed permission from the state to marry up until the 1950s. Now, gay and lesbian Australians were excluded from the institution. Marriage is an enduring institution, but it has never been frozen in time.[50] In Jane Austen's era, marriage had been mostly about money, family alliances and social position. All were thought to be more important than love.

She moved to the other side of the argument – coming from radicals who argued that marriage is an archaic institution, rooted in inequality, and therefore why should gays aspire to be married? Marriage had evolved, she said. Heterosexual people had changed it, so it was now chiefly about mutual support, intimacy and love. Why should gay people be excluded from that? 'Marriage has endured precisely because it has evolved, adapted and embraced change.'[51]

The argument from religion? Here she talked about her own faith: 'I don't think the God of my faith would be affronted by who I am, my relationship nor my family.'[52] She often quoted John Locke on the importance of freedom, including freedom from the imposition of religious belief. Locke had described homosexuality as 'promiscuous uncleanness'. But, she said, those who would quote Locke in support of discrimination against gays made 'a basic error in logic ... they can't distinguish principle from context. In my view, Locke identified a fundamental principle on which democratic politics is founded. It is the principle that matters, not who discovered it. One's own views should not determine the rights of others.'[53] She spoke about the changes in public opinion in her own time – how she now enjoyed the easy acceptance of her neighbour; the generosity of members of the public who stopped her in the street, at the airport, to tell her to press on; the good wishes received when her daughters were born, not only from friends but from strangers.[54]

*

The federal election was held on 2 July 2016. The result wasn't clear for days. Sitting on the ABC television panel on election night, Penny Wong said as the results rolled in: 'The people have spoken – we're just trying to work out what they said.'[55]

After a week of counting, neither party had a majority. Eventually, Turnbull achieved a one-seat majority. It was the second-closest election since 1961. Labor had come within a ghost of victory.

During the final fortnight of the campaign, the Labor Party had pushed hard against the plebiscite, instead touting Shorten's commitment – marriage equality in the first one hundred days of a Labor government, through a parliamentary vote. Activists in the marriage equality movement were now dedicated to opposing the plebiscite but preparing to win it if they had to. The government had the numbers to pass the necessary legislation in the lower house. The Senate was less certain. Labor took some time to make its position clear – although Penny Wong had already publicly opposed a plebiscite in the Lionel Murphy lecture. Over the second half of 2016, the Greens, Senator Derryn Hinch and the Nick Xenophon Team all announced that they would vote against the plebiscite, and in October Labor stated it would too.

In November the plebiscite legislation was defeated in the Senate 33–29. Penny Wong spoke during the debate, again emphasising the reality of hate speech and its impact. After the vote she felt satisfied, but not jubilant. She hoped the vote had succeeded in protecting vulnerable people. But the parliament, with its politics-as-usual approach, was no closer to delivering marriage equality.[56]

Wong and others began working on a way forward, which she assumed would succeed only under the next Labor government. The current government had released an exposure draft of a same-sex marriage bill sponsored by the Liberal senator Dean Smith. This was to be the vehicle for delivering the reform if the plebiscite succeeded. Wong lobbied for the bill to be put through the political process, and the Senate voted to establish a cross-party inquiry into the draft.

The resulting report was released in the week of Valentine's Day 2017. For the first time there was a cross-party consensus on the legislation. The bill would allow same-sex couples to marry but also protect the religious celebration of marriage. Wong told the Senate this was the first time 'the clouds of partisanship have parted ... We must now, together, take the next steps, to work together, to compromise, to end this debate and to achieve what is the will of the overwhelming majority of the Australian people.'[57] She told the media it was a 'historic agreement on how we can move forward and achieve marriage equality ... We ought to pause to consider the enormity of that achievement. [On] a debate so often mired in partisanship, mired in acrimony, a debate characterised by finger-pointing, we have a spirit of cooperation and the agreement around this report.'[58]

The emergence of a consensus bill gave more momentum to the debate. Corporate Australia joined in, with Qantas CEO Alan Joyce arguing that the parliament was falling behind the will of the people. Opinion polls showed increasing levels of popular support. Pressure was mounting on the government. On 9 August it brought the plebiscite bill forward again, and failed to get it to first base. Later that day it was announced that, instead of a plebiscite, which needed legislation, the government would instead have the Australian Bureau of Statistics conduct a postal survey.

A High Court challenge to disallow this failed. Over 16 million survey forms were mailed out from 12 September with a deadline for return of 7 November.

Wong hadn't wanted a plebiscite but, now the survey was inevitable, she decided along with the broader marriage equality movement that everything had to be thrown into winning it. She and others in Labor recommended to the two umbrella movements conducting the campaign for same-sex marriage – Australian Marriage Equality and Australians for Equality – that they recruit Tim Gartrell to lead the campaign. Wong had worked with Gartrell on several campaigns, including the 2007 effort that had brought Kevin Rudd to power. She told the lobbyists that Gartrell 'has the ability to think meta as well as details. So he sees the frame and the picture and the narrative and the emotional feel, but he's also good at the nuts and bolts. And very few people can do both.'[59]

While the High Court was still deliberating, Gartrell and the team assembled a campaign that reached out across the nation, including business, the union movement and community groups. There were rallies across Australia. Wong addressed a number of them. Meanwhile, when Wong was out with the children, Alexandra would count the number of cafés they passed with rainbow YES signs in the windows. Wong campaigned in Adelaide alongside the Greens' Sarah Hanson-Young and the Liberals' Christopher Pyne. On this issue, political differences were put aside.

When the results were released on 15 November, Wong was in a Senate committee room in Parliament House, television cameras trained on her and the other politicians gathered to watch the announcement on television. 'I'm nervous,' she said. She drank several glasses of water and joked that she wished it were gin. The volume on the television was turned up. 'These are the longest minutes of my life,' she said, closing her eyes for a short prayer.[60]

The chief statistician came on the screen and talked about the process of the survey. Penny Wong stood, her hand clasped tightly in a fist and held against her chest, chin up, eyes hard. She braced herself for the worst. She pursed her lips.

Then, at 10.03 am, the number of Yes votes was announced: 7,817,247. Penny Wong's face was animated. In a few seconds, she smiled, then frowned, then rocked from side to side. As the percentage of Yes votes was announced – 61.6 – she buried her face in her hands and turned away from the camera in tears. Labor senators Sam Dastyari and Pat Dodson patted her awkwardly on the back. Derryn Hinch put a rainbow flag around her shoulders.

In this moment, the political and the personal collided. Penny Wong's armour – her shield – collapsed. The Australian public had done what the parliament had been unable to do on its own. As the political journalist Katharine Murphy put it, 'The majority had spoken and they had accepted Penny Wong, her private and the public self. It was all OK.'[61]

The perpetual outsider, the Hakka descendant, the guest person, had been embraced and accepted – celebrated, even – and was now home.

*

At Wong's urging, action on the marriage equality bill began right away. An alternative bill containing stronger religious protections amounting to new forms of discrimination against same-sex couples was already before the parliament, sponsored by a conservative Liberal MP. Within hours of the plebiscite result, the *Marriage Amendment (Definition and Religious Freedoms) Bill 2017* – the Dean Smith Bill, now co-sponsored by a cross-party group including Penny Wong – was introduced in the Senate.

Wong spoke in the debate the next day. She pointed out that the Yes vote had been higher than any national two-party-preferred vote in the nation's history – marriage equality had more support than either of the two main political parties. It was 'a day of joy and a day of grace', she said. 'I chose to put my name in support of this bill because I believe this is the bill that can pass the parliament.' The Yes vote showed that fairness and equality in Australia grew ever stronger. 'This is the most personal of debates because it is about the people who matter most to us. It is about the people we love. So I say to Sophie, "Thank you for your love and commitment and for all you do." And I say to our beautiful daughters, Alexandra and Hannah, "I work for and fight for the world I want for you."'[62]

She sat down, accepted the hugs of her colleagues and some from the other side of the bench and, for the second time in forty-eight hours, the camera caught her brushing away tears.

Penny Wong made it clear to marriage equality campaigners that Labor would not support any amendments that amounted to new forms of discrimination – including changes to anti-discrimination laws to allow businesses to refuse services to gay couples.[63] On 29 November, the bill was passed by the Senate. None of the conservatives' amendments had been accepted. It passed the House of Representatives, also without amendment, on 7 December 2017.

The strategy – engineering a consensus bill through the Senate process – had worked. Politics had worked. And yet it had been done not by the parliament alone but by the people – by all those normally outside 'the room' in which decisions are made.

After the vote, Tim Gartrell said the result overturned conventional wisdom about the electorate's conservatism. He predicted it would energise the ambition of Australia's progressives on other fronts.[64] The 2019 federal election result has surely blunted that optimism. Many of the young people who enrolled to vote on same-sex marriage did not vote in the election.

So will Penny Wong and Sophie Allouache marry? Asked this question in early 2019, Wong said, 'Oh, who knows? That's something we will discuss together, and not in public.' It was never about her own desire to marry, she says, it was about her right to do so, and the right of everyone else like her.

When Sophie Allouache and Penny Wong filled out their survey forms, they did it with the children present. They walked together to the postbox. Penny Wong handed her form to the children, and they dropped it in. It was mostly about them, after all. 'For me, this really was wanting them to grow up not ever having society say to them that "your family is lesser".'[65]

13

A DANGEROUS PLACE

The 2019 federal election loss was devastating for Labor. The word was used often in the media to describe the events of 18 May, but it doesn't begin to capture the human reality of the disappointment.

Politicians don't attract much sympathy. They choose to play the game of thrones. Wong, at fifty years old, had spent most of her seventeen years in parliament preparing for power – for the ability to make a difference in government. In return she had had only the limited opportunities and plentiful frustrations of opposition, together with that brief, compromised six years of the Rudd–Gillard–Rudd government, with all its challenges and bitter unfulfilment. At a personal level, this loss was tragic.

The word 'tragedy' comes to us from the Greeks, where it meant a form of drama based on human suffering and the affairs of nations. In its true sense, the word is wrapped up with personal and political aspiration and human failings. According to Aristotle, the audience of a tragic play should leave the theatre cleansed and uplifted, with a heightened understanding of the ways of gods and humans. In tragedy, the lowest point comes before catharsis, which brings a lightening of the emotions, and fresh hope. At the time of the final interview for this book, on 9 July 2019, Penny Wong had not reached catharsis.

Wong did not expect the election defeat. 'It's the first election I haven't really judged correctly. But I don't think I'm an orphan in that,' she says. The Labor Party had been preparing for government. Public opinion polls had been predicting a Labor victory for almost three years, following the near win in 2016. Bill Shorten was never popular, but the party had, in public at least, united behind him. Meanwhile, the Coalition government had been in chaos, with Malcolm Turnbull deposed and Scott Morrison taking his job in August 2018.

Penny Wong had been preparing to be the minister for foreign affairs. After the 2016 election, she had requested the shadow portfolio. Over the next three years, overlapping with her work to build the case for legalising same-sex marriage, Penny Wong was working hard and quietly to construct what she described as a transformational foreign policy.

Foreign affairs, particularly at this moment in Australia's history, is arguably the most important job in government. It is also one of the lowest-profile domestically, and in election campaigns. Inevitably, there is a lot of bipartisanship between the major parties. The national interest demands it, which also means that policy disagreements are usually handled quietly. If foreign affairs hits the headlines, it is often evidence of crisis or failure. The work involves subtle language, negotiation and judgement calls. Yet in this portfolio, perhaps more than any other, there is the capacity to make a difference – the aim Wong has pursued ever since her teenage dreams of working for Médecins Sans Frontières. For Wong the anti-populist, the foreign affairs portfolio was a job that spoke to her talents and engaged her intellectually and emotionally. She brought to the preparation all her capacities and passion. The job was to be the pinnacle and the fullest expression of her career.

On election night she was part of the ABC panel commenting live on the results as they came in. She looked tired when the broadcast began at 6.00 pm. By shortly after 7.00 pm, it was clear to her that voting patterns were not playing out as expected. She texted Sophie, who was in a hotel room nearby with the children. 'I told her that I thought we were in trouble. I was trying to work out how long I would have to be there.'

It was 'horrible' to be on public display while dealing with such a shattering blow. Her fellow panel members, including Liberal senator Arthur Sinodinos, were 'gracious and decent', which helped. As is her way, she remained outwardly calm while in tumult. 'I thought to myself,

What's my job here, what should I do? and I thought that in part it was
to speak to those who voted for us and who were also disappointed.'

By 8.30 pm it was clear that a Labor defeat was likely. The ABC
election analyst Antony Green called the result as a Coalition victory
an hour later. Wong put in a three-hour-long display of grace under
pressure. She acknowledged a desire for a gin and tonic towards the
end. It was a 'very tough result' for Labor, she said.[1] She can't remember
whether she ever got the gin and tonic. She went back to the hotel, to
Sophie and the children.

The next morning, when Alexandra and Hannah woke up, they saw
Penny's face. 'Did you lose, Mum?' asked Alexandra. 'How are you?'

Penny replied that she was 'devo'.

'What does that mean?'

'Devastated. Very, very upset.'

The children set about trying to work out what they could do. 'They
made me a coffee and they gave me their last gingerbread man. I thought,
Greater love hath no child ...'

Alexandra recalled her earlier comment that she didn't want Labor
to win, and apparently felt guilty about it. 'She said, "Mum, I know I
said I didn't want you to win, but I *did* want you to win as well." I said,
"It's OK, darling. That's just how it happened."'

In the days that followed, Wong considered quitting politics. 'I had
to decide whether I wanted to stay. I don't want to be melodramatic
about it, but in these jobs you have to really commit and I had to ask
myself if I still could. The disappointment is not just personal – those
dashed hopes and dreams – and it's not just party political or tribal. It's
a sense of loss about what you want to be part of, about the meaning
of your life.

'When I was younger ... I wanted to do something in my life that
had some meaning ... There's a purpose to many, many jobs, but there's
a particular type of purpose to politics ... being part of something bigger than yourself and trying to contribute to shaping the country. And I
guess the question I had to ask was, 'Do I still have that in me?' Because
I think if you decide you don't then you should get out. And then there's

the question of whether, emotionally, you could do something else –
whether you would be content or satisfied in another kind of job.'

Her indecision did not last long. On 22 May, four days after the election, she called a media conference in which she announced her support
for Anthony Albanese to replace Bill Shorten as leader. Albanese was 'a
man of authenticity', she said, as well as describing him (of course) as the
outstanding parliamentarian 'of our generation'.[2] She looked exhausted –
she had dark circles under her eyes – but she was trademark Wong for the
cameras: calm, composed and forceful. By then, she had decided both
that she had what it took to stay in politics through the barren years of
opposition and that there was nothing else she wanted to do.

Her intervention came close to sealing the deal for Albanese. The
other contenders – Tanya Plibersek, Jim Chalmers and Chris Bowen –
dropped out of the race shortly afterwards.

Otherwise, Wong virtually disappeared from the headlines. She expressed no opinion on the reasons for the defeat, beyond what she had said
on election night about the impact of Clive Palmer's wall-to-wall advertising and the Coalition's preference deals with One Nation. Although
she had not voted for Shorten as leader, she offered no public blame for
either the policies Labor carried to the election, the unpopularity of the
leader, nor the campaign. Not all her colleagues were so restrained.

Simultaneously, this book was reaching its final stages. I had seen
her on 7 March for our last interview before the election. I had asked
for a final interview after the election, expecting that she would by then
be the minister for foreign affairs and we would talk foreign policy. As
was her way, she had neither guaranteed that interview nor refused me,
but I was led to expect it would happen.

But in the post-election period, communications temporarily broke
down. The time was fast approaching when it would be too late for a
final interview to inform this book, but no date was offered. On the
grapevine I heard that Wong was not in a good way. The publisher
stretched the deadlines.

On 2 July – the first day the federal parliament sat after the election –
Penny Wong was there but, as political journalist Katharine Murphy

commented, 'Wong lacked her characteristic vigour. She was in full possession of her poker face, but the disappointment at Labor's circumstances was etched in her body language.'[3]

The day before, she had given one of her first extended media interviews since the defeat, to Fran Kelly on Radio National's *Breakfast*. She talked mainly about how Labor would handle the government's tax cut legislation; on this she did a competent political job, not committing to anything and doing what she could to turn the pressure back on the government. Then the discussion turned to foreign affairs. Donald Trump had stepped over the North Korean border to shake the hand of leader Kim Jong-un. Wong commented that Trump liked to try engineering historically significant moments, but the true importance of this would depend on what followed – would Kim denuclearise? Asked about a truce in the US–China trade war, she said trade wars had no winners. Australia's interests were not served by bilateral trade arrangements between the United States and China: 'What we want is open, fair multilateral agreements.'

Finally, she was asked about unrest in the Middle East between the United States and Iran. US secretary of state Mike Pompeo had called on Australia to adopt a tougher stance to increase global pressure on Iran. Prime Minister Scott Morrison had not ruled out Australian participation in any military conflict. What would Labor's attitude be? Wong pointed out that no request had yet been received from Washington. Labor had sought a briefing from the government; she said she expected that to happen in the coming week, and went on: 'We don't believe military conflict is in anyone's interests.' The situation demanded that both sides de-escalate. Would Labor support military collaboration with the United States if asked? No such request had been made, she reiterated.[4]

Here were hints of the kind of foreign minister she would have been. It was possible to imagine the contours of what she might have said to Kelly had she been speaking not from opposition, but from government – the subtle shifts that, to the community that knows how to do the textual analysis, would have been significant.

Finally, at the very last moment it could inform this book, I was granted a final interview.

When we met, I suggested to Penny Wong that after tragedy there is catharsis.

'Is there?' she responded grimly.

Deciding to stay in politics did not mean she had recovered from the blow of the election defeat. 'I don't think this stuff is linear. I've never found emotional events in my life were dealt with in a linear way. It's much more organic.'

Certain aspects were harder than she had expected, others easier. Asked if there was any part of her that had not wanted to be the minister for foreign affairs in a Shorten government, Wong said, 'I was really worried about how we would manage, how I would protect and maintain and nurture my personal relationships.'

During the campaign, Alexandra, now seven years old, had been very focused on how much her mother was home. 'She was always asking, "When are you coming back? How many nights will you be gone? Will you be gone before I go to sleep? Will you be here when I wake up?" And now the kids have stopped asking, because I am just around. That's very nice. Really, really nice.'

Our interview took place the day after she had appeared on the ABC's *Q&A*, in which she talked again about foreign affairs. We were in a sterile meeting room at the Commonwealth Parliament Offices in central Sydney. The two events together – granting this interview and her *Q&A* appearance – signalled that Penny Wong was back in the game, still 'in the room'.

*

Penny Wong's preparation in foreign policy had begun in the shadow trade portfolio, which she held between the 2013 and 2016 election defeats. Once given the foreign affairs remit after the 2016 election, the preparation intensified.

Early on, she spent time with Gareth Evans, foreign minister in the Hawke and Keating governments from 1988 to 1996. Evans is remembered as one of Australia's most ambitious and successful foreign ministers, whose tenure straddled the end of the Cold War.

In theory, what is generally referred to as the 'international rules-based order' – the system of trade agreements, international treaties and compacts sponsored and led by the United States – dates from World War II and its immediate aftermath. In reality, it had its fullest expression in the burst of optimism and the potential for a better world that followed the fall of the Berlin Wall. Evans increased Australia's involvement with Asia and shifted the emphasis away from our traditional alliance with the United States. His was a structured, analytical approach. He articulated the concepts of Australia as a middle power and insisted that practising what he called 'good international citizenship' should be considered not just worthy in a moral sense but as an essential part of the national interest. His achievements included the initiation of a United Nations peace plan for Cambodia; Australia's crucial role in the international Chemical Weapons Convention, which outlaws the production and stockpiling of chemical weapons; and establishing both the Asia-Pacific Economic Cooperation (APEC) forum and the ASEAN Regional Forum. His was an activist foreign policy.

Today, Gareth Evans remembers that he offered Penny Wong 'an opportunity to throw ideas around' almost immediately after she was appointed. He thought highly of Wong but hadn't worked closely with her. In the months that followed her appointment they talked both detail and overarching principle. Penny Wong nominates 'Gareth' as the foreign minister she most admires, while also acknowledging that he presided over 'a different time – not as disruptive'. For Evans, working for outcomes within the rules-based order was possible. Now, across the world, from Britain to China and Donald Trump's United States, the dominant powers are moving away from the rules and the treaties that represent the best chance of security for middle-sized powers such as Australia.

Evans encouraged Wong to spend time thinking through the intellectual framework for foreign policy. She recalls, 'I took that on board. And I went back and looked at a lot of what he had done, his early writings in opposition and then also in government ... he had worked through quite systematically an intellectual framework ... and that appealed to me.'[5] Evans remembers that in their early conversations he urged her to think through and articulate the 'national interest' – a phrase often thrown around by politicians but rarely defined. As Penny Wong was later to remark, John Howard as prime minister had used an undefined notion of 'the national interest' to shut down conversation when he sent Australian military forces to join the United States in the 2003 invasion of Iraq.[6] Evans suggested to Wong that while the international climate had fundamentally changed, the national interest had not. He character-ised the national interest as consisting of security, prosperity and a sound economy. He also talked to her about 'good international citizenship'. These were the foundations on which she should build, he suggested.

Penny Wong talked to many other foreign policy specialists. She had discussions with Hugh White, professor of strategic studies at the Australian National University and the author of several books argu-ing that Australia will increasingly be forced to choose between the United States, our traditional ally, and China, our largest trading part-ner. White has argued that the regional power balance has already shifted towards China, and that the United States is a less-than-reliable ally that might not come to Australia's aid in the future. In the contest for regional supremacy, he has said, 'America will lose, and China will win,' so Australia had better work out how to deal with that. White imagines Australia forced to cope alone in a region where conflict between two superpowers is playing out. His latest book examines whether Austra-lia could defend itself in the absence of US assistance – and what that would entail.[7] White remembers Wong as a 'charming and gracious per-sona and an appealing interlocutor'. He was left with the impression that she disagreed with his analysis, but 'clearly understood what I was saying and was at grips with what was going on and why I thought as I did'.

She talked to Michael Fullilove, the executive director of the Lowy Institute, and to Peter Drysdale, an emeritus professor at the ANU's Crawford School of Public Policy and an expert on China's growing eco-nomic strength. She had meetings at the university's Australian Centre on China in the World and launched its 2017 yearbook. She consulted

Allan Gyngell, director of the Crawford Australian Leadership Forum and Fullilove's predecessor. Gyngell's 2017 book *Fear of Abandonment* argues that Australian foreign policy has always presupposed dependence on a great power – first Britain, and then the United States. Until recently, Australia's strategic partners have also been our main economic partners, but with China our biggest trading partner, for the first time we are economically dependent on a country that is not an ally. Australia is at a turning point, Gyngell argues. The 'globalisation engine is now spluttering'.[8] He criticises 'Australia's occasional lack of ambition and reluctance to wield the power available to it; its preference for hunkering down in the company of allies; its diplomatic caution'. In future, he says, the slipstream of the superpowers will be a dangerous place. Australia needs to be bolder and more vigorous.

Penny Wong listened, and was later to quote some of his ideas. Of all the experts she consulted, she singles out Gyngell as the one who probably influenced her the most. He is a 'clean thinker', she says – which from Wong is very high praise. 'He writes as I would like to write.' Gyngell, meanwhile, describes Wong as probably the best-prepared foreign-minister-in-waiting Australia has ever had.

She also read widely among the international foreign policy periodicals and academic papers. A PhD student specialising in India at the University of Melbourne was surprised one day by a contact from Penny Wong's office requesting a chat about the subcontinent.

Allan Behm was brought on to her staff as the senior adviser on foreign policy. She had first encountered him when he was Greg Combet's chief of staff. Behm had spent thirty years in the public service, specialising in international relations, defence strategy, and counterterrorism and law-enforcement policy. He was highly respected within the foreign policy community, and renowned for the character of his approach – intellectual, reflective and values-driven, rooted in his Jesuit education. When Wong's speeches began to contain references to Enlightenment figures, people interpreted it as Behm's influence.

Today, Behm says Wong has one of the best policy minds he has encountered among the many politicians he has served. She is, he says, 'certainly in the league of Gareth Evans and Kim Beazley'. Behm, who joined her staff in March 2017, remembers his brief was to 'offer a set of propositions to help her hammer out her ideas. If she didn't agree with me she would argue with me. It was a synergistic process.' They both loved intellectual combat. 'We had a lot of them. Never did they come anywhere near anger or irritation. Penny has never been the slightest bit short with me. But she is forensic. She's a lawyer, and she approaches any issue in a relentlessly logical way.' Behm was also dispatched to talk to other foreign policy thinkers, some of whom Wong had already spoken to. He prepared summaries of what the various thinkers said, highlighting areas of agreement and disagreement and detailing their reasoning.

They both remember early conversations about ways of thinking through problems. Their approaches were very different. She was structured, logical and deductive. His thinking was inductive or, as he puts it, when confronted with a problem he would consider it laterally: imagine what the world would look like without that problem in it, and work out how to get closer to that world. With Behm, Wong thought through how to frame issues differently, and how to attempt to persuade other countries to act in a way that met Australia's interests, rather than focusing only on our own actions. Wong says she worked on her speeches in a structured way – starting with boxes of concepts branching out into collections of ideas. To her, Behm seemed to be 'stream of consciousness', but together they worked in a way that was multidimensional. She says, 'I think about it as a meta-analysis. I try to think through the particulars in terms of what it means.'

Elements of this 'meta-analysis' approach were already visible in her brand of intellectual engagement with an issue. It could be seen in her repeated rejection of binary thinking, dating back to her period as the minister for climate change and water, if not before. It could be seen from the 2013 John Button address on in her adoption of the concept of the counterfactual as a way of thinking through policy dilemmas and alternative trajectories. It could be seen in the speeches she was giving on same-sex marriage, overlapping with the period in which she was working out her approach to foreign policy. It was visible in the framing of same-sex marriage as about love rather than aberration, and in the way she addressed the argument that marriage was an archaic institution by pointing out how it had changed over history.

Today, she says it is evident in her attitude to the debate over religious freedom in the wake of the homophobic comments made by Christian rugby union star Israel Folau. In her July 2019 *Q&A* appearance, she talked not about a legal response but about the kind of society we should seek to be – tolerant and respectful: 'Surely we want to come out of this improving that and not diminishing it.'[9] In our interview the following day, she said, 'I always find this religious freedom debate quite intellectually frustrating. We seem to move from the right for people to have belief to the idea that we abrogate the concept of equality before the law as a consequence of belief. That is a substantial step for a liberal democracy, but people just jump that step without understanding the meaning of it.'

Her rejection of binary thinking and conventional solutions, though, reached its apogee in her approach to the most urgent and difficult foreign policy issue of our time: how to handle our relationship with China and the United States. Is Australia to be meat in the sandwich? Does China's rise represent an opportunity or a threat? Do we have to choose between our traditional ally and the country on which so much of our economy depends?

On 8 November 2016, when Penny Wong had been in the shadow foreign affairs job about four months, Donald Trump won the US election. During the campaign Bill Shorten had described Trump as 'barking mad'.[10] Penny Wong, invited to agree during a television interview, was much more diplomatic. He was, she said 'an interesting candidate', and acknowledged that Labor's policies – against protectionism, in favour of multilateral trade agreements and a rules-based international order – were at variance with Trump's positions.[11]

Trump had made it clear he was a nationalist and a protectionist. He was contemptuous of the Trans-Pacific Partnership Agreement, the engine of former president Barack Obama's promised 'pivot to Asia'. Later, Trump was to withdraw from the agreement and start an episodic trade war with China. Australia's former ambassador to Washington, Kim Beazley, commented that if Trump pursued his objectives 'it will effectively suspend American leadership in global free trade and in the global order'.[12] Penny Wong wrote an opinion piece for *The Sydney Morning Herald* predicting a 'substantive shift' in US foreign policy. 'It is in Australia's interest to continue to assert our values and interests, and we should always be prepared to make clear our disagreement with political leaders who undermine them,' she wrote.[13] For that she was criticised by Prime Minister Malcolm Turnbull, who claimed Labor was trying to weaken the foundation of national security: the Australia–US defence alliance.[14]

But the problems with US policy towards China preceded Trump. President Obama had proclaimed his 'pivot' but failed to push back credibly when China established a military presence around the disputed Scarborough Shoal, which the international courts later recognised as belonging to the Philippines. That apparently emboldened the Chinese, who began to fortify and build islands in disputed areas the following year. The United States had attempted to draw a line, and then failed to enforce that line. The countries of the region had to work out how to respond. Following the 2016 election of Rodrigo Duterte as president of the Philippines, that nation did not pursue its rights under the international courts ruling, and instead grew closer to China. If the United States was not going to enforce the line, the Philippines was hardly able to do so on its own. Conciliation was the only option. This was part of the environment in which Wong sought to work out her 'transformational' approach to foreign policy.

The language of diplomacy is nuanced. Political bipartisanship in the national interest means that differences are communicated in ways missed by most ordinary people – and, for that matter, by most daily journalism. The foreign policy community, and the diplomats of foreign nations, examine the entrails of speeches and public statements, and do the textual analysis, looking for shifts in attitude or emphasis. For example, when Penny Wong said, as she did in most of her speeches from early 2017 onwards, that Australia would always follow its national interest, it was probably read by most as a statement of the obvious. But in the contexts Wong used it, the message received in the foreign policy community was loud and clear. It was about a more independent stance – that the United States should by no means assume that Australia would be in lockstep should it choose to confront Beijing in the South China Sea.

One of her first significant speeches as shadow minister for foreign affairs was delivered in March 2017 to the Global Heads of Mission – Australia's senior diplomats – who had been gathered by foreign minister Julie Bishop as part of the consultation process for a Foreign Policy White Paper. Wong talked about the 'discontinuity' in world affairs. She preferred this term to 'disruption' because it highlighted the fact that almost nothing in the current environment could be counted as a continuation of business as usual. Few of the traditional rules or assumptions still applied.

In particular, she described China's rise as having altered the rules of how strategic power was acquired. Previously, it had been about military might, and economic strength translated smoothly into military power. China, though, was 'seeking strategic power through economic dominance'. It was a new and challenging dynamic. She went on to catalogue the troubles of the world – Brexit, the unpredictability of Trump, civil war from North Africa to Afghanistan. Then she came to the main message she wanted to deliver to these senior diplomats. Australian foreign policy, said Wong, should be driven not by fear, but by optimism and confidence: 'In times of uncertainty, first-mover advantage lies with whoever sets the agenda. And that is exactly what we should seek to do, practically and confidently.'

She signalled a pragmatic approach to China. Labor would 'begin with what China actually is, rather than through the lens of risk management'. It was a form of words that recurred – the idea that China was portrayed or characterised in various ways but none captured its true nature. Later, she developed the idea that China's own idea of itself might not always be accurate. Labor would not deal with China from an ideological or fixed position.[15] For example, Australia did not need to either wholly reject or embrace China's Belt and Road Initiative, the wide-ranging international infrastructure program. Labor would approach it 'with an eye to identifying points of mutual interest and complementarity rather than reflexive negativity'.[16]

Wong was rejecting the idea that Australia had to choose – or rather, as she put it in later speeches, she thought we should be continually involved in a pragmatic, enlightened process of 'choosing for us'. This would involve a transformation of both Australia's key relationships – that with the United States, as well as that with China.

She had been Julie Bishop's guest at the Global Heads of Mission Meeting, and did not criticise her directly. But in later speeches she characterised the Coalition's approach to foreign affairs as 'transactional' – mere reactive management of events. Labor, she said, would be 'transformational' – taking the lead and the initiative to bring about change. Transaction and transformation were not binaries, she suggested. Both management and strategy were needed. But Labor sought, within its sphere of influence, to change the world.[17] Bishop had said in the 2016 election campaign that her approach to foreign affairs was marked by realism: 'We deal with the world as it is, not as we would wish it to be.' In a later speech, Wong picked up those words and used them against her: Labor would 'deal with the world as it is, and ... seek to change it for the better – to shape, as best we can, the world in which we live'.[18] This declaration appeared in most of her speeches from then on.

In the months after the Global Heads of Mission Meeting, Wong laid out her foreign policy approach in a series of addresses. The first two, conceived as a pair, were described in her office as 'the interests speech' and 'the values speech'. Behm had wanted the values speech delivered first – as the foundation of all that followed – but Wong was instead keen to establish the national interests that would drive Labor's foreign policy, and concerned not to appear romantic or sentimental. The values speech therefore took many careful drafts, which meant the interests speech came first for practical reasons. Titled 'Australia's national interests in a time of disruption', it was delivered at the Lowy Institute on 6 July 2017. The values speech, titled 'Australian values in a time of disruption', was delivered at Griffith University almost exactly a month later.[19] After these two came another pigeon pair – an address about Australia's relationship with China, delivered on 16 October 2017, and one about the foundations and future of Australia's connection with the United States, again almost exactly a month later.[20] The following January, she brought all these ideas together for an international audience in a speech at the Lee Kuan Yew School of Public Policy in Singapore.[21] According to Allan Behm, Kim Beazley described this as the best address ever given by an Australian foreign minister or shadow. Two more speeches about China followed in the ensuing year as events developed.

Wong worked on all these herself. In the conference room of her Adelaide office she would sit across the desk from Behm, who recalls, 'She will fight every bloody sentence and every word if she needs to. She owns her own thinking. She battles it out.'

In the interests speech she set out, as Gareth Evans had urged her, to articulate and define the national interest. These were, she said, 'the security of the nation and its people; economic prosperity, enabled by frameworks that allow Australia to take advantage of international economic opportunities; a stable, cooperative strategic system in our region anchored in the rule of law; and constructive internationalism supporting the continued development of an international rules-based order.'[22] This was largely the framework articulated by Evans, but Wong had changed his language in a significant way. What he had described as 'good international citizenship' had become 'constructive internationalism' – a more precise term adopted for these less optimistic times. The logic, Behm says, was that in disruptive times it is hard to tell what 'good' means; much easier to see whether something has been constructive or not.

She then picked up on each element in turn. Wong broadened the conventional understanding of security to include not only defence and counterterrorism but also economic and financial security – issues such as 'quality child-care, affordable healthcare and the secure prospect of a dignified retirement ... In a disrupted world, security concerns are expanding in their scope. People remain worried by war and the threat of war. But they are also increasingly worried by the political and social impacts of growing economic inequality.'

To increase economic prosperity, Wong argued, Australia should be working towards a cooperative relationship between China and the United States. Integral to this was an open trading system. Labor would eschew Trump's isolationism. For middle powers, a rules-based system was essential to security and economic interests, she said. She quoted Gyngell's comments about the danger of lingering in the slipstream of superpowers, and signalled an activist approach. 'Convergence of interests doesn't just happen. It has to be worked at.' This meant working on not only multilateral and bilateral defence but also the relationship in every sector of society – trade and political consultations, as well as people-to-people connections through education and tourism. Development assistance to the Asia-Pacific was crucial: 'Cuts to development assistance not only worsen the lives of people living in poverty but contribute to instability – with consequences that impact on the stability of develop-ment assistance recipients and on our security interests more generally.'

As for constructive internationalism:

The most effective response to disruption ... is to deal with it actively and constructively, working in concert with like-minded nations while identifying and managing, as well as we can, the sources of disruption ... While this might appear, at one level, to be an expression of morality, it is in fact an expression of enlightened self-interest. For nations such as Australia, playing as we are in the second eleven of economies but with global interests, constructive internationalism is a core national interest that delivers fundamen-tal security and economic benefits.

She concluded by again asserting that Australia should be bold – it should seek to set the agenda 'modestly but confidently'.

The 'values' speech confirmed that Labor would pursue 'a transfor-mation in foreign policy'. This meant, Wong elaborated, a policy that was informed by values while pursuing national interests. 'Values define who we are. Values guide our behaviour as individuals and as nations, determining the moral compass that is as necessary for national leaders as it is for the individual.' She referred to her maiden speech, all those years before, and her description of compassion as the 'core value'. She had not changed her mind, she said.

So what were Australia's core values? Democracy was 'a political practice' rather than a value. It relied on the rule of law applying to all citizens. But 'at the core of the values to which we as Australians adhere' was 'the intrinsic worth and dignity of each person by virtue of their basic humanity – their fundamental right to exist, to live a life of worth and fulfilment, to chart their own course through life and to pursue happiness'. This, she said, was what the rule of law meant, and from where it drew its legitimacy.

The foreign-minister-still-in-waiting combatted the notion that values were a 'kind of stalking horse' behind which '"the West" ... seeks to assert and defend a form of political dominance'. She used her own heritage in a manner no previous Australian shadow foreign minister could have done:

> Just as my family inherited two cultural traditions, so too did it comprehend two religious traditions, Christianity and Buddhism, both of them traditions which situate the individual in the context of family and community. Values underpin the common experience of humanity ... there are common threads such as community, respect, hospitality, honour, care and dignity, the observance of which depends on a fundamental acceptance of human worth.

The idea that defending human rights is a Western notion, or part of neo-colonialism, is often suggested when the human rights record of countries of our region is brought into question. Wong's personal background meant she was uniquely able to combat it.

The worth of each individual human was the basis, she said, for the rule of law, and therefore the international rules-based order. 'The alternative to a values-inspired foreign policy is a purely power-based foreign policy ... The twentieth century is littered with examples of the failure of power-based foreign policy.'

In her speech about Australia's relationship with the United States, Penny Wong reiterated the centrality of the rule of law. Behm describes this address as one of the most radical ever given on foreign affairs – but it was almost entirely overlooked by the media at the time. 'Never mind,' he says. 'The Americans understood what she was saying, loud and clear.'

The traditional convention of Australian politicians' speeches about the US–Australian partnership is to begin with the ANZUS Treaty as foundational and express gratitude for the defence provided by our great and powerful friend. Wong didn't mention ANZUS until more than halfway through. Instead, she laid out an alternative understanding of the relationship's foundation: constitutionality and the rule of law.

Wong went back to 1770, when Captain Cook sailed the *Endeavour* into Botany Bay, with a New Yorker, James Matra, as one of his midshipmen. Our two nations' histories were linked, she asserted. She did not use the term 'kindred offspring', the term once used to describe the parallels between Australia and Borneo, her countries of origin, but she was talking about that idea: the United States and Australia as progenies of the British colonial endeavour. 'The decision taken by the government of George III to establish the colony of New South Wales owed much to the American Revolution,' she noted. 'The loss of the American colonies meant that the British government had to find somewhere else for the pickpockets, poachers and political prisoners.'

She tracked forward through the American presence at the gold rushes, and referenced US businessman Herbert Hoover, who arrived in Albany in 1897 and soon persuaded his principals in London to establish the Sons of Gwalia mine – which survived into the twenty-first century and at one point was Australia's third-largest gold producer. She spoke of the trade relationship: despite China's dominance in bilateral trade, in terms of two-way investment the United States was Australia's top partner.

But more important were the countries' links through their constitutions. Britain had no written constitution, but on opposite shores of the Pacific, constitutions went 'to the core of how Australia and the US organise our democracies and shape our political lives'. This, she said, was 'a foundation of our continuing partnership'.

It was in this context that Penny Wong finally mentioned ANZUS. 'The salient feature about alliances is this: they are not about warfare. They are about common interests.' She called for the operating principles of the ANZUS Treaty – consultation and action – to apply not only to defence but 'across the entire bilateral relationship'.

What did the Americans understand from this speech? According to Behm, they got the message that 'its importance notwithstanding, ANZUS does not define our relationship with you. We are about more than that.'

The pair to this address was one on China. Evans had urged Wong to view China as not necessarily a threat. Behm says: 'China is growing its power. It's finding it difficult to grow its authority. And when it can't have authority it's a bit inclined to lash out and be a bit ham-fisted and actually act against its own interests.'

Evans says today that China's challenge to the international order can be overstated. In his view, China is busy asserting its right to be not only a rule-taker but also a rule-maker. 'But it doesn't mean it wants to tear up the entire system. That just means that it wants to be part of the rule-making process.' The main 'barefaced challenge' to the rules-based order, he says, is China's aggression in the South China Sea. But even there, he points out, the lack of regard for international rules relates to both sides. The United States has not ratified the United Nations Convention on the Law of the Sea, under which international courts adjudicate competing claims in the area. Evans believes the threat China poses in the South China Sea must be addressed, but 'it's at least as much the responsibility of the Americans to accept the reality of China's rise and not try to exercise ... a dominant role in the region'.

Wong, at least initially, was optimistic about China. Behm sees her heritage as important here. Raised in Chinese culture, she has an inherent respect for it. 'She understands what China has achieved. She understands what China's priorities are.' In the China speech, Wong called for a 'step change' in engagement with Asia – 'not tinkering, not gradualism, but a fundamental whole-of-government, indeed whole-of-nation, effort to deepen and broaden our engagement with Asia ... If we want to get it right with Asia, we need to get it right with China.'

She described the 'binary thinking' of the economic and security worlds, 'each of which is populated by disparate groups, each with their particular mindsets, that either talk past each other or simply do not connect at all'. Labor's policy, she said, would not start or finish by deciding between China and the United States, but instead by 'continually deciding for us'. 'For those who remain attracted to the linearity implied in the so-called "inevitability" of a choice between Washington and Beijing,' she noted, 'let me remind them that a disrupted world is non-linear, and for that reason it is not only option-rich, it is choice- and decision-rich.'[23]

In these two speeches Wong had announced an intention to transform both of Australia's key international relationships, and to chart its own course – seeking to escape the dangerous slipstream.

Wong's acclaimed address in Singapore at the beginning of 2018, bringing many of these foreign policy ideas together, was both a continuation and introduced new elements. She revisited the ideas of national interest and values, and the rule of law. But her earlier optimism about managing the relationship with China was tempered. She emphasised that China differed from Australia on many values – most significantly, it was not a democracy. Nevertheless, she said, Australia would deal with China 'on the basis of respect, not fear'. In later addresses, Wong's optimism about the relationship with China had further decreased. In 2018, she issued what could be interpreted as a caution to China:

We should be consistent and clear about our support for multi-lateral and transparent trade arrangements. We should be clear that Australian sovereignty is beyond politics and never up for negotiation. We should respect the role China has in the region. So, too, we should expect China to respect the core elements that define the characteristics of a stable, peaceful and prosperous region.[24]

By the time of the 2019 election campaign, she was acknowledging that it would get more difficult, not easier, to manage.[25] In the final interview for this book she stated that, while China's clear desire to be among the rule-makers was reasonable, it was unclear how fundamental the changes it wanted to the international rules-based order would be. In notes she wrote in preparation for her *Q&A* appearance she said that both the United States and China were 'in different ways ... challenging the status quo. This means the playbook of the last decades isn't fit for purpose.' A stable and prosperous region would mean 'a multipolar region in which the US remains deeply and constructively engaged, in which China is a positive contributor and in which there is broad support amongst the countries of the region for these rules and norms'.

The new element here – a change of emphasis rather than of approach – was the role of the rest of the region. Perhaps it was in fostering this that Australia could take the initiative.

So much for the intellectual foundations of foreign policy. What would Penny Wong's policy stance have meant in action, if she were foreign minister? What will Labor's attitude be as the Morrison government deals with the challenges? What, for example, would be the response if the United States wanted support for a military freedom-of-navigation operation in the South China Sea, or for Australia to join a coalition taking military action against Iran?

Wong was understandably constrained in answering questions about these matters in our interview. There is no such thing as a dialogue with only the Australian readers of this book. It will be read by allies and rivals internationally.

But, reading between the lines of what she says, it is clear she would be pragmatic. She would not make the decision until it was necessary to do so. There would be no blanket guarantees or statements of 'all the way with the USA'. Australia would 'decide for us'. The ghost of this approach was seen in her interview with Fran Kelly when asked about military action in Iran. No request had been received. No further comment needed to be made.

She would identify the national interests in play. In the South China Sea, she would ask what other countries more directly affected – Japan, the Philippines, Vietnam, Indonesia, Malaysia, South Korea – were doing. This would be a determining part of the context in which Australia's decisions would be made.

Wong says she thinks too much emphasis can be given to the tensions in the South China Sea. They tend to be symbolic for China hawks and doves (another unhelpful binary). But at some point, she thinks, there is likely to be a flashpoint, an occasion that will require the countries of the region to make their support for freedom-of-navigation explicit. Rather than thinking of this in terms of US-led action that Australia might be called on to join, she emphasises the importance of action by those regional states that have a direct stake in the territorial disputes.

Action by such regional players might not be military. In 2016, Indonesian leader Joko Widodo sailed to the Natuna Islands and held a cabinet meeting in waters where his nation's interests and rights overlap with China's. The move was described by Indonesian officials as the strongest message the nation had sent to China – but there were no soldiers, no sabre-rattling, no obvious increase in tension.[26]

According to Wong, 'The question ultimately is how do you shape China's behaviour? And we're all searching for that. My instinct is that you don't shape China's behaviour only by Australia and the US doing something. I think China's behaviour needs to be shaped by a recognition that there are other countries in the region who support the law of the sea and freedom of navigation.'

As for action against Iran, she says Australia's interests are served neither by military escalation nor by a nuclear-armed Iran. We should support attempts to find a way through under the present deal whereby Iran limits its nuclear ambitions in return for a lifting of trade embargoes.

But, should push come to shove, it is clear that Wong would not necessarily support joining US military action. She refers to the history of wars in the Middle East, and the fact that Labor opposed Australia's involvement in the invasion of Iraq, which was 'the right call'.

Other commentators suggested in interviews for this book that if a Coalition government wanted to support aggressive US action in the South China Sea, it could be expected to lead to a dispute in shadow cabinet. Richard Marles, the deputy leader and shadow minister for defence, would want to support the United States. So would other figures on the Right. Wong, on the other hand, might favour a different approach. The outcome would be unclear. Asked about this, Wong simply says, 'You know I won't talk about that.'

Penny Wong's final speech on foreign policy before the election was given at the Lowy Institute at the beginning of May. It was in some ways more partisan than is normal for foreign affairs, perhaps not surprisingly given the election context. She accused the government of damaging the perception of Australia in the region by refusing to preference One Nation last, thus reviving memories of the White Australia policy. She spoke about the main foreign policy plan Labor was taking to the election – a FutureAsia program that included support for improving Asian capacity in business and increasing education in Asian languages.

Again, there was cooled optimism on China. Managing the relationship would become more challenging, but 'it is hard to think of an important issue for Australia's future where China will not be an influential player ... We also recognise that China has a right to develop, and a right to a role in the region alongside other regional powers.'

For the first time, at the end of the speech, she spoke about what difference her personal background and ethnicity would make should Labor be elected. 'What is significant ... is not my personal attributes. Rather, what would be significant about an Asian-Australian being our foreign minister is what it says about us.' The fact of her holding this key position, Wong said, would be a powerful demonstration of Australia having overcome its racist past. It would be an exemplar of Australia as a confident multiracial nation. 'South-East Asia is not just our region, it is where I was born. I grew up with stories of the Fall of Singapore, the occupation of Malaya and the unique American contribution to peace in the Pacific. China's rise and its future place in the world was far more likely a topic of discussion than nostalgia over the Anglosphere.'

If elected, her first overseas visit as foreign minister, she announced, would be to Indonesia, and then to Malaysia – 'the country of my birth'.

The plan was for her to make a rapid tour of the region, visiting the ASEAN nations and including a made-for-media return to Kota Kinabalu, the city of her birth. It would have been a powerful illustration of her personal story and connections, a statement of Australia's place in Asia and a public relations coup not within the reach of any previous Australian foreign minister.

But then came the election defeat.

So what did Australia miss out on through Penny Wong not becoming the minister for foreign affairs in 2019? The key distinction is not so much on the aims of foreign policy – the commitment to the rules-based order is bipartisan. Rather, it is her commitment to activism, and to not only manage but take the initiative in building coalitions in our region, making this a priority independent of the relationship with the United States.

In July 2019, the new US ambassador to Australia, Arthur Culvahouse, signalled that the United States would expect Australia to be 'even more supportive' of US policy in the Pacific. 'That may include calling out malign influences where they see them.' He called on Australia to play 'a great power leadership role' in the region, and said the Australia–US alliance was 'solemn and unbreakable' and the United States would 'absolutely' come to Australia's aid if it were threatened by a foreign power.

Culvahouse's words could be read as an encouragement for Australia to remain in the US slipstream. Certainly, they telegraphed that the nation expected Australia to choose between the United States and China, and assumed that choice would be for the United States.[27]

If Penny Wong had been foreign minister, it is reasonable to expect that she might, ever so politely and carefully, have pushed back – or at least made another speech affirming the need for the United States to stay engaged with the region, but pointing out what other work needed to be done.

*

Penny Wong voted for Anthony Albanese to be leader of the Labor Party in 2013. Albanese won 60 per cent of the vote among rank-and-file party members, but lost in the caucus.[28]

So what was it like for Penny Wong over the next six years, working for a leader she had not supported in the ballot? Commentators generally saw the relationship between Shorten and Wong as positive. Insiders confirm the communication between their offices was good. She was credited with being one of his key advisers, part of a trusted 'inner circle'.[29] She did not leak; she did not undermine. There were occasional rumblings that Albanese was doing the numbers, both after the 2016 election defeat and in the lead-up to the Super Saturday raft of by-elections in mid-2018. Shorten's performance in both quashed any nascent leadership speculation. There was never any suggestion that Wong was anything but loyal to her leader during this time.

Yet there is a curious fact about Wong's role in the Shorten opposition that has gone largely unremarked. Early after the 2016 election she withdrew from the Opposition Expenditure Review Committee – the part of the policymaking framework that examines tax and spending policy. Given she was a former finance minister and the third most senior person in the parliamentary party, her withdrawal was significant. Wong rejoined shortly before the 2019 election, but for the period when the spending and taxation policies were presumably being devised, she was not on this committee. There is clearly a backstory – but not one that Wong will share.

Asked about the election loss, she is careful to make clear she regards herself as responsible, together with the rest of the leadership team, for the policies and the campaign. 'I am not trying to duck anything,' she says. 'I don't think it's ethical to do so, and I was part of the leadership group. We decided together on these things, and we all signed off on the policy package.'

In the media conference after the 2019 election at which she backed Albanese for the leadership, and again in the final interview for this book, she resisted too rapid an assessment of what had gone wrong for Labor. The election loss is now being reviewed by Jay Weatherill, her old friend and ally – although she says she did not suggest his name – and Craig Emerson. Wong says she thinks all the policies will have to be reviewed, together with the impact of the campaign and the leadership.

Yet her withdrawal from the ERC tempts the conclusion that she was not always comfortable with the decisions of the committee.

Against this, there has been a line of media commentary in the wake of the defeat that part of the problem for Labor was that Shorten, although from the Right, bought into and prosecuted a Left agenda – and that the Left is now too powerful in the parliamentary party. In this argument, Wong is sometimes mentioned explicitly, sometimes implicitly.

I put this view to Wong. She responded that it was completely wrong: 'I am a lot more fiscally conservative than a lot of my colleagues. Haven't they noticed that?'

When I tell her that Gareth Evans has suggested it is a 'category error' to see her as from the Left, she laughs uproariously, then says, 'I've been finance minister. I know that when you spend money you have to work out how to pay for it. Of course I'd love to spend more on health and education, but that inevitably has implications for how you raise the revenue, and that has political consequences too.'

She continues, 'I was always part of the leadership. So we agreed this policy framework and obviously it didn't work. So all of us take responsibility.' And further than that she will not go.

As for her relationship with Shorten, she says, 'I was Bill's Senate leader and I didn't engage with him, or he with me, thinking that I would then talk publicly about it. So I am not going to do that.'

Penny Wong was on form as the election approached. On 20 March it was announced that she would receive a major award for political leadership – the McKinnon Prize. It was bestowed 'for her leadership and advocacy in promoting a more tolerant and inclusive Australia, and for shaping Australia's foreign policy dialogue', the media release stated.[30] The judging panel that awarded her the gong included former prime ministers Julia Gillard and John Howard. Gillard's involvement was apparent evidence against Rudd's claim, published in his memoir a few months before, that she held Wong in contempt. Howard, on the other hand, had been the focus of Wong's criticism many times. Perhaps significantly, he did not appear on the video reel of the judges saying positive things about her. Other judges in the thirteen-member panel included Business Council of Australia chief executive Jennifer Westacott, former defence secretary Dennis Richardson and the University of Melbourne provost, Professor Mark Considine, who told the media that Wong was 'remarkable' for having been able to innovate from opposition.[31]

In her acceptance speech, the winner who would soon lose was upbeat about politics. The prize affirmed democracy, she said. She went on to lay out what democracy meant, and how it related to racism. She was speaking two weeks after the Christchurch mosque shootings, in which Muslim men, women and children had been gunned down by a white racist extremist while at prayer. The perpetrator was an Australian but, said Wong, he did not represent our values.

> Hate speech is inimical to democracy; it must not be normalised; it cannot be defended on grounds of freedom of speech because it inflicts real and direct harm. A central element of the way prejudice works is by dehumanising, by singling out people as outsiders, as second-class citizens, not deserving the protections and dignity afforded to full members of the community.

Australia was poorer and its democracy more fragile for the debate on Asian immigration, hate speech and the *Racial Discrimination Act*, she said. The Coalition should preference One Nation last.

Wong went on to address the question of the times – the one that I have suggested underlies her career. Can Australian democracy and political processes deliver on the needs of the times?

'Many Australians feel that their political leaders are out of touch and that the political system is increasingly dysfunctional, incapable of addressing everyday concerns, let alone longer-term challenges,' she said. The reasons were many, but among them were 'hyper-partisanship' that went beyond the healthy contest of ideas. This was driven by the conduct of political leaders, but also by the rise of social media.

She mounted a defence of democratic values that, in the light of the 2019 election defeat, is almost poignant. Democracy had allowed the advance of women's rights, defended the rights of minorities and created an international system that underpinned the world order, she noted. 'In my first speech in Parliament, I said that prejudice and distrust cannot build a community, but they can tear one apart. Unfortunately, that observation remains as relevant today as it was in 2002 … My hope is that people from across the political landscape will once again work together to articulate and defend the values and principles that underpin who we are and what we believe.'[32]

*

As Paul Keating might have said, a few days later she was throwing the switch to vaudeville.

She and her opposite number, Leader of the Government in the Senate, Mathias Cormann, were doing their customary double act in the parliament as she pressed him on when the election might be called.

Cormann: 'I'm not inside the Prime Minister's mind.'
Wong: 'It might be a little more ordered if you were!'

And then:

Wong: 'You're going to call the election this weekend …'
Cormann: 'I'm not going to call the election.'
Wong: 'You, plural; vous.'
Cormann: 'We're speaking French now?'[33]

She used Senate Estimates to challenge the cost of taxpayer-funded government advertising in the lead-up to the election – an old chestnut that she had prosecuted in every attempt to defeat Coalition governments since she entered the parliament.

The poll was finally called on 11 April, scheduled for 18 May.

Penny Wong was well used during the fray. She campaigned once again with Steve Georganas, now contesting the seat of Adelaide following Kate Ellis's retirement and an electoral redistribution. She appeared with Bill Shorten on a stage in Box Hill, Melbourne: the centre of the city's Chinese community. She toured the centres of ethnic Chinese populations, and spoke out about fake news on WeChat. Penny Wong was the face of the campaign in South Australia. In Labor's mail-outs it was her picture, not the unpopular Shorten's, that featured prominently.

But, this time round, Penny Wong was not the campaign spokesperson – her role since the 2007 election. Instead that job was taken by Jim Chalmers. She says this was at her suggestion: she felt the time had come for a fresh face, Chalmers was a good media performer and was from Queensland, which didn't hurt. As shadow minister for finance, he was across all the portfolios and issues.

This meant that Wong was not, as in previous years, at campaign headquarters. Each morning she took part in a telephone hook-up of the leadership team. She shared the general view that the first two weeks of campaigning were wobbly, and she was part of measures taken to address that. 'I thought we retrieved it,' she says. She was not excluded from the campaign strategy, but at the same time was clearly not as central to it as she had been in previous years.

On 8 May, a few days before the election, there came a personal low point. It was one of few occasions when Wong's weakness – her temper and ill-judged aggression – showed in public.

She was part of a debate in Adelaide including other South Australian senators. At the end of the event, trade minister Simon Birmingham was discussing former prime minister Paul Keating's comment that Australia's security and intelligence agencies were 'nutters' for their hostility to China. Birmingham suggested Labor was weak on China, mentioning former foreign minister Bob Carr. As Birmingham spoke, Wong was interrupting, shaking her head, accusing him of 'desperate politics' and saying it wasn't in the national interest to be using foreign policy for political advantage. Her eyebrows were in overdrive.

When the debate wrapped up, she pointedly refused to shake his hand, but did shake the hands of all other senators on stage. Birmingham offered his hand, started when she refused it, and then shrugged. Whatever point Wong was trying to make was overshadowed by what looked like petulance. Her evident lack of good grace was prominent in the news cycle for the day.

Probably it would have dominated the campaign week, were it not for Bill Shorten on the same day making a tearful speech about his mother after Sydney's *Daily Telegraph* falsely suggested he had distorted an account of her career.

After the election defeat, right-wing magazine *The Spectator* likened Wong's failure to shake Birmingham's hand to Mark Latham's infamous aggressive handshake with John Howard in the 2004 election campaign, which cemented doubts about his character in the public mind.[34] *The Spectator*, never Labor's friend, was surely over-egging the incident – but there was a grain of truth. Had it not been for Shorten and his mum, Wong's lack of good grace could have been a campaign-damaging moment: a rare public display of a less electorally appealing Penny Wong.

In our final interview, Wong was unapologetic about the incident, and seemingly oblivious to its impact. She said she was 'furious' with Birmingham for politicising the relationship with China. There had been conversations between them about how to handle the hold-up of coal exports to China. Together, they'd talked to business and other stakeholders. 'We'd been incredibly non-partisan about it because there was a national interest there. And in the debate that day I got a question on the China relationship and I gave a bipartisan answer and he went the low road – and he was the trade minister. He should have known better.'

Her decision to shun his proferred hand was not calculated, she says, but taken in the moment.

Would she do it again?

She shrugged. 'Who knows?'

I told her it looked terrible.

She shrugged again. 'That's your view.'

Birmingham and Wong both live in Adelaide. They have known each other for years – at least since 2004, when he was contesting the seat of Hindmarsh and she was managing Georganas's campaign. There is no getting away from each other in such small circles. They ran into each other in an airport lounge and discussed the incident, and again, ironically, when they were both dropping their children off at the same Mandarin language class. Wong says they shook hands and made up.

Looking forward, she hopes to be able to talk to Birmingham and the rest of the government on how to have a frank conversation with the Australian people about foreign policy without resorting to accusations of being too close to China, or too cosy with the United States – tired political tropes not suited to the times. This would include acquainting the Australian people with what the costs of preserving our sovereignty might be as China rises.

Does she think such a conversation will be possible? She shrugs. 'I don't know. We'll see how we go.'

*

The question everyone asks when they know you are writing a book about Penny Wong is whether she will ever be prime minister, and if not, why not.

The simple answer is that she is in the wrong house – the Senate – when prime ministers must sit in the House of Representatives. But couldn't she change house?

The better answer is that she has never aspired to the job. Many people have urged her to consider it over the years, including some of her closest allies and friends. She has been entirely consistent, rejecting the idea in private as in public. Partly this is due to her fear of the impact of prejudice: she judges the nation not ready for a gay Asian woman as prime minister. There are two sides to this concern. On the one hand she fears the electoral impact – the percentage of Australians who would change their vote because of her. On the other side, she fears what it would mean for her personally. As she puts it, 'Why would I do it to myself and my family?'

But it is also a keen assessment of her own talents, limitations and abilities. She has learned to campaign, and to perform for the media and the public, but it will never be her natural or preferred game. It drains her. As prime minister, selling the government message and performing in public would be an unavoidable and dominant responsibility.

Nevertheless, some wonder whether she will reconsider if the party's success seems to depend on it, and when her children are older. Comments John Faulkner, phlegmatically, 'How long are you going to condemn her to sit in parliament?'

Perhaps because she is different from other politicians, Penny Wong tends to be what one of her staffers described as 'a floating signifier' – a symbol with no agreed meaning. She absorbs meaning as well as projecting it. In these populist times, people tend to see her as what they wish her to be, rather than what she is. Thus, she is popular – at least with lefties – without being populist. There is a cult of Penny Wong. There is a Twitter account devoted to her eyebrows. She is assumed to be more conventionally left-wing than she really is, and somehow above or outside the dirty business of politics when one of the central points of this book is that she is decidedly in the room, inside and of politics. One of the first things she published as an adult was the *On Dit* article in which she argued that professional political representation was the most important service. That remains her vocation.

Yet the cult of Penny Wong has enduring power because it is not built on fiction. Intellectually, Penny Wong is clearly head and shoulders above most of her colleagues. She is one of the most significant political talents of our times – or, as she might put it, 'of our generation'. She is both principled and pragmatic. In all of Labor's troubles since she entered the Australian parliament, Penny Wong has emerged from each stage with her reputation enhanced and her influence increased. Her political judgement has usually been acute.

We tend to idealise politicians who appear different from the pack, and then tear them down when they inevitably disappoint. Despite her talents, it is easy to imagine this happening to Penny Wong if she were in the top job. Racism, misogyny and homophobia aside, the aspects of her character that constitute her chief weakness – the sometimes ill-judged aggression – would likely be more apparent. She is charming, but also cutting. She is fiercely intellectual, yet also emotional. Her Senate colleagues talk ruefully about her temper. One told me that 'repair work' had to be done after a Wong display of temper against her own.

Whether or not Wong has a clear-eyed view of her weaknesses, she certainly understands her strengths. Her natural strength is policy and strategy. In other words, she is well suited to the leadership of the party in the Senate.

So Penny Wong will almost certainly never be prime minister. Yet she will lead. The opposition is now dominated by her allies. Albanese is leader largely because of her support. Asked why she backs him, she says she believes he has the capacity for a strong relationship with the Australian people. His principles are visible in his support of gay rights, long before it was popular. As well, she credits him with 'holding the government together' during the years of minority government under Gillard. 'I think that's sometimes taken for granted. We would not have stayed in government without Albo. Gillard certainly cut the deal with the independents, but he retained the majority in the house. That was by dint of his capacity, his procedural understanding, his rhetorical capacity and his personal relationships.' In caucus, she says, Albanese is 'consultative and strategic'. She thinks his leadership will evolve into an election winner.

And, around Albanese, Penny Wong's allies and collaborators are grouping. Her alliance with Mark Butler is enduring, and important to the party. In addition to Jay Weatherill heading up the election review, Tim Gartrell, the man who ran the same-sex marriage campaign, is now Albanese's chief of staff.

Against this, some in the parliamentary party speculate that Kristina Keneally's ascent to the position of deputy leader of the Opposition in the Senate is not necessarily good for Penny. Keneally replaced Don Farrell in that position. Despite all their differences over same-sex marriage, Penny Wong never had to fear that Farrell aspired to her job as Senate leader. Keneally, on the other hand, is an ambitious contemporary of

Wong's, just a few weeks younger, a former premier of New South Wales and a good media performer. Despite being from the Right, Keneally backed Albanese to be leader, and he insisted on her promotion to the frontbench, making a colleague from the Right, Ed Husic, stand aside to give way. Keneally is now shadow minister for home affairs, up against Peter Dutton. Farrell also had to make way, despite earlier making it clear he wanted to keep the deputy's job, and thinking he had the numbers to do so. Largely, this was about gender balance, with Albanese and Richard Marles as leader and deputy leader in the lower house. The two women in the Senate were to maintain balance in the leadership team, as Plibersek and Shorten had epitomised before the election.

Wong rejects any view of herself and Keneally as rivals. They are allies, she says, and Keneally has earned her place. 'She is a very good performer. I think she knows how to throw a political punch. She's got political courage ... I think it was important for the Labor Party to have another woman in the leadership.' Others, perhaps falling into the misogynistic trope that senior women must necessarily be adversaries, suggest that for the next three years Wong may have to look over her shoulder. The stability of the arrangement is one of the questions surrounding Labor's immediate political future.

What happens if Labor doesn't win the next election, expected in 2022? By then Wong, at fifty-three, will have been in the Senate for twenty years – a long and exhausting run. Will she quit politics if Labor fails next time around?

She doesn't answer the question.

She says her father was the member of the family who used to construct long-term plans. 'I remember always thinking that he had five-year plans and seven-year plans, and I just did the next thing, and then the next. You can have all these plans, and then life does something different and you have spent all this mental energy on complex plans that are entirely in your head ... That sounds a bit fatalistic, but it's also a sort of weariness, I think, that comes with being fifty.'

*

In our final interview, Penny Wong reflected on this book and her initial opposition to it.

'I know I was pretty hard on you,' she said. 'And in a perfect world I would prefer that this wasn't being done. But I hope there is something about whatever story you write that has some benefits.'

I asked her what she thought those benefits might be.

She responded there was the obvious thing – a high-profile gay person as a role model for others and 'that meaning something to vulnerable people – but you don't have to do a book for that'.

I said that as the book had proceeded I had come to think of it as being about politics itself: how hard it is, the price that is paid in the struggle to make change, and both the necessity and inevitability of compromise, even when – as with climate change – such compromise may do us in. I was thinking that perhaps, as with a tragic play, the audience might leave with a greater understanding of the human affairs it depicted. Perhaps they might also grasp the humanity behind the headlines – and what it meant for a person of talent, passion and principle to devote herself to delivering the service of political representation.

She agreed. 'There are pretty fundamental questions about democracy right now, and maybe my career is just a small way in which we can have that discussion about what we hope and expect of political representatives and the polity, and what we can do better. Not just me and my colleagues, but the media and the broader community.'

Did she still believe that it was possible to meet the needs of the nation through democratic political processes?

'I have to,' she said. 'What is the other path? We see the rise of authoritarianism and nationalism. These are bad things. History should remind us of that. So what's the alternative? We have only this path.' She quoted Churchill's famous saw about democracy being the worst form of government, except for all the others.

Penny Wong had come to our interview without having had breakfast. She had been up late because of her *Q&A* appearance, woken, done a work-out in her hotel and gone straight to a meeting. While we spoke she consumed a honey sandwich out of a brown paper bag.

Now she was late for her next meeting. The following week she was going on holiday with her kids.

And then there would be the next thing, and the next.

She swigged the dregs of a coffee, balled up her brown paper bag and swept the table clear of crumbs.

Acknowledgements

A book like this incurs many debts of gratitude for its author. First, I would like to thank Senator Penny Wong for her cooperation, despite her antipathy to the idea of the book and the near certainty that she will not be entirely happy with the result. I would also like to thank – or perhaps apologise to – her family, who have had to put up with the slipstream from a project they did not welcome.

Also to be thanked are Senator Wong's staff, both for practical assistance and for their forbearance and wisdom.

I am indebted to those who agreed to be interviewed, as acknowledged in the list of interview subjects, and to those who gave of their time and perspectives but asked not to be identified.

Ken Haley compiled fearsome books of clippings for me at the beginning of this project, and assisted with fact-checking and chasing down elusive bits and pieces towards the end. Gary Dickson was, as always, assiduous in tracking down information and sorting my references. Natasha Sim visited the archives for me in Sabah, Malaysia.

Thanks are due to the staff of the State Library of South Australia, the University of Adelaide archives, Mr Ramlin Alim at the Sabah State Archives, the researchers at Genealogy SA and Mr Alex Pouwbray, archivist at Scotch College, Adelaide. Thanks, as well, to the staff of Coromandel Valley Primary School and Scotch College for the tours and insights they gave me.

I am indebted to Judith Ajani, Maryanne Slattery and Allan Behm for commenting on drafts of relevant chapters. Ramona Koval and Denis Muller helped by reading proofs.

My colleagues in the School of Media, Film and Journalism at Monash University were consistently understanding and supportive. My family are now experienced in putting up with book projects. They are very good at it, and I thank them.

My agent, Lyn Tranter, looked after my interests with characteristic skill and judgement. Finally, thanks to Aviva Tuffield, who pestered me to do this book in the first place, and to the team at Black Inc.: as always, Chris Feik, and particularly Julia Carlomagno, who saw the project through to completion with care and patience.

Any errors or misjudgements are, of course, entirely my responsibility.

Notes

1: KINDRED OFFSPRING

1 Rhiannon Elston, 'First day: Penny Wong's journey from shy student to senator', *SBS News*, 27 January 2017.

2 Fiona Scott-Norman, 'Penny Wong', *Bully for Them: Outstanding Australians on Hard Lessons Learned at School*, Affirm Press, Melbourne, 2014, pp. 217–27.

3 ibid., p. 223.

4 Jane Cadzow, 'The pair who have cleaned every prime minister's office since Bob Hawke', *Good Weekend*, 26 January 2019.

5 Peter Scriver and Amit Srivastava, 'Institutionalising the profession in post-colonial Malaysia: the role of Australian-trained architects in the establishment of PAM (Pertubuhan Akitek Malaysia)', *Proceedings of the Society of Architectural Historians, Australia and New Zealand: 32, Architecture, Institutions and Change*, SAHANZ, 2015, pp. 582–91.

6 Mary Penelope Mayo, *The Life and Letters of Colonel William Light*, F.W. Preece and Sons, Adelaide, 1937, pp. 108–10, and Robert Gouger, 'Some rough notes of a voyage from Gravesend to South Australia in the Africaine', entry for 19 November 1836, State Library of South Australia, PRG 1012/1.

7 The records are inconsistent on Samuel Chapman's age, with his obituary suggesting he was born in 1802. However, his wife's obituary suggests that he was born in 1815, which is also confirmed by records sourced through Ancestry.com.

8 South Australian Colonization Commission, 'Appendix 1', Annual report of the Colonization Commissioners of South Australia to His Majesty's Principal Secretary of State for the Colonies, London, House of Commons, 1837.

9 Boyle Travers Finniss, 'Sunday 15 May 1936', Borrow Collection, Special Collections, Flinders University Library.

10 Mary Penelope Mayo, *The Life and Letters of Colonel William Light*, p. 100.

11 Miles Fairburn, 'Wakefield, Edward Gibbon', *Dictionary of New Zealand Biography*, Te Ara – the Encyclopedia of New Zealand, 2014.

12 R.M. Gibbs, *A History of South Australia* (third edition), Peacock Publications for Southern Heritage, Mitcham, 1999, pp. 24–25.

13 *South Australian Register*, Robert Thomas and Co., Adelaide, 11 September 1839, p. 10.

14 ibid., 28 November 1849, p. 3.

15 ibid., 27 October 1849, p. 3.

16 ibid., 15 December 1849, p. 1.

17 ibid., 15 April 1882, p. 2.

18 *The Observer*, John Stevens, Adelaide, 2 March 1912, p. 41.

19 Samuel William Chapman Papers, State Library of South Australia, PRG 698.

20 ibid.

21 Danny Wong Tze-Ken, 'The Chinese in Sabah: an overview', in Lee Kam Hing and Tan Chee-Beng (eds), *The Chinese in Malaysia*, Oxford University Press, Kuala Lumpur, 2000, pp. 381–403.

22 Sharon Carstens, 'Form and content in Hakka Malaysian culture', in Nicole Constable (ed.), *Guest People: Hakka Identity in China and Abroad*, University of Washington Press, Seattle, 1996.

23 Richard W. Braithwaite and Yun-Lok Lee, *Dark Tourism, Hate and Reconciliation: The Sandakan Experience*, Global Educators' Network of the International Institute for Peace through Tourism, IIPT Occasional Paper No. 8, March 2006.

24 Danny Wong Tze-Ken, 'Chinese migration to Sabah before the Second World War', *Archipel*, vol. 58, no. 3, 1999, p. 144.

25 ibid., pp. 131–58.

26 Francis Yit Shing Wong Papers, Sabah State Archives, ANS/KSP/FWYS/C/99/1.

27 Australian War Memorial, 'Stolen years: Australian prisoners of war', 2017.

28 K.G. Tregonning, *A History of Modern Sabah 1881–1963*, University of Malaya Press, Kuala Lumpur, 1965; also cited in Richard Braithwaite and Yun-Lok Lee, *Dark Tourism, Hate and Reconciliation*.

29 Danny Wong Tze-Ken, 'Kinabalu guerrillas: the Inanam-Menggatal-Telipok Basel Church connections', in Chong Tet Loi (ed.), *The Hakka Experiment in Sabah*, Sabah Theological Seminary, Kota Kinabalu, 2007, pp. 166–88.

30 ibid.

31 Penny Wong, 'Embracing our common humanity', 2014 Angelo Roncalli Lecture, Canberra, 21 August 2014.

32 Penny Wong, 'Maiden speech', Parliament of Australia, Canberra, 21 August 2002.

33 Irene Obon, 'A man for all seasons', *New Sabah Times*, Sunday 18 July 1999, p. 2.

34 'Photograph of Francis Wong with his mother taken when he was in Form One', Francis Yit Shing Wong Papers, ANS/KSP/FWYS/G/99/25.

35 'Photograph of Francis Wong as a teenager', Francis Yit Shing Wong Papers, ANS/KSP/FWYS/G/99/24.

36 Francis Yit Shing Wong Papers, no item number.

37 ibid.

38 Francis Yit Shing Wong, Student Cards, University of Adelaide Archives, SC85952 and SC85953.

39 No author, 'University award to Asian', *The Advertiser*, 2 September 1965.

40 No author, 'A future Sabah architect', *Sabah Times*, 1964, Sabah State Archives, ANS/KSP/FWYS/G/99/32.

41 Peter Scriver and Amit Srivastava, 'Institutionalising the profession in post-colonial Malaysia', p. 587.

42 ibid.

43 ibid., p. 589.

44 Howard Salkow, 'Australian experience builds global perspective', *Lumen*, Summer 2005, p. 13.

45 Paul Keating, 'Anzac Day, Ela Beach, Port Moresby', Speech, 25 April 1992.

46 Rhiannon Elston, 'First day'.

2: BUTTERFLIES AND BULLIES

1 Passenger Arrival Card, Penelope Ying-Yen Wong, National Archives of Australia Series A1197, Item 11574375; Passenger Arrival Card, Barbara Jane Wong, National Archives of Australia Series A1197, Item 11574375.

2 Greg Sheridan, *God Is Good for You*, Allen & Unwin, Sydney, 2018, p. 194.

3 Rachel Hancock, 'Banging out a sense of pride', *The Sunday Mail*, 10 March 2002, p. 15.

4 Penny Wong, 'Maiden speech'.

5 Irene Obon, 'A man for all seasons', pp. 2–3.

6 No author, 'History of KIS', *Kinabalu International School*, 2019.

7 Jane Rocca, 'Four prominent women on why they are proud to be Australian', *The Sydney Morning Herald*, 19 January 2018.

8 Gwenda Tavan, *The Long, Slow Death of White Australia*, Scribe Publications, Melbourne, 2005, p. 216 and Siew-Ean Khoo and Charles A. Price, *Understanding Australia's Ethnic Composition*, Australian Government Publishing Service, Canberra, 1996.

9 Irene Obon, 'A man for all seasons', pp. 2–3.

10 Chok Sim Yee, 'Sabah-born Aussie minister always aims for the best', *The Borneo Post*, 19 September 2010, p. B1, in Francis Yit Shing Wong Papers, ANS/KSP/FWYS/G/99/22.

11 'Wong family tree', in Francis Yit Shing Wong Papers, ANS/KSP/FWYS/C/99/1.

12 'Penny Wong', *Kitchen Cabinet*, ABC-TV, 6 March 2012.

13 No editor, 'Our recipe to win – favourite recipes of Labor parliamentarians serving in the 45th parliament', compiled by the campaign for Gilmore, 2016.

14 'Penny Wong', *Kitchen Cabinet*.

15 Peter Read and Alex Pouw-Bray, *Ninety Years at Torrens Park: The Scotch College Story*, Wakefield Press, Adelaide, 2010, pp. 337–39.

16 *Cluaran*, Scotch College, vol. LXIV, 1981.

17 Chok Sim Yee, 'Sabah-born Aussie minister always aims for the best'.

18 *Cluaran*, Scotch College, vol. LXVI, 1983.

19 ibid., vol. LXVII, 1984.

20 ibid., vol. LXVIII, 1985.

21 ibid.

22 ibid.

23 Jane Chapman and Sue Park, 'Marital therapy and feminism', *Australian Journal of Family Therapy*, vol. 5, no. 4, 1984, pp. 259–65.

24 Stilgherrian has only one name – making him mononymous.

25 Annabel Crabb, 'Freakish powers of a formidable operator', *The Sydney Morning Herald*, 8 December 2017.

26 Greg Sheridan, *God Is Good for You*, p. 195.

3: BECOMING LABOR

1   Julia Gillard, *My Story*, Knopf Australia, Sydney, 2014, p. 118.
2   Adelaide University Union board minutes, University of Adelaide Archives, series 64, boxes 2, 19 and 21.
3   Mark Batistich, 'Students heckle minister during Wran tax protest', *The Advertiser*, 12 May 1988, p. 58.
4   'Adelaide University Student Union Election statements 1998', University of Adelaide Archives, 1988, RC371.810994A228e.
5   Andrew Markus, *Race: John Howard and the Remaking of Australia*, Allen & Unwin, Sydney, 2001, pp. 85–89.
6   No author, 'ALP conference delayed by dispute', *The Advertiser*, 13 August 1988, p. 13.
7   Peter Haynes, 'Student tax "no" beats Bannon', *The Advertiser*, 15 August 1988, p. 1.
8   ibid. and Edmund Doogue, 'SA Labor Party rebuffs Hawke government on tertiary tax', *The Age*, 15 August 1988, p. 18.
9   George Karzis, 'Letter to the editor', *On Dit*, 14 May 1989, p. 7.
10 James Greentree, 'Letter to the editor', ibid.
11 Adelaide University Union board minutes, box 19.
12 Penny Wong, 'Political representation – the undervalued service', *On Dit*, 31 July 1989, p. 9.

4: BOLKUS LEFT

1   Katharine Murphy, 'Leaks and loose lips undermine Labor unity ahead of campaign postmortem', *The Guardian*, 22 June 2019 and Sarah Martin, 'Jay Weatherill asked to conduct "warts-and-all" review of Labor's election loss', *The Guardian*, 5 June 2019.
2   Craig Clarke, 'The federal election: Labor's lipstick warriors', *The Sunday Mail*, 7 October 2001.
3   Louise Milligan, 'Women come to the rescue', *The Australian*, 12 November 2001.
4   Susie O'Brien, 'SA senators: we're more than just pretty faces', *The Advertiser*, 12 November 2001, p. 12.
5   See Moira Rayner, 'Public discourse and the power of women', Papers on Parliament, no. 41, June 2004.
6   James Massola, 'Julia Gillard on the moment that should have killed Tony Abbott's career', *The Sydney Morning Herald*, 23 June 2015.
7   For example, Penny Wong, 'Light on the Hill address', 20 September 2014.
8   Carol Johnson, *Social Democracy and the Crisis of Equality: Australian Social Democracy in a Changing World*, Springer, Singapore, 2019.
9   See Kevin Rudd, *The PM Years*, Pan Macmillan, Sydney, 2018, p. 381 and Julia Gillard, *My Story*, p. 120.
10 Catherine Bauer, 'New president booed during racism debate', *The Advertiser*, 12 July 1993, p. 10.
11 Gary Wagener v Moinalwar Pty Ltd t/a K. and S. Dixon [1994] SAIRC 71 (23 December 1994); Industrial Relations Commission Decision 125/1994 [1994] AIRC 15 (18 January 1994); Industrial Relations Commission Decision 208/1994 [1994] AIRC 85 (9 February 1994); Industrial Relations Commission Decision 1028/1993 [1993] AIRC 1033 (6 September 1993); Industrial Relations

Commission Decision 209/1994 [1994] AIRC 79 (8 February 1994); Industrial Relations Commission Decision 1220/1994 [1994] AIRC 1182 (2 August 1994).

12 Brander v Ryan and Messenger Press Newspapers No. SCGRG-99-199 [2000] SASC 2 (12 January 2000).

5: INTO THE WOODS

1   Judith Ajani, *The Forest Wars*, Melbourne University Press, Melbourne, 2007, p. 16.
2   Margaret Simons, *Latham's World: The New Politics of the Outsiders*, Quarterly Essay 15, Black Inc., Melbourne, 2004.
3   Don Watson, *Recollections of a Bleeding Heart: A Portrait of Paul Keating, PM*, Random House Australia, Sydney, 2002, pp. 538–40.
4   Greg Sheridan, *God Is Good for You*, pp. 191–97.
5   The account here of federal government actions draws heavily on Judith Ajani, *The Forest Wars*, Chapters 1, 10 and 14.
6   A coupe is an area of forest that can be harvested in one go – typically between 30 and 60 hectares.
7   Quoted in Judith Ajani, *The Forest Wars*, p. 135.
8   Adam Gartrell, 'Meet Michael O'Connor, now the country's most powerful union boss', *The Sydney Morning Herald*, 6 March 2018.
9   Julia Gillard, 'Maiden speech', Parliament of Australia, Canberra, 11 November 1998.
10 Matt Peacock, 'NSW State Election', *Background Briefing*, ABC Radio, 19 March 1995.
11 ibid.
12 Bob Carr, *Thoughtlines*, Viking Press, Sydney, 2002, p. 317.
13 Quoted in Matt Peacock, 'NSW State Election'.
14 ibid.
15 Judith Ajani, *The Forest Wars*, p. 279.
16 ibid., p. 280.
17 Annie Lewis, 'Elvis Presley "The King" lives on in Wagga', *The Daily Advertiser*, 28 June 2018.
18 No author, 'Obituary: Gavin Maxwell Hillier', *The Daily Advertiser*, 5 December 2018.
19 Quotes from Bill Kelty eulogy provided to the author by Kim Yeadon.
20 Kevin Rudd, 'Building a better world together', Speech at Kyoto University, Japan, 9 June 2008.
21 WorkCover Corporation/HIH Winterthur Workers Compensation (SA) Ltd (Eldercare Inc.) v Marlene Keen [1997] SAWCAT 23 (7 March 1997).
22 Health Services Employees Award [1997] SAIRComm 26 (18 April 1997).
23 John Smith v. South Australia Meat Corporation [1996] SAWCT 3 (18 December 1996).
24 Ramsey v Royal Flying Doctor Service of Australia (Central Section Inc.) [1998] SAIRC 19 (30 April 1998).
25 Olsen v WorkCover Corp. v MMI Workers Comp. (SA) Ltd (V.S.L. Prestressing Aust. Pty Ltd) [1998] SAWCT 89 (13 November 1998).
26 Lyell McEwin Hospital v Childs [1998] SAWCT 79 (16 October 1998).
27 Baker v WorkCover Corp. v HIH Winterthur Workers Compensation (SA) Ltd (Pacific Waste Management Pty Ltd) [1999] SAWCT 12 (19 February 1999).

28 Christine Francis v WorkCover Corp./HIH Winterthur (Kate Cocks Child Care Centre) [1998] SAWCT 7 (29 January 1998).

29 No author, 'Driver's landmark win', *The Advertiser*, 9 March 1998, p. 3.

30 No author, 'ALP lawyer scores prize Senate spot', *The Advertiser*, 14 May 1998, p. 36.

31 Dunk & Aust. Liquor, Hospitality & Miscellaneous Workers' Union v SA Health Commission [1998] SAIRC 63 (6 November 1998).

32 Buttercup Bakeries South Australia Continuous Improvement Agreement 1997 (Renegotiation Dispute) [2000] SAIRComm 1 (10 January 2000).

33 Caretakers and Cleaners Award (Menzies International Australia Pty Ltd v ALHMWU) [2002] SAIRComm 15 (3 April 2002).

34 Department of Education, Training and Employment v O'Brien [2001] SAIRC 10 (5 March 2001).

35 Hancock v Sanctuary Farm Child Care Centre & Kindergarten Pty Ltd [2000] SAIRC 30 (30 October 2000).

36 Neil G. Wolfendale v Pilkington Australia Ltd [1994] SAIRC 21 (15 April 1994).

6: CHOSEN

1 Greg Sheridan, *God Is Good for You*, p. 196.

2 Gary Johns, 'Clarke v Australian Labor Party', *Australian Journal of Political Science*, vol. 35, no. 1, 2000, pp. 137–42.

3 Carol Altmann, 'Tensions stack up on Labor', *The Australian*, 24 March 2000, p. 5.

4 Interview with Ralph Clarke MHA, 27 October 1999, cited in Gary Johns, 'Clarke v Australian Labor Party', pp. 137–42.

5 Quoted in Matthew Abraham, 'Bulk sign-ups thwart ALP factional trouble', *The Australian*, 9 March 1999, p. 6.

6 Quoted in Carol Altmann, 'Tensions stack up on Labor', p. 5.

7 Richard McGregor and Matthew Abraham, 'ALP racked by membership "rorts"', *The Australian*, 23 April 1999, p. 2.

8 Clarke v ALP (SA branch), Hurley & Ors & Brown No. SCGRG-99-874 Judgement No. S365 [1999] SASC 365 (2 September 1999).

9 No author, 'I paid to shore up the faction', *The Advertiser*, 8 September 1999, p. 2.

10 Miles Kemp, 'Individual signed 878 in branch stacking', *The Advertiser*, 30 October 1999, p. 19.

11 David Eccles, 'Wong wins her ticket to political prominence', *The Advertiser*, 10 April 2000, p. 6.

12 Wong, Penny, Citizenship Register, Parliament of Australia, Canberra.

13 Liz Burke, 'Who's who in the citizenship saga', *news.com.au*, 24 August 2017.

14 No author, '4000 march on racism', *The Advertiser*, 6 August 1998, p. 6.

15 David Marr and Marian Wilkinson, *Dark Victory*, Allen & Unwin, Sydney, 2003.

16 No author, 'Labor's policy on asylum seekers', *Australian Labor Party*, no date, https://www.alp.org.au/asylumseekers

7: A NEW VOICE

1 Lenore Taylor, 'The minister of cool', *Weekend Australian Magazine*, 23 May 2009, p. 12.

2 'Wong, Toby', Death notices, *The Advertiser*, 27 November 2001.

3   Penny Wong, 'Maiden speech'.

4   ibid.

5   Tony Walker and Mark Davis, 'Federal parliament like being on a spaceship', *Australian Financial Review*, 17 January 2003, p. 10.

6   Samantha Maiden, 'Linda Kirk and Penny Wong: new housemates', *The Advertiser*, 10 August 2002, p. 7.

7   Lyle Allan, 'ALP modernisation, ethnic branch stacking, factionalism and the law', *People and Place*, vol. 10, no. 4, 2002, p. 50.

8   Samantha Maiden, 'Labor women: the rise and rise of Penny Wong', *The Advertiser*, 8 October 2002, p. 19.

9   Kelvin Thomson, 'Howard government allows increase in land clearing in Queensland', Media release, 29 May 2003 and Kelvin Thomson, 'Government confirms 67% cut to greenhouse programs', Media release, 29 May 2003.

10 Commonwealth of Australia, *Senate Select Committee on Ministerial Discretion in Migration Matters Report*, March 2004; Cynthia Banham, 'Star visa witness misses Senate date', *The Sydney Morning Herald*, 18 November 2004, p. 5; Peta Donald, 'Philip Ruddock: 30 years in parliament marred by cash-for-visa allegations', *PM*, ABC Radio, 22 September 2003.

11 Mark Latham, *Civilising Global Capital: New Thinking for Australian Labor*, Allen & Unwin, Sydney, 1998; Mark Latham, *From the Suburbs*, Pluto Press, Annandale, 2003; Mark Latham, *The Enabling State: People Before Bureaucracies*, Pluto Press, Annandale, 2001.

12 Mark Latham, 'Wedge politics and the culture war in Australia', Menzies Lecture, 17 September 2002, published by the Menzies Centre for Australian Studies, King's College, London, 2003.

13 Paul Starick, 'South Australia's 10 most poisonous political feuds', *The Advertiser*, 21 May 2014.

14 'Nick Bolkus interviewed by Peter Donovan in the Old Parliament House political and parliamentary oral history project', National Library Political and Parliamentary Oral History Project Sound Recording, ORAL TRC 6100/17. The interview took place on 18, 19 and 29 March 2010 in Adelaide, South Australia.

15 Malcolm Farr and Mark Phillips, 'The raffle without a price was a rort', *Daily Telegraph*, 26 June 2003, p. 9.

16 Bolkus v Nationwide News [2005] SADC 138 (13 October 2005).

17 'Nick Bolkus interviewed by Peter Donovan in the Old Parliament House.'

18 'The Adjournment Debate', *Insiders*, ABC-TV, 22 February 2004, ABC Archives ID T557443.

19 ibid., 21 March 2004, ABC Archives ID T560060.

20 ibid., 23 May 2004, ABC Archives ID T572593.

21 ibid., no day, August 2004, ABC Archives ID T572593.

8: STAYING IN THE ROOM

1   Carol Johnson, Sarah Maddison and Emma Partridge, 'Australia: parties, federalism and rights agendas', in Mann Tremblay, David Patternote and Carol Johnson (eds), *The Lesbian and Gay Movement and the State: Comparative Insights into a*

Transformed Relationship, Ashgate, Surrey, 2011, pp. 27–42.

2   No author, 'Not happy Nicola', *The Sydney Morning Herald*, 11 August 2004; No
     author, 'Govt to outlaw gay marriage', *ABC News*, 27 May 2004; Alex Greenwich
     and Shirleene Robinson, *Yes Yes Yes*, NewSouth, Sydney, 2018, pp. 16–17.

3   Marcus Priest, 'Labor supports gay bashing law', *Australian Financial Review*, 2 June
     2004, p. 4; Craig Clarke, 'Wong takes up fight over gays', *The Advertiser*,
     2 June 2004, p. 2; Misha Schubert, 'Labor MPs back leader's gay compromise plan',
     The Age, 2 June 2004.

4   Natasha Stott Despoja, 'Marriage Amendment Bill 2004', Senate *Hansard*,
     12 August 2004, p. 1034.

5   Deirdre McKeown, 'Chronology of same-sex marriage bills introduced into the
     federal parliament: a quick guide', Research Paper Series, 2017–18, Parliamentary
     Library, Department of Parliamentary Services, Canberra, 15 February 2018.

6   No author, 'Howard: election to be about trust', *The Sydney Morning Herald*,
     29 August 2004.

7   Mark Latham, *The Latham Diaries*, Melbourne University Press, Melbourne, 2005,
     p. 366.

8   No author, 'Gay rights movement welcomes Australia's first openly gay frontbencher',
     Agence France-Presse, 23 October 2004.

9   Jackson Sawatan, 'Father follows closely daughter's rise in Australia's politics',
     Bernama Daily, 24 October 2004.

10   No author, 'Sabah-born Malaysian woman is Labor Party "new star"', *Sin Chew
     Daily*, 24 October 2004.

11   Andrew Bolt, 'And another thing', *Sunday Herald Sun*, 24 October 2004, p. 21.

12   Stephen Loosley, 'Labor must bow to the people's verdict with grace', *Sunday
     Telegraph*, 24 October 2004, p. 1.

13   Jeremy Roberts, 'Gay senator prepared for when it gets personal', *The Australian*,
     28 October 2004, p. 2.

14   Maria Moscaritolo, 'Rudd won't stand, no word from Gillard, a surprise backer, it's
     a done deal', *The Advertiser*, 25 January 2005.

15   Patricia Karvelas, 'Gillard fights on against the odds', *The Australian*, 25 January
     2005, p. 2.

16   Mark Latham, 'No exit', *The Monthly*, November 2010.

17   'Budget Strategy and Outlook 2005–06: Budget Paper No. 1', Commonwealth of
     Australia, Canberra, 10 May 2005.

18   Penny Wong, 'Transcript of doorstop interview', Media release, 20 May 2006.

19   Penny Wong, 'Values and politics', Public lecture at the University of Adelaide,
     26 October 2006.

20   Penny Wong, *Reward for Effort: Meeting the Participation Challenge*, discussion paper on
     Australia's workforce participation issues, Australian Labor Party, November 2006.

21   Julia Gillard, *My Story*, pp. 5–6.

22   Fleur Anderson, 'Double shocks cast a sombre mood', *Australian Financial Review*,
     5 December 2006.

23   Kevin Rudd and Penny Wong, 'Federal Labor to lift standards on taxpayer-funded
     advertising: $1.7 billion spent by Howard government', Media release, 19 May 2007.

24 Penny Wong and Kim Wilkie, 'Transcript of doorstop interview', Media release, 9 August 2006.

25 Penny Wong, 'Who's been in the same chair too long?', Media release, 21 May 2007.

26 Penny Wong, 'Transcript of doorstop interview', Media release, 22 May 2007.

27 Penny Wong, '*Star Wars* epic pales into insignificance', Media release, 24 May 2007.

28 Darrell Giles, 'Who does he think he is – Linda Evangelista? Our $10,000-a-day pollie', *Sunday Mail*, 10 June 2007.

29 Penny Wong, 'Questions without notice', Senate *Hansard*, 14 June 2007, p. 89.

30 Anthony Albanese, 'Censure of the prime minister', House *Hansard*, 14 June 2007, p. 88.

31 Tony Wright, 'Team Rudd', *The Age*, 18 August 2007.

32 Barrie Cassidy, 'Barrie Cassidy talks to Penny Wong', *Insiders*, ABC-TV, 25 November 2007.

33 Paul Kelly, *Triumph and Demise: The Broken Promise of a Labor Generation*, Melbourne University Press, Melbourne, 2014, p. 108.

34 Lindsay Tanner and Penny Wong, 'Cleaning up government', Media release, 8 August 2007.

35 Penny Wong, 'Labor's approach to the Australian public service', Speech to the Institute of Public Administration Australia (ACT Division), Ainslie Football Club, 20 September 2007.

36 Penny Wong, 'Tony Jones talks to Labor's Penny Wong and Liberal Andrew Robb', *Lateline*, ABC-TV, 21 November 2007.

37 No author, 'Musa welcomes appointment of Saban-born Wong to Australian Cabinet', *Bernama Daily Malaysian News*, 30 November 2007.

38 Nick Squires, 'Rudd reveals his right on government', *Daily Telegraph*, 30 November 2007.

39 Annabel Crabb, 'Sit right back and you'll hear a tale of a fearless crew', *The Sydney Morning Herald*, 4 December 2007.

40 Mungo MacCallum, no title, *Crikey*, 3 December 2007.

41 Mia Handshin and Miles Kemp, 'Minister for saving the world', *The Advertiser*, 23 February 2008, p. 7.

9: PENNY WONG FAILS TO SAVE THE WORLD (PART 1)

1 Paul Kelly, *Triumph and Demise*, p. 497.

2 Rodney Tiffen, *Disposable Leaders: Media and Leadership Coups from Menzies to Abbott*, NewSouth, Sydney, 2014, p. 49.

3 Paul Kelly, *Triumph and Demise*, p. 498.

4 ibid.; Julia Gillard, *My Story*; Kevin Rudd, *The PM Years*; Wayne Swan, *The Good Fight: Six Years, Two Prime Ministers and Staring Down the Great Recession*, Allen & Unwin, Sydney, 2014; Greg Combet and Mark Davis, *The Fights of My Life*, Melbourne University Publishing, Melbourne, 2014; Tony Windsor, *Windsor's Way*, Melbourne University Publishing, Melbourne, 2016; Rob Oakeshott, *The Independent Member for Lyne: A Memoir*, Allen & Unwin, Sydney, 2014; Sarah Ferguson and Patricia Drum, *The Killing Season Uncut*, Melbourne University Publishing, Melbourne, 2016; Patrick Weller, *Kevin Rudd: Twice Prime Minister*, Melbourne University Publishing, Melbourne, 2014; Christine Milne, *An Activist*

Life, University of Queensland Press, Brisbane, 2017; Craig Emerson, *The Boy from Barcaldine*, Scribe Publications, Melbourne, 2018; Maxine McKew, *Tales from the Political Trenches*, Melbourne University Publishing, Melbourne, 2013; Bob Carr, *Diary of a Foreign Minister*, NewSouth, Sydney, 2014; Rodney Tiffen, *Disposable Leaders*; Philip Chubb, *Power Failure: The Inside Story of Climate Politics under Rudd and Gillard*, Black Inc., Melbourne, 2014.

5   Quoted in Paul Connolly, 'Penny Wong', *The Sydney Morning Herald,* 17 April 2011.

6   Patrick Weller, *Kevin Rudd*, p. 148.

7   ibid., p. 151.

8   Bret Walker SC, Commissioner, 'The Murray–Darling Basin royal commission report', South Australia, 29 January 2019.

9   'Pumped', *Four Corners*, ABC-TV, 24 July 2017. A useful summary is contained in Maryanne Slattery and Rod Campbell, *The Basin Files: Maladministration of the Murray–Darling Basin Plan: Volume I*, The Australia Institute, Canberra, June 2018.

10   Kathy Marks, '... As it dries up down under', *The Independent*, 22 June 2008 and AAP News, 'Fed. govt holds back advice on Murray lakes', Australian Associated Press, 1 September 2008.

11   Mark Kenny and Greg Kelton, 'No easy Murray options', *The Advertiser,* 3 September 2008, p. 1.

12   Penelope Debelle, 'Xenophon insists water be found', *The Age*, 11 August 2008, p. 4.

13   Bret Walker SC, 'The Murray–Darling Basin royal commission report', p. 22.

14   ibid., p. 17.

15   Australian Labor Party, 'Labor's national plan to tackle the water crisis', Election 2007 Policy Document, November 2007.

16   No author, 'Water buyback details outlined', *ABC News*, 26 February 2008.

17   Dean Jaensch, 'Morals washed away as states battle for water', *The Advertiser*, 12 March 2008, p. 18.

18   Greg Kelton, 'Dead in the water – last-minute manoeuvres that revived the Murray Deal', *The Advertiser*, 29 March 2008, p. 19.

19   ibid.

20   ibid.

21   Greg Kelton and Kim Wheatley, 'Dear SA: you were right but it took an extra billion dollars', *The Advertiser*, Metro, 27 March 2008, p. 1.

22   Kim Wheatley, 'Water rats: desperate farmers steal from Murray', *The Advertiser*, 30 June 2008, p. 1.

23   Productivity Commission, 'Market mechanisms for recovering water in the Murray–Darling Basin', Research report, Commonwealth of Australia, Canberra, RCE 496, March 2010; Gavan Dwyer, Matthew Clarke and Rod Carr, 'Economic effects of the Commonwealth water recovery programs in the Murrumbidgee Irrigation Area: final report prepared for the Department of Agriculture and Water Resources', Marsden Jacob Associates, Melbourne, Perth and Sydney, RCE 56, October 2017; Australian National Audit Office, 'Administration of the private irrigation infrastructure operators program in New South Wales', ANAO Audit Report No. 38 2011–12, 5 June 2012; Victorian Auditor-General's Report, 'Irrigation efficiency programs', PP no. 313, session 2006–10, Commonwealth of

Australia, Canberra, June 2010; Bret Walker SC, 'The Murray–Darling Basin royal commission report'.

24 CSIRO, 'Assessment of the ecological and economic benefits of environmental water in the Murray–Darling Basin: the final report to the Murray–Darling Basin Authority from the CSIRO', CSIRO Water for a Healthy Country National Research Flagship, Commonwealth of Australia and CSIRO, Australia, RCE 16, 28 March 2012; Productivity Commission, 'Murray–Darling Basin Plan: five-year assessment', Draft report, Commonwealth of Australia, Canberra, RCE 539, August 2018; Department of Agriculture and Water Resources (Cth), 'Murray–Darling Basin water infrastructure program', Commonwealth of Australia, Canberra, RCE 1015, 29 November 2018; Bret Walker SC, 'The Murray–Darling Basin royal commission report'.

25 Penny Wong, 'Water for the future', Speech to the Fourth Annual Australian Water Summit, Sydney Convention and Exhibition Centre, 29–30 April 2008.

26 Bret Walker SC, 'The Murray–Darling Basin royal commission report'.

27 'Commonwealth water recovering in the Murray–Darling Basin (as at 30 November 2018)', provided to the author by Penny Wong's office and compiled at her request by the Parliamentary Library, Canberra.

28 No author, 'Toorale deal won't help the lower lakes', *ABC News*, 11 September 2008.

29 Australian National Audit Office, *Restoring the balance in the Murray–Darling Basin*, Auditor-General Audit Report No. 27 2010–11 Performance Audit, Commonwealth of Australia, Canberra, 10 February 2011.

30 Productivity Commission, *National Water Reform*, Productivity Commission Inquiry Report No. 87, 19 December 2017.

31 'Commonwealth water recovering in the Murray–Darling Basin'.

32 The Australia Institute, *Moving Targets*, Canberra, 2018, and The Australia Institute, *That's Not How You Haggle*, Canberra, 2018.

33 Anne Davies, 'Questions over companies chosen for $200m of Murray–Darling water buybacks', *The Guardian*, 17 April 2019.

34 Sam Clench, 'Let me answer: Trioli's merciless grilling', *news.com.au*, 23 April 2019.

35 Verity Edwards, 'Tough Murray water plan to hit irrigators', *The Australian*, 21 May 2010, p. 2.

36 Bret Walker SC, 'The Murray–Darling Basin royal commission report', p. 172.

37 ibid.

38 ibid., p. 216.

39 Colin Bettles, 'Reflections of a basin peacemaker', *Farm Online*, 25 January 2015.

40 Ian Jones, 'MDBA visit hijacked by "bastardry"', *Goondiwindi Argus*, 8 February 2018.

41 Rachel Baxendale, 'Murray–Darling Basin Plan under threat', *The Australian*, 13 February 2018 and Tory Shepherd, 'Murray Plan in jeopardy', *The Advertiser*, 15 February 2018, p. 1.

42 Bret Walker SC, 'The Murray–Darling Basin royal commission report', p. 409.

43 ibid.

44 Natalie Kotsios and Tory Shepherd, 'SA Water Minister Ian Hunter in foul-mouthed tirade at fellow politicians', *Adelaide Now*, 18 November 2016.

45 Penny Wong and Tony Burke, 'Labor to repeal the 1500GL cap on buybacks in the Murray–Darling Basin', Media release, 13 February 2019.

46 Rosie Lewis, 'New water minister makes the Murray–Darling a priority', *The Australian*, 28 May 2019.

10: PENNY WONG FAILS TO SAVE THE WORLD (PART 2)

1   Julia Gillard, *My Story*; Kevin Rudd, *The PM Years*; Wayne Swan, *The Good Fight*; Greg Combet and Mark Davis, *The Fights of My Life*; Christine Milne, *An Activist Life*.

2   Sarah Ferguson and Patricia Drum, *The Killing Season Uncut*; Philip Chubb, *Power Failure*; Paul Kelly, *Triumph and Demise*.

3   Mark Butler, *Climate Wars*, Melbourne University Press, Melbourne, 2017.

4   Kevin Rudd, 'Speech at the high-level segment of the 13th conference of the parties', United Nations Framework Convention on Climate Change, Bali, Indonesia, 12 December 2007.

5   Kevin Rudd, *The PM Years*, p. 14.

6   Matthew Warren, 'Wong rewards leaders' faith', *The Australian*, 12 December 2007.

7   No author, 'Workaholic Wong just the ticket as a climate crusader', *The Canberra Times*, 12 December 2007.

8   Glenn Milne, 'Wong takes centre stage', *The Sunday Times*, 16 December 2007.

9   Penny Wong, 'From Copenhagen to Paris: climate change and the limits of rationality, multilateralism, and leadership', *Brown Journal of World Affairs*, vol. XXII, no. 1, Spring/Summer 2015, p. 268.

10 Julia Gillard, *My Story*, p. 369.

11 This anecdote is taken from Kevin Rudd, *The PM Years*, pp. 259–60.

12 Penny Wong, 'Water for the future'.

13 Ian Bailey, Iain MacGill, Rob Passey and Hugh Compston, 'The fall (and rise) of carbon pricing in Australia: a political strategy analysis of the carbon pollution reduction scheme', *Environmental Politics*, vol. 21, no. 5, 2012, pp. 691–711.

14 Paul Kelly, *Triumph and Demise*, p. 197.

15 Josh Gordon, 'Can Wong avert carbon-fuelled train wreck?' *The Sunday Age*, 6 July 2008.

16 Ross Garnaut, 'Australia counts itself out', *The Australian*, 20 December 2008, p. 21.

17 Mark Butler, *Climate Wars*.

18 Paul Kelly, *Triumph and Demise*, p. 242.

19 ibid., Chapter 16.

20 David Marr, *Power Trip: The Political Journey of Kevin Rudd*, Quarterly Essay 38, 2010.

21 ibid.

22 Kevin Rudd, *The PM Years*, p. 220.

23 ibid., p. 222 ff.

24 ibid., Chapter 18.

25 ibid., p. 227.

26 Cathy Alexander, 'Climate change summit disappoints Wong', AAP, 20 December 2009.

27 See Philip Chubb, *Power Failure*; Paul Kelly, *Triumph and Demise*; Greg Combet and Mark Davis, *The Fights of My Life*; Wayne Swan, *The Good Fight*; Julia Gillard, *My Story*.

28   Paul Kelly, *Triumph and Demise*, p. 279 ff.

29   ibid., p. 282.

30   No author, 'Carbon tax plan aims to break ETS deadlock', *The West Australian*, 14 April 2010, p. 10.

31   Christine Milne, *An Activist Life*, pp. 187–88.

32   Paddy Manning, *Inside the Greens: The Origins and Future of the Party, the People and the Politics*, Black Inc., Melbourne, 2019, p. 274.

33   Lenore Taylor, 'ETS off the agenda until late next term', *The Sydney Morning Herald*, 27 April 2010, p. 1.

34   Kevin Rudd, *The PM Years*, p. 262 ff.

35   Julia Gillard, *My Story*; Kevin Rudd, *The PM Years*; Paul Kelly, *Triumph and Demise*; Sarah Ferguson and Patricia Drum, *The Killing Season Uncut*.

36   Tom Arup, 'ETS needs consensus: Wong', *The Age*, 18 June 2010, p. 7.

37   'No leadership revolt against Rudd', AAP, 19 June 2010.

38   Kevin Rudd, *The PM Years*, p. 259.

39   Julia Gillard, *My Story*, p. 369.

40   Kevin Rudd, *The PM Years*, p. 317.

41   Julia Gillard, *My Story*, p. 69.

42   Michael Owen, 'Greens at odds with Wong on climate change', *The Australian*, 8 September 2010, p. 4.

43   No author, 'Wong tipped to move on from climate', AAP, 8 September 2010.

44   Christine Milne, *An Activist Life*, and interview with the author.

45   Greg Combet and Mark Davis, *The Fights of My Life*, p. 248.

46   Mark Butler, *Climate Wars*, pp. 28–29.

47   Greg Combet and Mark Davis, *The Fights of My Life*, pp. 257–58.

48   Julia Gillard, *My Story*, p. 368.

49   Ian Bailey, Iain MacGill, Rob Passey and Hugh Compston, 'The fall (and rise) of carbon pricing in Australia', pp. 691–711. This view is also advanced by some of the senior bureaucrats who served in the Department of Climate Change.

50   No author, 'Carbon tax: a timeline of its tortuous history in Australia', *ABC News*, updated 17 July 2014.

51   Philip Chubb, *Power Failure*.

52   Michael Shmith, 'A man of plain words', *The Age*, 3 October 2009, p. 10, and Jonathan Holmes, 'Journalists weather the changing climate', *ABC News*, 11 February 2010.

11: A WOMAN OF GOVERNMENT

1   Penny Wong, John Button Memorial Lecture 2010, Melbourne, 9 November 2010.

2   Media Monitors quoting from *Meet the Press*, Channel Ten, 25 July 2010. and No author, 'Wong backs Labor's anti-gay marriage stance', *The Sydney Morning Herald*, 25 July 2010.

3   Patricia Karvelas, 'Gays call Wong a hypocrite', *The Australian*, 26 July 2010.

4   No author, 'Wong horrifies Brown on gay call', AAP, 26 July 2010.

5   Mark Kenny, 'Rudd backed gay vote', *Daily Telegraph*, 17 November 2010.

6   Andrea Hayward, 'Labor MPs support change: Wong's gay win', *Geelong Advertiser*, 29 November 2010, p. 2.

7   Penny Wong, 'Speech to the South Australian Labor Convention', 27 November 2010.
8   Jeremy Thompson, 'Wong, partner expecting first child', *ABC News*, 9 August 2011.
9   Peter Jean, 'Mixed views on Wong baby news', *The Canberra Times*, 10 August 2011, p. 3.
10 ibid.
11 No author, 'Wong, gay partner expecting baby', *ABC News*, 14 August 2011.
12 Jihad el-Khazen, 'Ayoon wa Azan', *Al-Hayat*, 14 August 2011, p. 20.
13 Miranda Devine, 'Pregnancy of Penny Wong's partner no cause for mass celebration', *Daily Telegraph*, 14 August 2011.
14 Tom Ballard, 'Miranda Devine: What the f&*k are you talking about?', YouTube, 14 August 2011.
15 Penny Wong, Interview with Leigh Sales, *7.30*, ABC-TV, 15 August 2011.
16 Michelle Grattan, 'Pincer move on Gillard over gay marriage', *The Age*, 1 December 2011, p. 1.
17 Quoted in no author, 'What they said', *The Sunday Age*, 4 December 2011, p. 5.
18 Quoted in Graham Richardson, 'A little democracy goes a long way when you are managing a party', *The Australian*, 6 December 2011, p. 12.
19 Penny Wong, 'Address to ALP National Conference', Sydney, 3 December 2011.
20 Matthew Franklin, 'Wake-up call that drove PM towards tactical switch', *The Australian*, 5 December 2011, p. 8.
21 ibid.
22 Graham Richardson, 'A little democracy goes a long way'.
23 Deirdre McKeown, 'Chronology of same-sex marriage bills introduced into the federal parliament'.
24 ibid.
25 Penny Wong, 'Penny Wong talks of her support for equality in marriage', *Lateline*, ABC-TV, 18 September 2012.
26 Penny Wong, *Q&A*, ABC-TV, 14 May 2012.
27 Dennis Altman, 'Penny Wong, Joe Hockey and the dire state of political punditry', *The Conversation*, 15 May 2012.
28 Kevin Rudd, *The PM Years*, p. 490 and Julia Gillard, *My Story*, p. 86.
29 Michael Rowland, 'Australian government news: finance minister Wong speaks on media, minerals, resource rent tax, economy and Fair Work Australia', *News Breakfast*, ABC-TV, 1 February 2012.
30 No author, 'Gillard has my full support: Wong', AAP, 4 February 2012.
31 Matt Buchanan and Scott Ellis, 'The diary', *The Sydney Morning Herald*, 9 February 2012, p. 22.
32 Dennis Atkins, 'Wong a steady hand in unsteady ship of state', *The Courier-Mail*, 17 February 2012, p. 59.
33 Julia Gillard, *My Story*, p. 86 and Kevin Rudd, *The PM Years*, pp. 493–95.
34 Michael Rowland, 'Australian government news: finance minister Wong talks about leadership issues with ABC 891', *News Breakfast*, ABC Radio, 23 February 2012.
35 No author, 'Wong says Rudd must rule out second tilt', AAP, 24 February 2012.
36 Tony Jones, *Lateline*, ABC-TV, 2 July 2013.

37   Michael Koziol, 'Penny Wong calls for unity as she backs Anthony Albanese for
      Labor leadership', *The Sydney Morning Herald*, 22 May 2018.

38   Kevin Rudd, *The PM Years*; Wayne Swan, *The Good Fight*, 2014; Paul Kelly,
      Triumph and Demise.

39   Paul Kelly, *Triumph and Demise*, pp. 295ff.

40   Julia Gillard, *My Story*; Kevin Rudd, *The PM Years*; Wayne Swan, *The Good Fight*;
      Paul Kelly, *Triumph and Demise*, pp. 279 ff.

41   Wayne Swan, *The Good Fight*, p. 277.

42   Paul Kelly, *Triumph and Demise*.

43   Penny Wong, 'Finance minister delves into mining tax and budget talk', *7.30*,
      ABC-TV, 13 March 2012.

44   Penny Wong, 'Penny Wong defends ditching the budget surplus', *7.30*, ABC-TV,
      20 December 2012.

45   Penny Wong, 'Finance minister Penny Wong discusses the budget', *Lateline*,
      ABC-TV, 14 May 2013.

46   No author, 'Labor factions at odds over SA Senate', AAP, 29 October 2012.

47   ibid.

48   No author, 'Penny Wong to lead Labor's SA Senate ticket after Don Farrell gives
      up spot', AAP, 30 October 2012.

49   Simon Benson, 'Who's running: former PM wants backing of senior ministers',
      Herald Sun, 17 June 2013, p. 2.

50   Julia Gillard, *My Story*, p. 369.

51   Mary Delahunty, *Gravity: Inside the PM's Office During Her Last Year and Final
      Days*, Hardie Grant, Melbourne, 2014.

52   Mark Kenny and Jessica Wright, 'Labor in crisis: Gillard on back foot after
      ministers quit', *Sun Herald*, 3 February 2013, p. 8.

53   Kevin Rudd, *The PM Years*, p. 539.

54   Benjamin Law, *Moral Panic 101: Equality, Acceptance and the Safe Schools Scandal*,
      Quarterly Essay 67, 2017, p. 7.

55   Samantha Maiden, 'Voyage of the damned', *The Advertiser*, 1 September 2013,
      p. 8 and Samantha Maiden, 'Loose rein on Rudd's campaign', *The Advertiser*,
      8 September 2013.

56   ibid.

57   Laurie Oakes, 'Rudd's big blunder ensures Labor's number is up', *The Mercury*,
      31 August 2013, p. 34.

58   Tony Walker, 'The Rudd experiment has failed', *Australian Financial Review*,
      31 August 2013, p. 16.

59   Sarah Martin, 'Farrell loss ignites a bitter factional brawl', *The Australian*,
      9 September 2013, p. 4.

60   Sarah Martin, 'Wong blamed for "not trying hard enough"', *The Australian*,
      12 September 2013, p. 6.

61   Penny Wong, 'Inside words from a brutal campaign', *The Advertiser*, 18 July 2016,
      p. 21.

62   'South Australia', in 'Senate results by state, 2016 federal election', AEC Tally
      Room, *Australian Electoral Commission*, 5 August 2016.

63 Penny Wong quoted in Natalie Whiting, 'The Nick Xenophon Team could become a new political force', *7.30*, ABC-TV, 9 June 2016.

64 Sabra Lane, 'Wong says Labor needs to put more resources into winning Senate seats', *The World Today*, ABC Radio, 17 September 2013.

12: ARRIVAL

1 Bill Shorten, 'Statement to the Labor campaign rally', Box Hill Town Hall, Melbourne, 29 April 2019.

2 No author, 'Government seizes on Beazley slip', AAP, 20 April 2006.

3 Mark Kenny, 'Report card', *The Advertiser*, 20 December 2008, p. 81.

4 Lenore Taylor, 'The minister of cool', p. 12.

5 No author, 'Cathy Freeman is Australia's most admired woman', PR Newswire Asia, 11 October 2011.

6 No author, 'That eyebrow tho', *BuzzFeed Australia*, 25 October 2015.

7 James Jeffrey, 'Strewth: brows beaten', *The Australian*, 18 October 2016, p. 11.

8 Amy Remeikis, 'Penny Wong: the politician you really don't want to cross during an Estimates hearing', *The Sydney Morning Herald*, 18 October 2016.

9 Brigid Delaney, 'Julia Gillard the movie: who would you cast', *The Guardian*, 8 November 2013.

10 Kaz Cooke, Twitter, 27 February 2018, https://twitter.com/reallykazcooke/status/968673806293221376

11 Quoted in *Crikey*, 'Tips and rumours', 22 June 2017.

12 No author, 'George Brandis tells Penny Wong she is becoming hysterical', AAP, 11 August 2015.

13 Amy Remeikis, 'Penny Wong'.

14 Rory Callinan, 'Had training for this? Hands up', *The Australian*, 31 May 2017.

15 Penny Wong, 'Questions without notice: *Racial Discrimination Act*', Senate *Hansard*, 24 March 2014, p. 1797.

16 Henry Martyn Lloyd, *The Drum*, ABC-TV, 22 April 2014 and Henry Belot, 'George Brandis takes aim at Penny Wong', *ABC News*, 13 February 2017.

17 Penny Wong, 'Human Rights Legislation Amendment Bill 2017', Senate *Hansard*, 28 March 2017, p. 2352.

18 Penny Wong, 'Speech to the Chifley Research Centre', 3 November 2013.

19 Katharine Murphy, 'Penny Wong's composure cracked in a moment of relief too big to be contained', *The Guardian*, 15 November 2017.

20 Chris Uhlmann, 'Labor's Senate leader defends budget attacks', *AM*, Radio National, 22 May 2014.

21 Penny Wong, 'Australia's future is in the world – and there is no turning back', Speech at the Economic and Social Outlook Conference, Melbourne, 3 July 2014.

22 Penny Wong, 'Tackling global climate change from Copenhagen to Paris and COP21', Speech at the University of Pennsylvania Law School, Philadelphia, 17 November 2015.

23 Penny Wong, 'Speech to the Australian Fabians Forum', Melbourne, 13 June 2015.

24 Phillip Coorey, 'ChAFTA: China free trade deal to pass after Labor deal', *Australian Financial Review*, 21 October 2015.

25 Wayne Errington and Peter van Onselen, *The Turnbull Gamble*, Melbourne University Publishing, Melbourne, 2016, Chapter 3.

26 Anne Hyland, 'Team Shorten', *Australian Financial Review*, 14 May 2016.

27 Penny Wong, Twitter, 17 May 2013, https://twitter.com/senatorwong/status/335183161954807808?lang=en

28 Alex Greenwich and Shirleene Robinson, *Yes Yes Yes*.

29 Penny Wong, 'Maiden speech'.

30 Penny Wong, 'Plebiscite (Same-Sex Marriage Bill) 2016', Senate *Hansard*, 7 November 2016, p. 1882.

31 Penny Wong, 'Why I am proud to march at my first Mardi Gras', *The Guardian*, 6 March 2014.

32 Michael McGuire, 'Senator's Mardi Gras debut', *The Advertiser*, 3 March 2014, p. 12.

33 Penny Wong in Michaela McGuire and Marieke Hardy (eds), *From the Heart: A Collection from Women of Letters*, Viking, Melbourne, 2015 (first read aloud at a Women of Letters event on 25 November 2013).

34 No author, 'China's emissions reductions aren't a gigantic landmark', *The Australian*, 19 November 2014, p. 15.

35 No author, 'Australian defence minister back-paddles on canoe comment', Agence France-Presse, 26 November 2014 and No author, 'Government treating people like mugs', AAP, 23 November 2014.

36 No author, 'Pyne determined to continue fight on unis', AAP, 3 December 2014.

37 May Slater, 'Penny Wong announces she is expecting her second child with partner Sophie', *Daily Mail*, 6 December 2014.

38 Paul Millar, '2014 Crikeys: arsehat, person of the year and sexiest pollies', *Crikey*, 19 December 2014.

39 Deirdre McKeown, 'Chronology of same-sex marriage bills introduced into the federal parliament'.

40 Emily Crane, 'Senator Wong and partner announce the arrival of their second child', *Daily Mail*, 8 April 2015.

41 Quoted in Natalie Whiting, *The World Today*, ABC Radio, 5 June 2015.

42 No author, 'Labor transformed – almost', *The Canberra Times*, 28 July 2015.

43 Penny Wong, 'Speech to the Australian Labor Party Conference', 26 July 2015.

44 Alex Greenwich and Shirleene Robinson, *Yes Yes Yes*, p. 127.

45 Rob Taylor, 'Australia's Abbott under fire after gay marriage vote blocked', *The Wall Street Journal*, 12 August 2015.

46 Peter Hartcher, 'He sold everything he believed in: the price Turnbull paid to become prime minister', *The Sydney Morning Herald*, 28 March 2019.

47 Leadership debate, ABC-TV, 17 June 2016.

48 Penny Wong, Lionel Murphy Memorial Lecture, 21 June 2016.

49 ibid.; Penny Wong, 'It's time', *The Monthly*, February 2016; Penny Wong, Frank Walker Memorial Lecture, 17 May 2017.

50 Penny Wong, 'Plebiscite Same-Sex Marriage Bill 2016'.

51 Penny Wong, 'It's time'.

52 ibid.

53 Penny Wong, Frank Walker Memorial Lecture.

54 Penny Wong, Lionel Murphy Memorial Lecture.

55 Alex Greenwich and Shirleene Robinson, *Yes Yes Yes*, p. 123.

56 Penny Wong, Senate *Hansard*, 15 February 2017.

57 Penny Wong, 'Exposure Draft of the Marriage Amendment (Same-Sex Marriage) Bill Select Committee', Senate *Hansard*, 15 February 2017, p. 1034.

58 Lane Sainty, '"Historic agreement" moves the marriage equality debate forward', *BuzzFeed*, 15 February 2017.

59 Alex Greenwich and Shirleene Robinson, *Yes Yes Yes*, pp. 204–05.

60 Katharine Murphy, 'Penny Wong's composure cracked in a moment of relief too big to be contained'.

61 ibid.

62 Penny Wong, 'Marriage Amendment (Definition and Religious Freedoms) Bill 2017', Senate *Hansard*, 16 November 2017.

63 Alex Greenwich and Shirleene Robinson, *Yes Yes Yes*, p. 279.

64 Peter Hartcher, 'The five key lessons to emerge from the same-sex marriage result', *The Sydney Morning Herald*, 15 November 2017.

65 Alex Greenwich and Shirleene Robinson, *Yes Yes Yes*, p. 226.

13: A DANGEROUS PLACE

1   Henry Belot, 'Election 2019: Scott Morrison says "I have always believed in miracles" as Coalition retains power', *ABC News*, 19 May 2019.

2   Guardian Australia, 'Penny Wong endorses Anthony Albanese', YouTube, 21 May 2019.

3   Katharine Murphy, 'Adani protest echoes in void as parliament without a compass sets sail', *The Guardian*, 2 July 2019.

4   Fran Kelly, '"Scott Morrison is standing in the way": Penny Wong on Coalition tax cuts', *RN Breakfast*, ABC Radio National, 1 July 2019.

5   Penny Wong, 'Australian values, Australia's interests – foreign policy under a Shorten Labor government', Speech at the Lowy Institute, Sydney, 1 May 2019.

6   ibid.

7   See Hugh White, *Power Shift*, Quarterly Essay 39, 2010; Hugh White, *Without America: Australia in the New Asia*, Quarterly Essay 68, 2017; Hugh White, 'The United States or China: "We don't have to choose"', in Mark Beeson and Shahar Hamerri (eds), *Navigating the New International Disorder: Australia in World Affairs 2011–2015*, Oxford University Press, Melbourne, pp. 93–108; Hugh White, *How to Defend Australia*, Black Inc., Melbourne, 2019.

8   Allan Gyngell and Sam Roggeveen, 'A dialogue on Australian foreign policy past and future', Speech at the Lowy Institute, 31 May 2017.

9   Interview with Tony Jones, *Q&A*, ABC-TV, 8 July 2019.

10 Fergus Hunter, 'Election 2016: Shorten's description of Donald Trump as "barking mad" draws ire of Malcolm Turnbull', *The Sydney Morning Herald*, 27 May 2016.

11 Michael Brissenden, 'Labor and Coalition share "very similar" approach to foreign policy: Penny Wong', *AM*, ABC Radio, 27 July 2016, and Brendan Nicholson, 'We must think global: Wong', *The Australian*, 30 July 2016, p. 6.

12 Katharine Murphy, 'After the US result the instinct of Australia's politicians was to soothe. That says a lot', *The Guardian*, 9 November 2016.

13   Penny Wong, 'Our alliances need an update', *The Sydney Morning Herald*,
     16 November 2016, p. 19.
14   Evan Vucci, 'Updated: Donald Trump', *The Australian*, 16 November 2016.
15   Penny Wong, 'Australian values, Australia's interests'.
16   Penny Wong, 'Foreign policy in a time of disruption', Address at the Global Heads
     of Mission Meeting, Canberra, 29 March 2017.
17   Penny Wong, 'Australia's national interests in a time of disruption', Speech at the
     Lowy Institute, Sydney, 6 July 2017; Penny Wong, 'Australian values in a time of
     disruption', Griffith University's Asia Institute, Brisbane, 3 August 2017; Penny
     Wong, 'Australian values, Australia's interests'.
18   Penny Wong, 'Australian values in a time of disruption'.
19   Penny Wong, 'Australia's national interests in a time of disruption'; Penny Wong,
     'Australian values in a time of disruption'.
20   Penny Wong, 'FutureAsia: engaging with China', Australian Institute of
     International Affairs annual conference, Canberra, 2017; Penny Wong, 'Australia
     and the US in the age of disruption', Cranlana Centre for Ethical Leadership,
     Melbourne, 22 November 2017.
21   Penny Wong, 'Peace and prosperity in a time of disruption', Lee Kuan Yew School
     of Public Policy, Singapore, 24 January 2018.
22   Penny Wong, 'Australia's national interests in a time of disruption'.
23   Penny Wong, 'FutureAsia'.
24   Penny Wong, 'Managing the Australia–China relationship', 2018 Outlook
     Conference, 12 October 2018.
25   Penny Wong, 'Australian values, Australia's interests'.
26   Ben Otto, 'Indonesia's Widodo wades into the South China Sea dispute', *The Wall
     Street Journal*, 23 June 2016, and Wahyudi Soeriaatmadja, 'Indonesian president
     Joko Widodo's trip to South China Sea islands a message to Beijing, says minister',
     The Straits Times, 23 June 2016.
27   Ben Packham, 'US ambassador's message for Morrison: embrace power role in the
     Pacific', *The Australian*, 2 July 2019.
28   Brad Norington, 'The Left's right man', *Weekend Australian*, 23 May 2019.
29   Shannon Molloy, 'The power four: inside Bill Shorten's tight and trusted inner
     circle', *news.com.au*, 21 April 2019.
30   No author, 'Penny Wong and Jordan Steele-John celebrated for political leadership',
     The McKinnon Prize in Political Leadership, March 2019.
31   Michael Koziol, '"She's quite remarkable": Penny Wong awarded major prize for
     political leadership', *The Sydney Morning Herald*, 20 March 2019.
32   Penny Wong, 'McKinnon Prize in Political Leadership Oration', University of
     Melbourne, Melbourne, 29 March 2019.
33   Penny Wong and Mathias Cormann, Finance and Public Administration
     Legislation Committee, Senate *Hansard*, 4 April 2019, pp. 30, 50.
34   Mark Powell, 'Ten more reasons Labor lost the unlosable election', *The Spectator
     Australia*, 23 May 2019.

INTERVIEWS

Unless otherwise referenced, information and quotations in this book are sourced from the interviews listed below. There were an additional eight interviews conducted on the understanding that the subjects would not be identified.

Albanese, Anthony, 29 September 2018.
Behm, Allan, 15 June 2019.
Bennett, Dascia, 10 July 2018.
Bolkus, Nick, 28 March 2018.
Boswell, Lois, 14 December 2018.
Butler, Mark, 2 May 2018, 15 May 2018, 10 July 2018.
Durkin, Anthony, 29 May 2018.
Evans, Gareth, 21 June 2019.
Faulkner, John, 21 November 2018.
Frater, Don, 10 July 2018.
Garnaut, Ross, 27 June 2018.
Georganas, Steve, 7 March 2019.
Grant, Shane, 27 March 2018.
Greentree, James, 4 April 2018.
Gyngell, Alan, 31 January 2019.
Hamilton, Andrew, 21 March 2018.
Hannon, Peter, 7 March 2019.
Jackson, Sharryn, 14 March 2019.
Johnson, Caroline, 7 March 2019.
Karzis, George, 25 March 2018.
Lamb, Andrew, 20 March 2018.
Lawrence, Carmen, 10 May 2018.
Macklin, Jenny, 4 June 2018.
Milne, Christine, 12 April 2019.
Ogiers, Richard, 20 February 2018.
Olenich, John, 1 August 2018, 8 August 2018, 12 September 2018, 4 December 2018.
Pedler, Kim, 20 March 2018.
Penberthy, David, 9 May 2018.
Schacht, Chris, 21 March 2018.
Slattery, Maryanne, 27 May 2019.
Stilgherrian, 19 March 2019.
Wakefield, Wendy, 19 January 2018.
Weatherill, Jay, 11 July 2018.
White, Hugh, 31 January 2019.
Wong, Penny, 4 September 2018 (preliminary conversation regarding cooperation), 12 December 2018, 13 December 2018, 6 February 2019, 7 February 2019, 7 March 2019, 9 July 2019.
Yeadon, Kim, 15 May 2018.
Yuan, Mel, 15 May 2018.

Index

Margaret Simons is an award-winning journalist and the author of thirteen books, including a biography of Malcolm Fraser that won the Book of the Year and the Douglas Stewart Prize at the 2011 NSW Premier's Literary Awards. She is the recipient of the 2015 Walkley Award for Social Equity Journalism and has been honoured with several Quill Awards for Journalistic Excellence. Simons is an associate professor in the School of Media, Film and Journalism at Monash University, and a board member of the Public Interest Journalism Initiative.